Requiem
of the
Rose King

16

AYA KANNO

Based on *Henry VI* and *Richard III*
by William Shakespeare

STORY THUS FAR

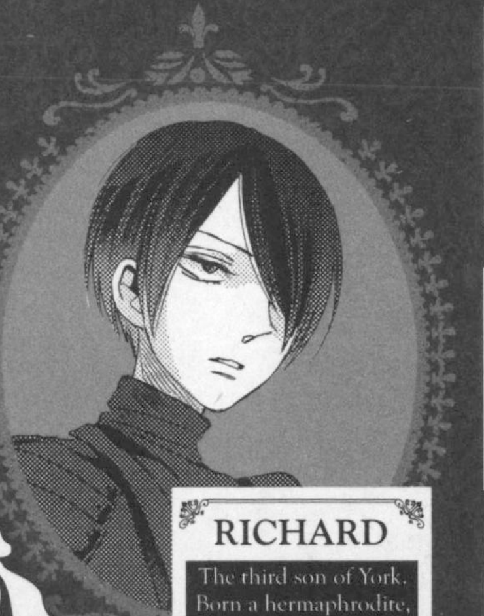

RICHARD

The third son of York. Born a hermaphrodite, he has been shunned by his mother since childhood.

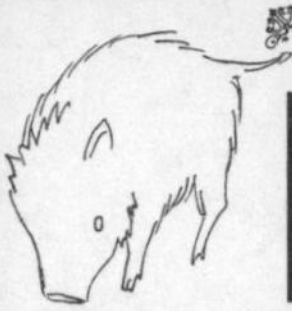

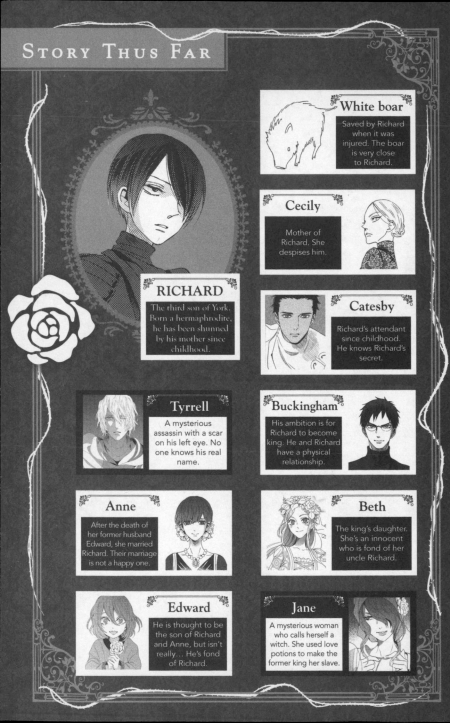

White boar

Saved by Richard when it was injured. The boar is very close to Richard.

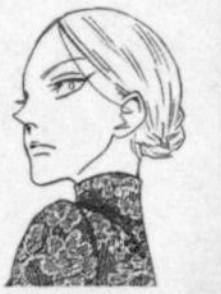

Cecily

Mother of Richard. She despises him.

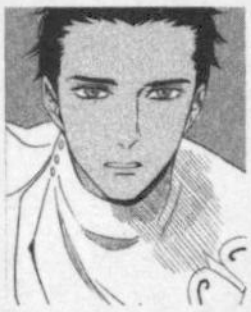

Catesby

Richard's attendant since childhood. He knows Richard's secret.

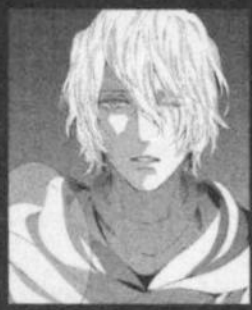

Tyrrell

A mysterious assassin with a scar on his left eye. No one knows his real name.

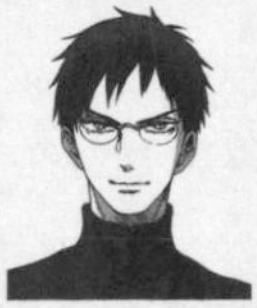

Buckingham

His ambition is for Richard to become king. He and Richard have a physical relationship.

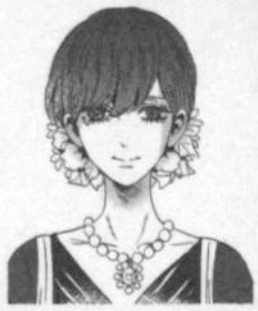

Anne

After the death of her former husband Edward, she married Richard. Their marriage is not a happy one.

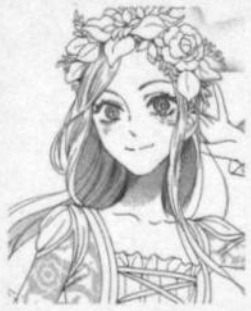

Beth

The king's daughter. She's an innocent who is fond of her uncle Richard.

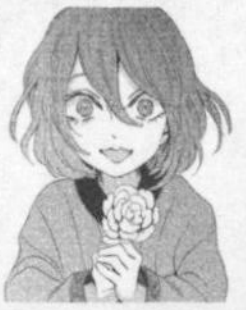

Edward

He is thought to be the son of Richard and Anne, but isn't really... He's fond of Richard.

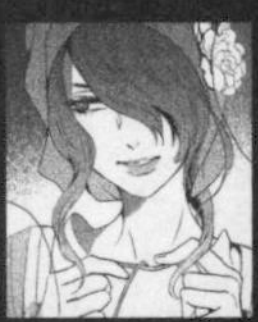

Jane

A mysterious woman who calls herself a witch. She used love potions to make the former king her slave.

Characters &

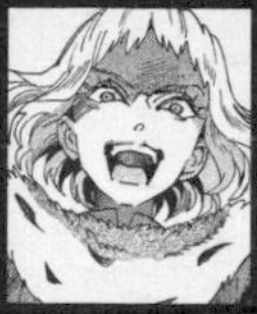

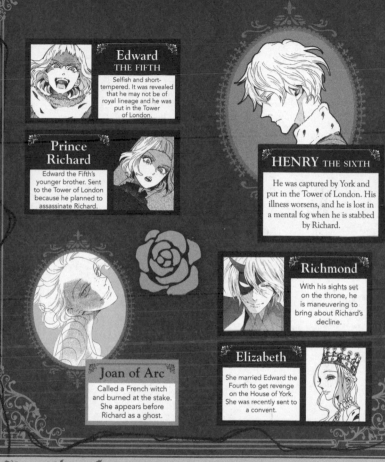

Edward THE FIFTH

Selfish and short-tempered. It was revealed that he may not be of royal lineage and he was put in the Tower of London.

Prince Richard

Edward the Fifth's younger brother. Sent to the Tower of London because he planned to assassinate Richard.

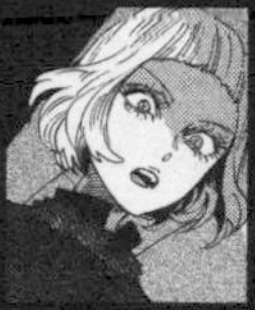

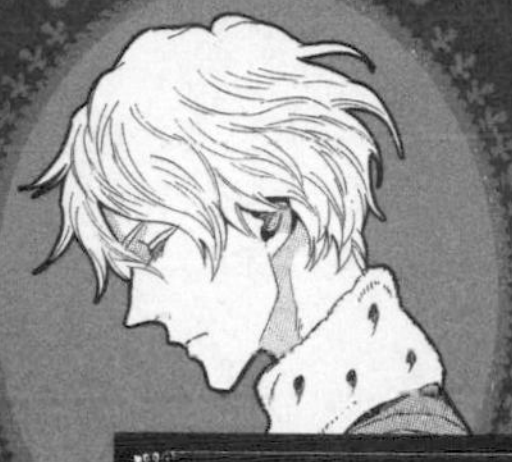

HENRY THE SIXTH

He was captured by York and put in the Tower of London. His illness worsens, and he is lost in a mental fog when he is stabbed by Richard.

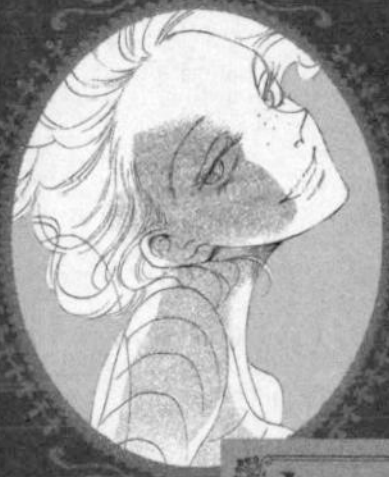

Joan of Arc

Called a French witch and burned at the stake. She appears before Richard as a ghost.

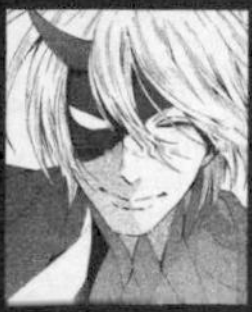

Richmond

With his sights set on the throne, he is maneuvering to bring about Richard's decline.

Elizabeth

She married Edward the Fourth to get revenge on the House of York. She was recently sent to a convent.

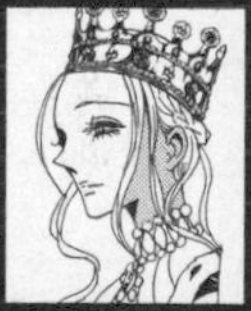

Story thus far...

England, the Middle Ages. Richard has at last obtained his long-desired throne.

Richard confesses to Buckingham that Edward is not his actual son. Buckingham becomes irate and proposes that Richard disinherit Edward, but Richard refuses. As preparations are made for the coronation in York, Richard goes to Buckingham's estate to tell him that Jane has suggested he might be pregnant. Buckingham locks Richard up and says they should abandon the throne and live together. Richard, who has dreamed of being king for many years, brushes aside Buckingham's outstretched hand and heads for York.

Upon arriving, Richard is inspired by the example of his father and renews his resolve to be king. Buckingham does not come to York, but instead sends an ultimatum, leaving Richard unable to decide whether to choose the throne or his other half.

While he wrestles with this dilemma, the rebellion begins at last. His advisers appeal to his duty as king, and Richard braces himself to put down Buckingham's revolt. With a mix of complicated emotions in his heart, Richard prepares to cross swords with Buckingham...

Requiem
— of the —
Rose

King

Contents

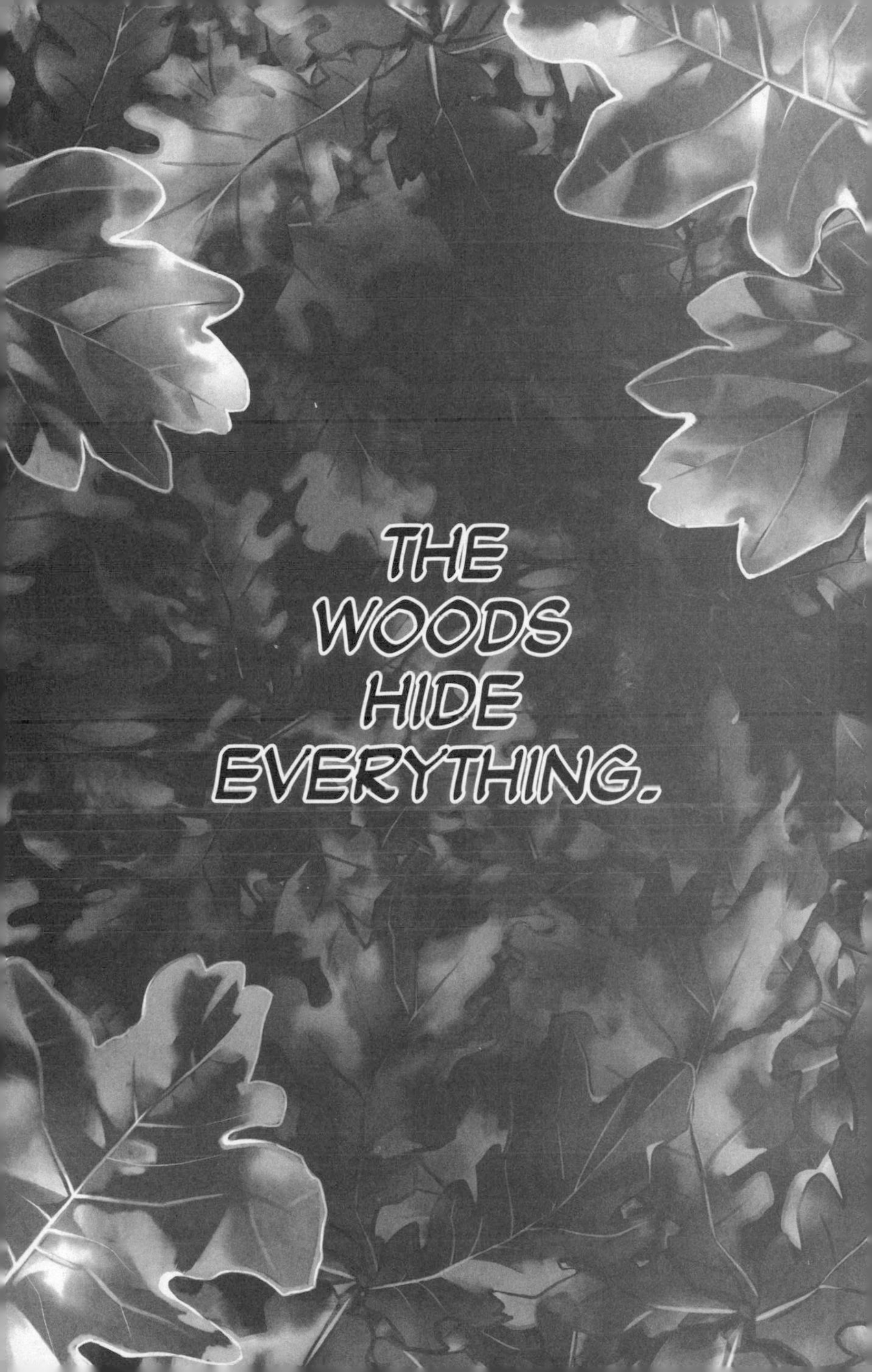
THE WOODS HIDE EVERYTHING.

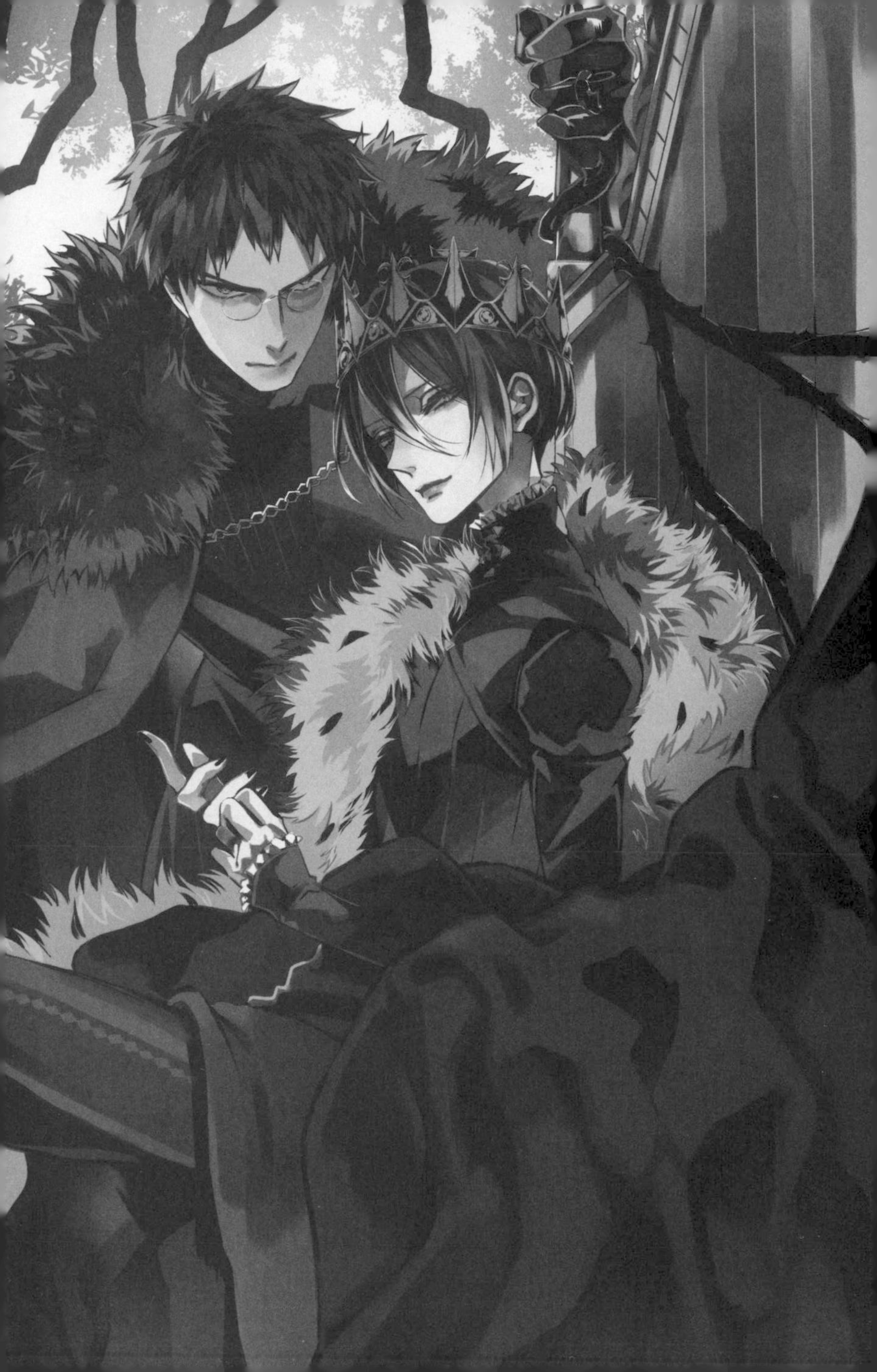

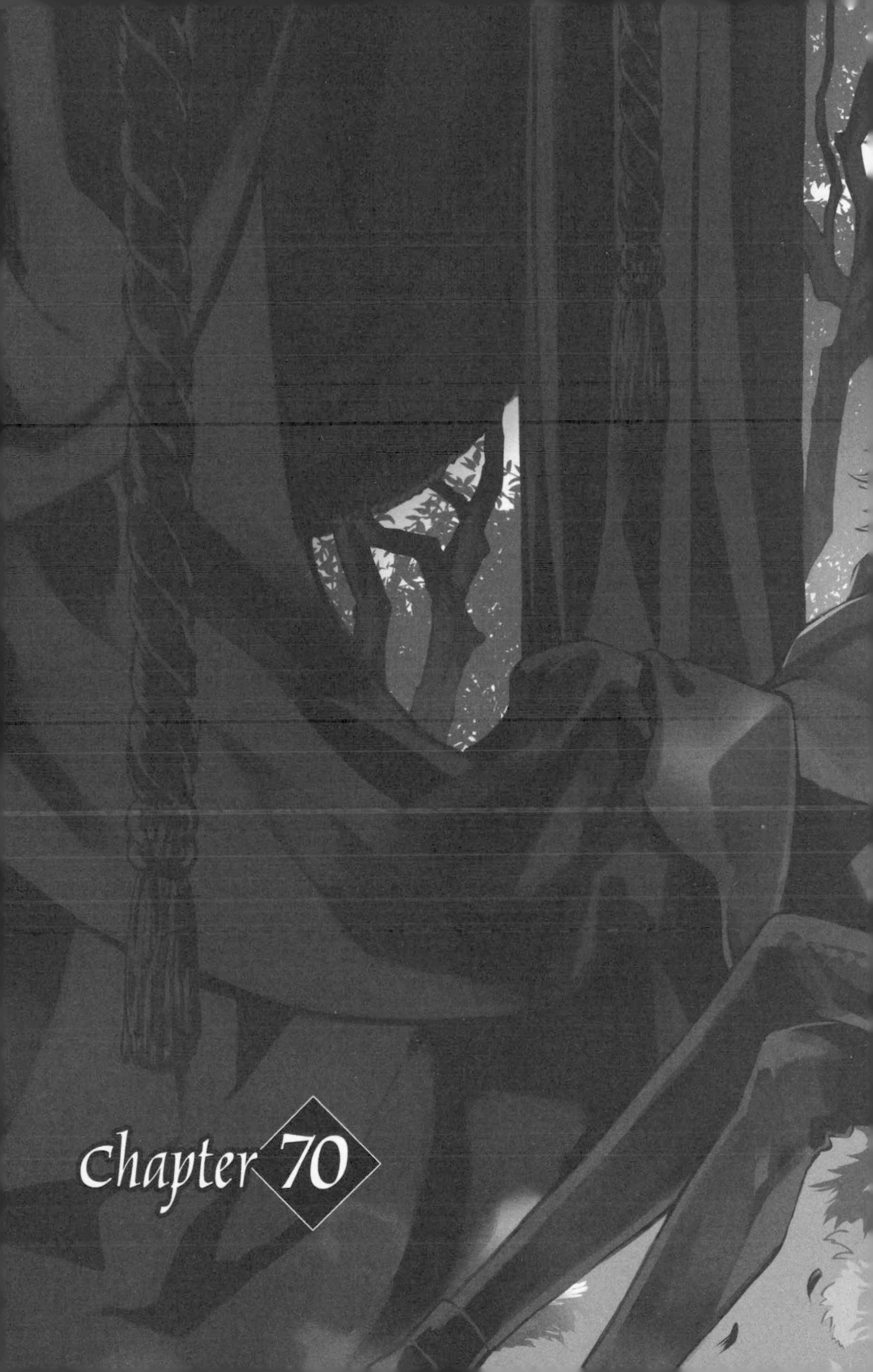
Chapter 70

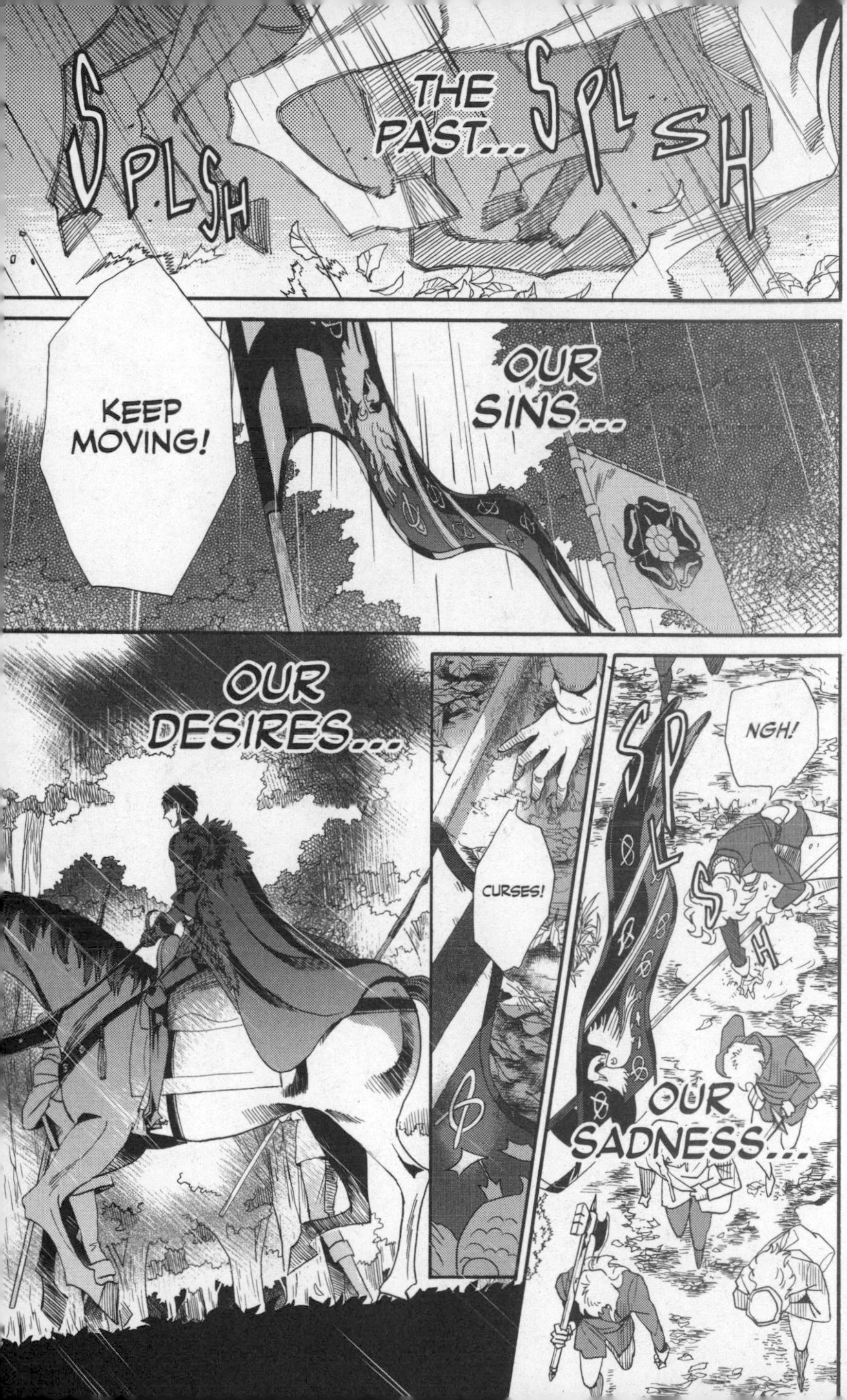
SPLSH
THE PAST...
SPLSH
OUR SINS...
KEEP MOVING!
NGH!
SPLSH
SPLSH
OUR SADNESS...
CURSES!
OUR DESIRES...

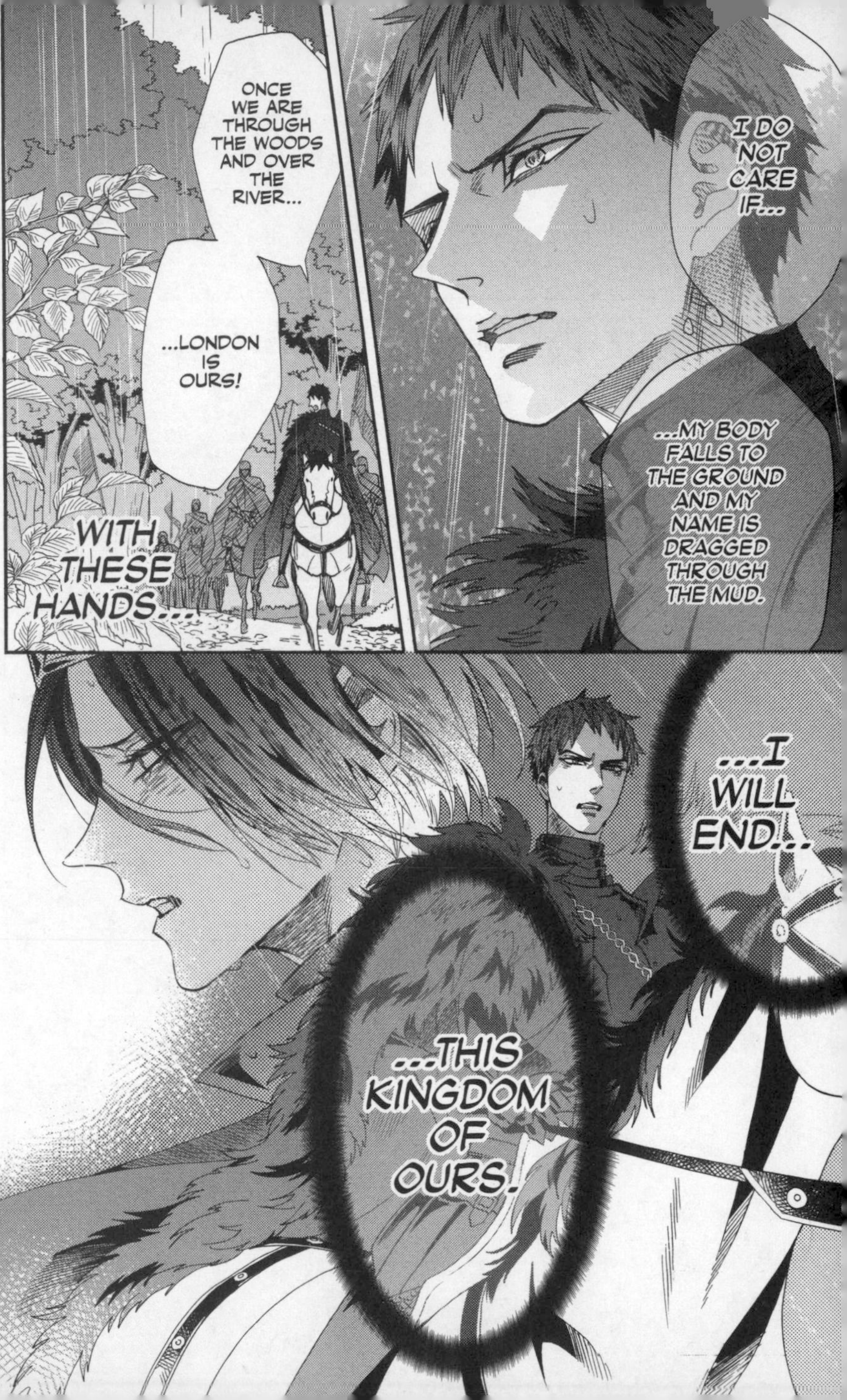
I DO NOT CARE IF...
...MY BODY FALLS TO THE GROUND AND MY NAME IS DRAGGED THROUGH THE MUD.
ONCE WE ARE THROUGH THE WOODS AND OVER THE RIVER...
...LONDON IS OURS!
WITH THESE HANDS...
...I WILL END...
...THIS KINGDOM OF OURS.

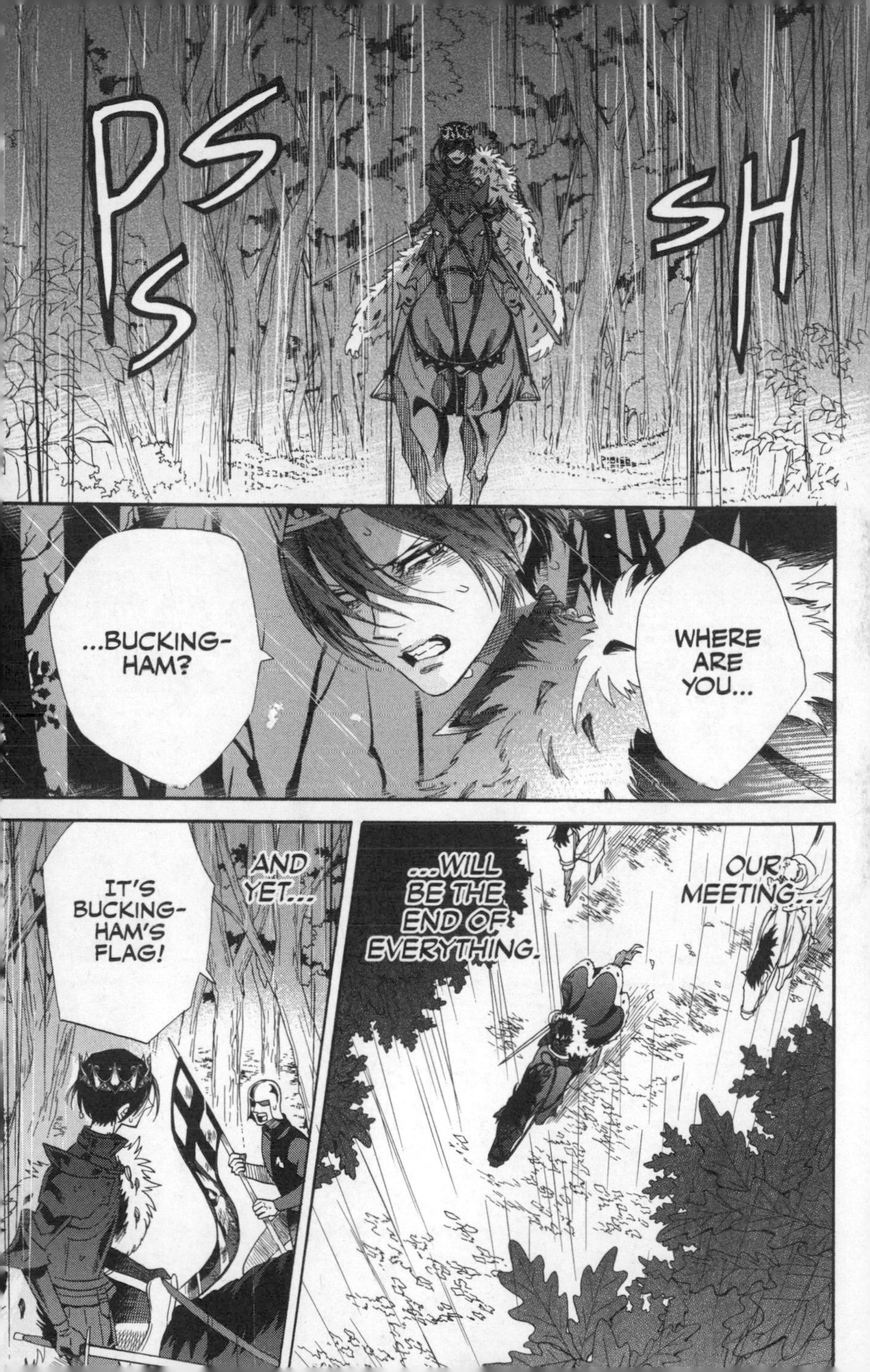
PSSSH
WHERE ARE YOU...
...BUCKING-HAM?
OUR MEETING...
...WILL BE THE END OF EVERYTHING.
AND YET...
IT'S BUCKING-HAM'S FLAG!

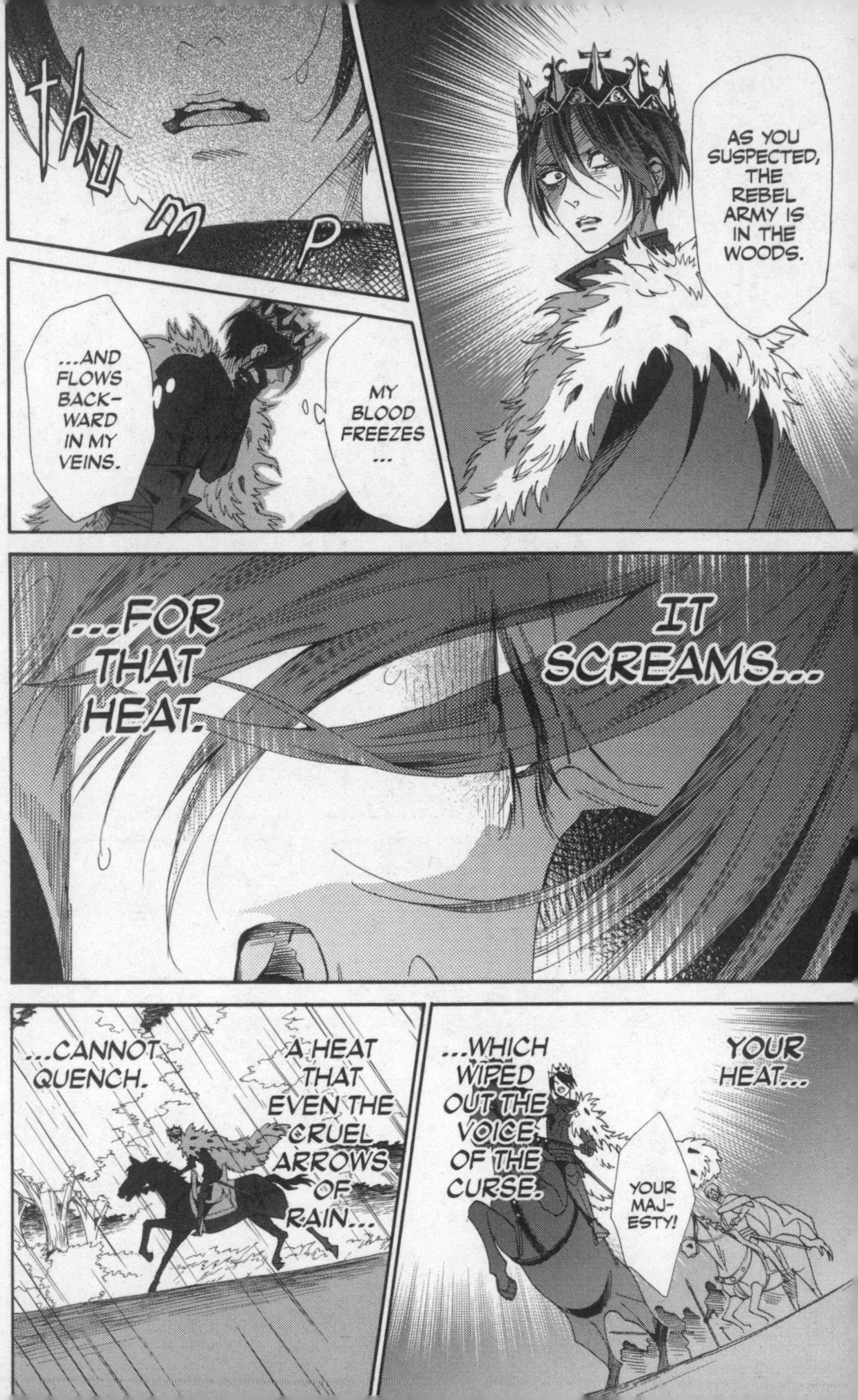
AS YOU SUSPECTED, THE REBEL ARMY IS IN THE WOODS.
thump
MY BLOOD FREEZES...
...AND FLOWS BACK-WARD IN MY VEINS.
IT SCREAMS...
...FOR THAT HEAT.
YOUR HEAT...
...WHICH WIPED OUT THE VOICE OF THE CURSE.
YOUR MAJ-ESTY!
A HEAT THAT EVEN THE CRUEL ARROWS OF RAIN...
...CANNOT QUENCH.

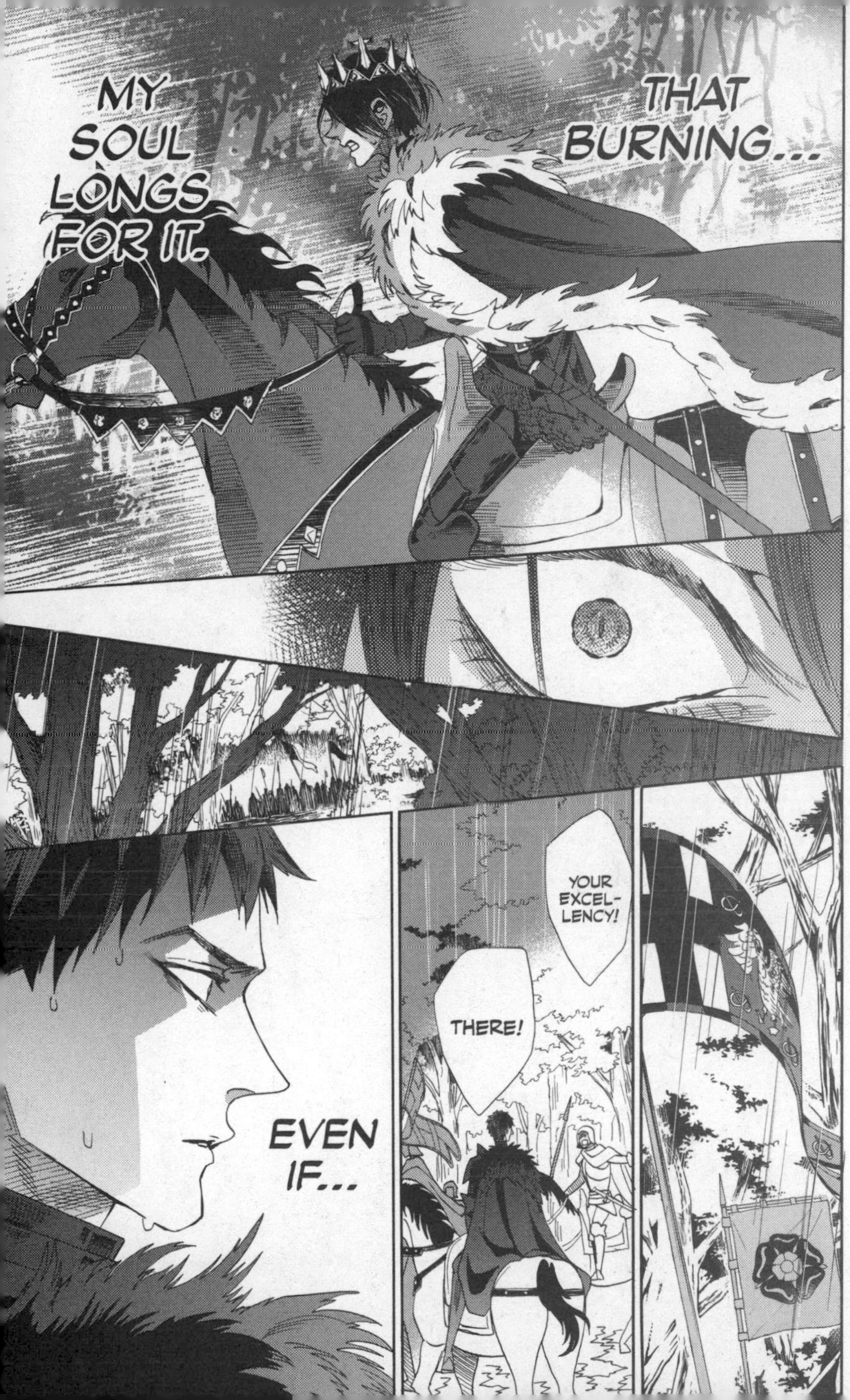
THAT BURNING...
MY SOUL LONGS FOR IT.
YOUR EXCEL-LENCY!
THERE!
EVEN IF...

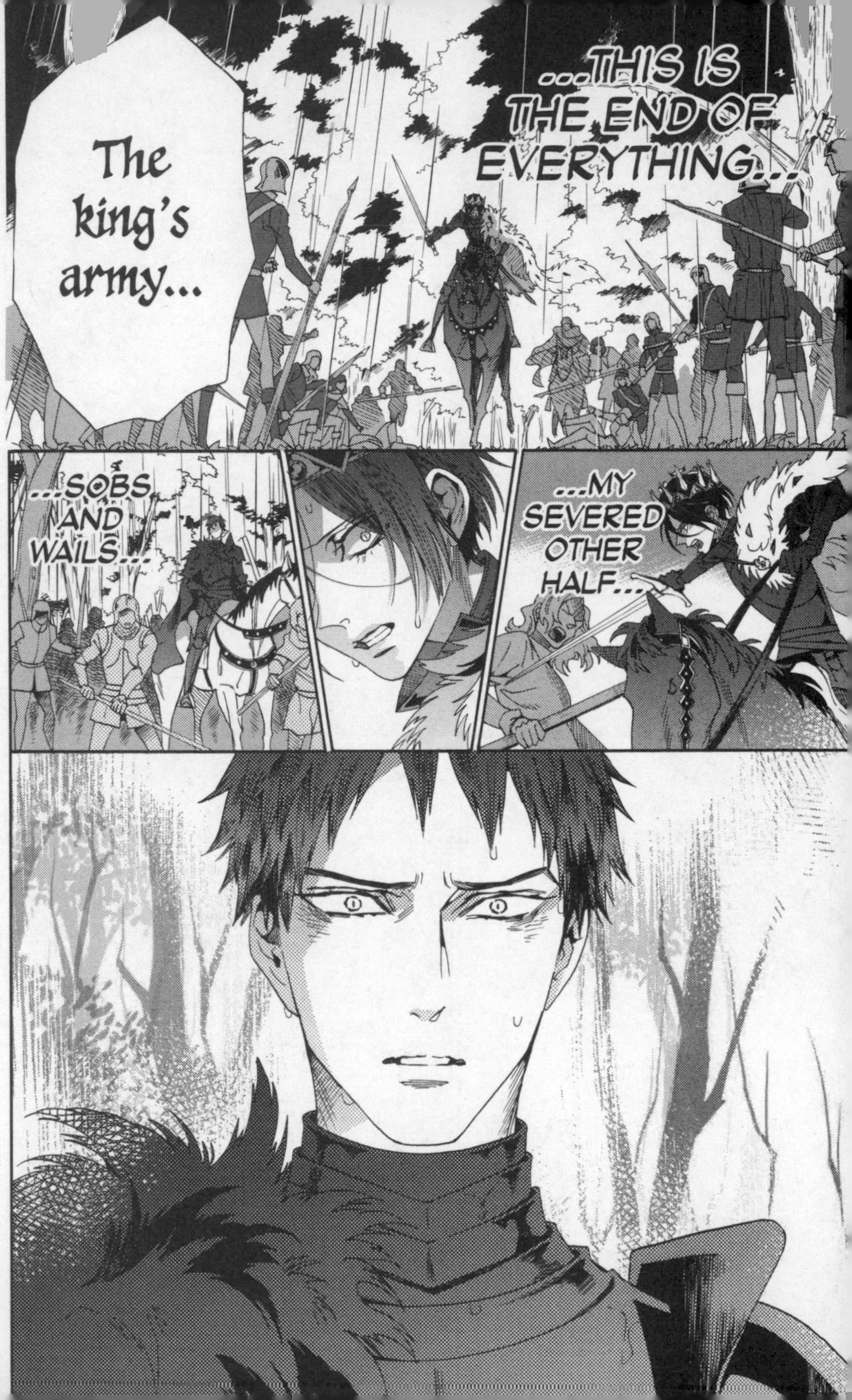
...THIS IS THE END OF EVERYTHING...
The king's army...
...MY SEVERED OTHER HALF...
...SOBS AND WAILS...

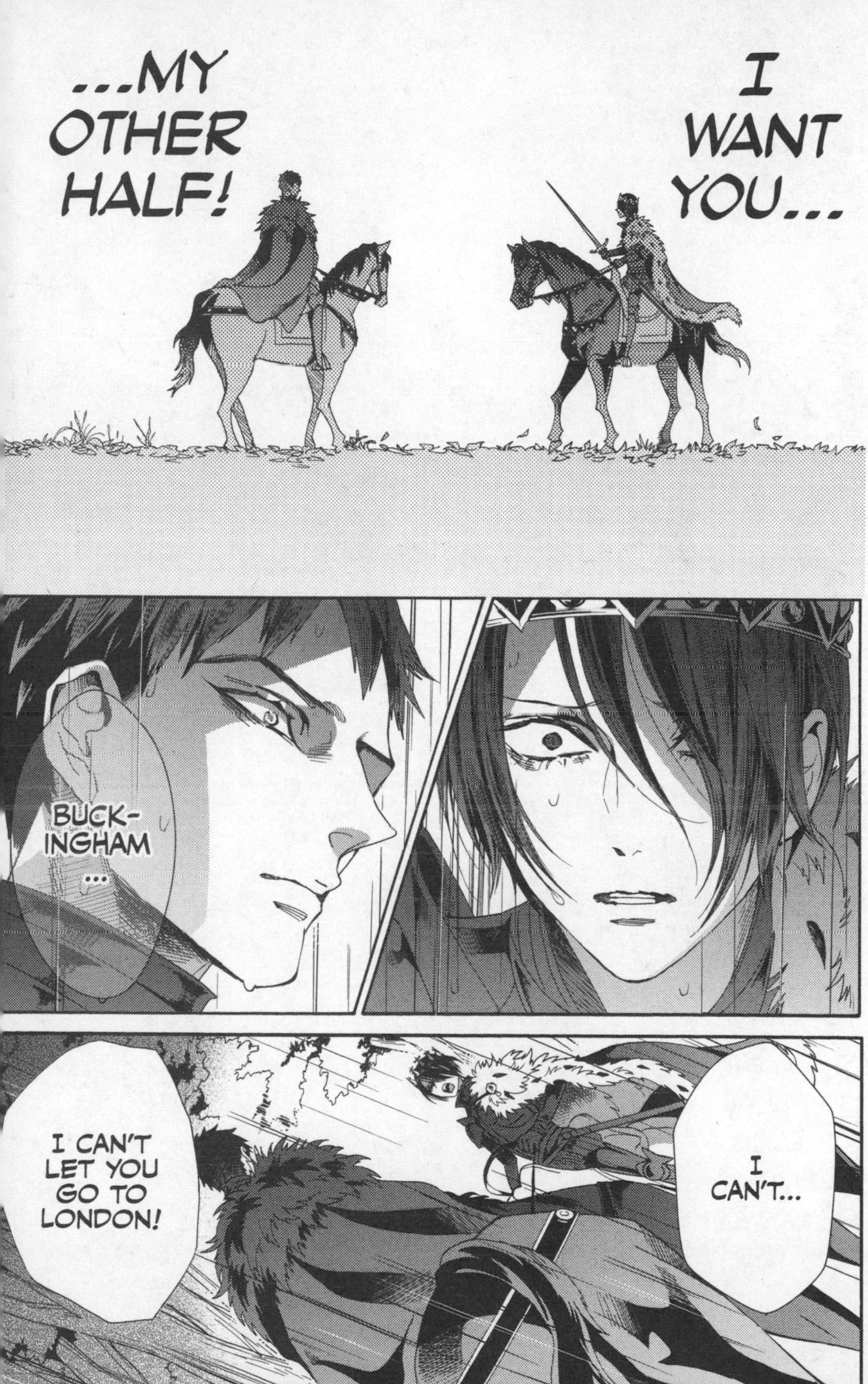
I WANT YOU...
...MY OTHER HALF!
BUCK-INGHAM...
I CAN'T...
I CAN'T LET YOU GO TO LONDON!

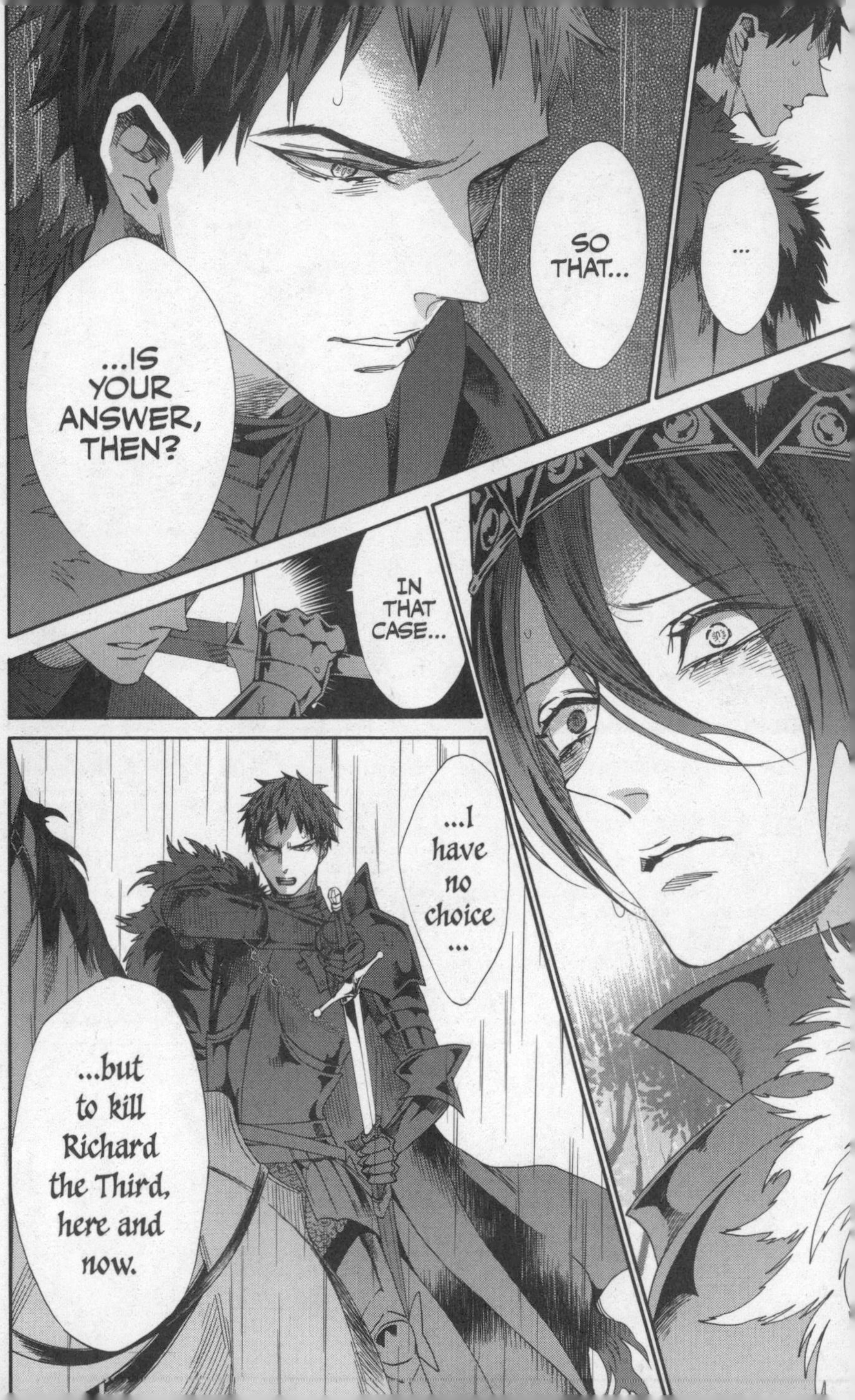
...
SO THAT...
...IS YOUR ANSWER, THEN?
IN THAT CASE...
...I have no choice...
...but to kill Richard the Third, here and now.

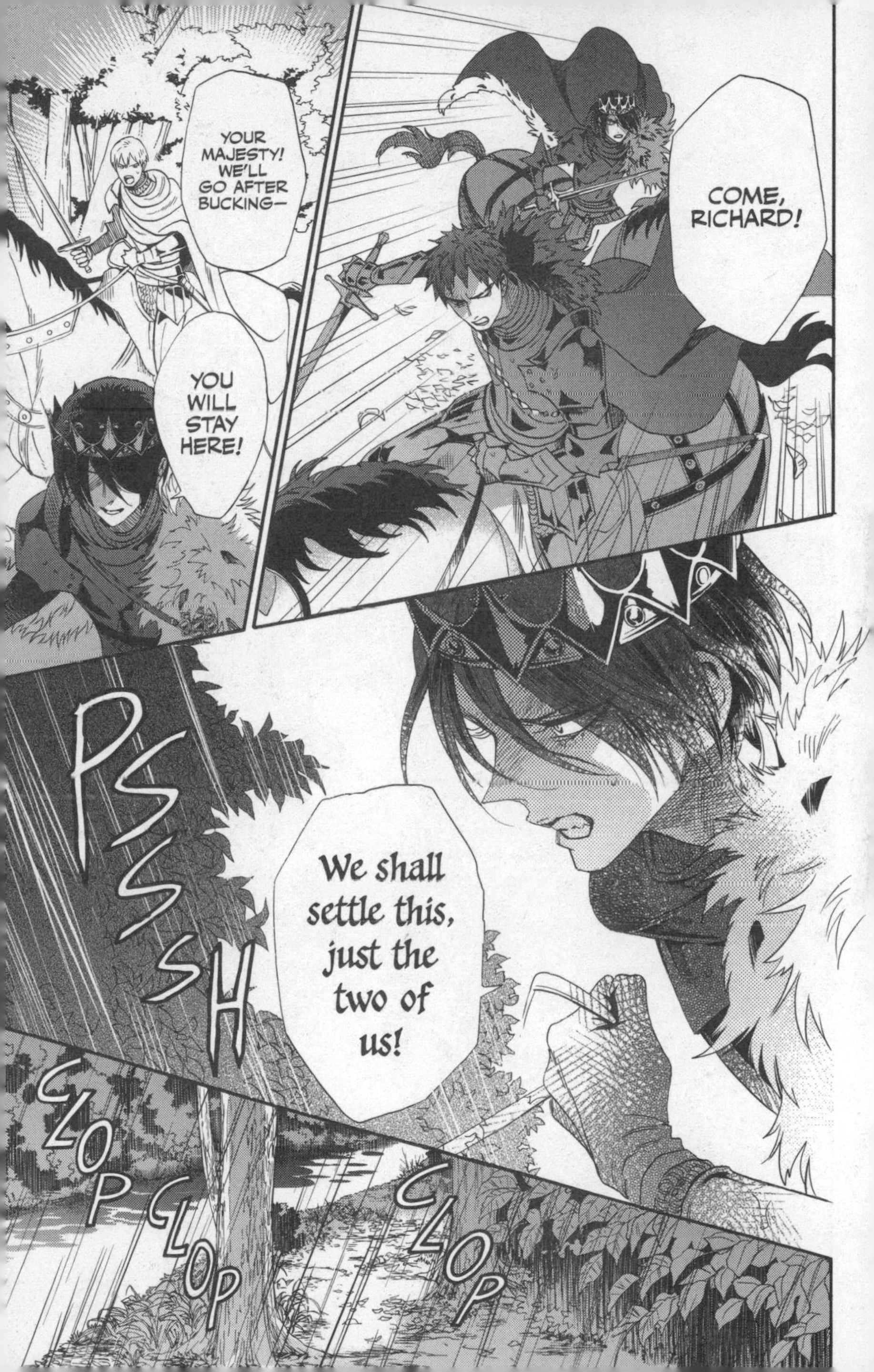
COME, RICHARD!
YOUR MAJESTY! WE'LL GO AFTER BUCKING—
YOU WILL STAY HERE!
We shall settle this, just the two of us!
PSSSH
CLOP
CLOP CLOP

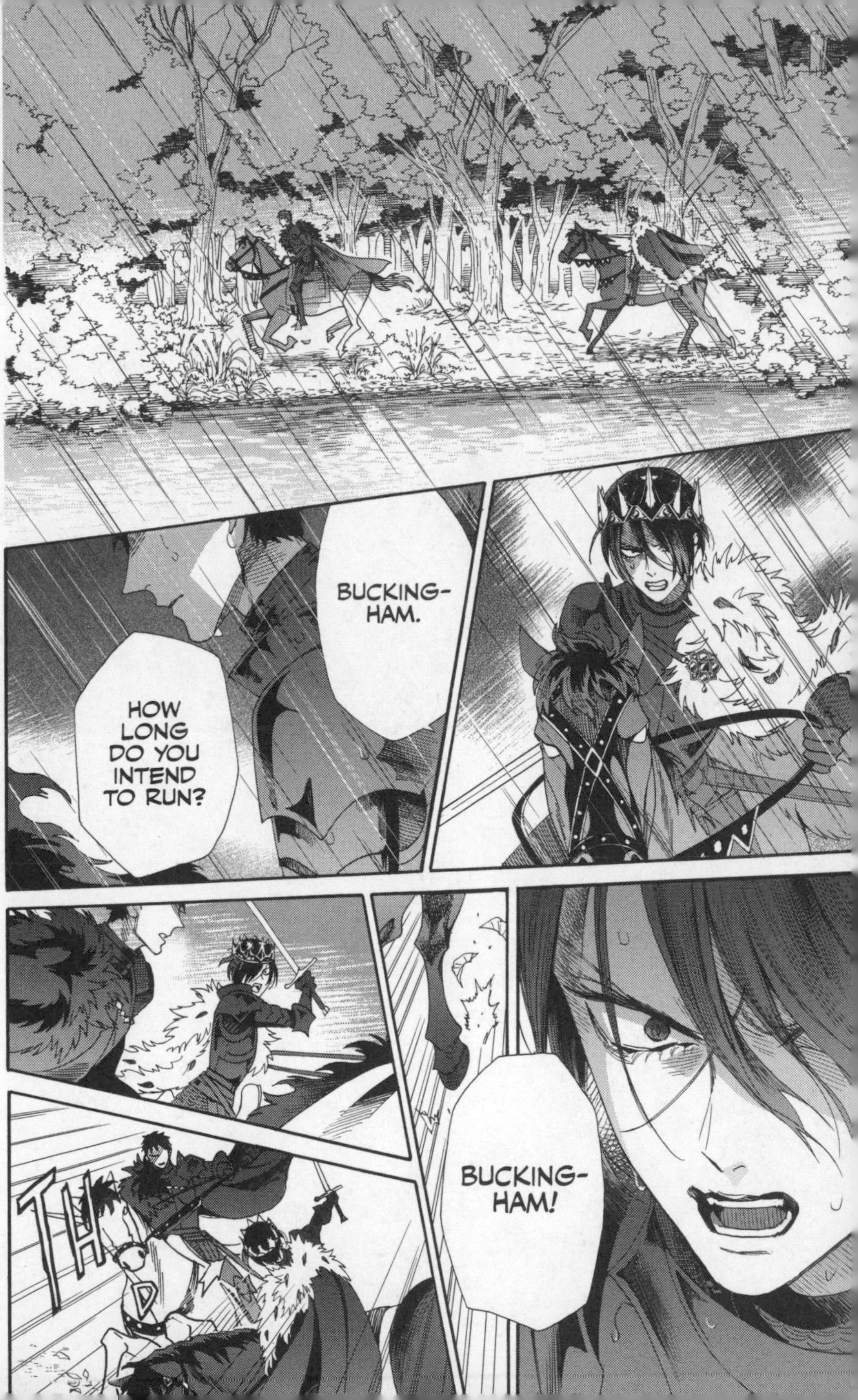
BUCKING-HAM.
HOW LONG DO YOU INTEND TO RUN?
BUCKING-HAM!
THD

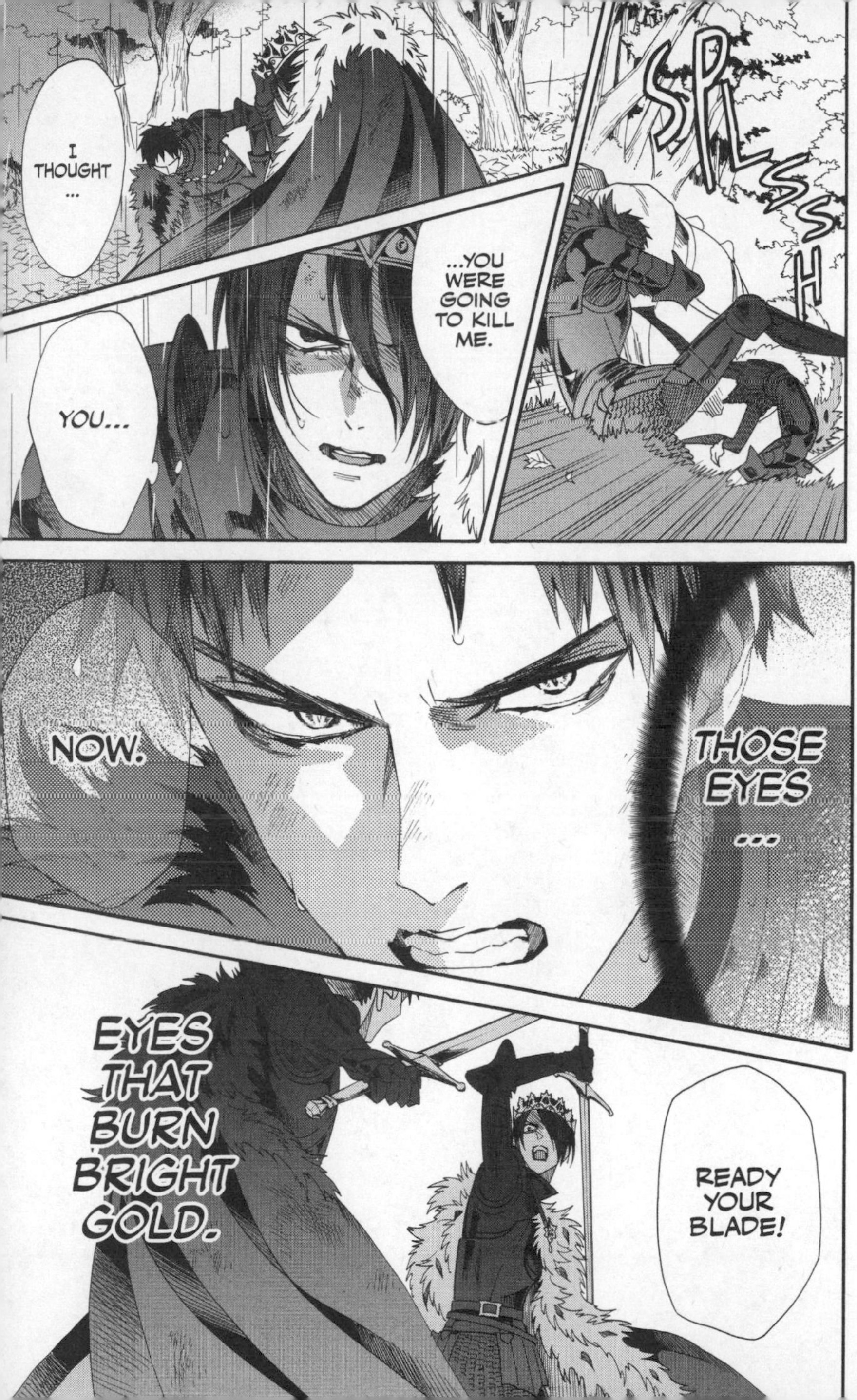
SPLSSH
I THOUGHT ...
...YOU WERE GOING TO KILL ME.
YOU...
THOSE EYES ...
NOW.
READY YOUR BLADE!
EYES THAT BURN BRIGHT GOLD.

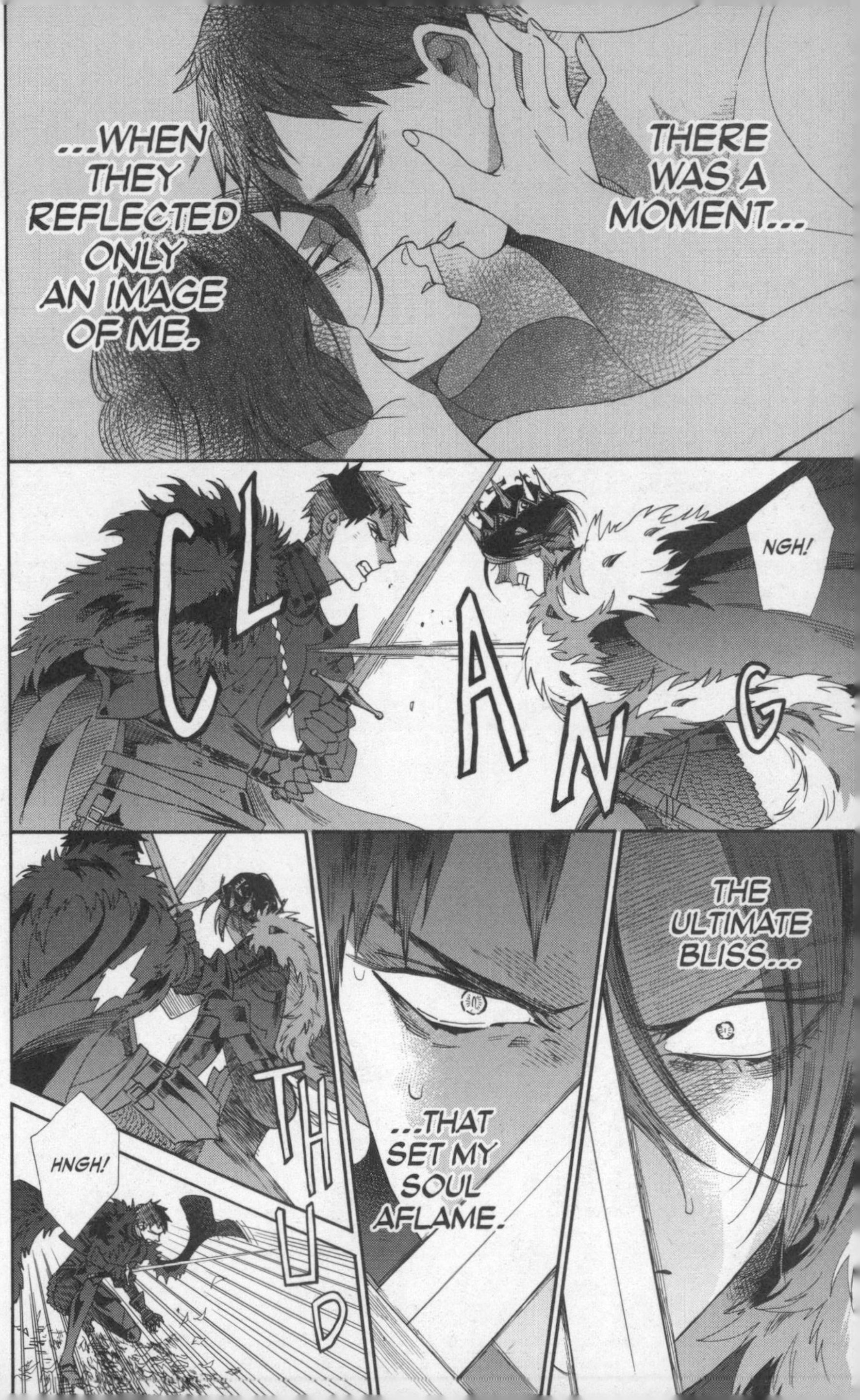
THERE WAS A MOMENT...
...WHEN THEY REFLECTED ONLY AN IMAGE OF ME.
NGH!
CLANG
THE ULTIMATE BLISS...
...THAT SET MY SOUL AFLAME.
THUD
HNGH!

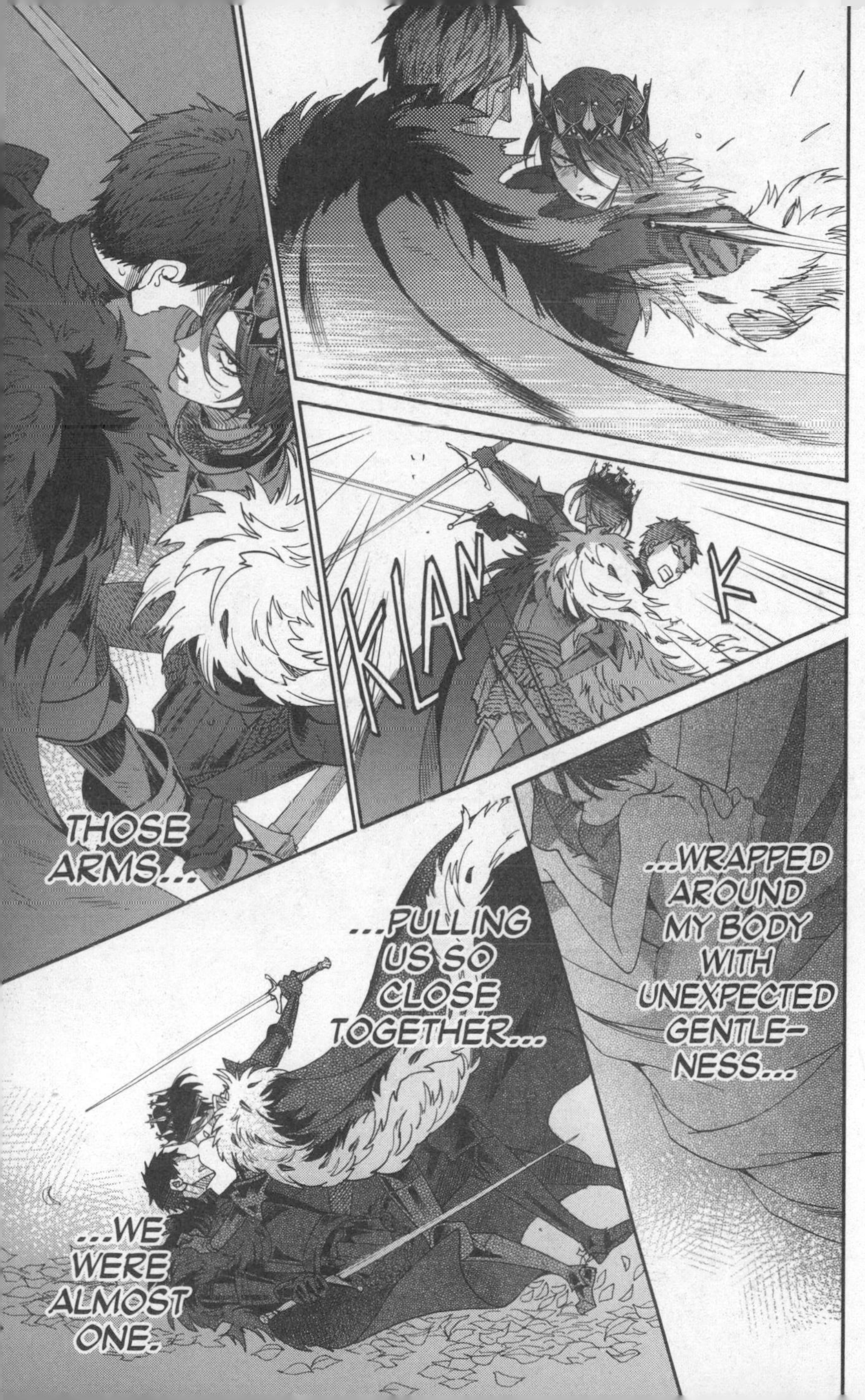
KLANK
THOSE ARMS...
...WRAPPED AROUND MY BODY WITH UNEXPECTED GENTLE-NESS...
...PULLING US SO CLOSE TOGETHER...
...WE WERE ALMOST ONE.

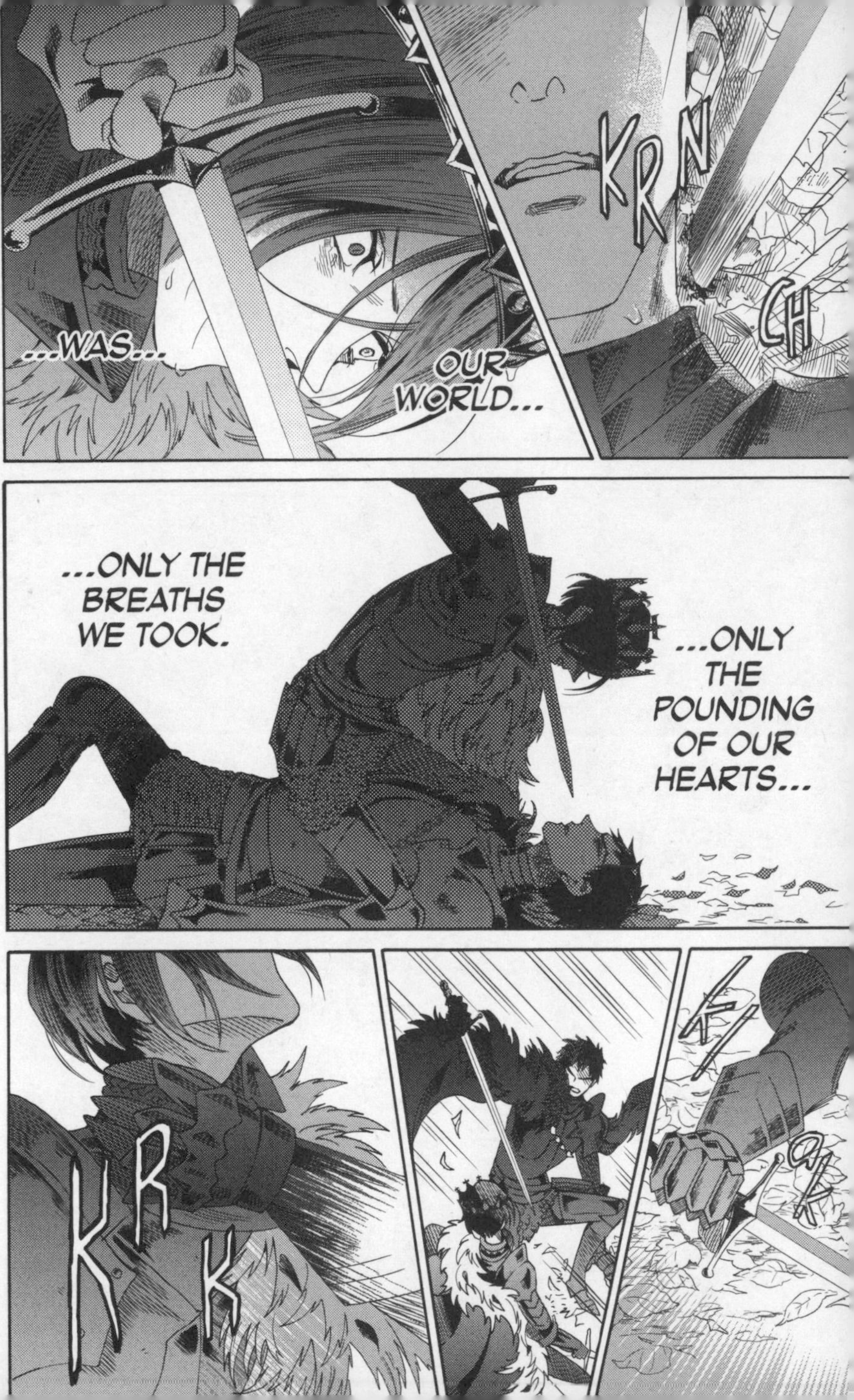
KRNCH
OUR WORLD...
...WAS...
...ONLY THE POUNDING OF OUR HEARTS...
...ONLY THE BREATHS WE TOOK.
KRK

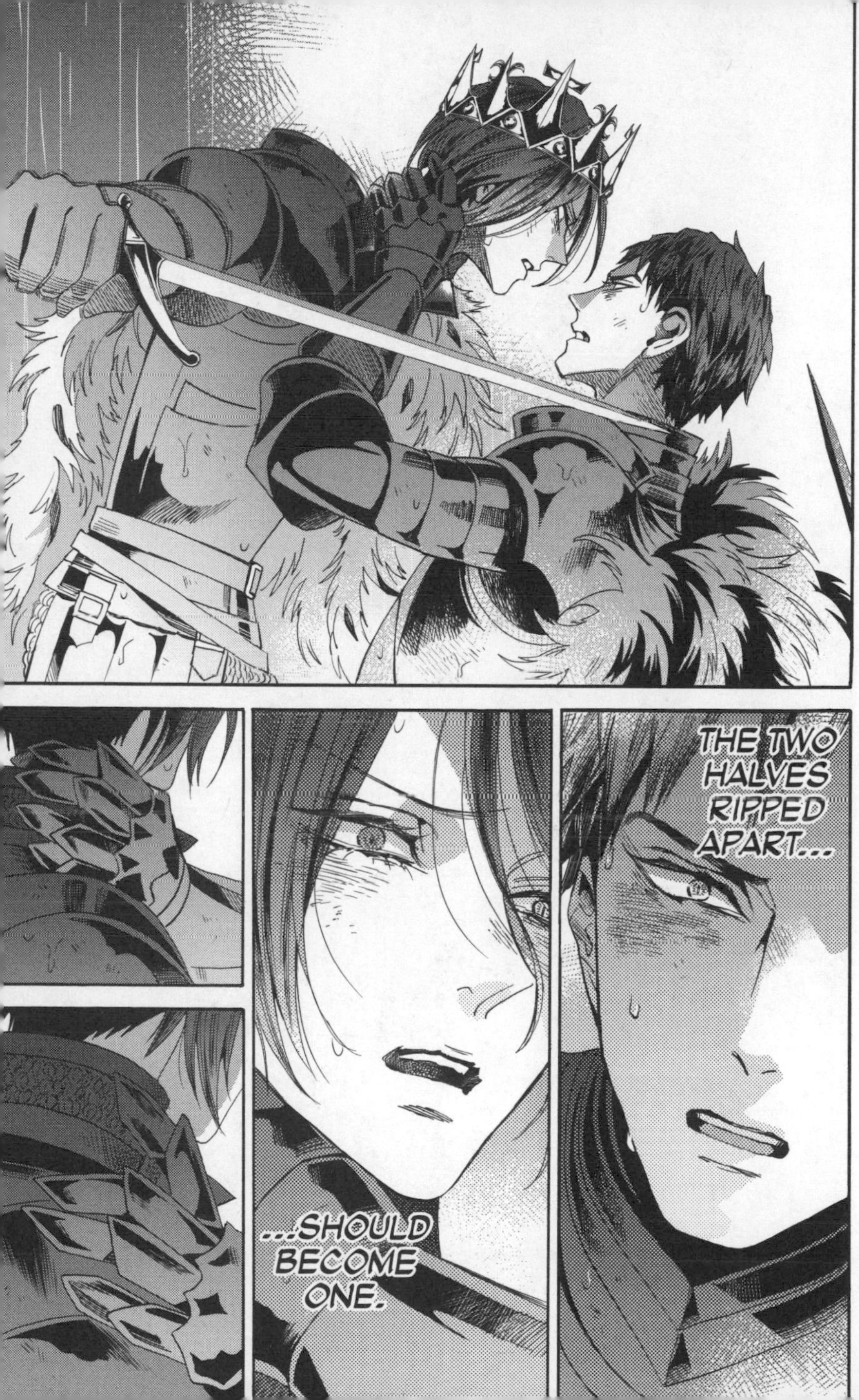
THE TWO HALVES RIPPED APART...
...SHOULD BECOME ONE.

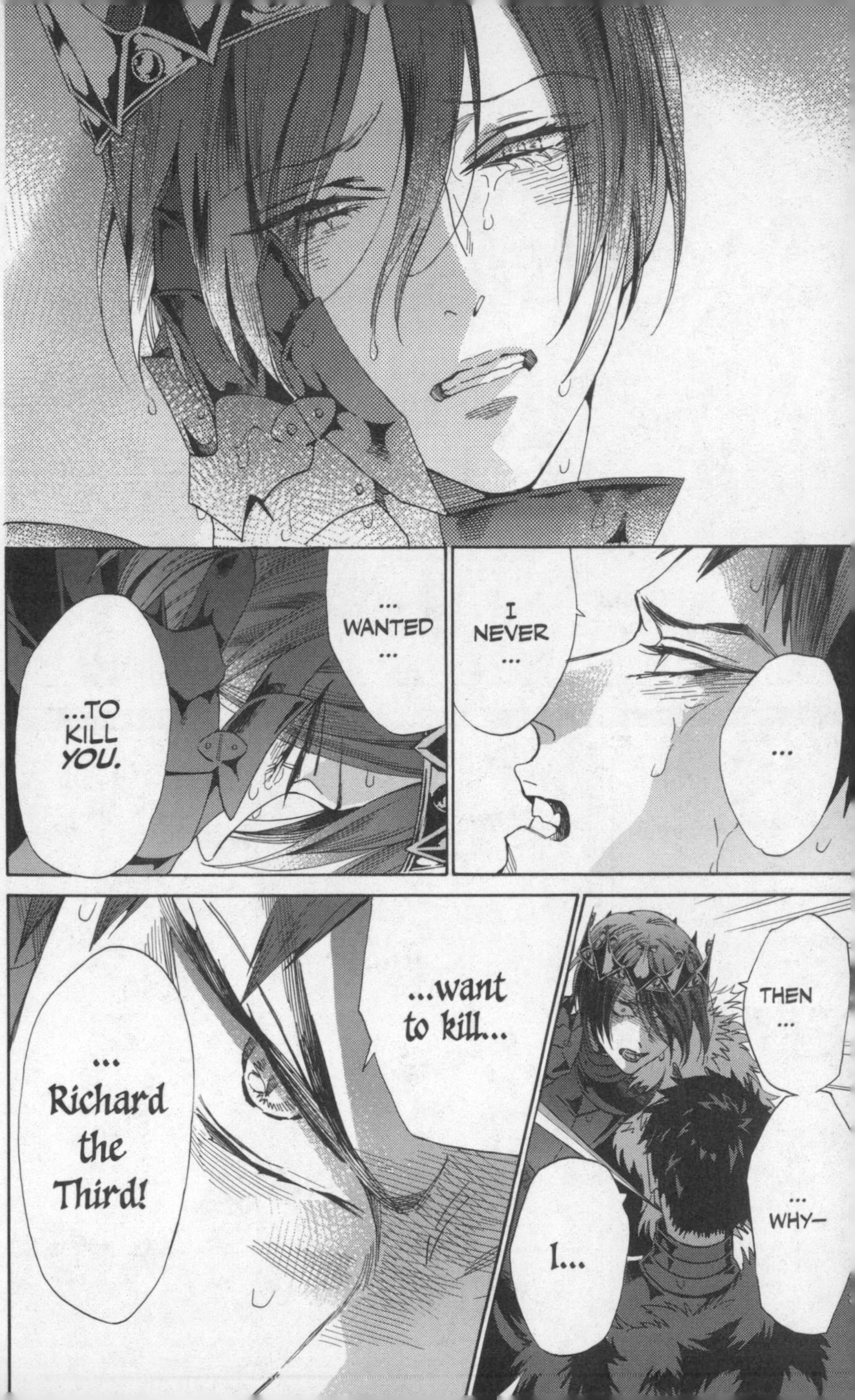
...
I NEVER ...
... WANTED ...
...TO KILL YOU.
THEN ...
... WHY—
I...
...want to kill...
... Richard the Third!

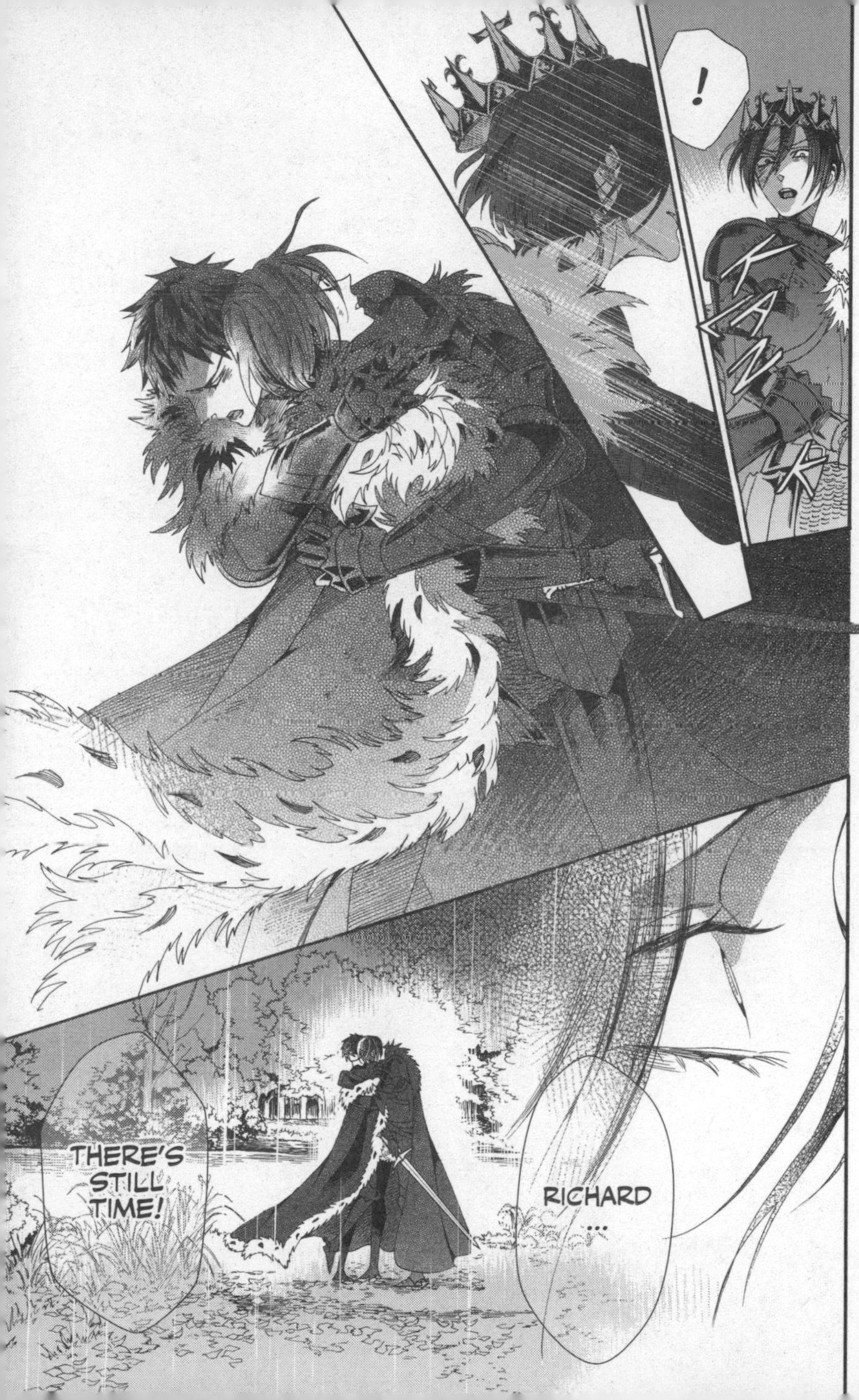
!
KANK
RICHARD ...
THERE'S STILL TIME!

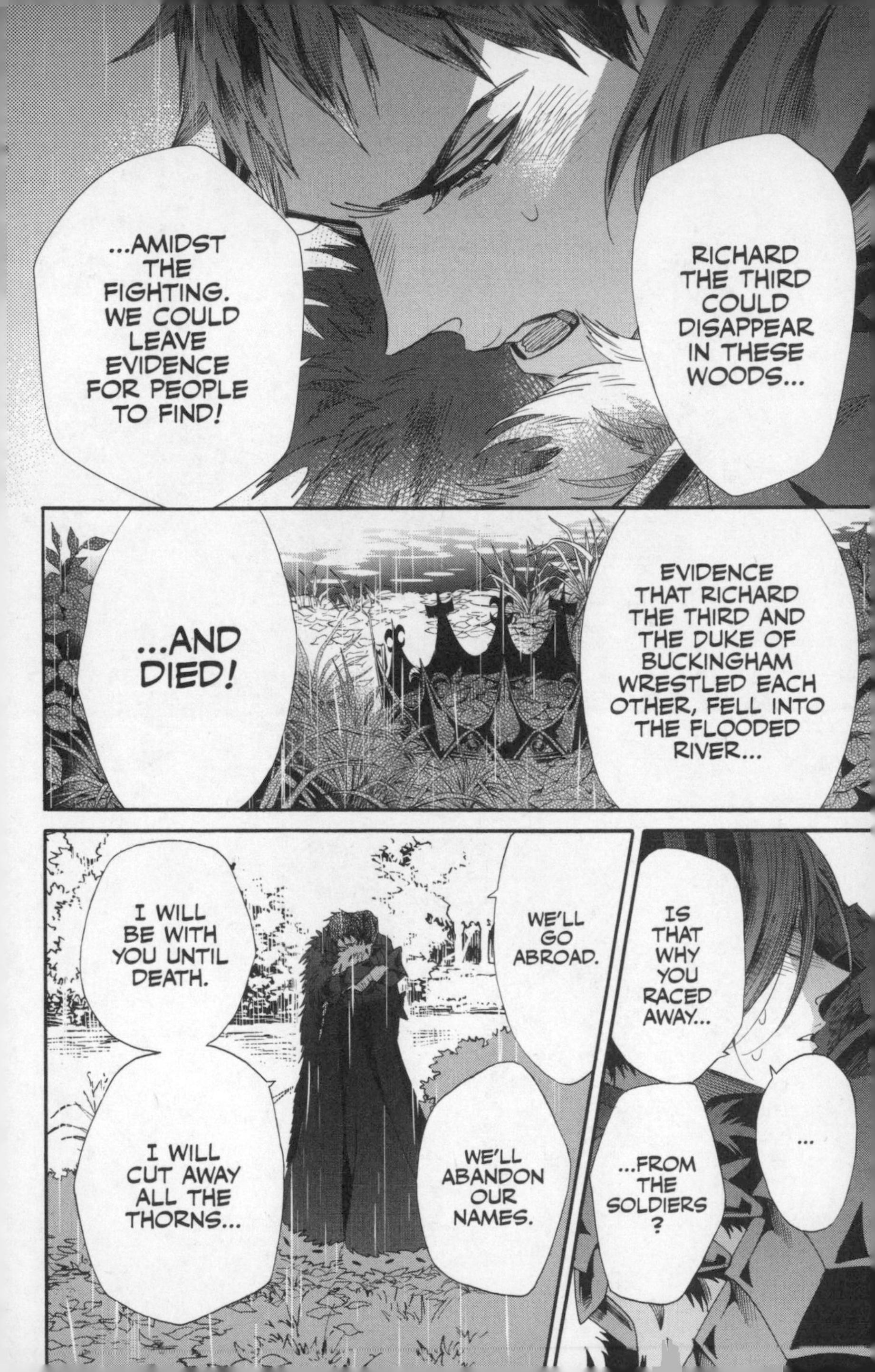
RICHARD THE THIRD COULD DISAPPEAR IN THESE WOODS...
...AMIDST THE FIGHTING. WE COULD LEAVE EVIDENCE FOR PEOPLE TO FIND!
EVIDENCE THAT RICHARD THE THIRD AND THE DUKE OF BUCKINGHAM WRESTLED EACH OTHER, FELL INTO THE FLOODED RIVER...
...AND DIED!
IS THAT WHY YOU RACED AWAY...
...FROM THE SOLDIERS?
...
WE'LL GO ABROAD.
WE'LL ABANDON OUR NAMES.
I WILL BE WITH YOU UNTIL DEATH.
I WILL CUT AWAY ALL THE THORNS...

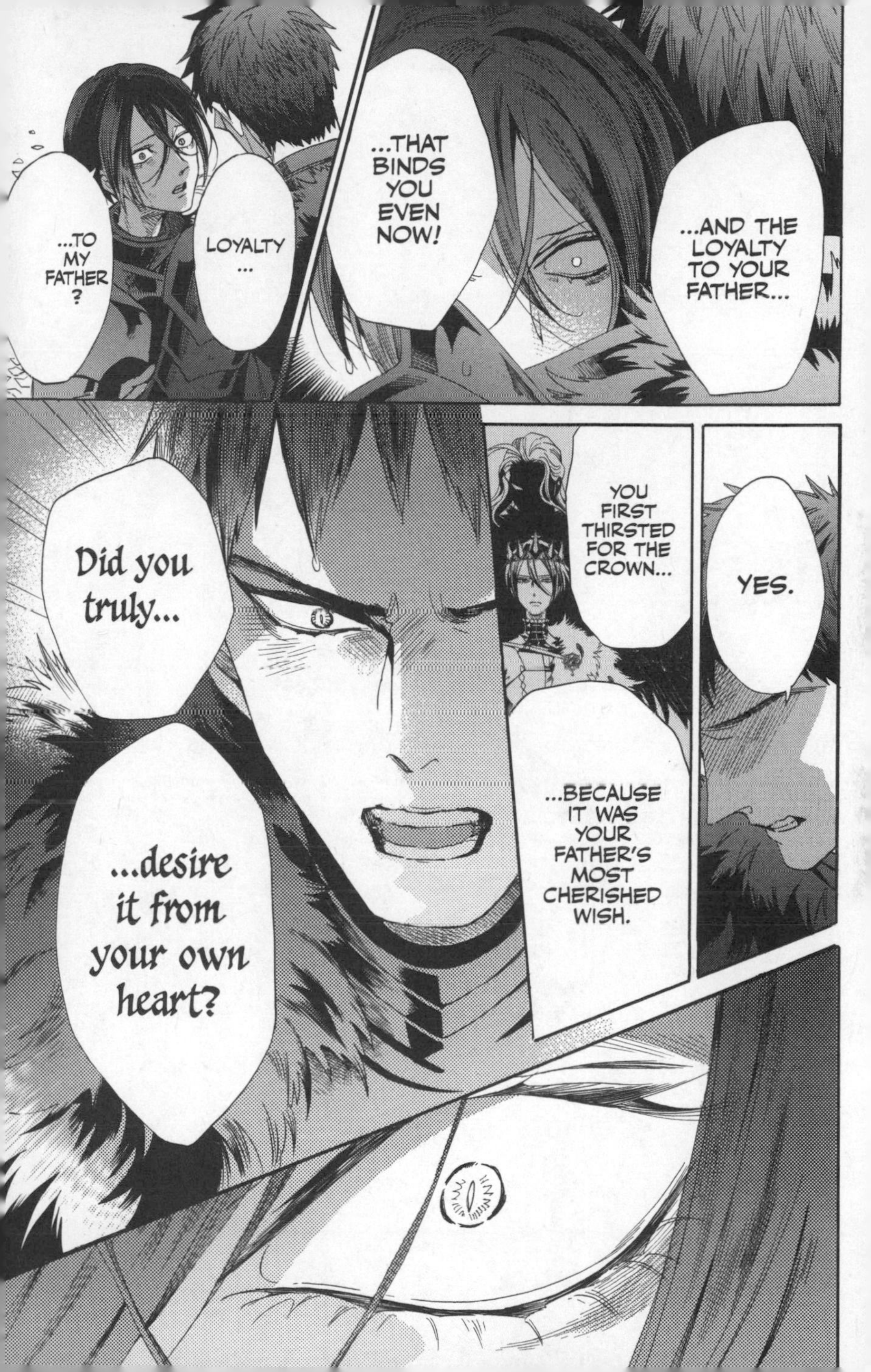
...AND THE LOYALTY TO YOUR FATHER...
...THAT BINDS YOU EVEN NOW!
LOYALTY ...
...TO MY FATHER ?
YES.
YOU FIRST THIRSTED FOR THE CROWN...
...BECAUSE IT WAS YOUR FATHER'S MOST CHERISHED WISH.
Did you truly...
...desire it from your own heart?

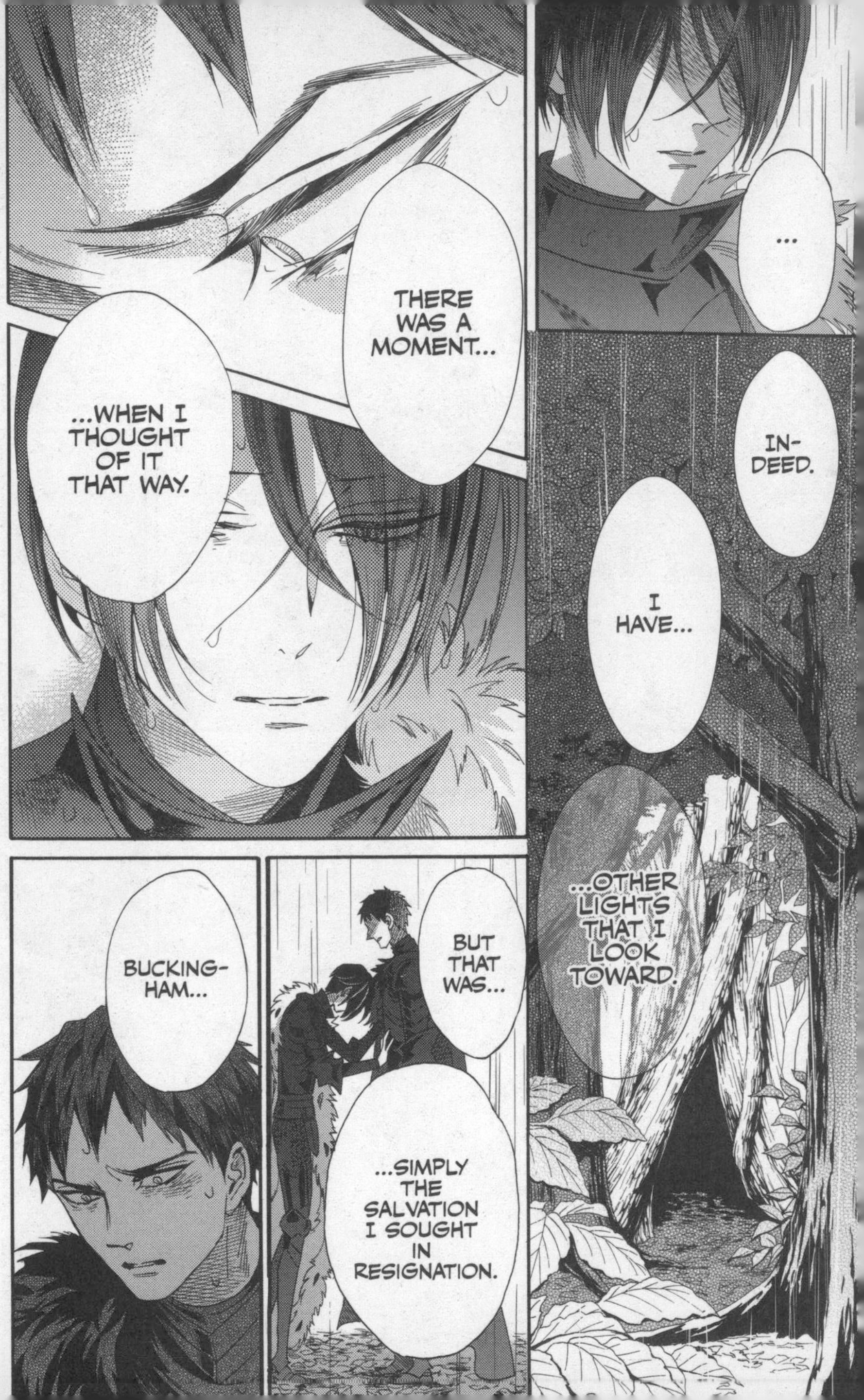
...
THERE WAS A MOMENT...
...WHEN I THOUGHT OF IT THAT WAY.
BUT THAT WAS...
...SIMPLY THE SALVATION I SOUGHT IN RESIGNATION.
BUCKING-HAM...
IN-DEED.
I HAVE...
...OTHER LIGHTS THAT I LOOK TOWARD.

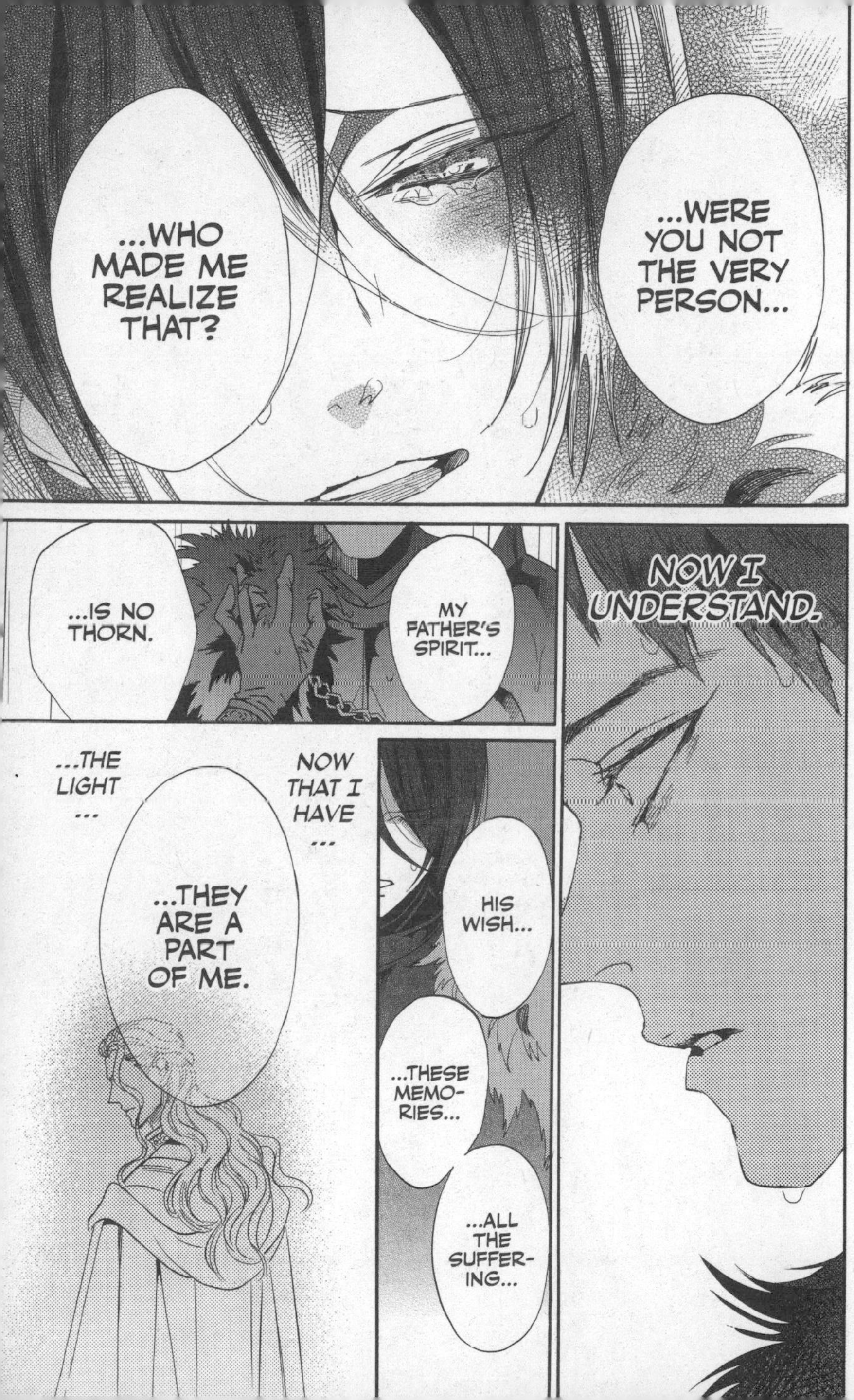
...WERE YOU NOT THE VERY PERSON...
...WHO MADE ME REALIZE THAT?
NOW I UNDERSTAND.
MY FATHER'S SPIRIT...
...IS NO THORN.
HIS WISH...
...THESE MEMO-RIES...
...ALL THE SUFFER-ING...
NOW THAT I HAVE ...
...THE LIGHT ...
...THEY ARE A PART OF ME.

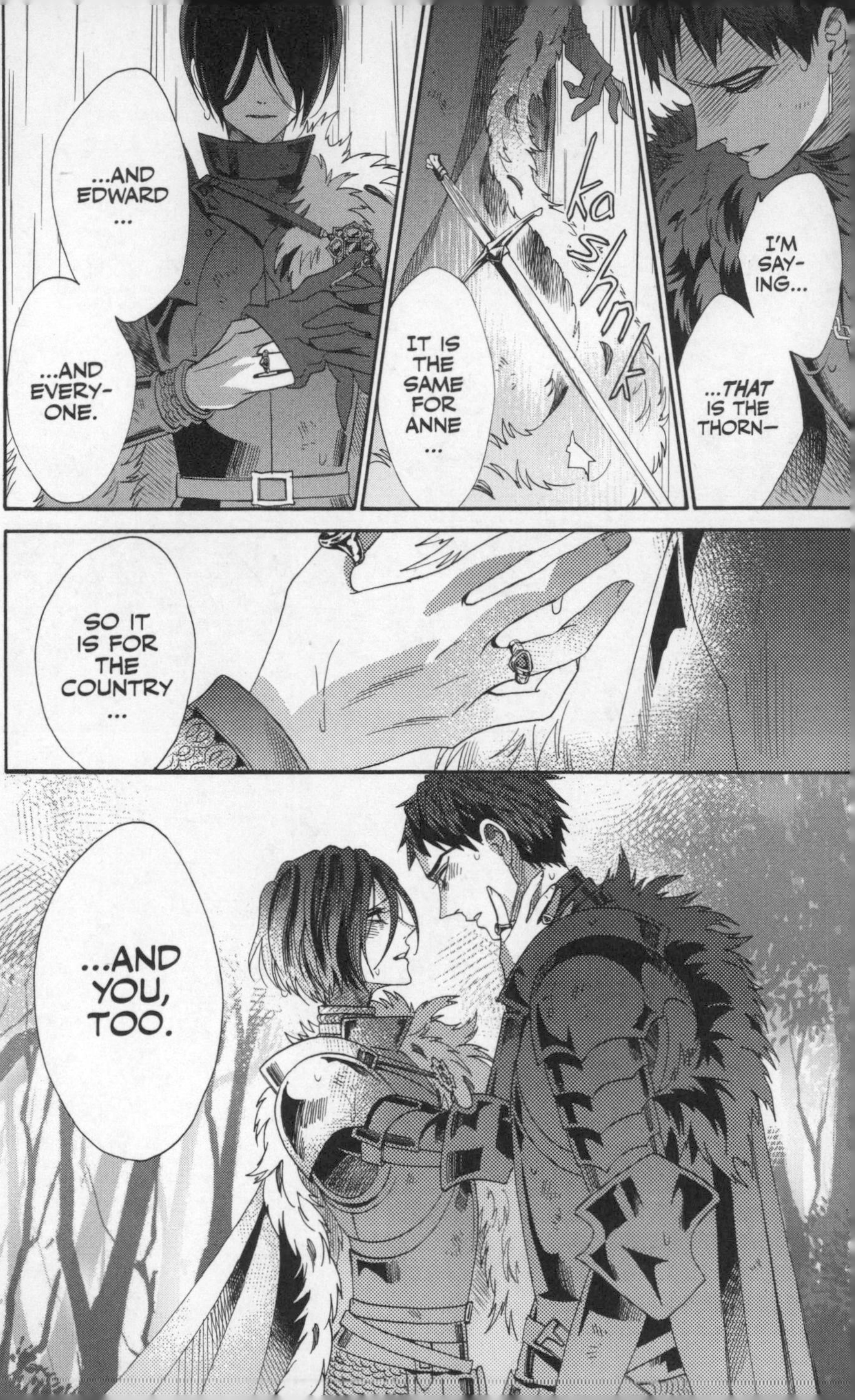
I'M SAYING...
...THAT IS THE THORN—
kashnk
IT IS THE SAME FOR ANNE...
...AND EDWARD...
...AND EVERYONE.
SO IT IS FOR THE COUNTRY...
...AND YOU, TOO.

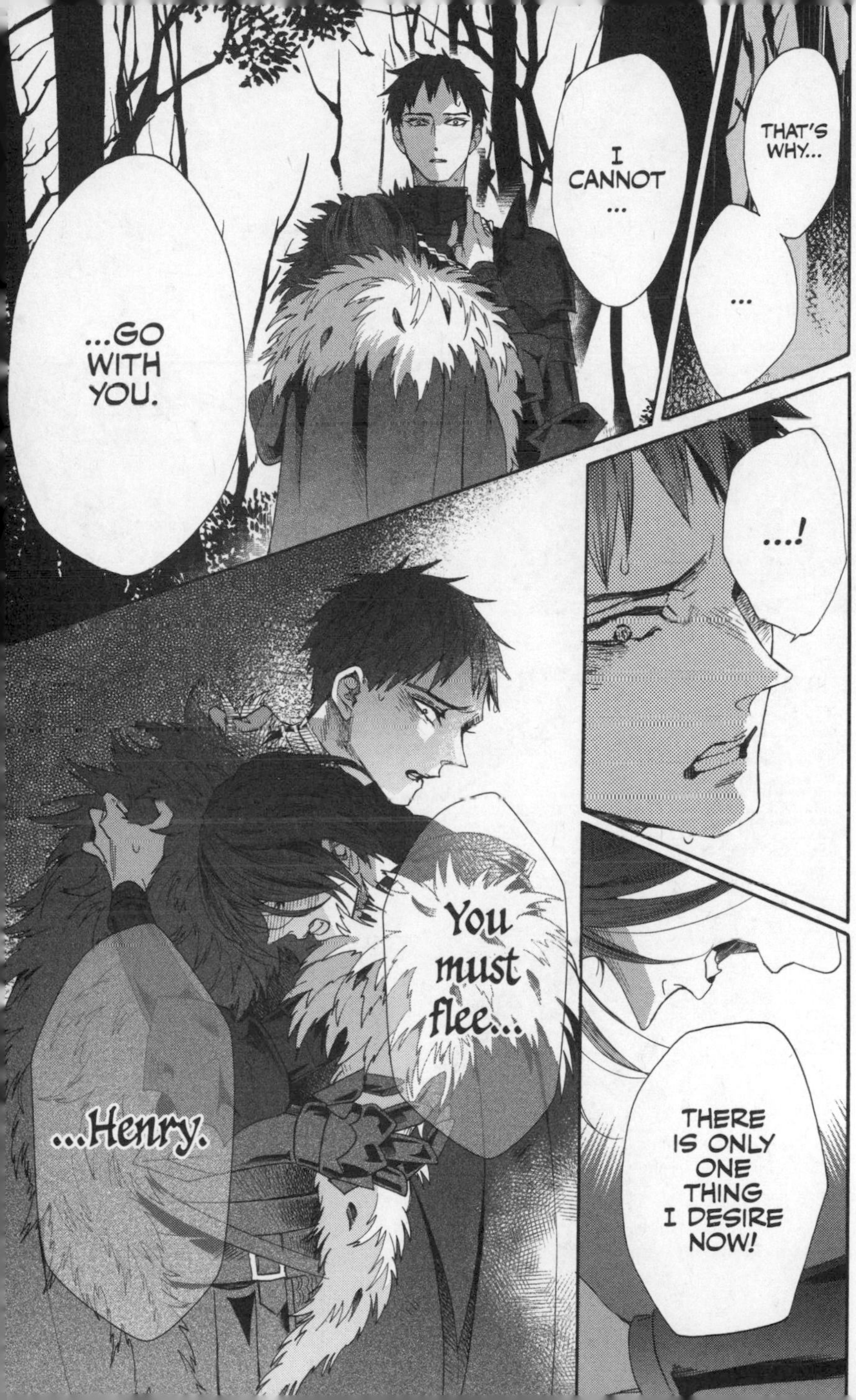
THAT'S WHY...
...
I CANNOT ...
...GO WITH YOU.
...!
THERE IS ONLY ONE THING I DESIRE NOW!
You must flee...
...Henry.

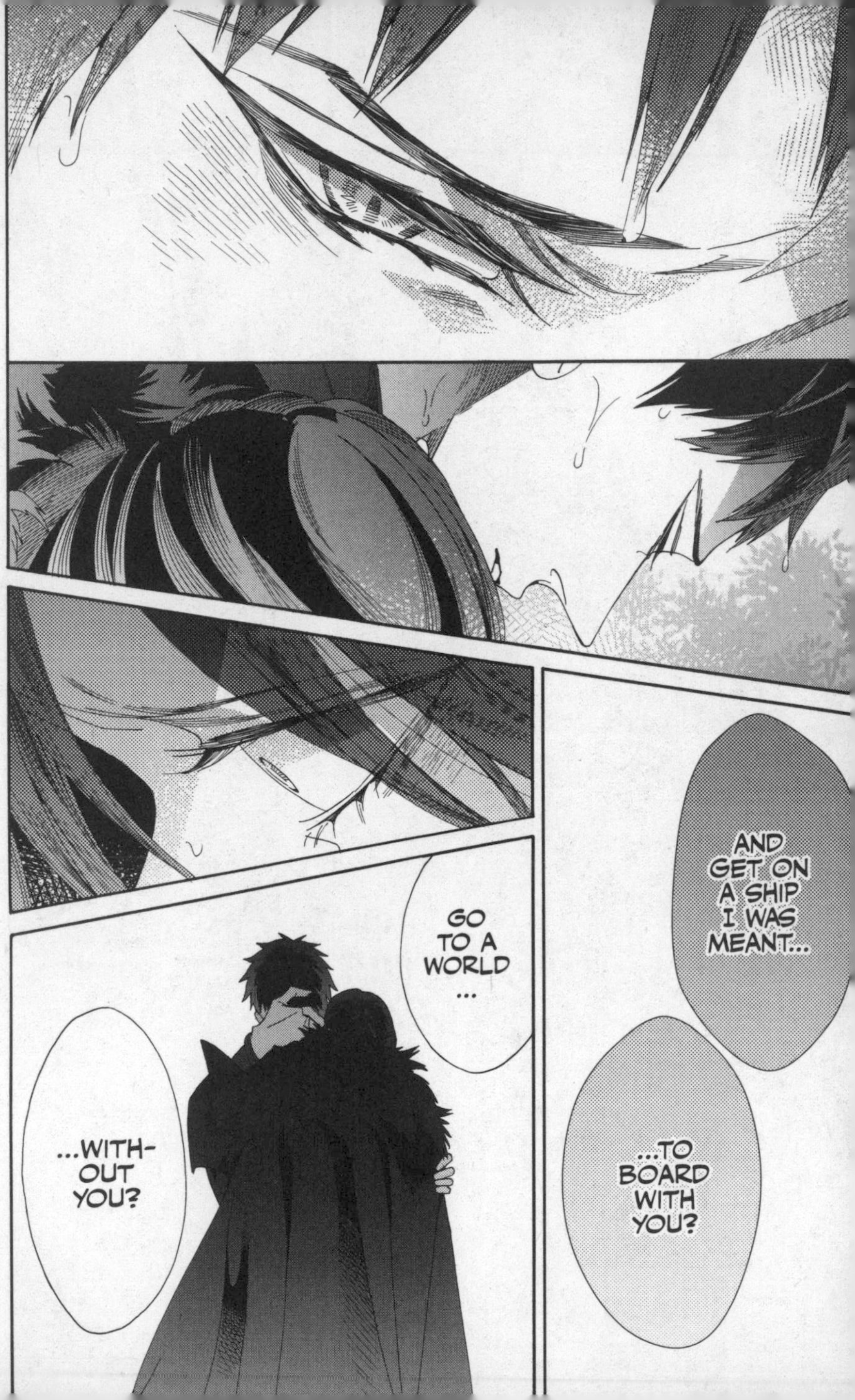
AND GET ON A SHIP I WAS MEANT...
...TO BOARD WITH YOU?
GO TO A WORLD ...
...WITH-OUT YOU?

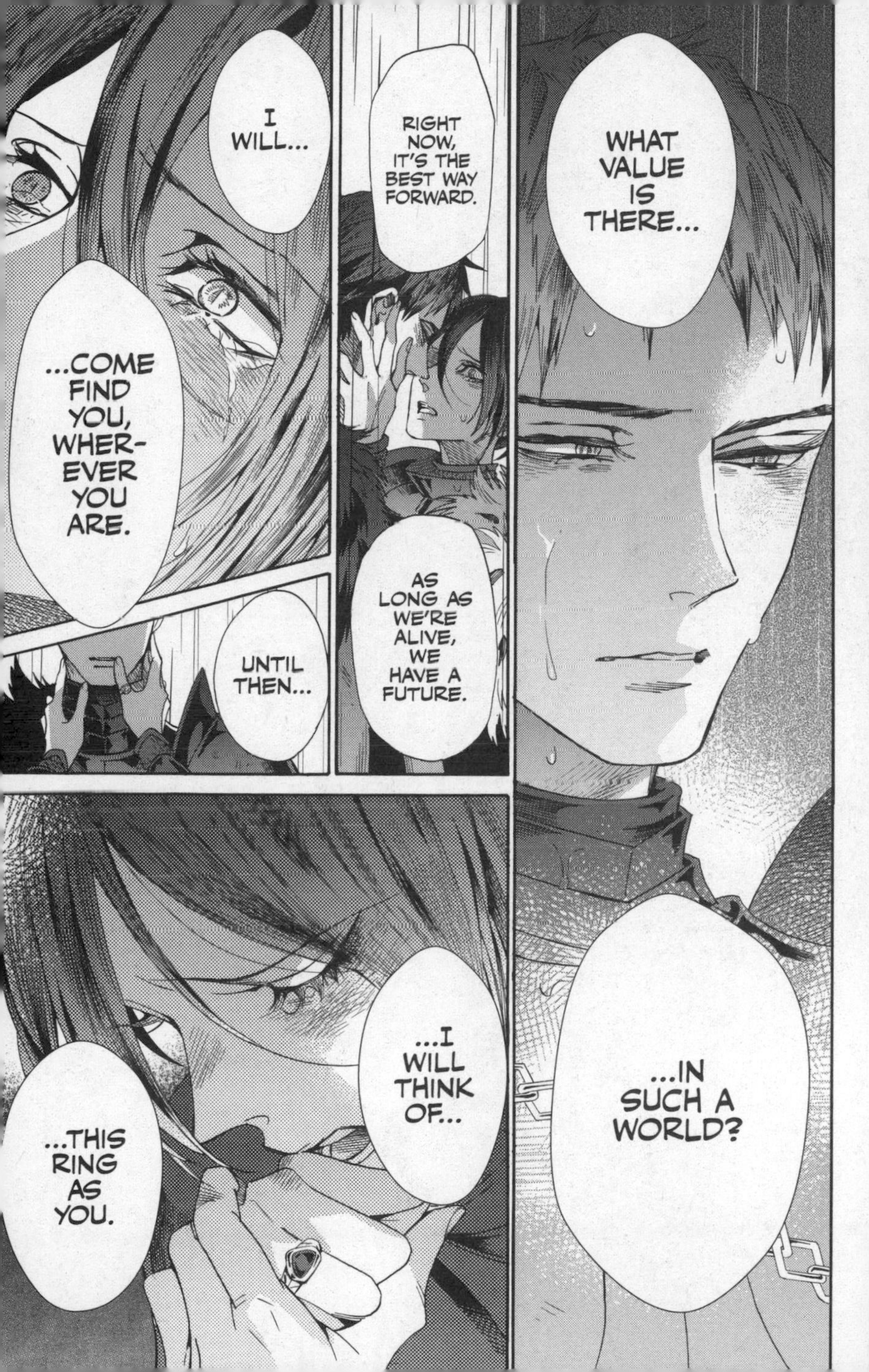
WHAT VALUE IS THERE...
...IN SUCH A WORLD?
RIGHT NOW, IT'S THE BEST WAY FORWARD.
AS LONG AS WE'RE ALIVE, WE HAVE A FUTURE.
I WILL...
...COME FIND YOU, WHER-EVER YOU ARE.
UNTIL THEN...
...I WILL THINK OF...
...THIS RING AS YOU.

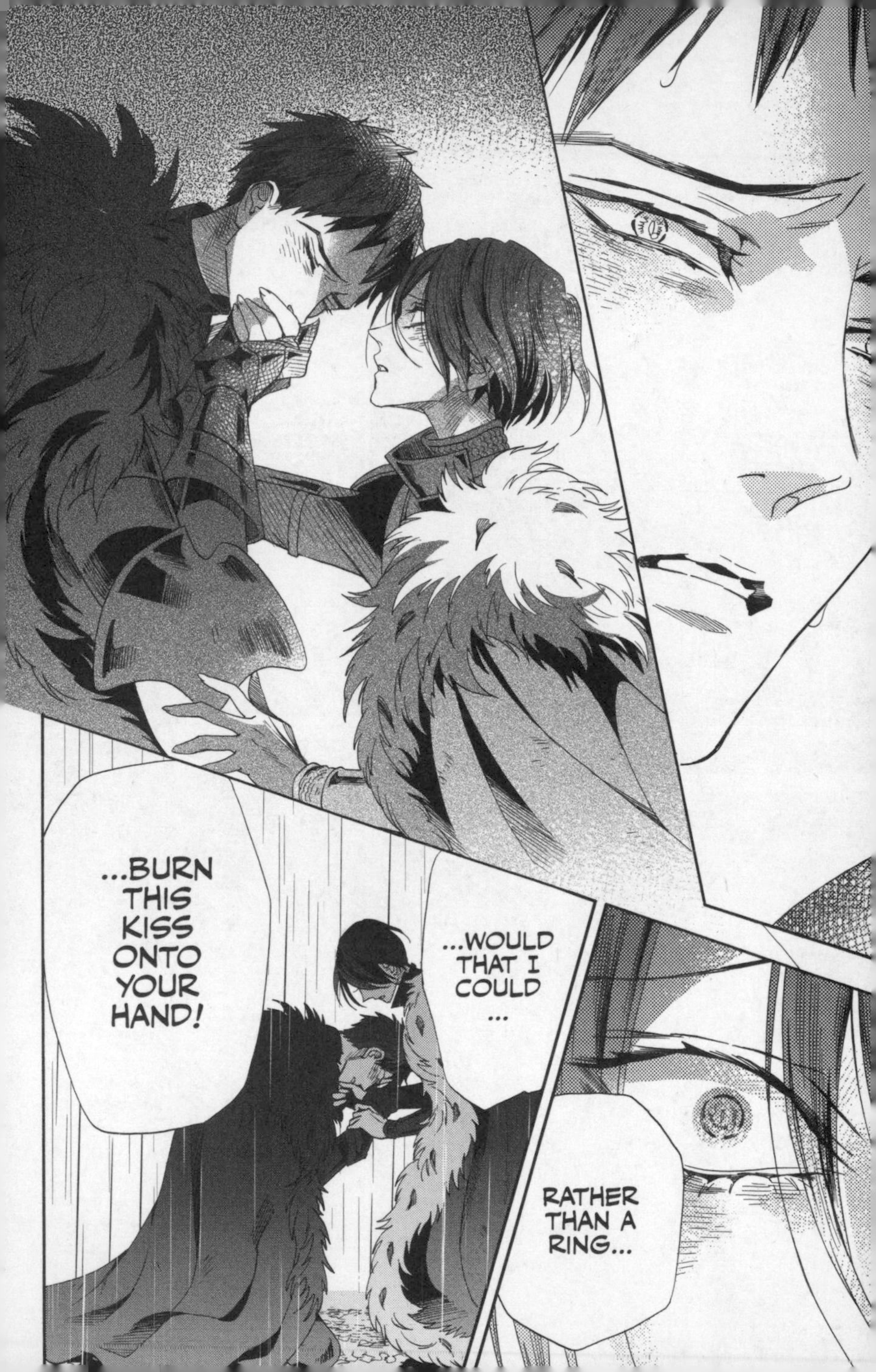
RATHER THAN A RING...
...WOULD THAT I COULD ...
...BURN THIS KISS ONTO YOUR HAND!

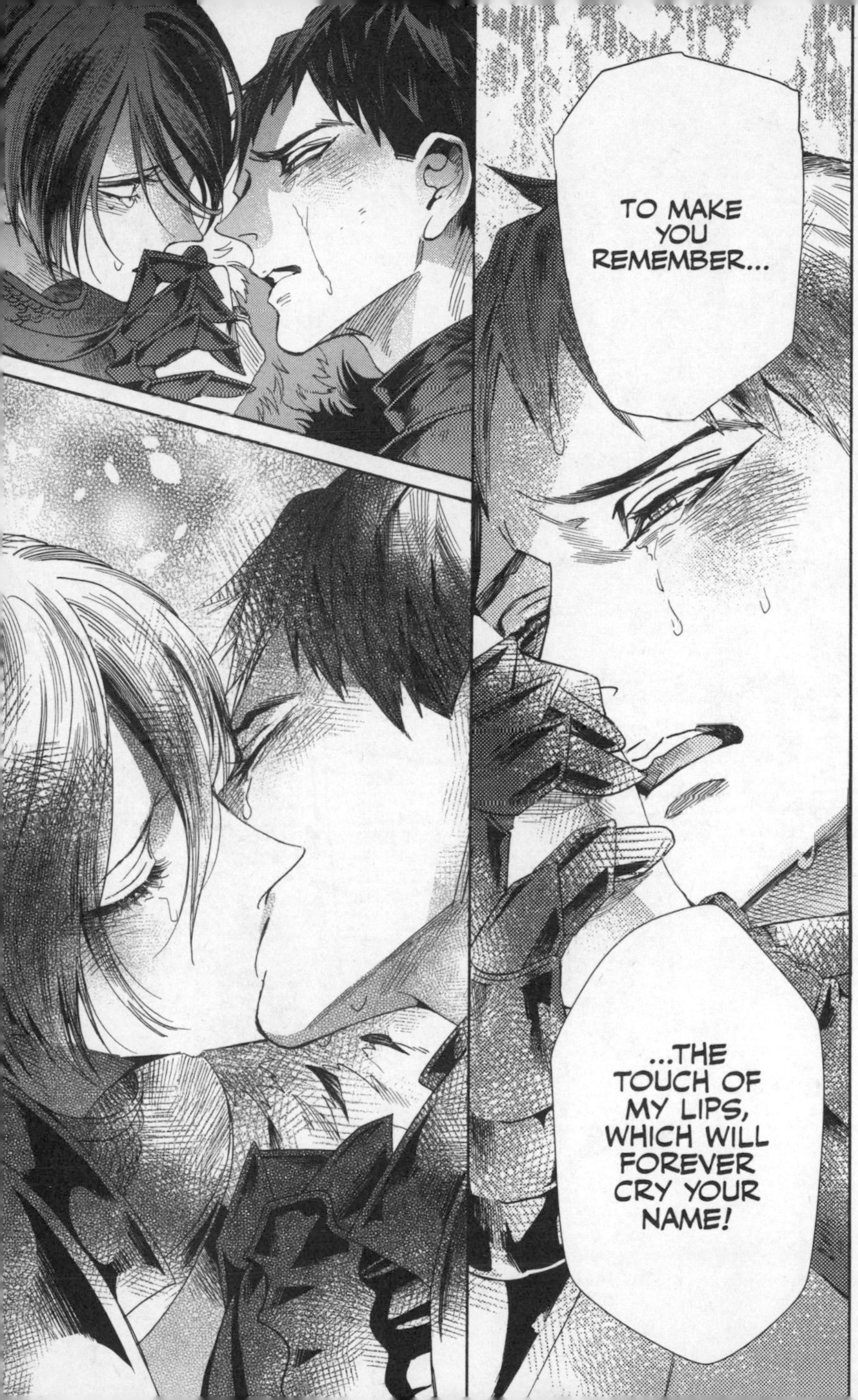
TO MAKE YOU REMEMBER...
...THE TOUCH OF MY LIPS, WHICH WILL FOREVER CRY YOUR NAME!

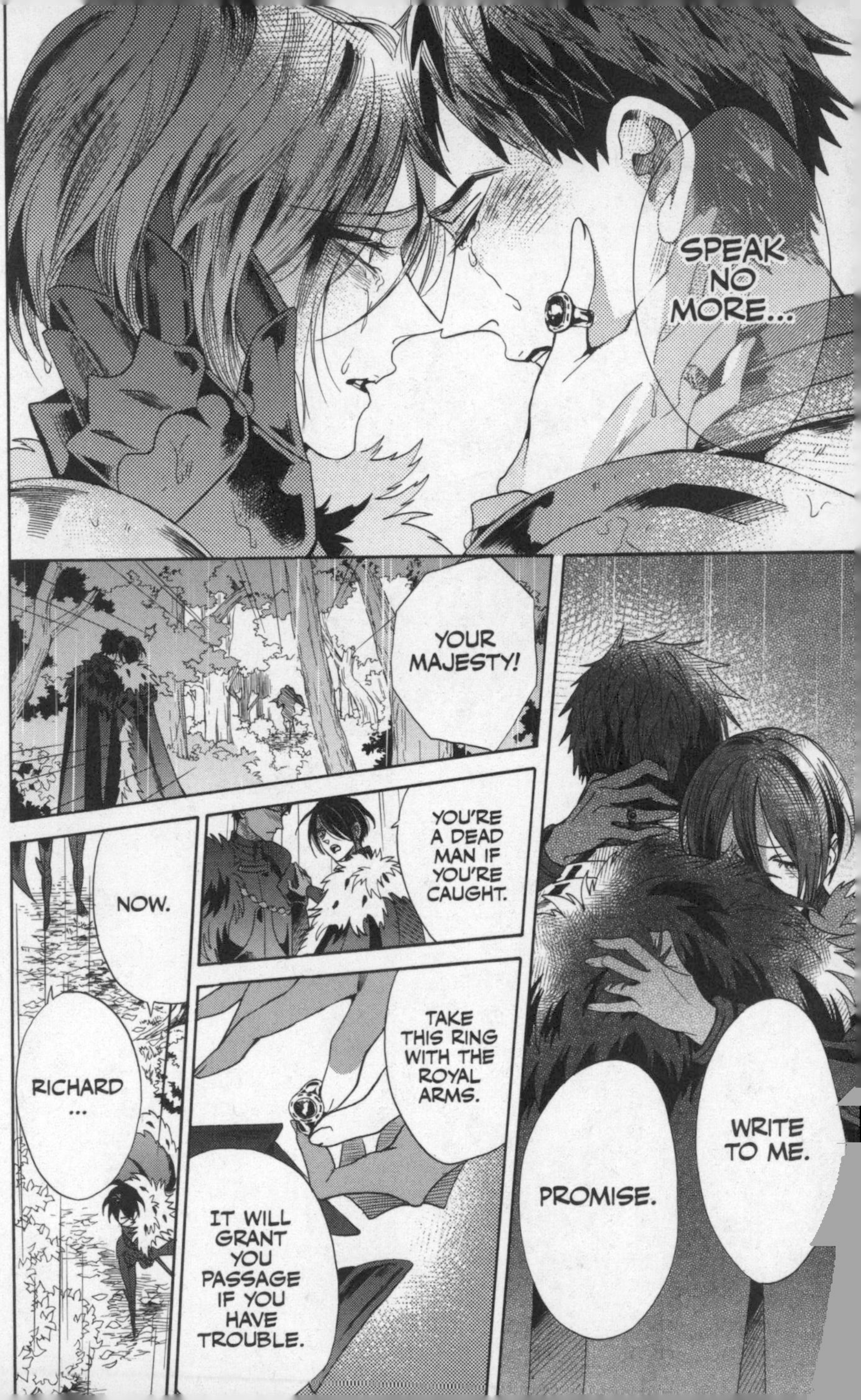
SPEAK NO MORE...
WRITE TO ME.
PROMISE.
YOUR MAJESTY!
YOU'RE A DEAD MAN IF YOU'RE CAUGHT.
TAKE THIS RING WITH THE ROYAL ARMS.
IT WILL GRANT YOU PASSAGE IF YOU HAVE TROUBLE.
NOW.
RICHARD ...

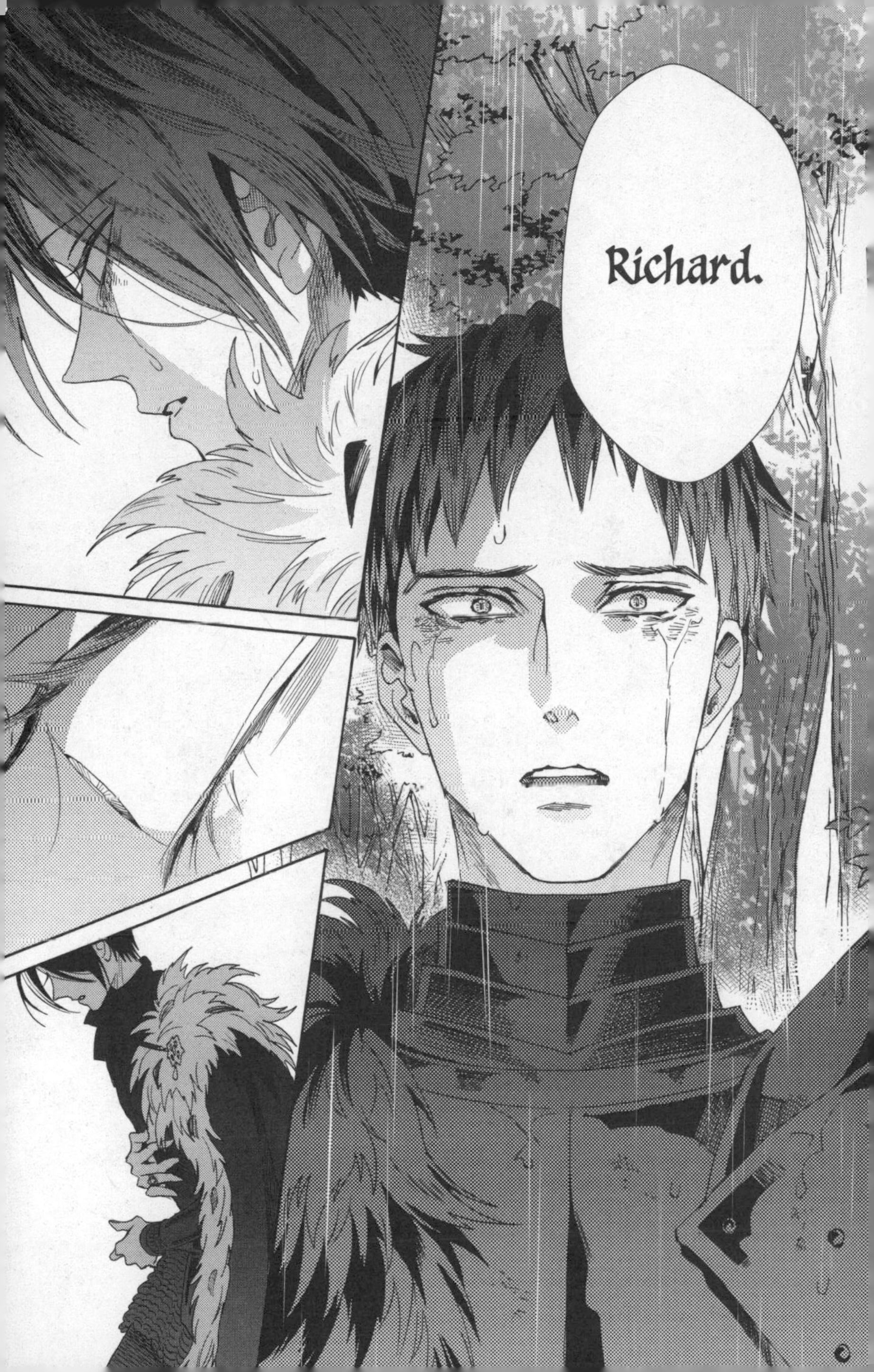
Richard.

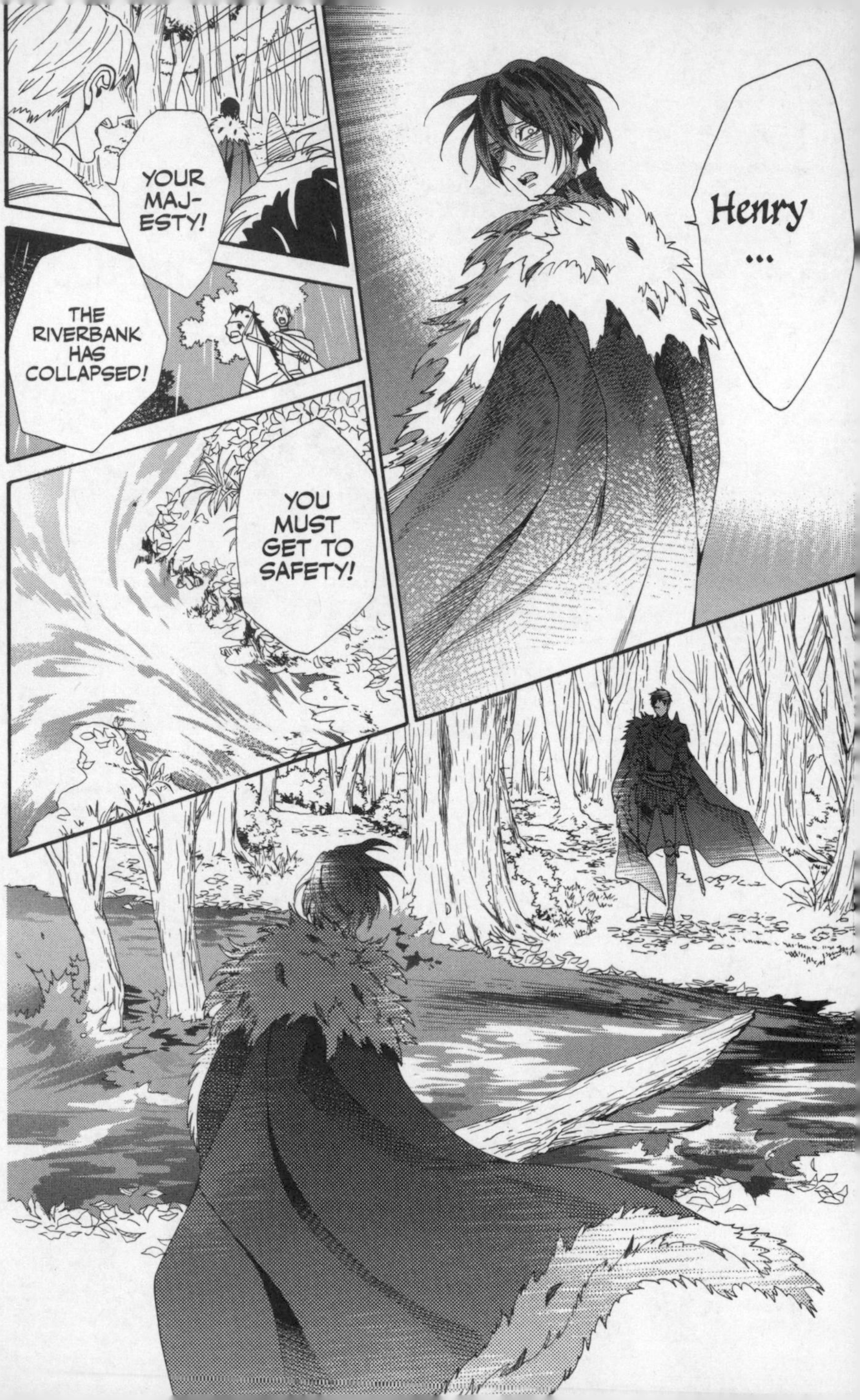
Henry ...
YOUR MAJ-ESTY!
THE RIVERBANK HAS COLLAPSED!
YOU MUST GET TO SAFETY!

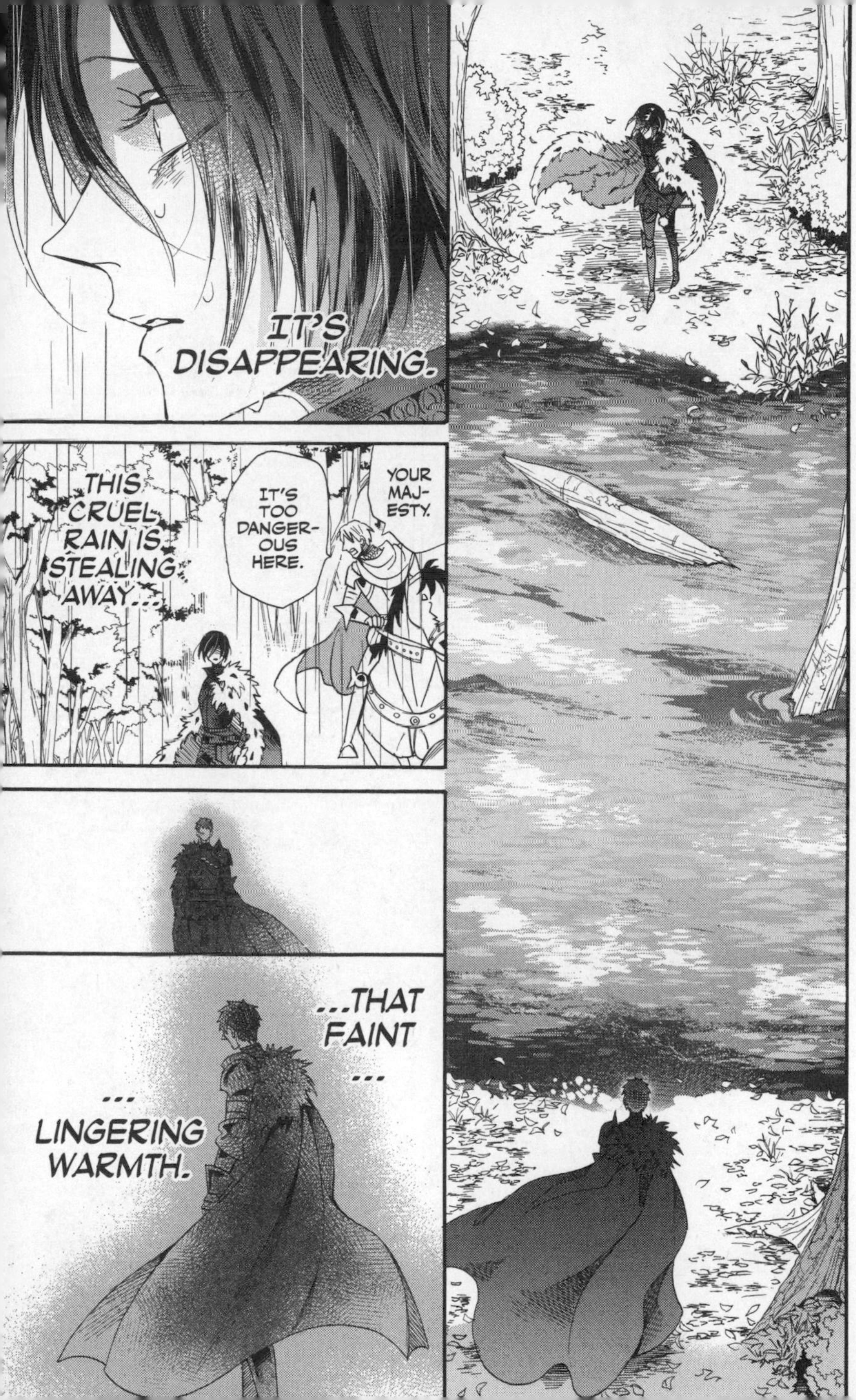
IT'S DISAPPEARING.
YOUR MAJ-ESTY.
IT'S TOO DANGER-OUS HERE.
THIS CRUEL RAIN IS STEALING AWAY...
...THAT FAINT ...
... LINGERING WARMTH.

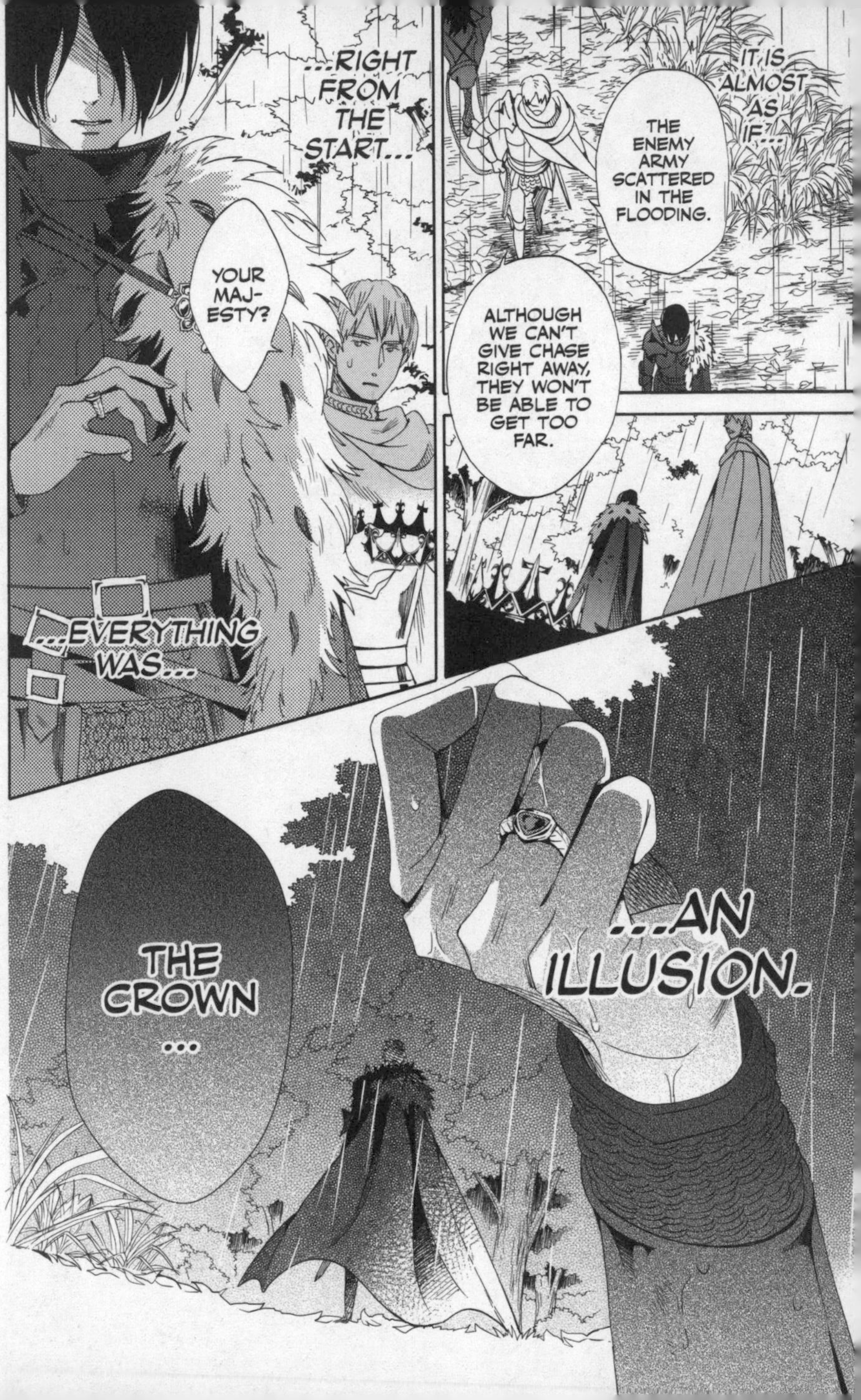

...IT IS ALMOST AS IF...
THE ENEMY ARMY SCATTERED IN THE FLOODING.
ALTHOUGH WE CAN'T GIVE CHASE RIGHT AWAY, THEY WON'T BE ABLE TO GET TOO FAR.
...RIGHT FROM THE START...
YOUR MAJ-ESTY?
...EVERYTHING WAS...
...AN ILLUSION.
THE CROWN ...

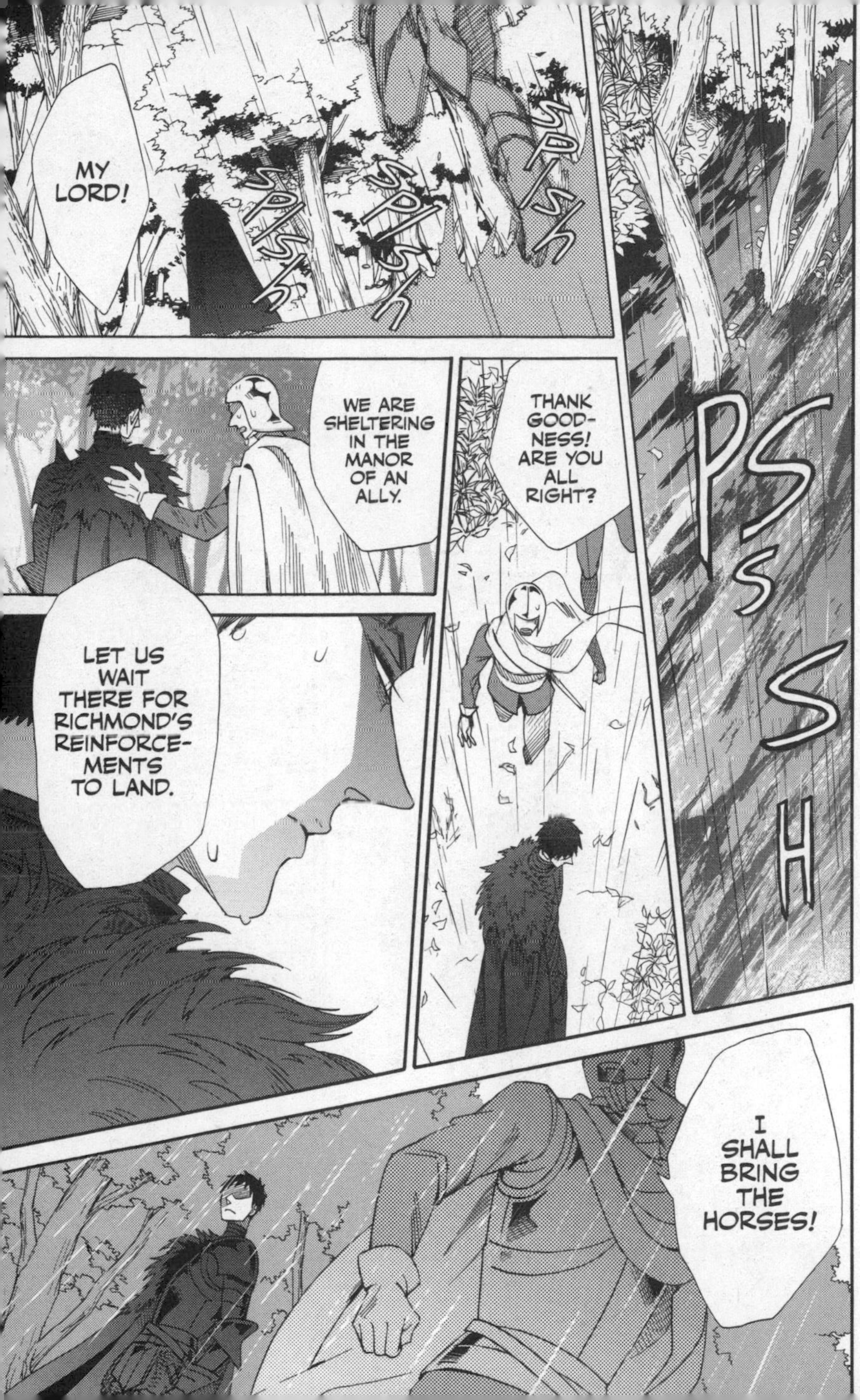
PSSSH
SPISH
SPISH
SPISH
MY LORD!
THANK GOODNESS! ARE YOU ALL RIGHT?
WE ARE SHELTERING IN THE MANOR OF AN ALLY.
LET US WAIT THERE FOR RICHMOND'S REINFORCEMENTS TO LAND.
I SHALL BRING THE HORSES!

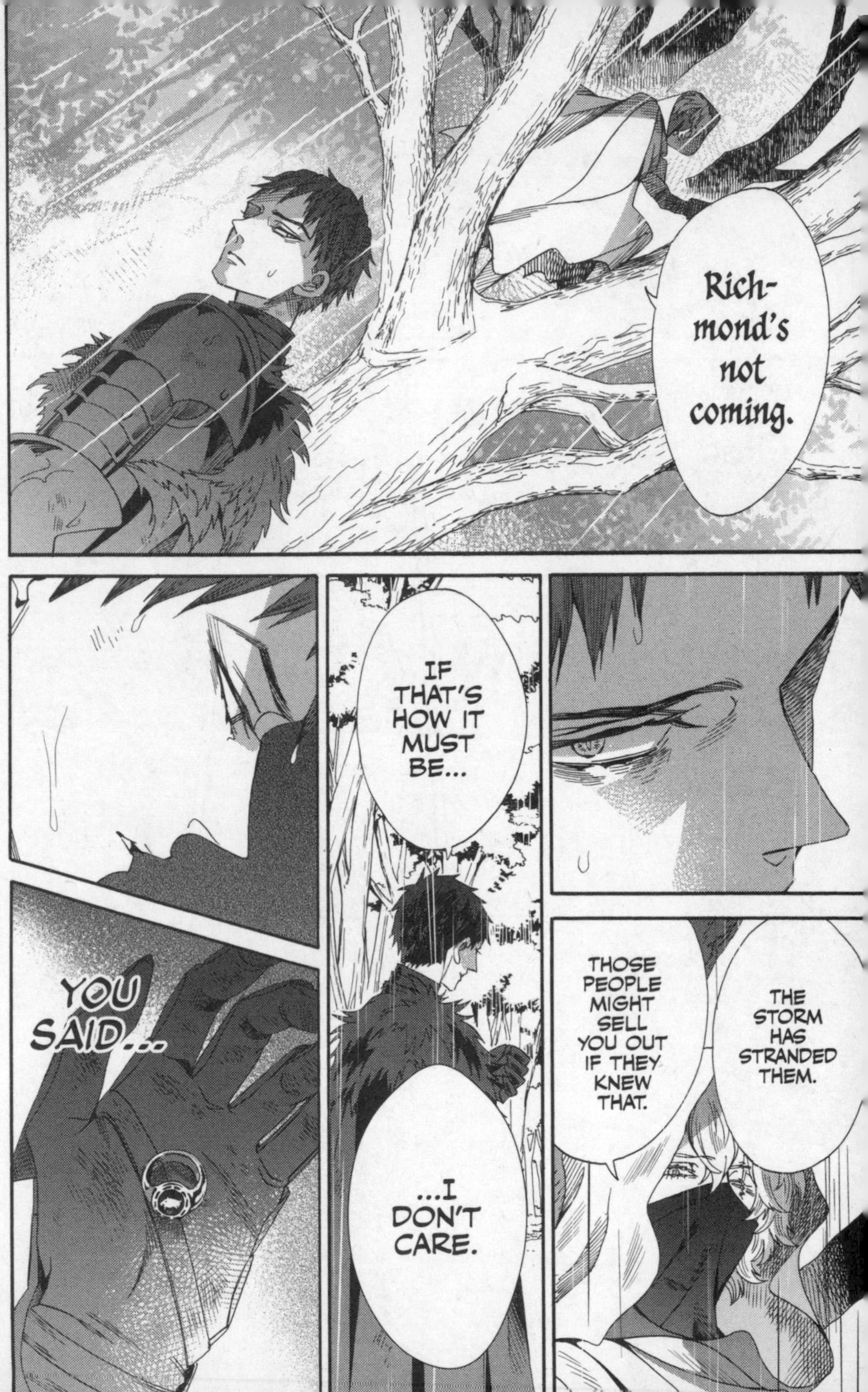
Rich-mond's not coming.
THE STORM HAS STRANDED THEM.
THOSE PEOPLE MIGHT SELL YOU OUT IF THEY KNEW THAT.
IF THAT'S HOW IT MUST BE...
...I DON'T CARE.
YOU SAID...

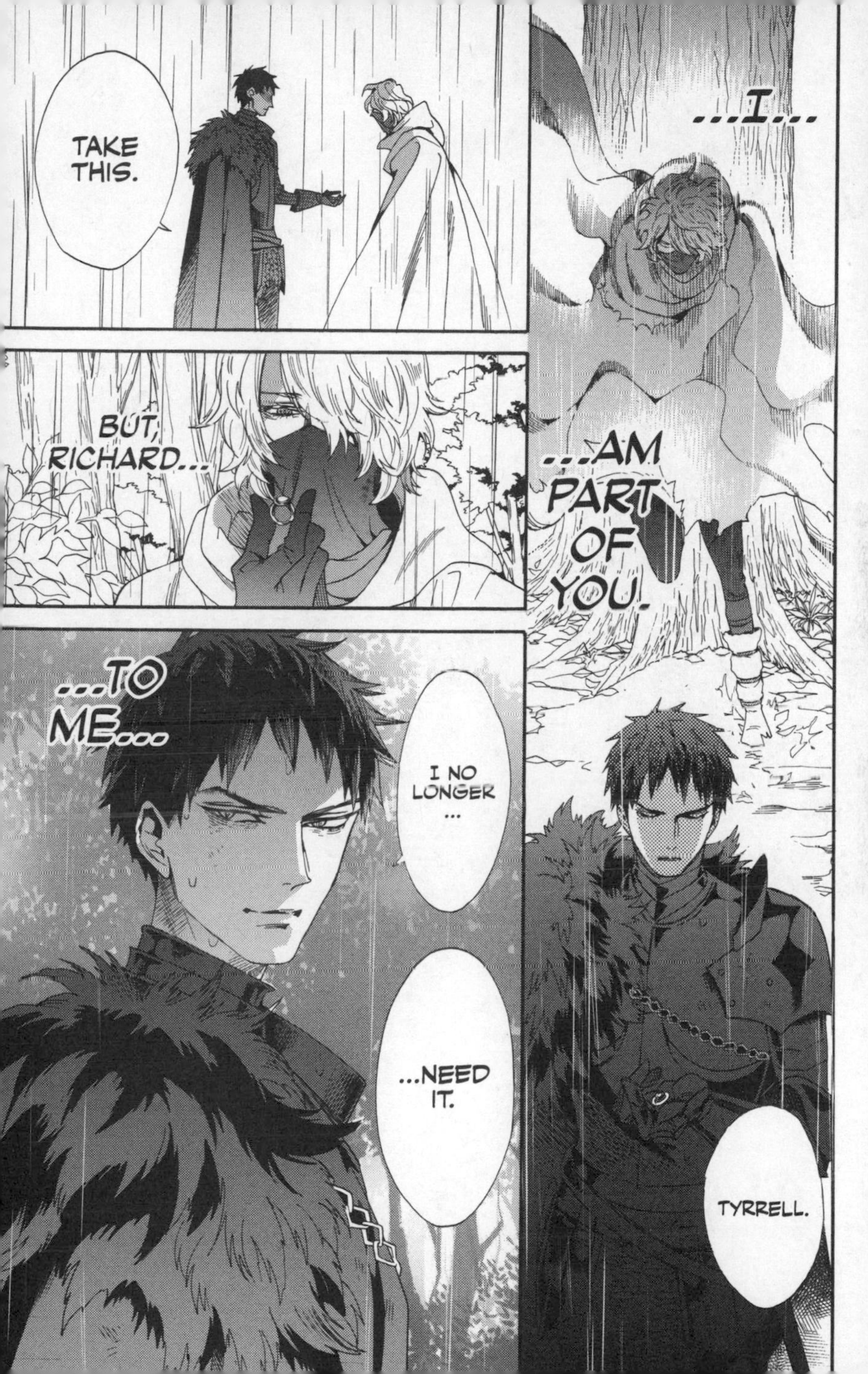
...I...
...AM PART OF YOU.
TAKE THIS.
BUT, RICHARD...
TYRRELL.
...TO ME...
I NO LONGER ...
...NEED IT.

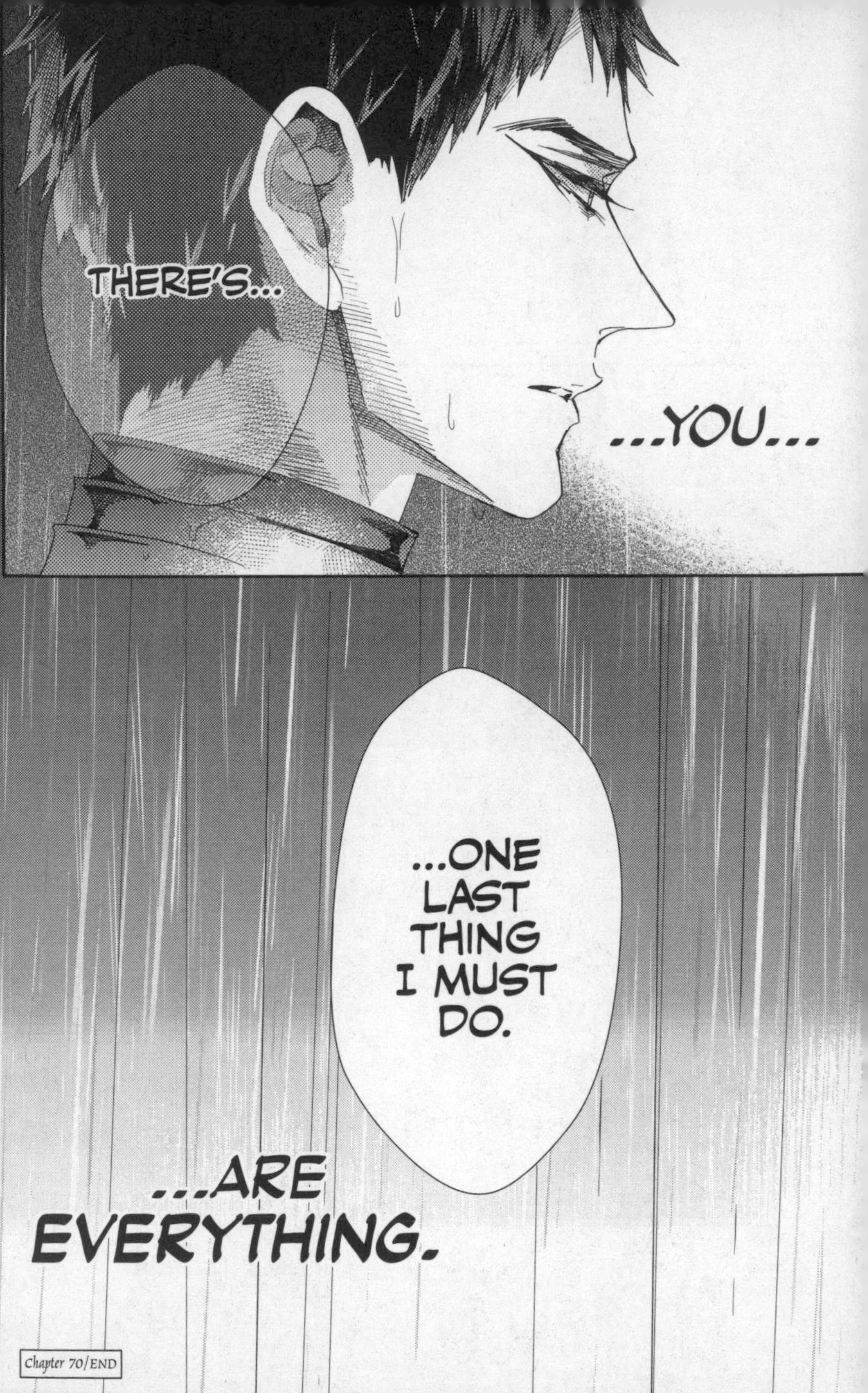
THERE'S...
...YOU...
...ONE LAST THING I MUST DO.
...ARE EVERYTHING.

Chapter 70/END

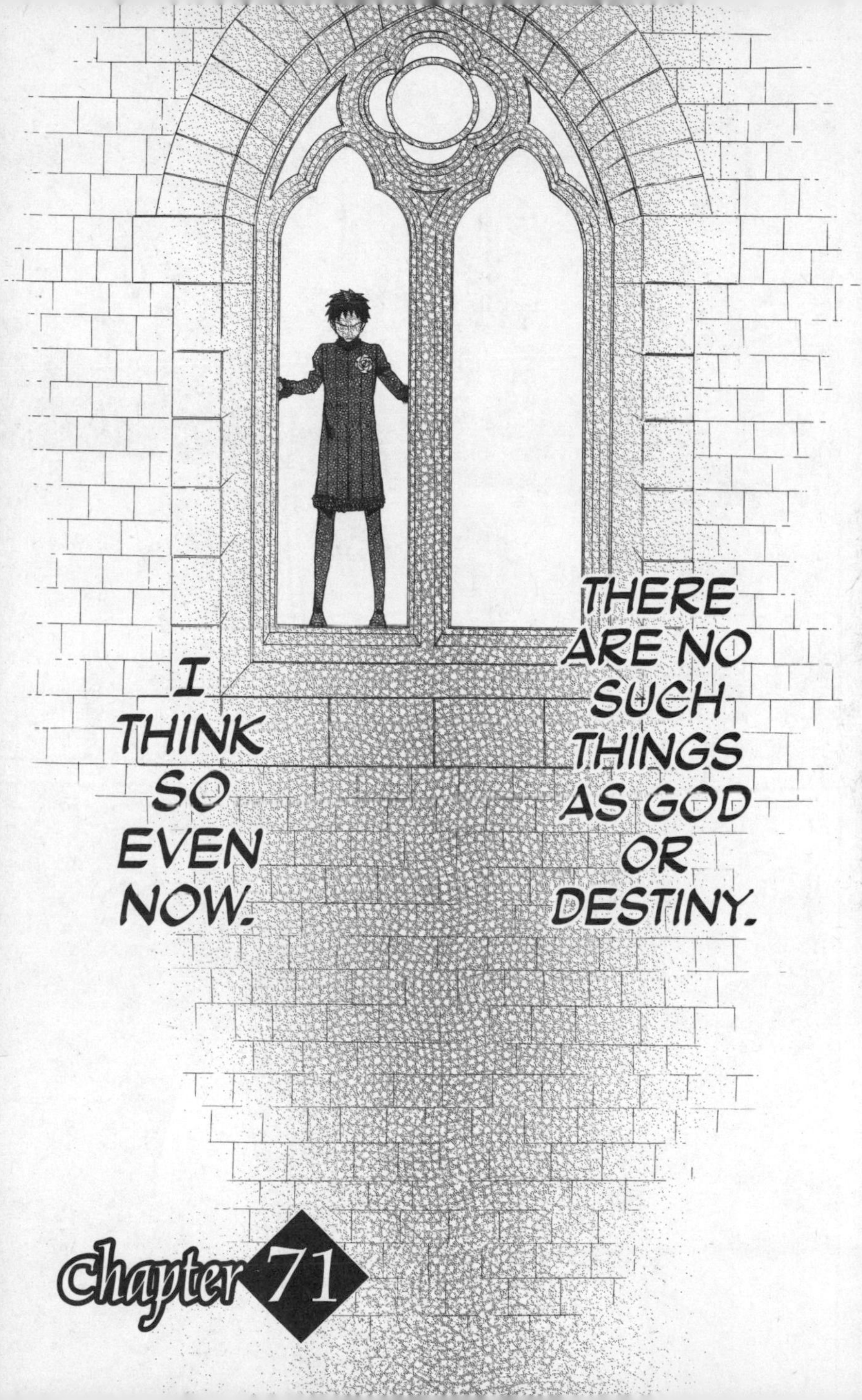
THERE ARE NO SUCH THINGS AS GOD OR DESTINY.
I THINK SO EVEN NOW.

Chapter 71

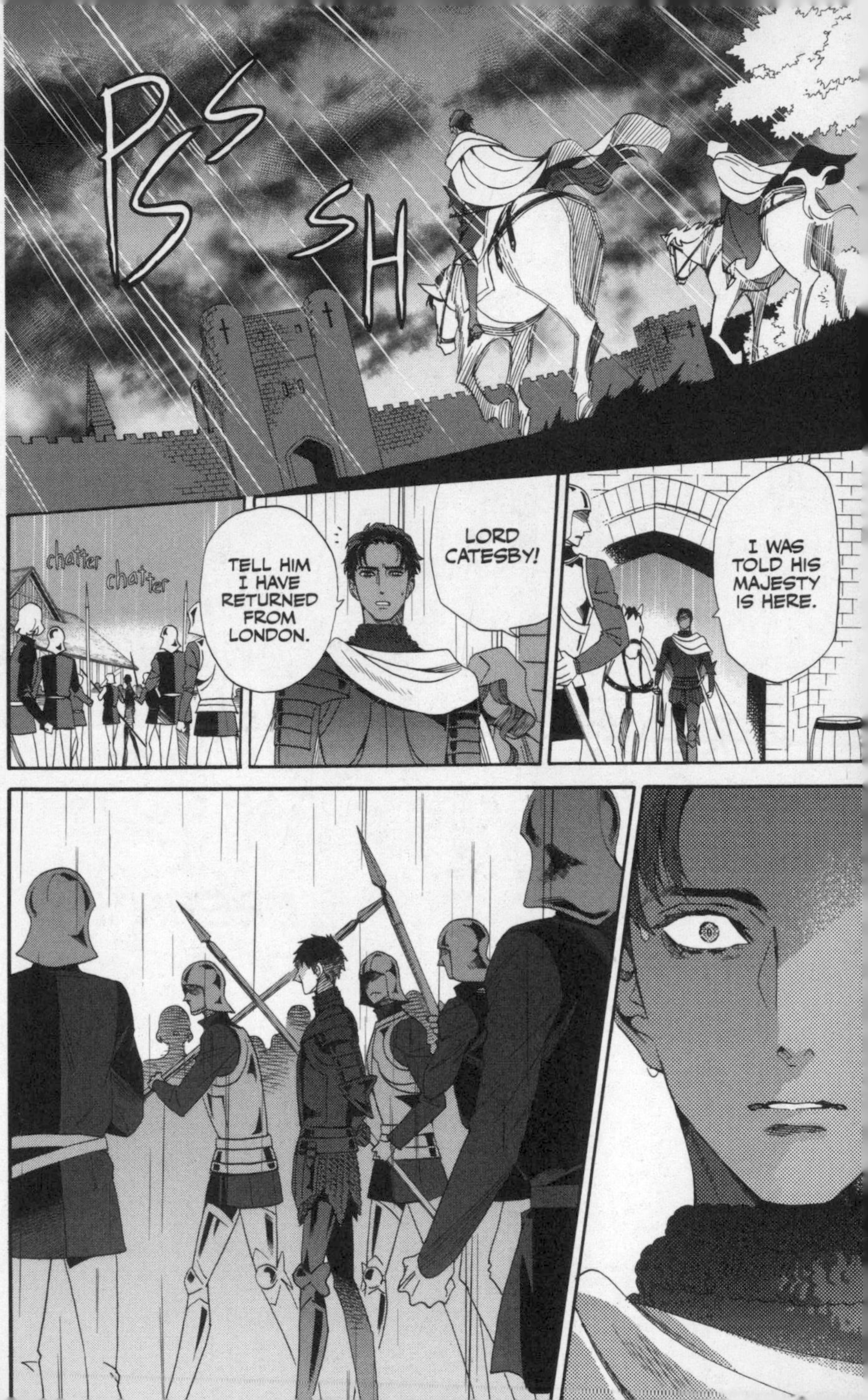
PSSSH
I WAS TOLD HIS MAJESTY IS HERE.
LORD CATESBY!
TELL HIM I HAVE RETURNED FROM LONDON.
chatter chatter

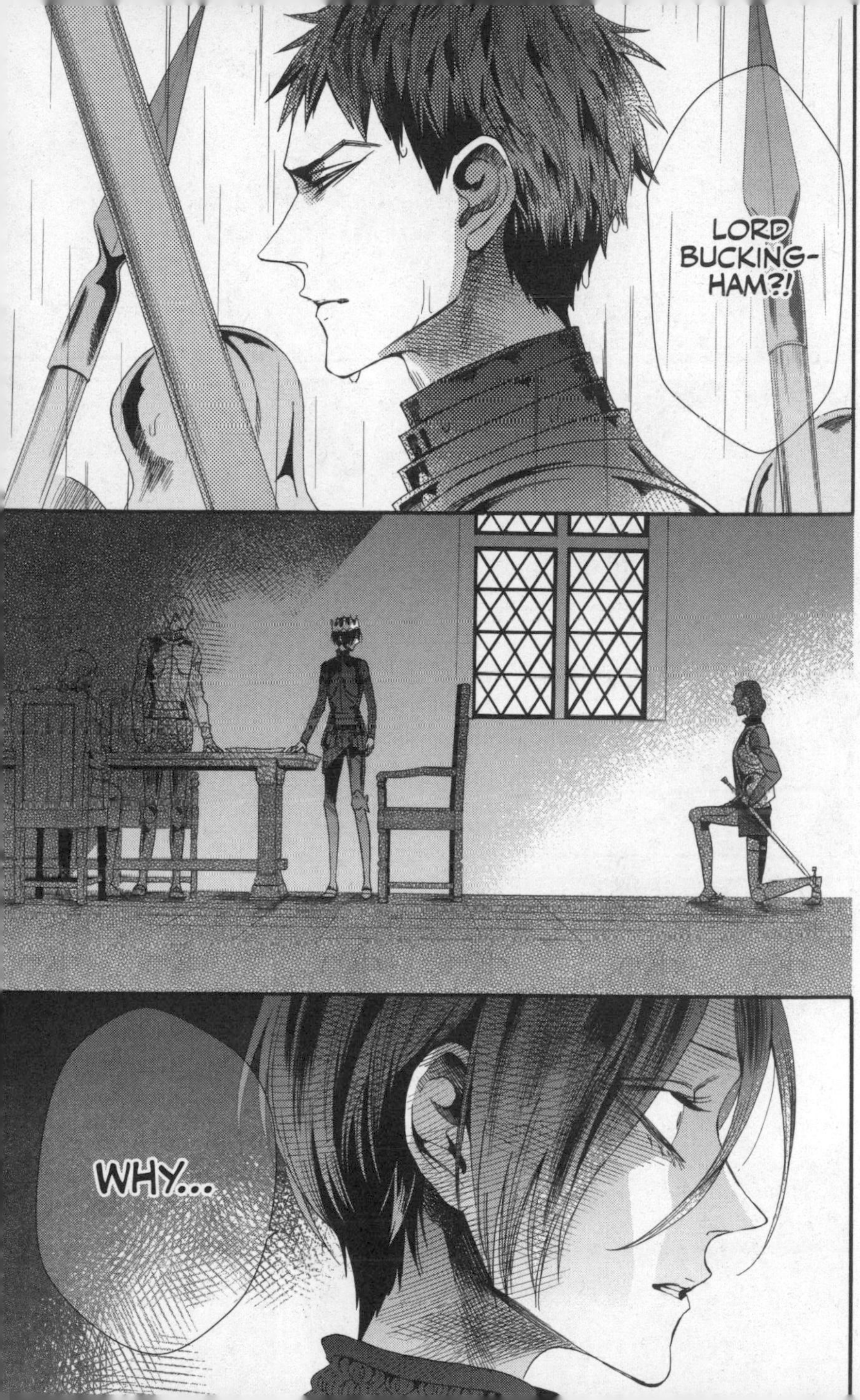
LORD BUCKING-HAM?!
WHY...

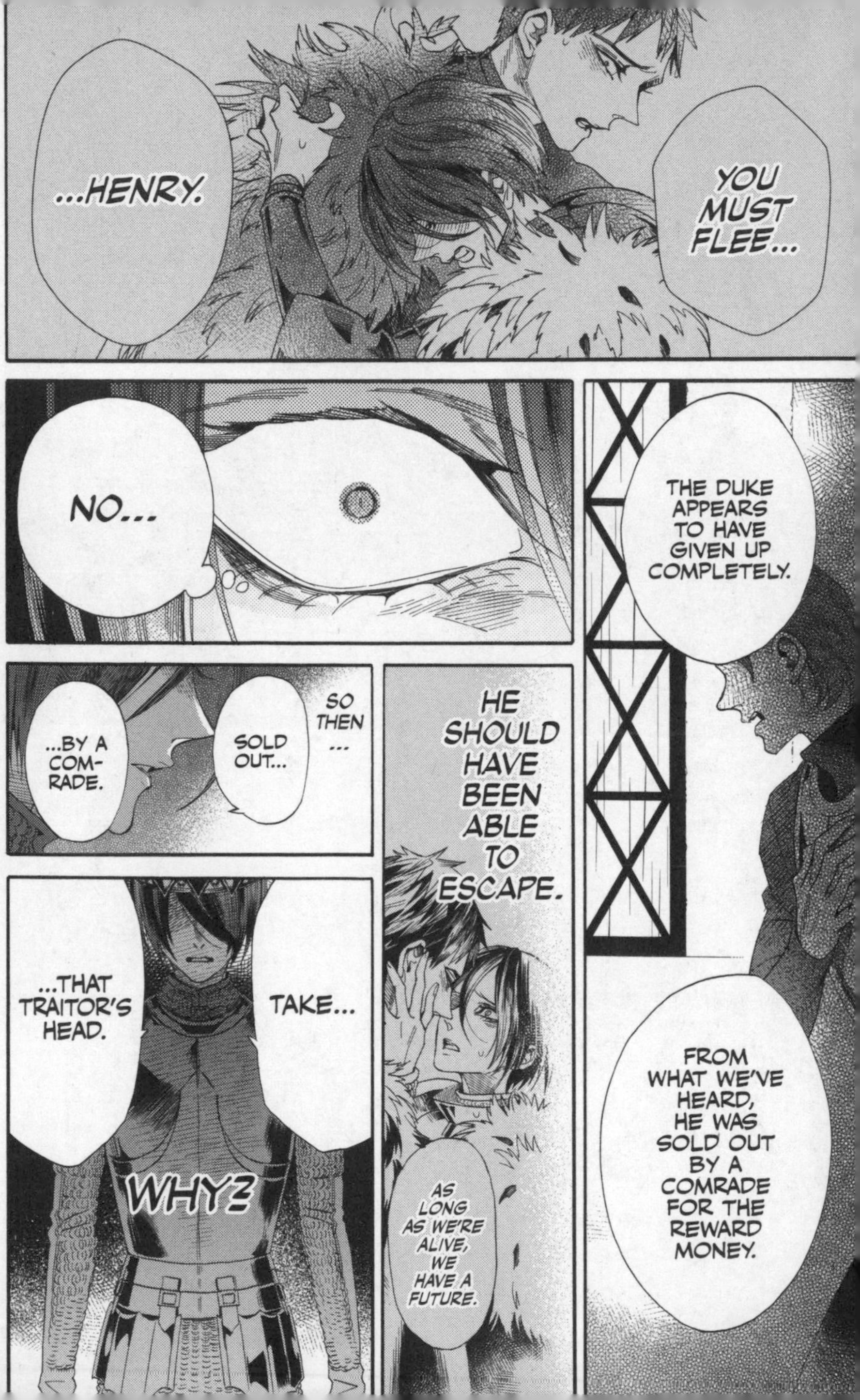
YOU MUST FLEE...
...HENRY.
THE DUKE APPEARS TO HAVE GIVEN UP COMPLETELY.
FROM WHAT WE'VE HEARD, HE WAS SOLD OUT BY A COMRADE FOR THE REWARD MONEY.
NO...
HE SHOULD HAVE BEEN ABLE TO ESCAPE.
AS LONG AS WE'RE ALIVE, WE HAVE A FUTURE.
SO THEN ...
SOLD OUT...
...BY A COM-RADE.
TAKE...
...THAT TRAITOR'S HEAD.
WHY?

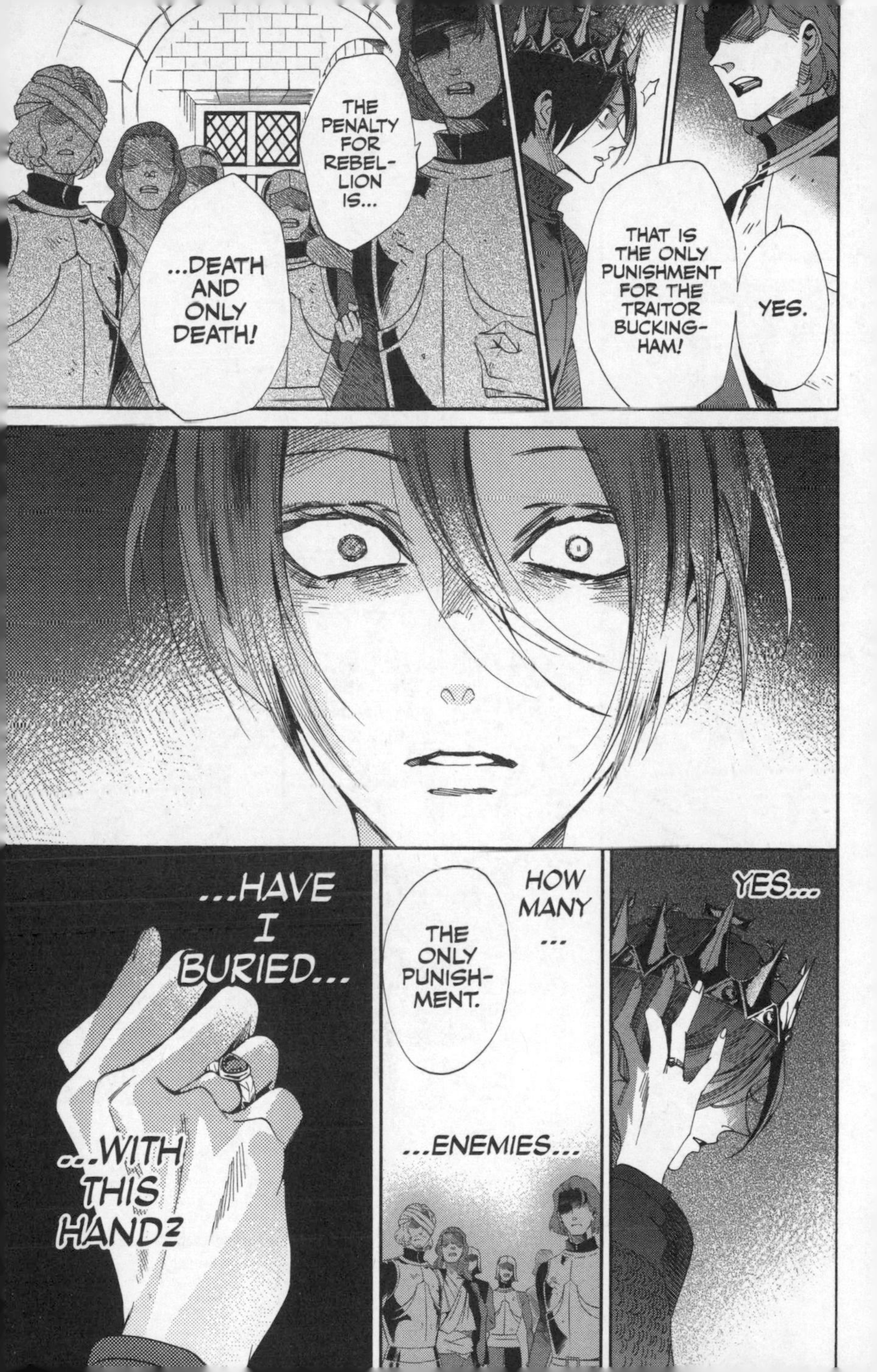
YES.
THAT IS THE ONLY PUNISHMENT FOR THE TRAITOR BUCKINGHAM!
THE PENALTY FOR REBELLION IS...
...DEATH AND ONLY DEATH!
YES...
HOW MANY ...
THE ONLY PUNISHMENT.
...ENEMIES...
...HAVE I BURIED...
...WITH THIS HAND?

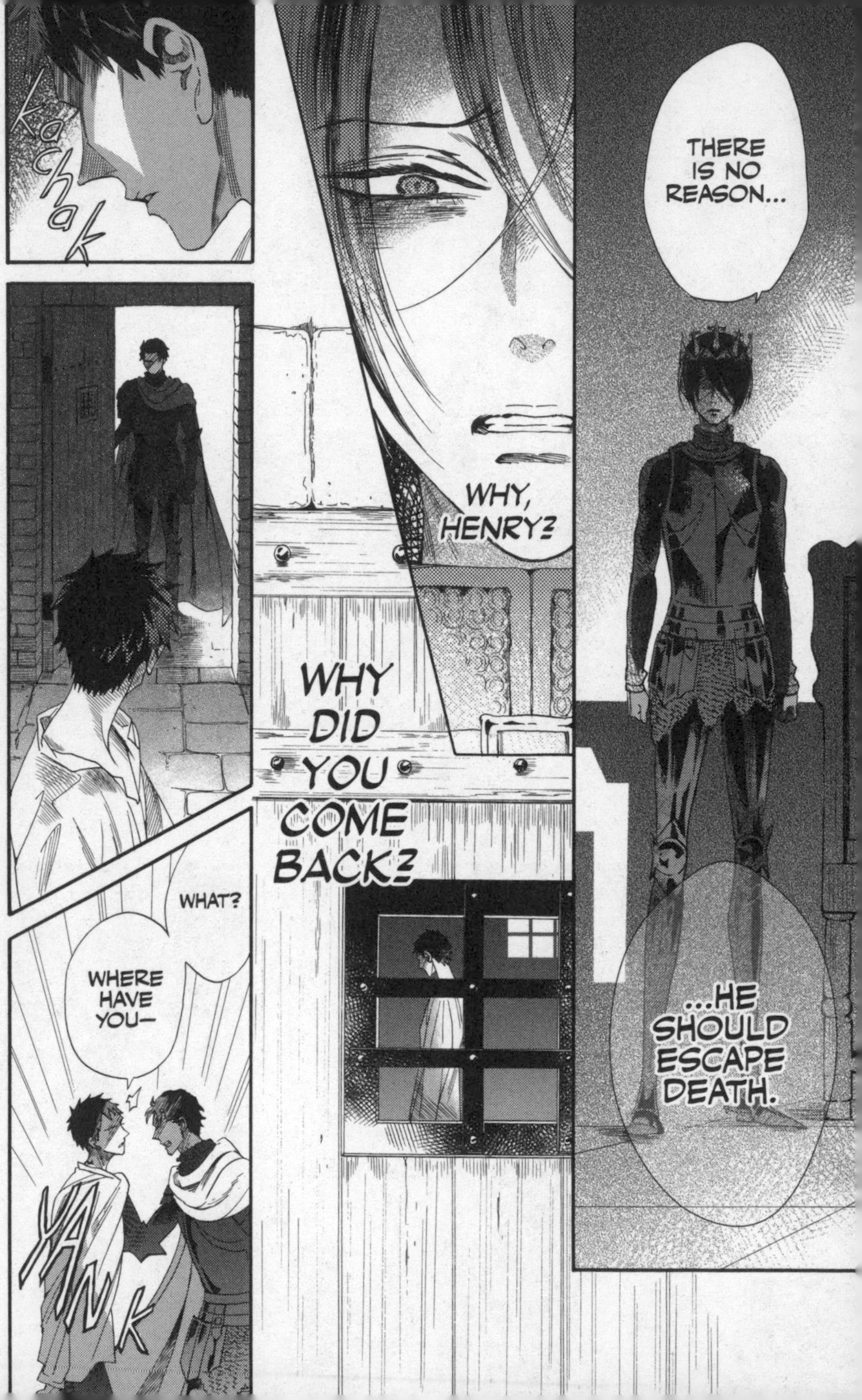
THERE IS NO REASON...
...HE SHOULD ESCAPE DEATH.
WHY, HENRY?
WHY DID YOU COME BACK?
kachak
WHAT?
WHERE HAVE YOU—
YANK

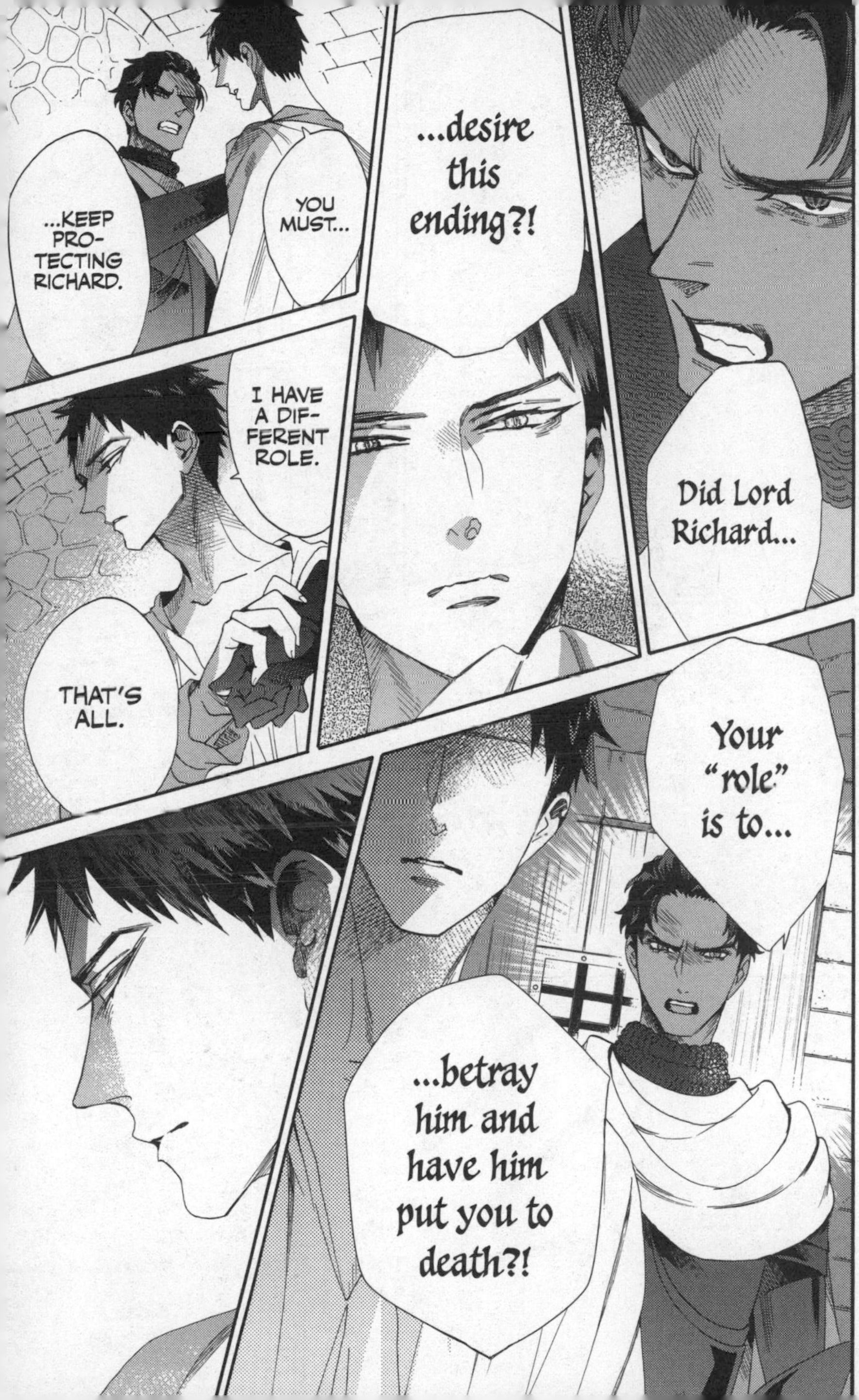
Did Lord Richard...
...desire this ending?!
YOU MUST...
...KEEP PRO-TECTING RICHARD.
I HAVE A DIF-FERENT ROLE.
THAT'S ALL.
Your "role" is to...
...betray him and have him put you to death?!

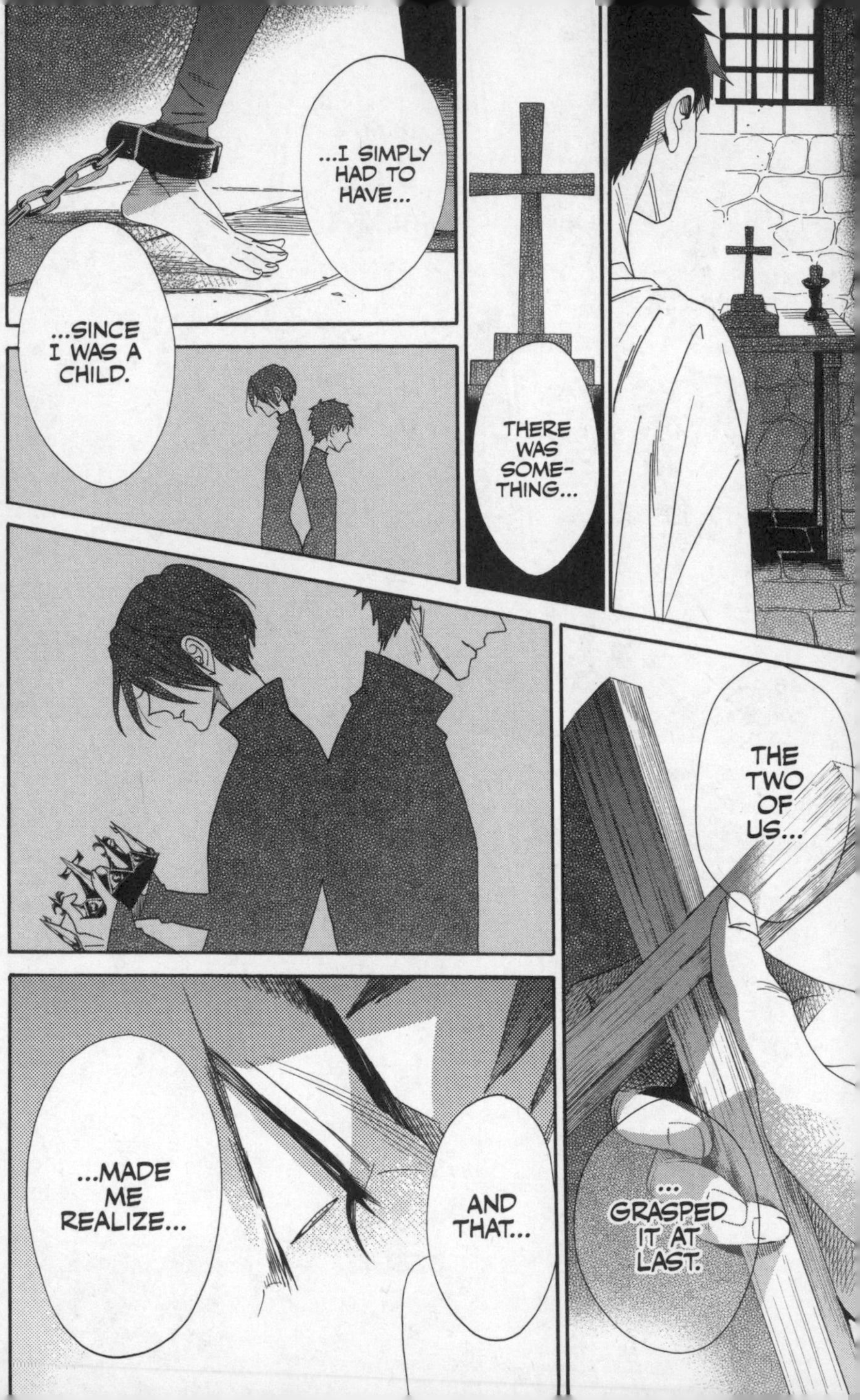
THERE WAS SOMETHING...
...I SIMPLY HAD TO HAVE...
...SINCE I WAS A CHILD.
THE TWO OF US...
...GRASPED IT AT LAST.
AND THAT...
...MADE ME REALIZE...

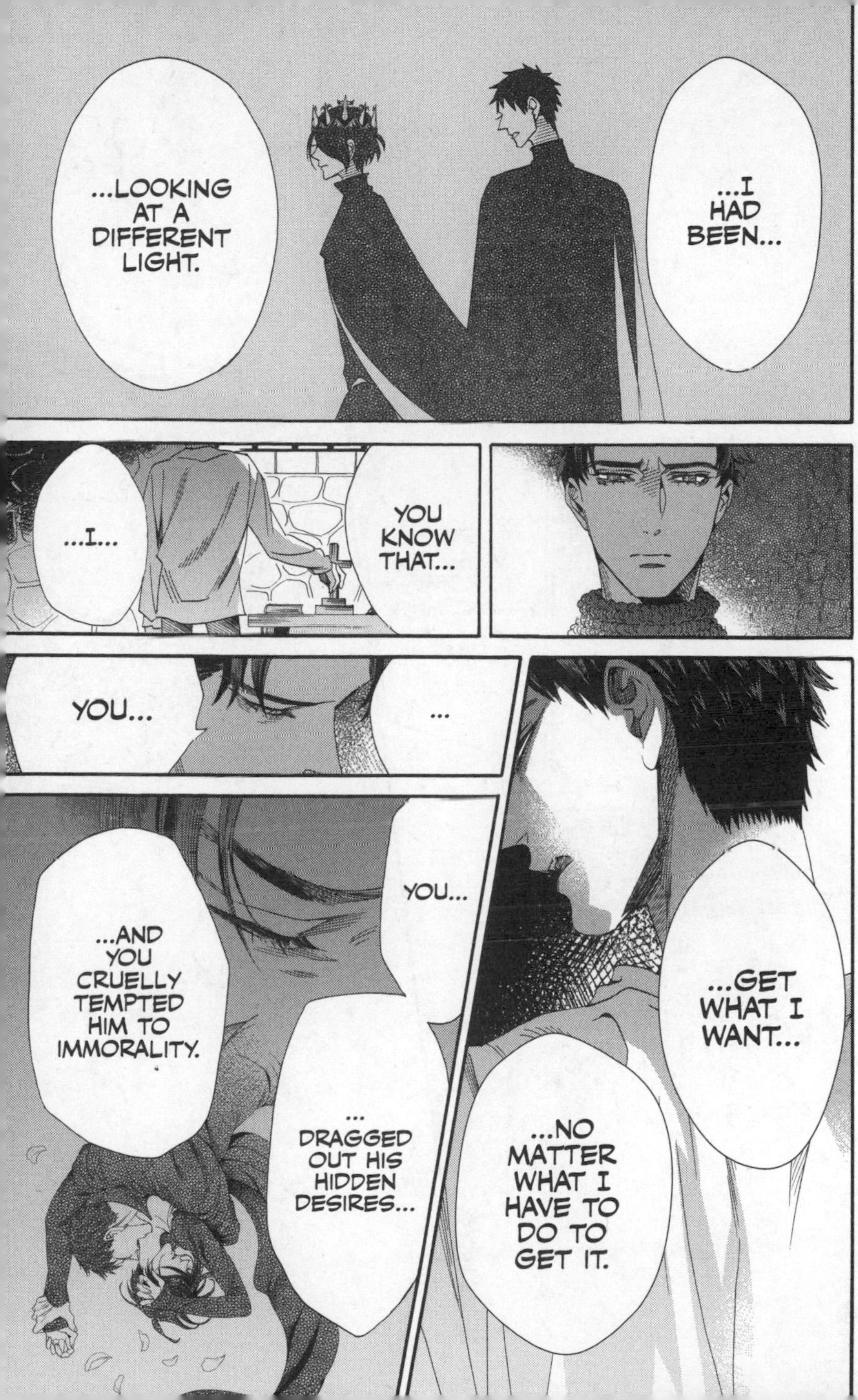
...I HAD BEEN...
...LOOKING AT A DIFFERENT LIGHT.
YOU KNOW THAT...
...I...
...GET WHAT I WANT...
...NO MATTER WHAT I HAVE TO DO TO GET IT.
...
YOU...
YOU...
...DRAGGED OUT HIS HIDDEN DESIRES...
...AND YOU CRUELLY TEMPTED HIM TO IMMORALITY.

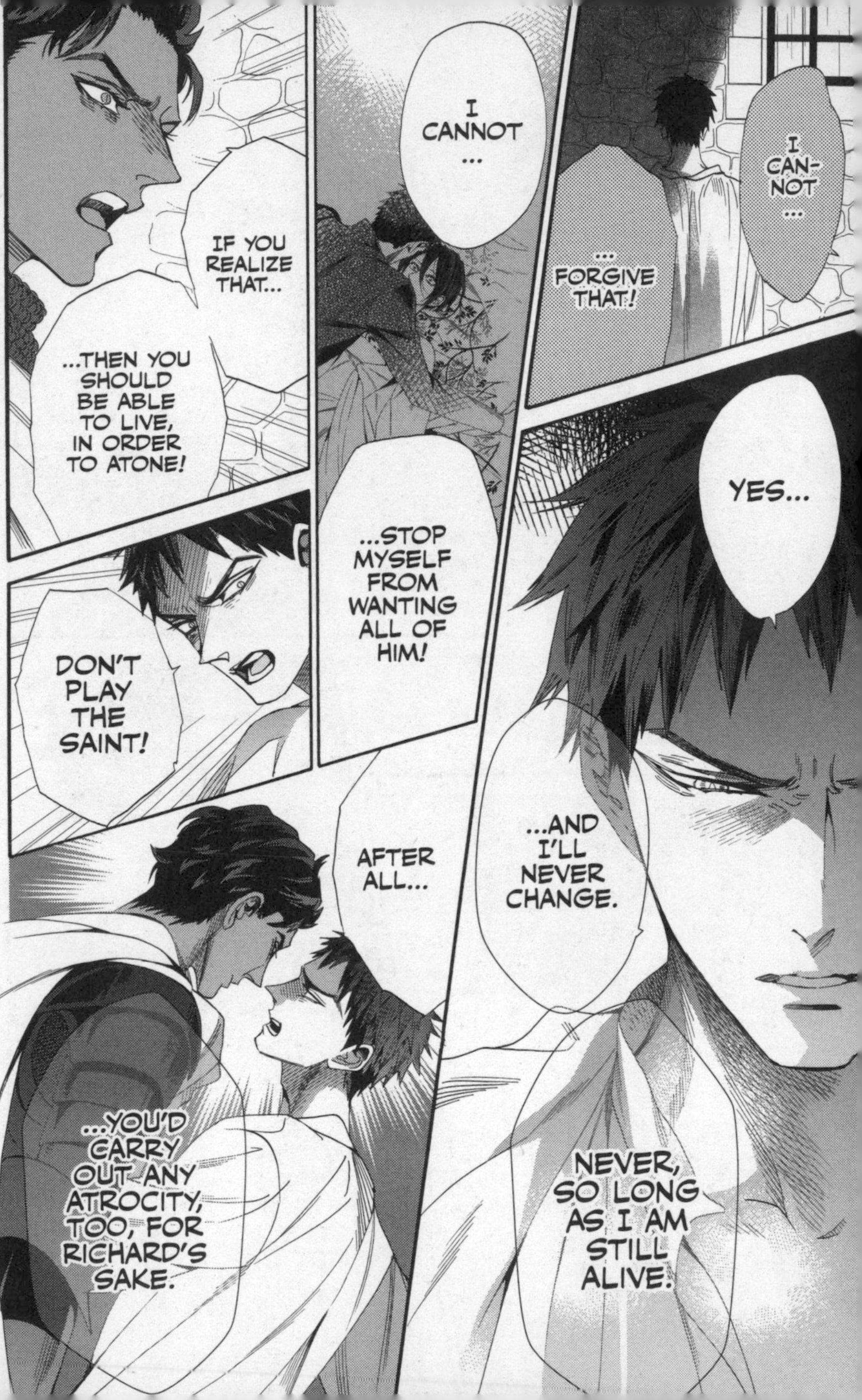
I CAN-NOT ...
... FORGIVE THAT!
I CANNOT ...
...STOP MYSELF FROM WANTING ALL OF HIM!
IF YOU REALIZE THAT...
...THEN YOU SHOULD BE ABLE TO LIVE, IN ORDER TO ATONE!
DON'T PLAY THE SAINT!
YES...
...AND I'LL NEVER CHANGE.
NEVER, SO LONG AS I AM STILL ALIVE.
AFTER ALL...
...YOU'D CARRY OUT ANY ATROCITY, TOO, FOR RICHARD'S SAKE.

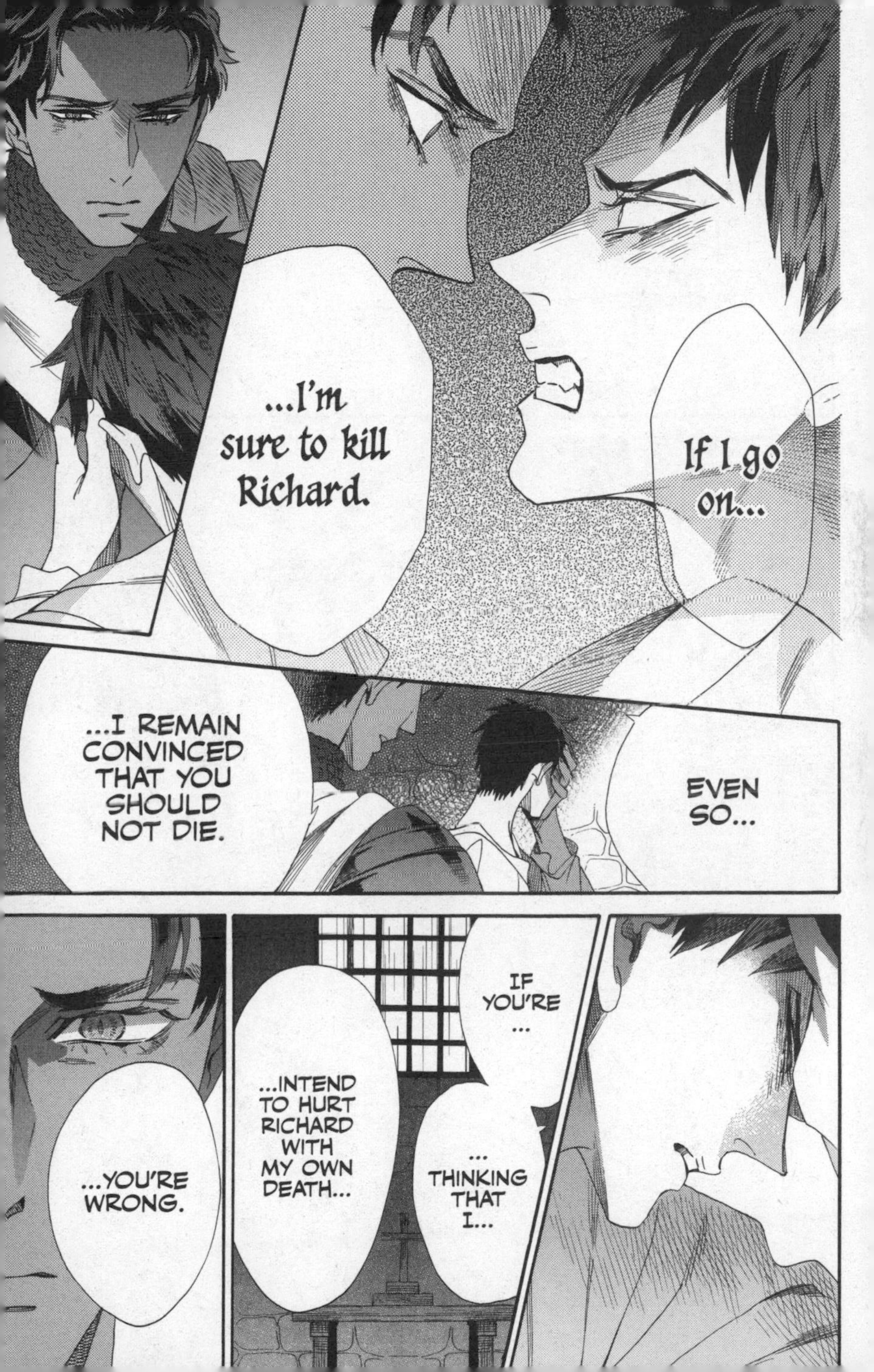
If I go on...
...I'm sure to kill Richard.
EVEN SO...
...I REMAIN CONVINCED THAT YOU SHOULD NOT DIE.
IF YOU'RE ...
... THINKING THAT I...
...INTEND TO HURT RICHARD WITH MY OWN DEATH...
...YOU'RE WRONG.

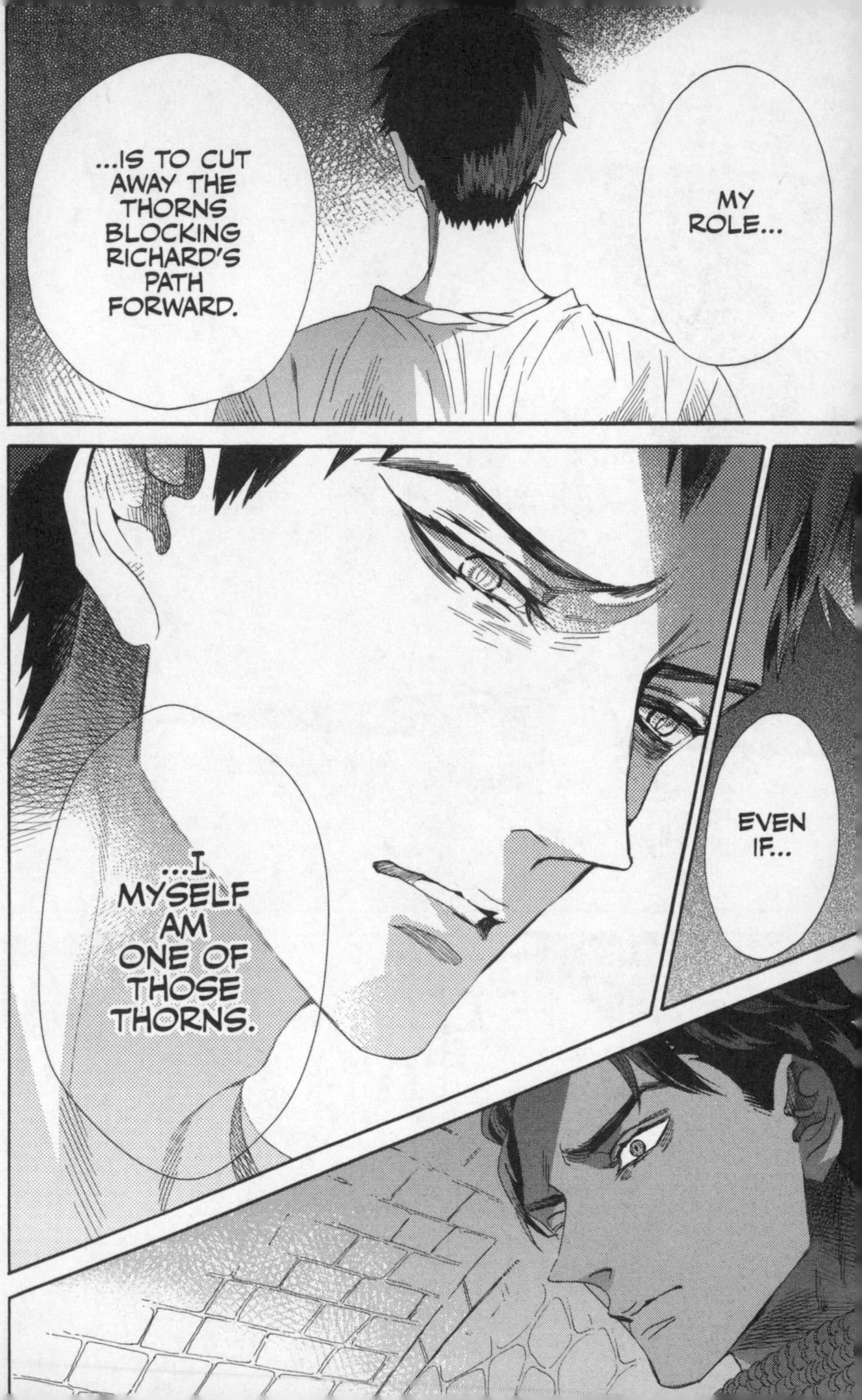
MY ROLE...
...IS TO CUT AWAY THE THORNS BLOCKING RICHARD'S PATH FORWARD.
EVEN IF...
...I MYSELF AM ONE OF THOSE THORNS.

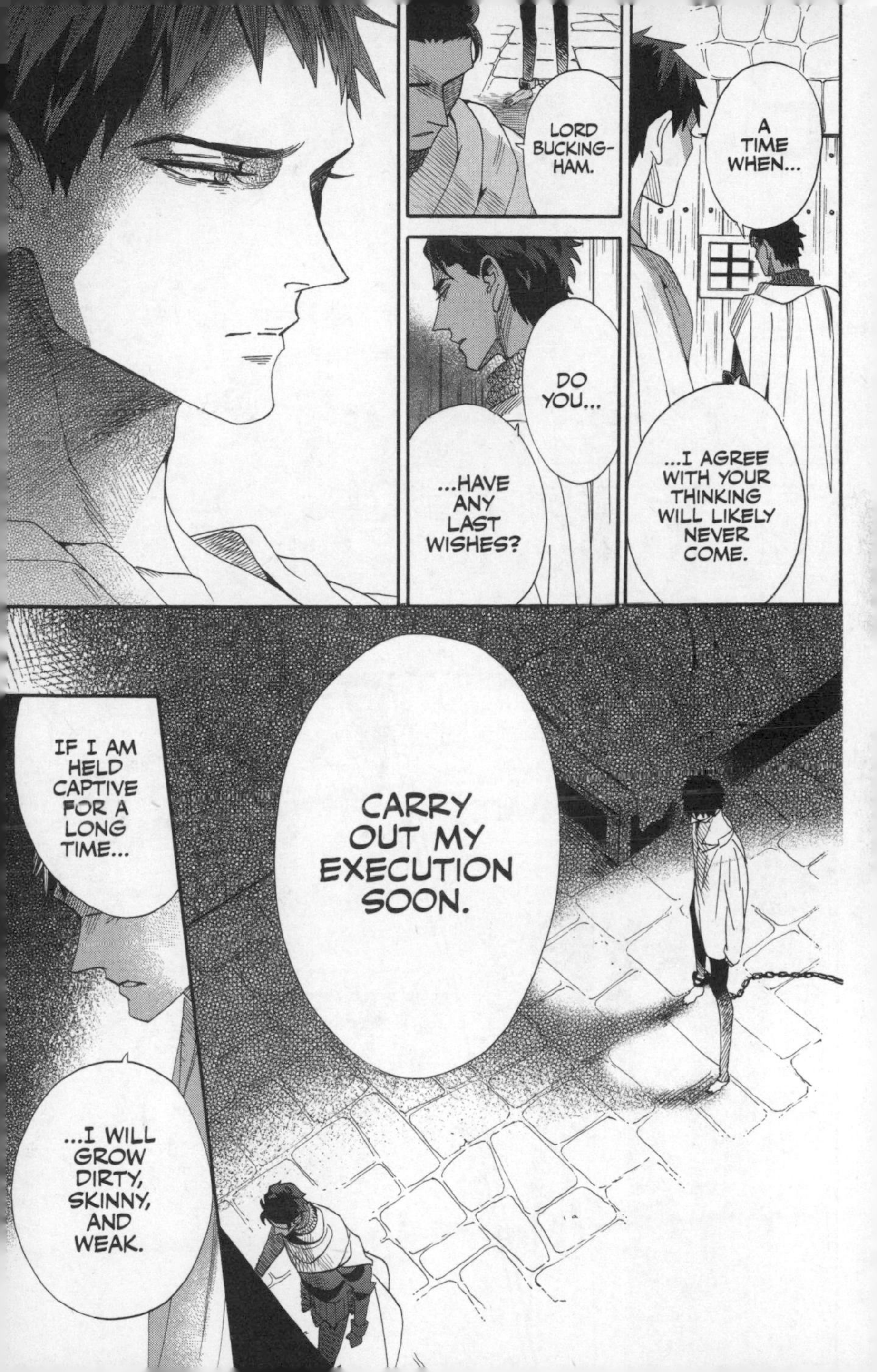
A TIME WHEN...
...I AGREE WITH YOUR THINKING WILL LIKELY NEVER COME.
LORD BUCKINGHAM.
DO YOU...
...HAVE ANY LAST WISHES?
CARRY OUT MY EXECUTION SOON.
IF I AM HELD CAPTIVE FOR A LONG TIME...
...I WILL GROW DIRTY, SKINNY, AND WEAK.

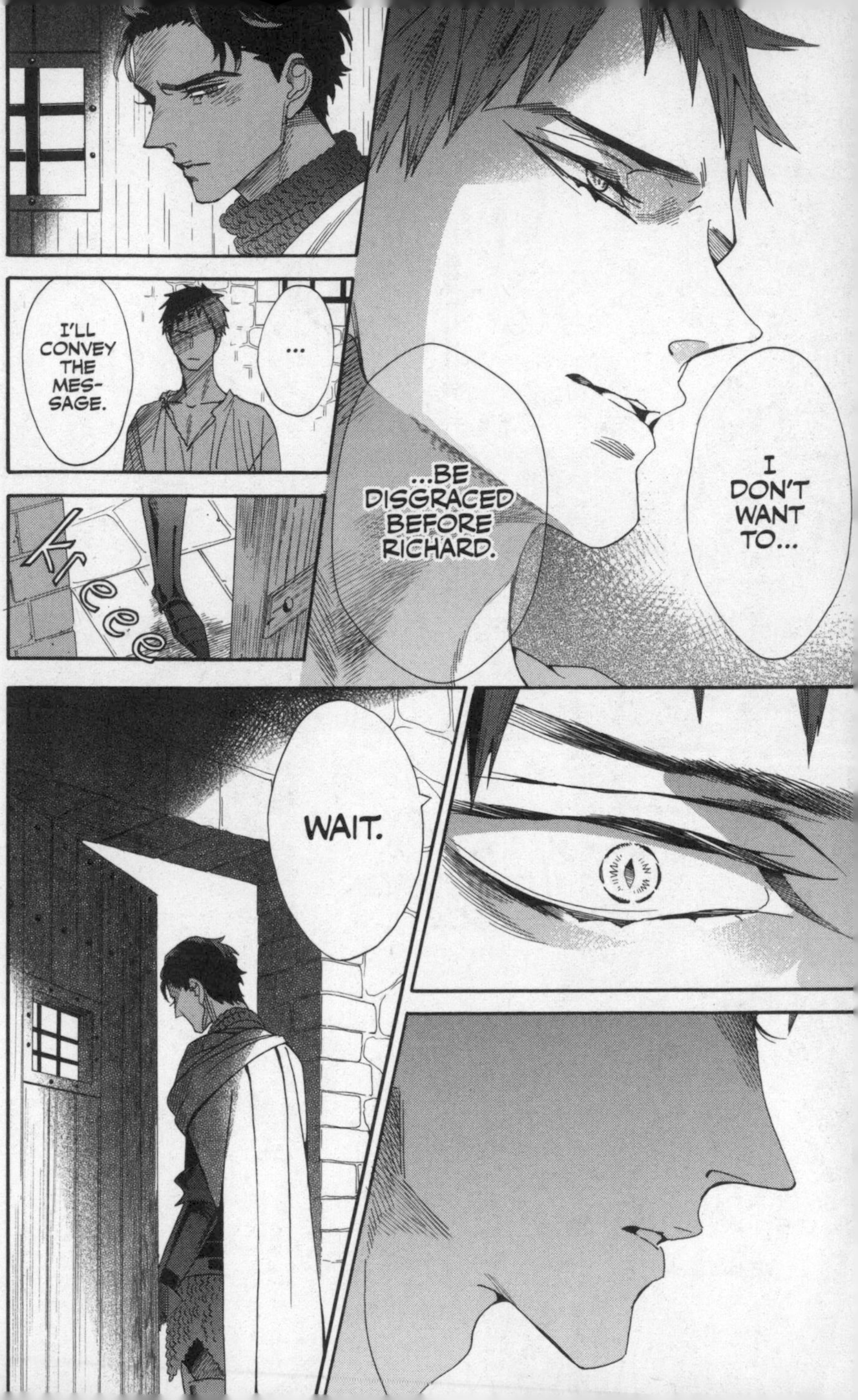
I DON'T WANT TO...
...BE DISGRACED BEFORE RICHARD.
...
I'LL CONVEY THE MES-SAGE.
kreee
WAIT.

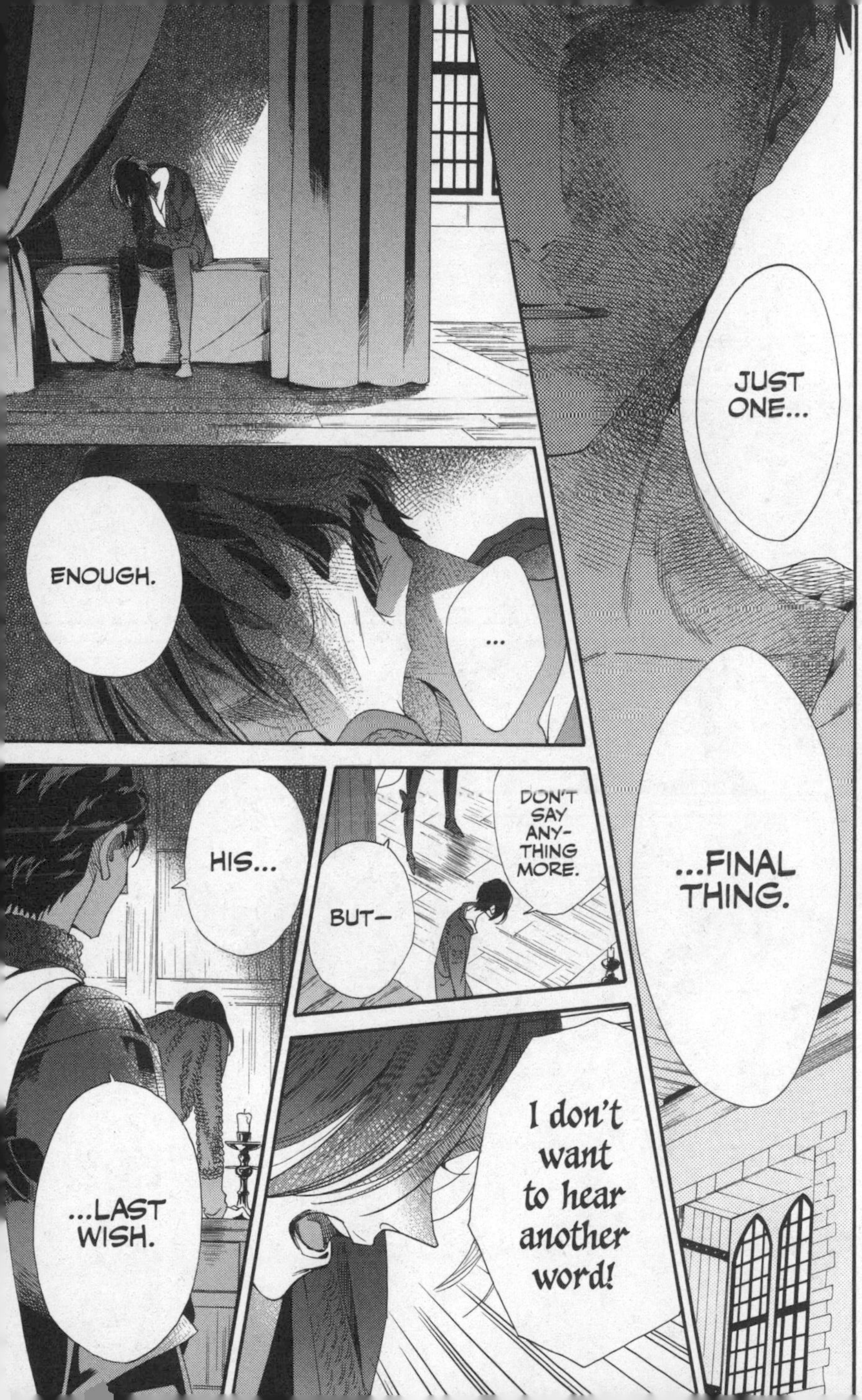
JUST ONE...
...FINAL THING.
...
ENOUGH.
DON'T SAY ANY-THING MORE.
BUT—
I don't want to hear another word!
HIS...
...LAST WISH.

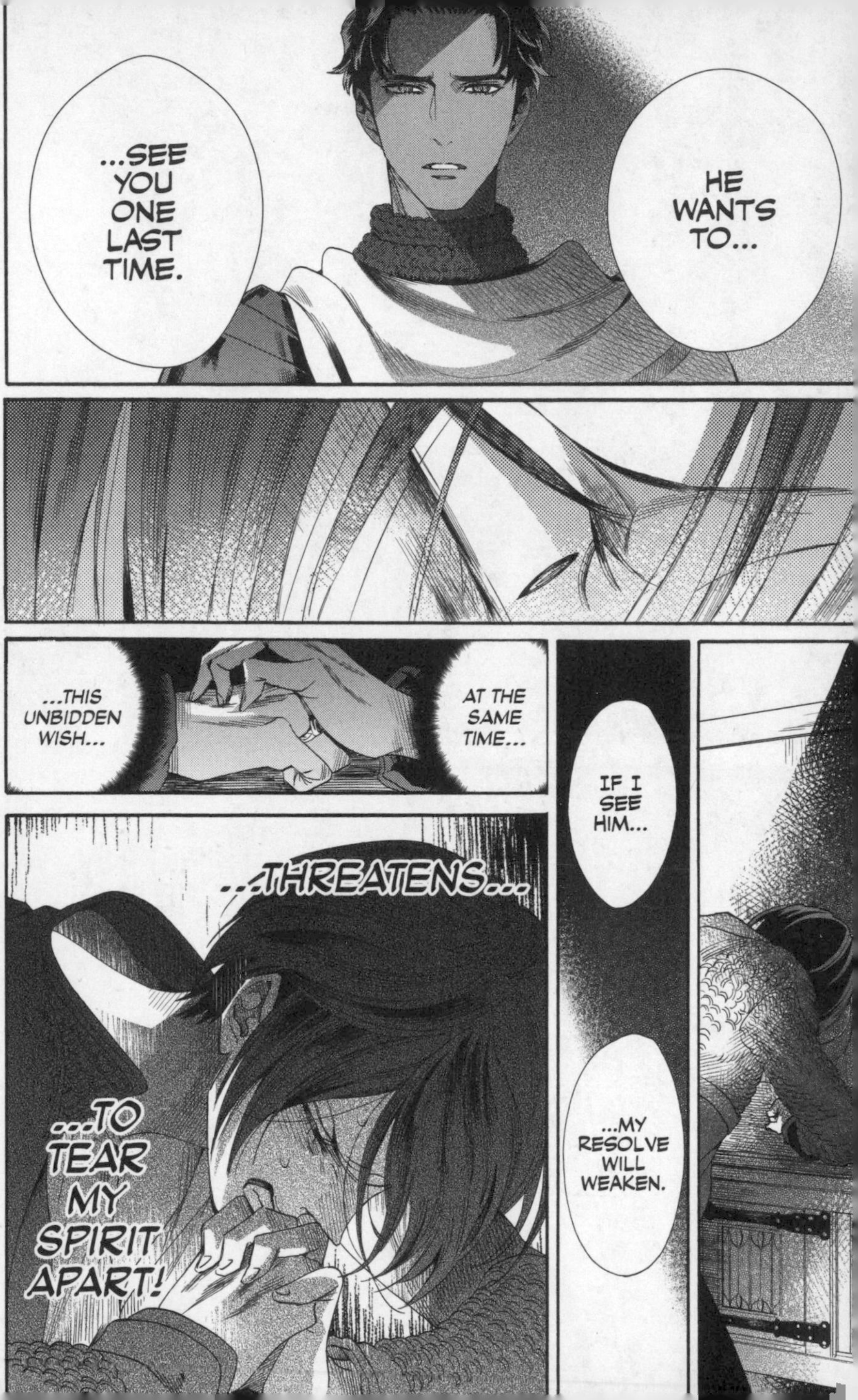
HE WANTS TO...
...SEE YOU ONE LAST TIME.
IF I SEE HIM...
...MY RESOLVE WILL WEAKEN.
AT THE SAME TIME...
...THIS UNBIDDEN WISH...
...THREATENS...
...TO TEAR MY SPIRIT APART!

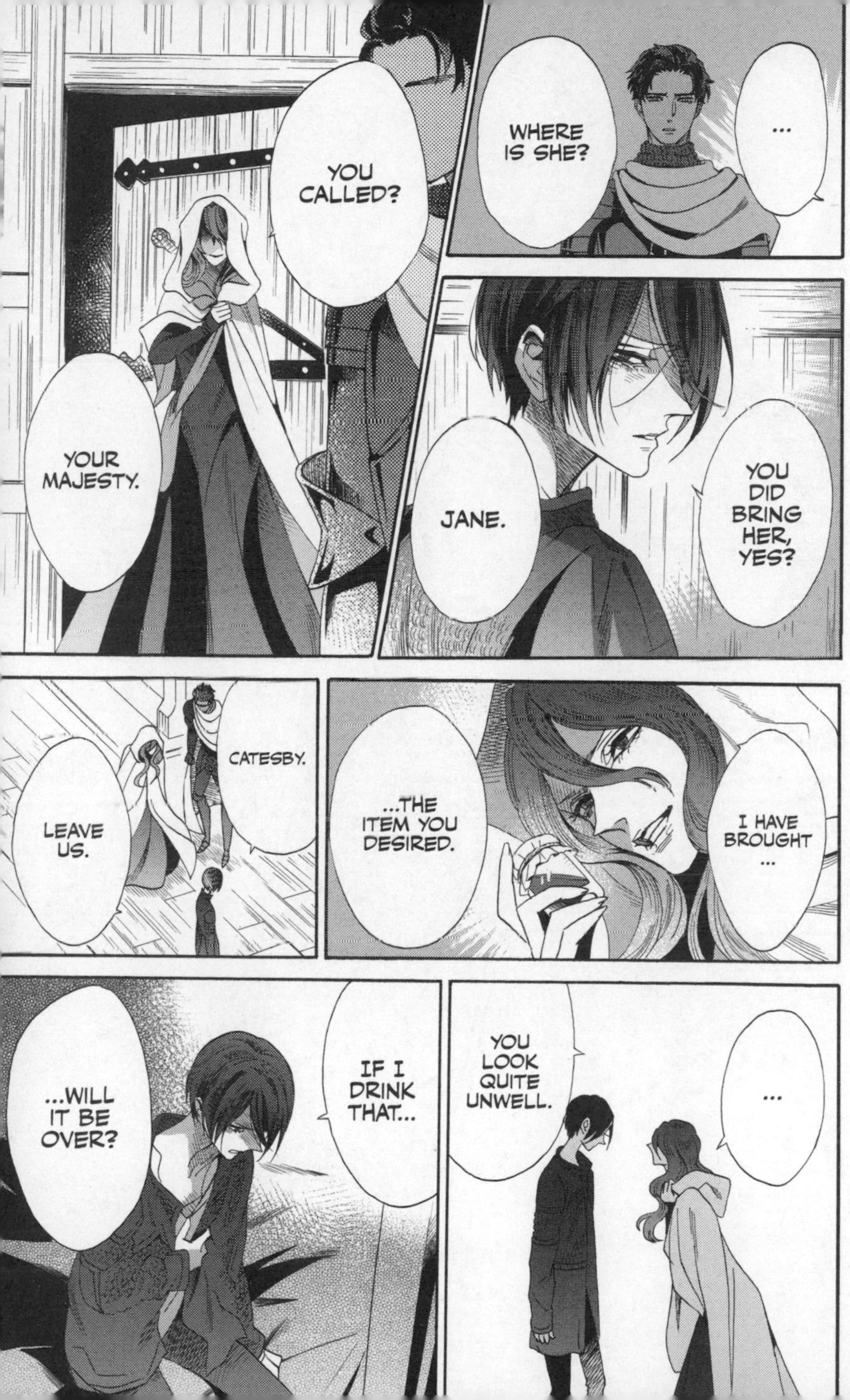
...
WHERE IS SHE?
YOU DID BRING HER, YES?
JANE.
YOU CALLED?
YOUR MAJESTY.
I HAVE BROUGHT ...
...THE ITEM YOU DESIRED.
CATESBY.
LEAVE US.
...
YOU LOOK QUITE UNWELL.
IF I DRINK THAT...
...WILL IT BE OVER?

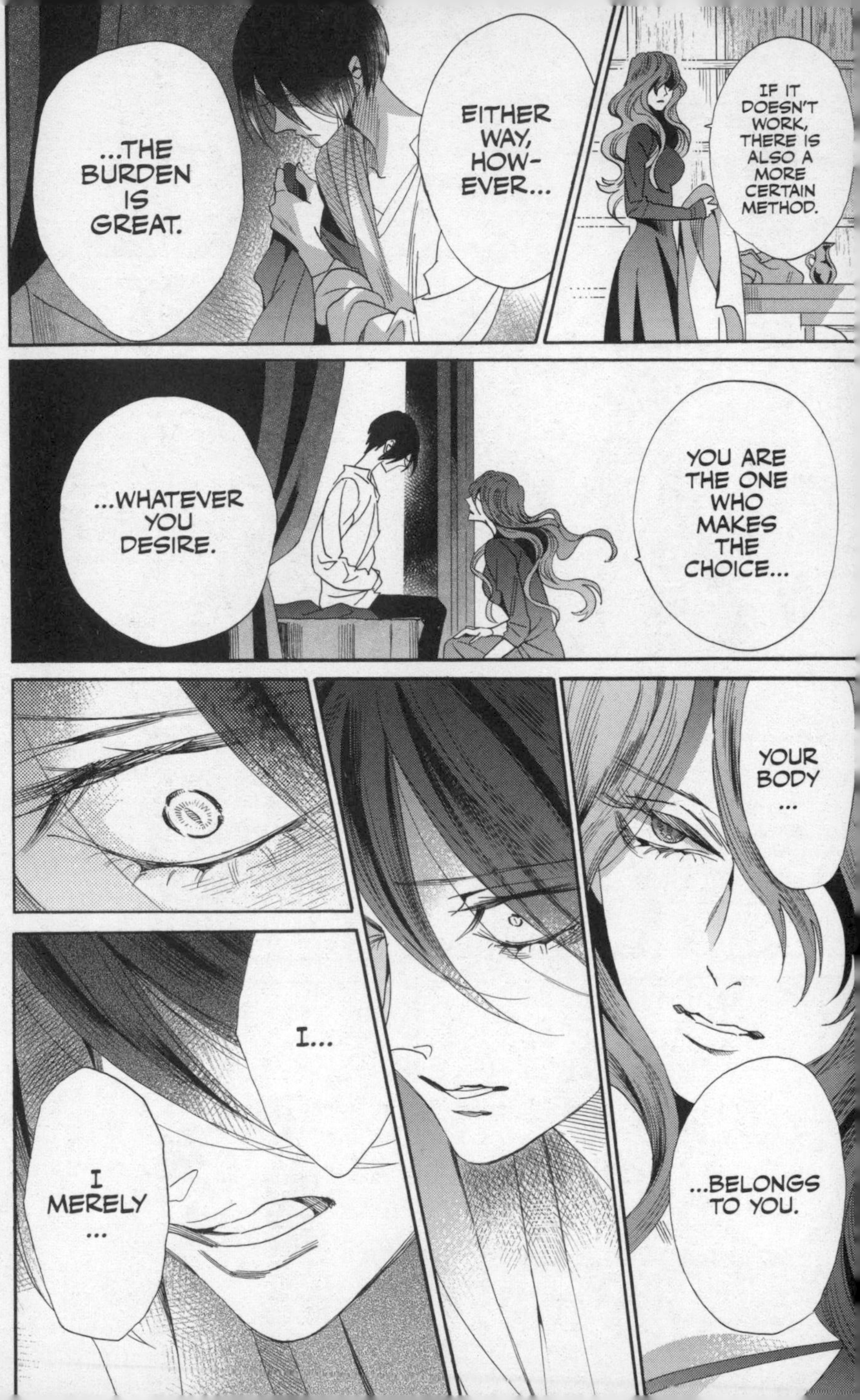
IF IT DOESN'T WORK, THERE IS ALSO A MORE CERTAIN METHOD.
EITHER WAY, HOW-EVER...
...THE BURDEN IS GREAT.
YOU ARE THE ONE WHO MAKES THE CHOICE...
...WHATEVER YOU DESIRE.
YOUR BODY ...
...BELONGS TO YOU.
I...
I MERELY ...

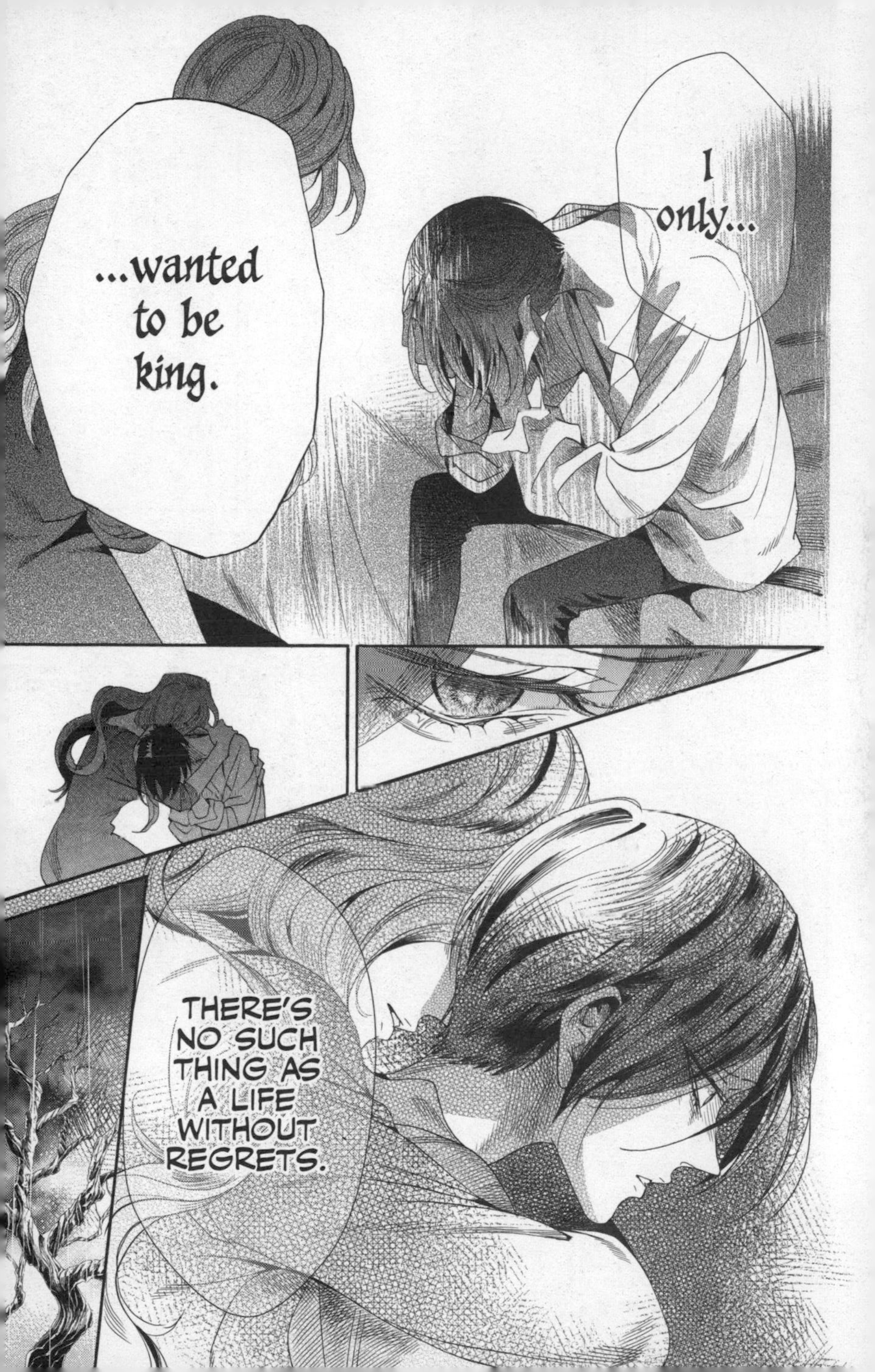
I only...
...wanted to be king.
THERE'S NO SUCH THING AS A LIFE WITHOUT REGRETS.

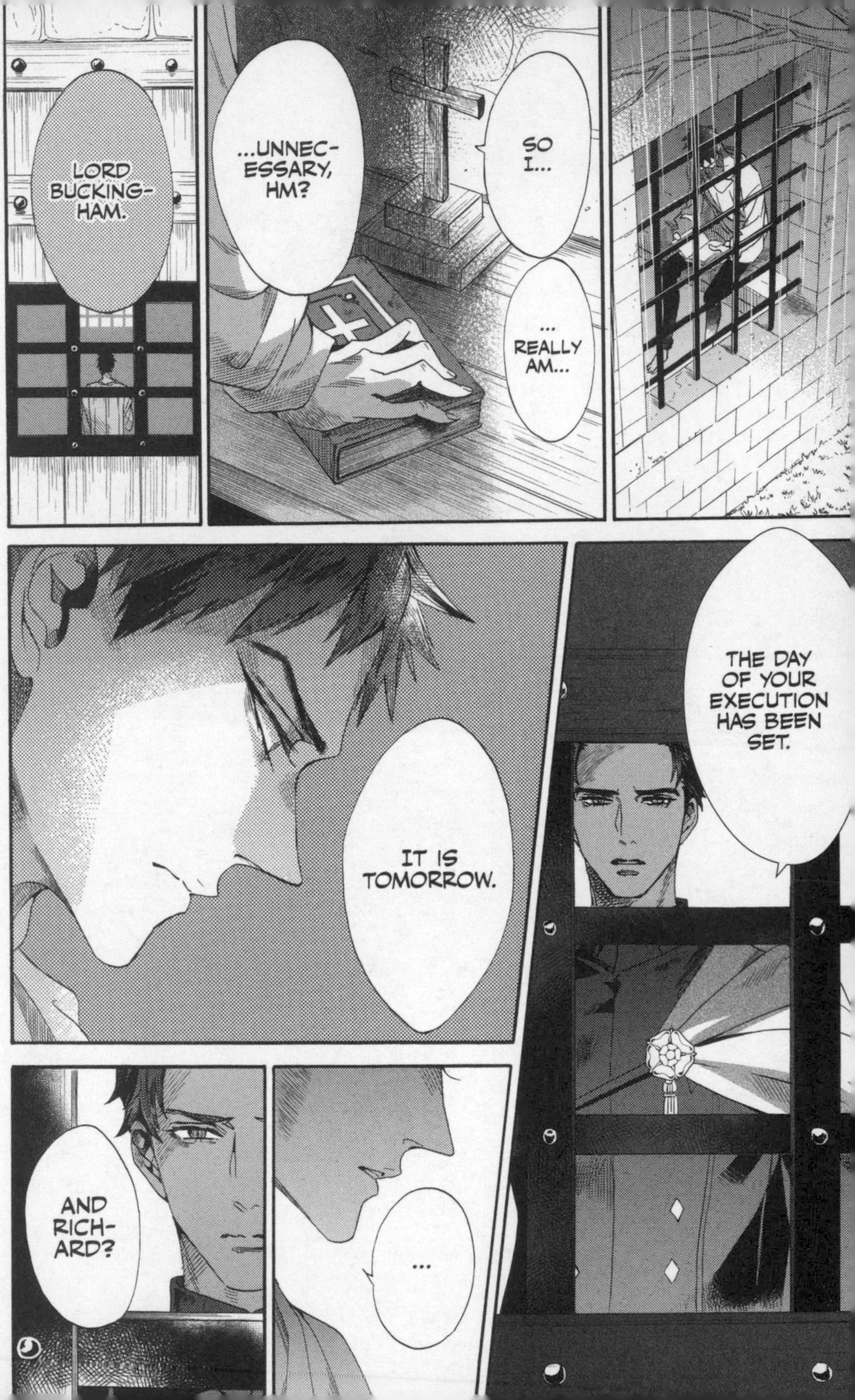
SO I...
...REALLY AM...
...UNNEC-ESSARY, HM?
LORD BUCKING-HAM.
THE DAY OF YOUR EXECUTION HAS BEEN SET.
IT IS TOMORROW.
...
AND RICH-ARD?

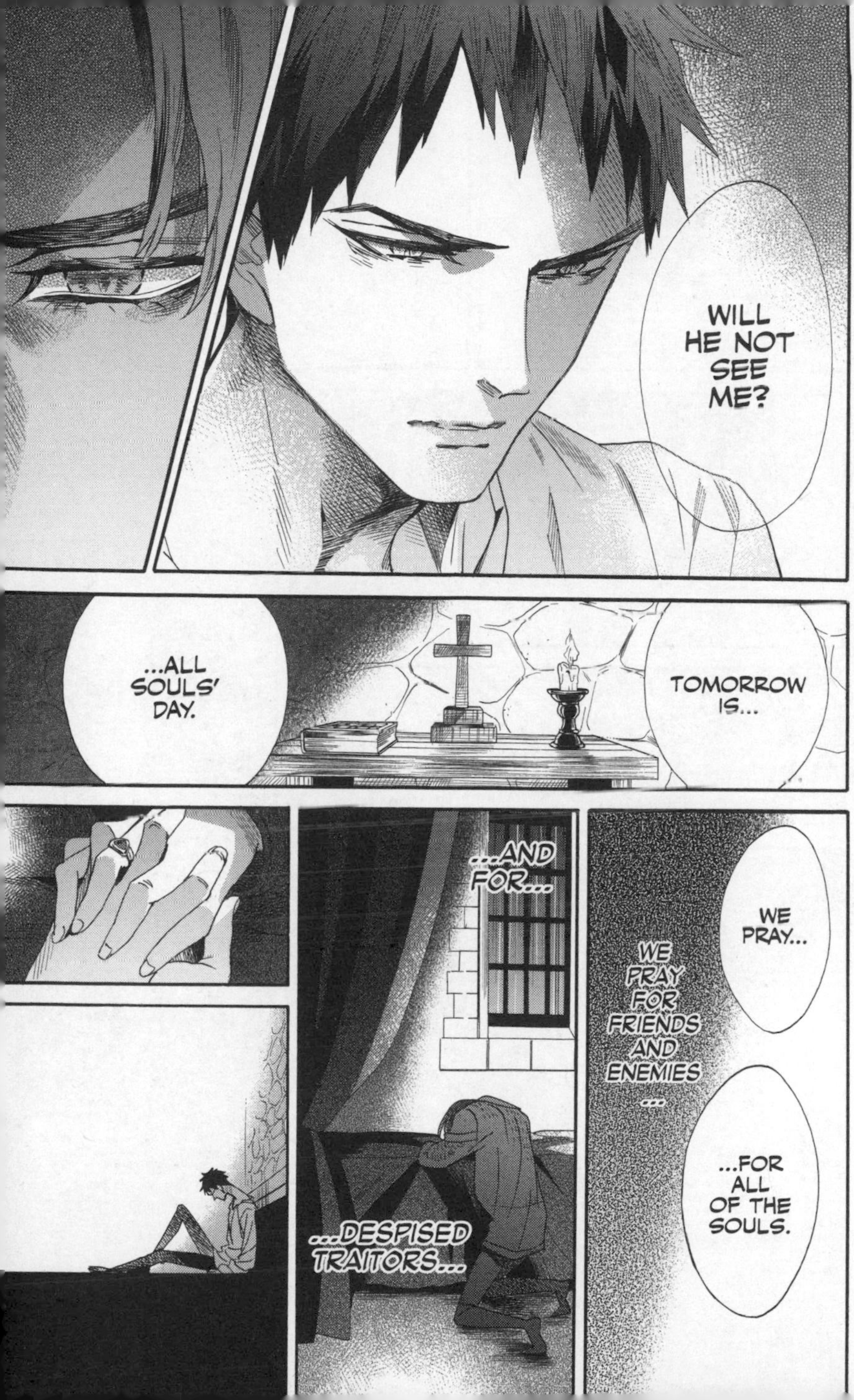
WILL HE NOT SEE ME?
TOMORROW IS...
...ALL SOULS' DAY.
WE PRAY...
WE PRAY FOR FRIENDS AND ENEMIES...
...FOR ALL OF THE SOULS.
...AND FOR...
...DESPISED TRAITORS...

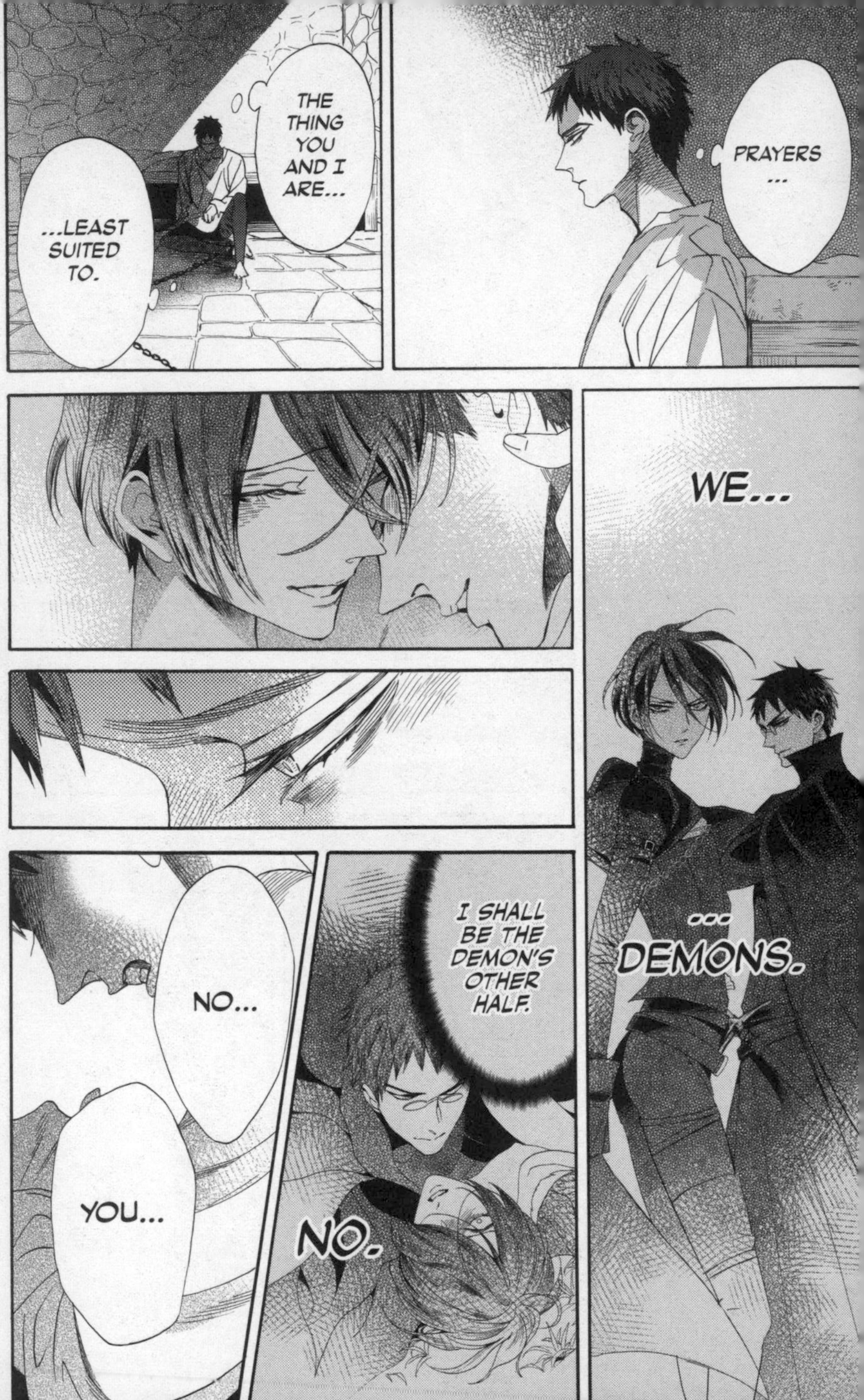
PRAYERS ...
THE THING YOU AND I ARE...
...LEAST SUITED TO.
WE...
...DEMONS.
I SHALL BE THE DEMON'S OTHER HALF.
NO.
NO...
YOU...

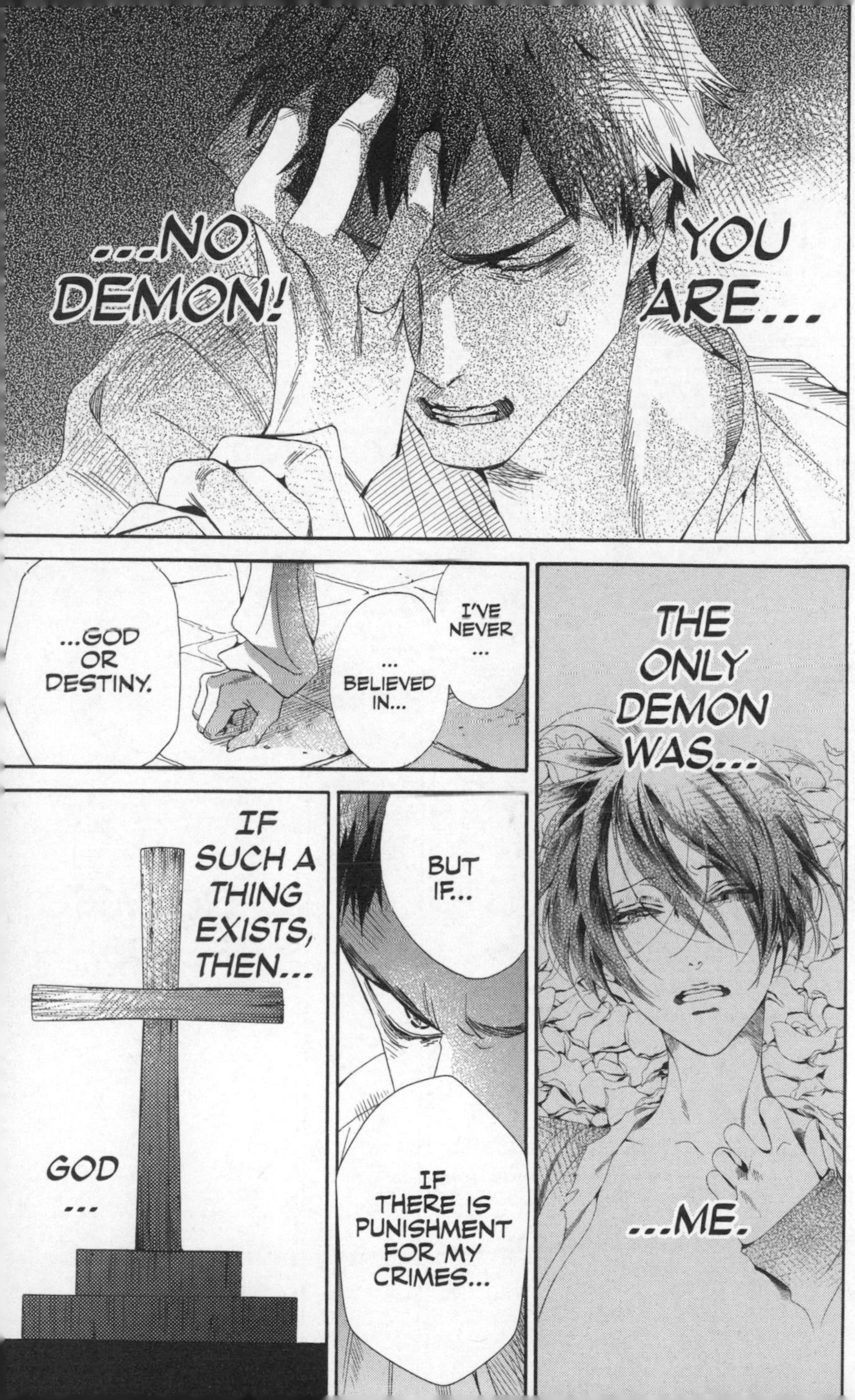
YOU ARE...
...NO DEMON!
THE ONLY DEMON WAS...
...ME.
I'VE NEVER... ... BELIEVED IN...
...GOD OR DESTINY.
BUT IF...
IF THERE IS PUNISHMENT FOR MY CRIMES...
IF SUCH A THING EXISTS, THEN...
GOD ...

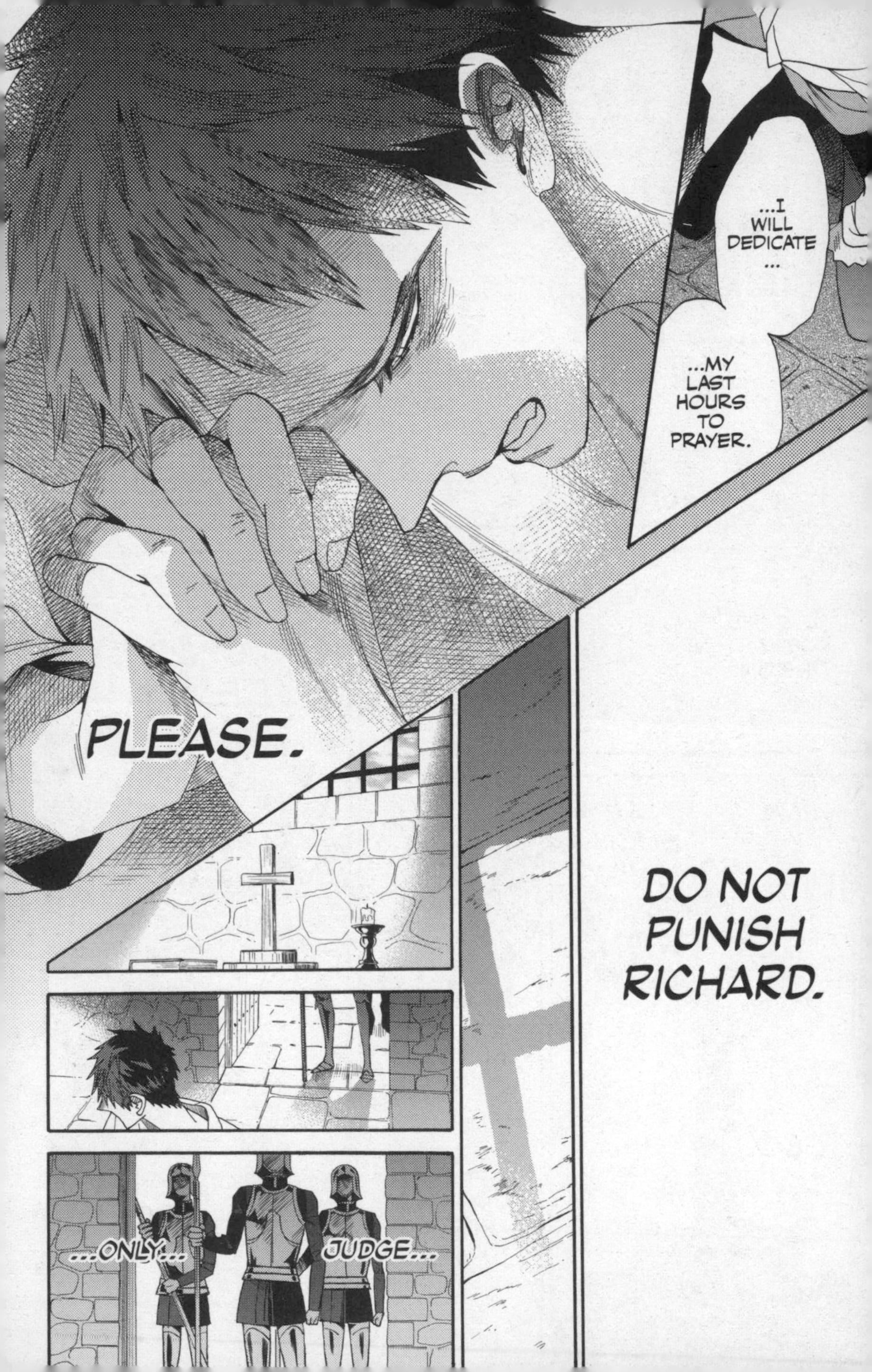
...I WILL DEDICATE ...
...MY LAST HOURS TO PRAYER.
PLEASE.
DO NOT PUNISH RICHARD.
...ONLY...
JUDGE...

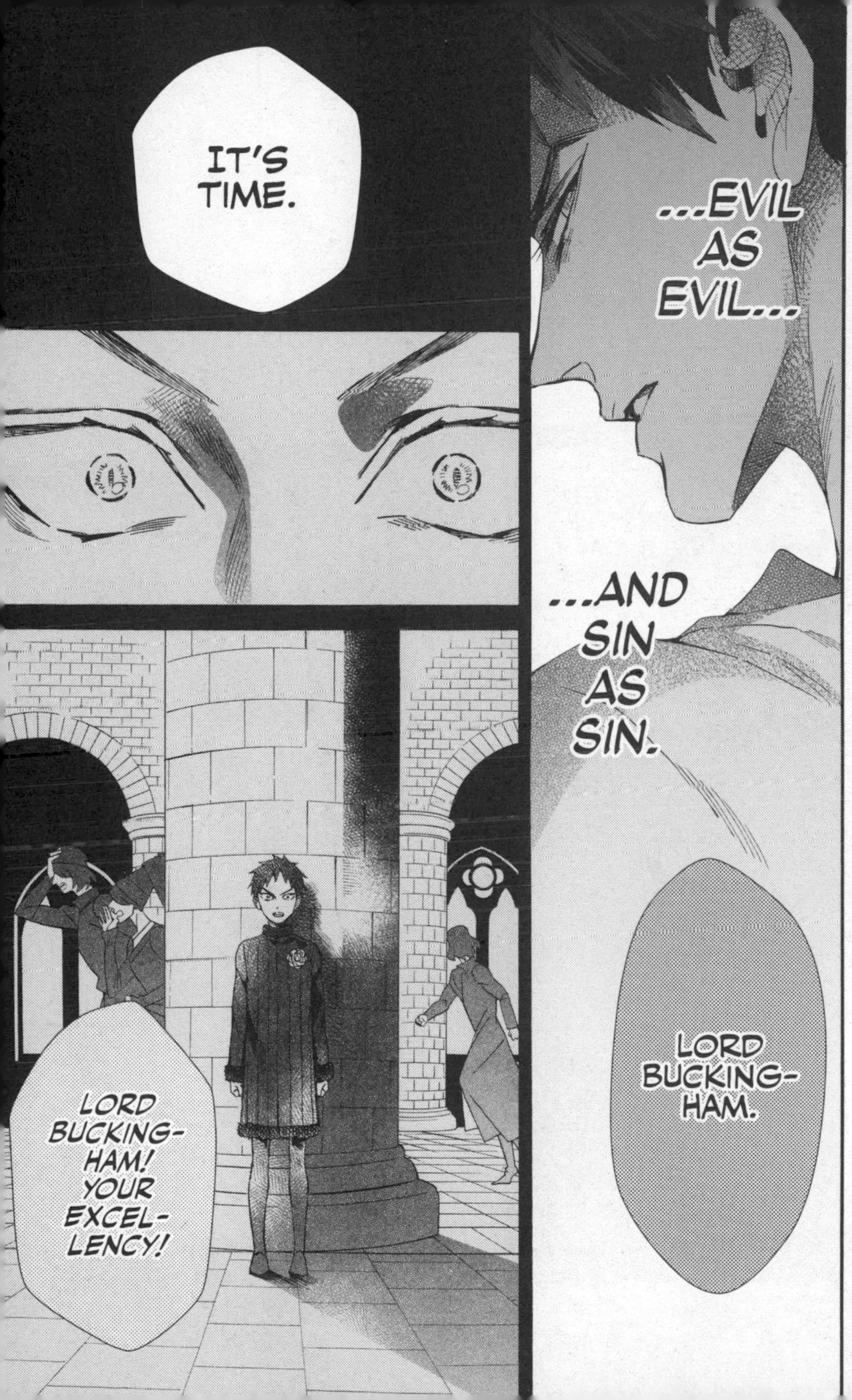
...EVIL AS EVIL...
...AND SIN AS SIN.
LORD BUCKING-HAM.
IT'S TIME.
LORD BUCKING-HAM! YOUR EXCEL-LENCY!

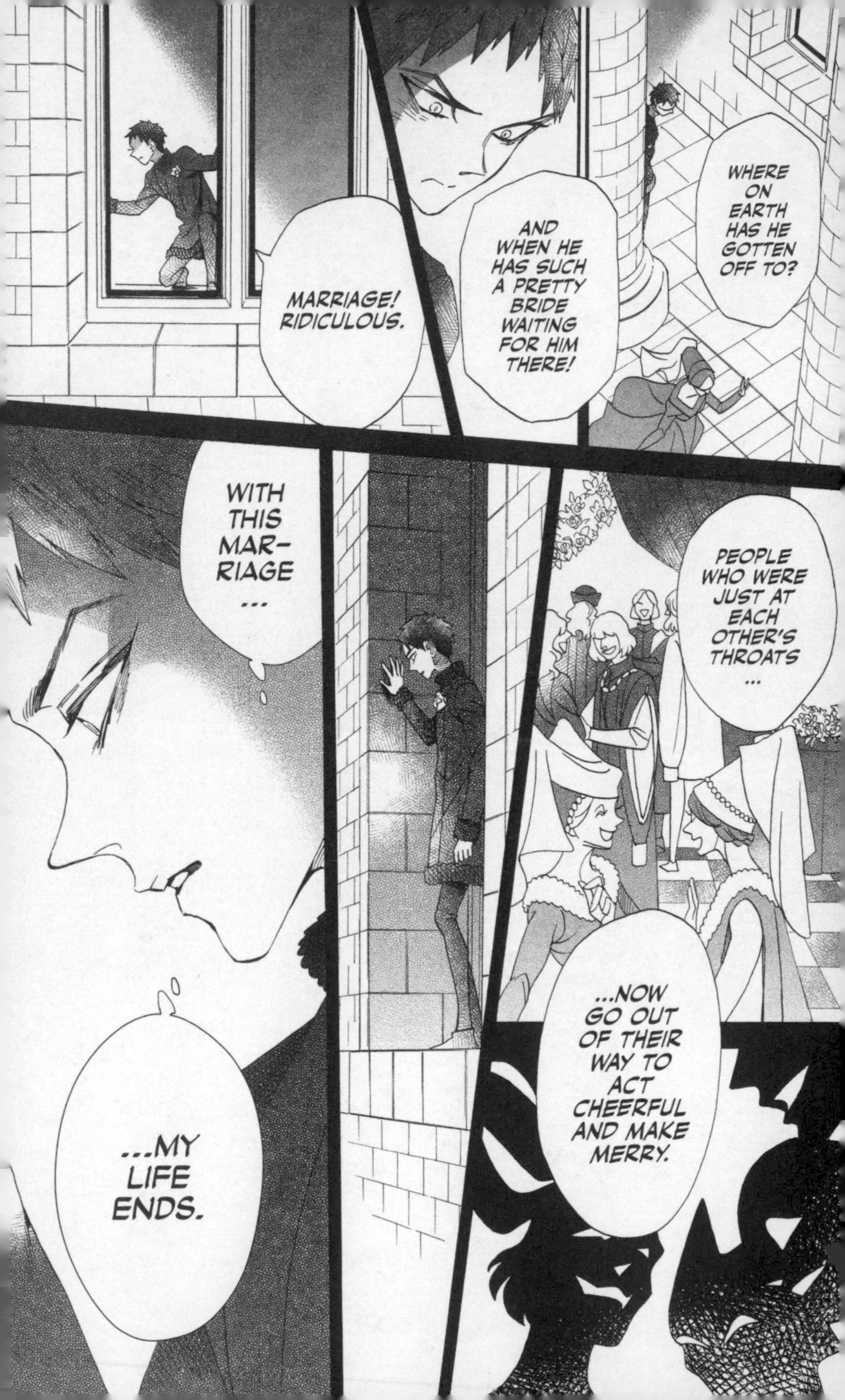
WHERE ON EARTH HAS HE GOTTEN OFF TO?
AND WHEN HE HAS SUCH A PRETTY BRIDE WAITING FOR HIM THERE!
MARRIAGE! RIDICULOUS.
PEOPLE WHO WERE JUST AT EACH OTHER'S THROATS...
...NOW GO OUT OF THEIR WAY TO ACT CHEERFUL AND MAKE MERRY.
WITH THIS MAR-RIAGE...
...MY LIFE ENDS.

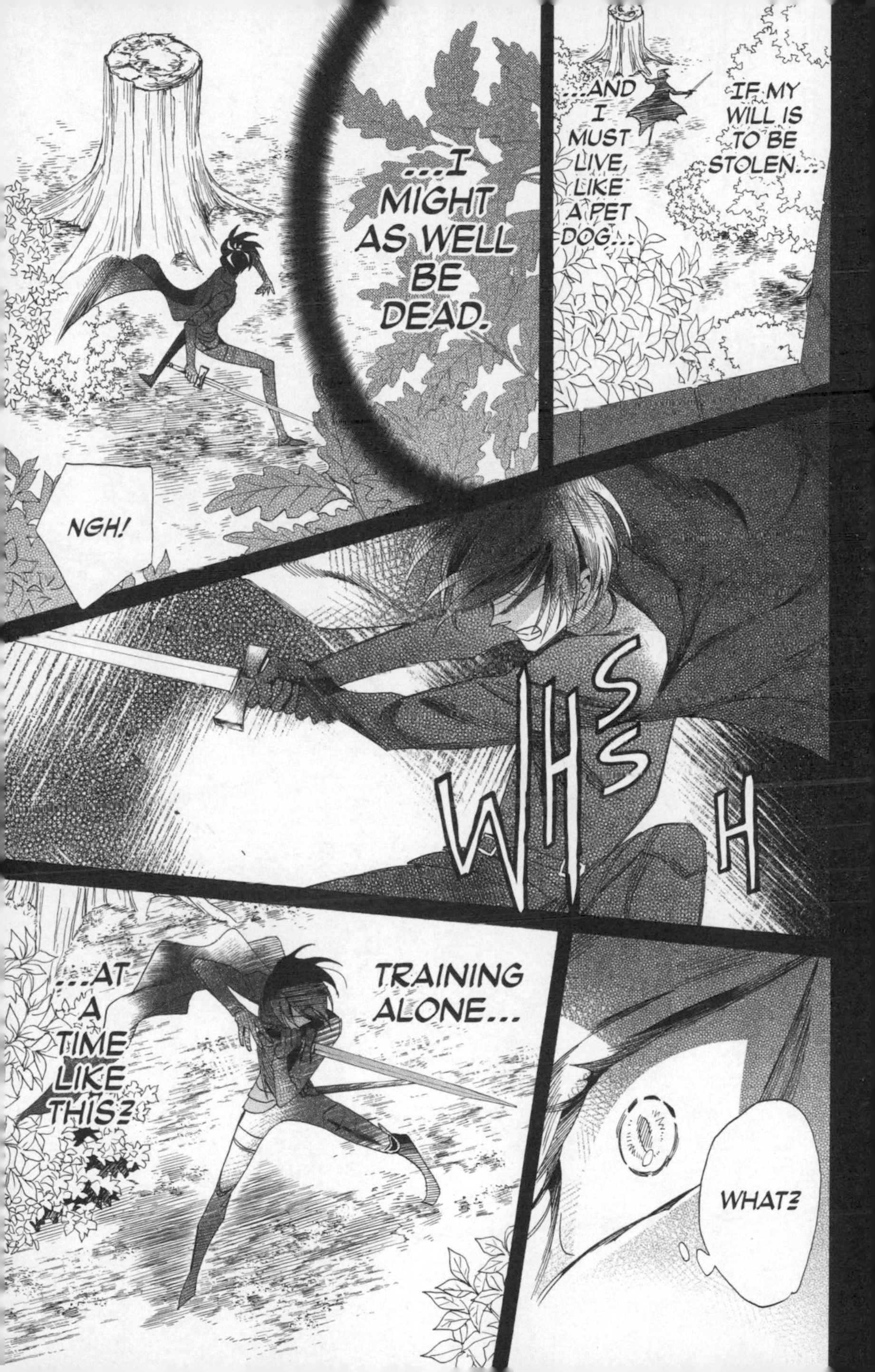
IF MY WILL IS TO BE STOLEN...
...AND I MUST LIVE LIKE A PET DOG...
...I MIGHT AS WELL BE DEAD.
NGH!
WHSSH
WHAT?
TRAINING ALONE...
...AT A TIME LIKE THIS?

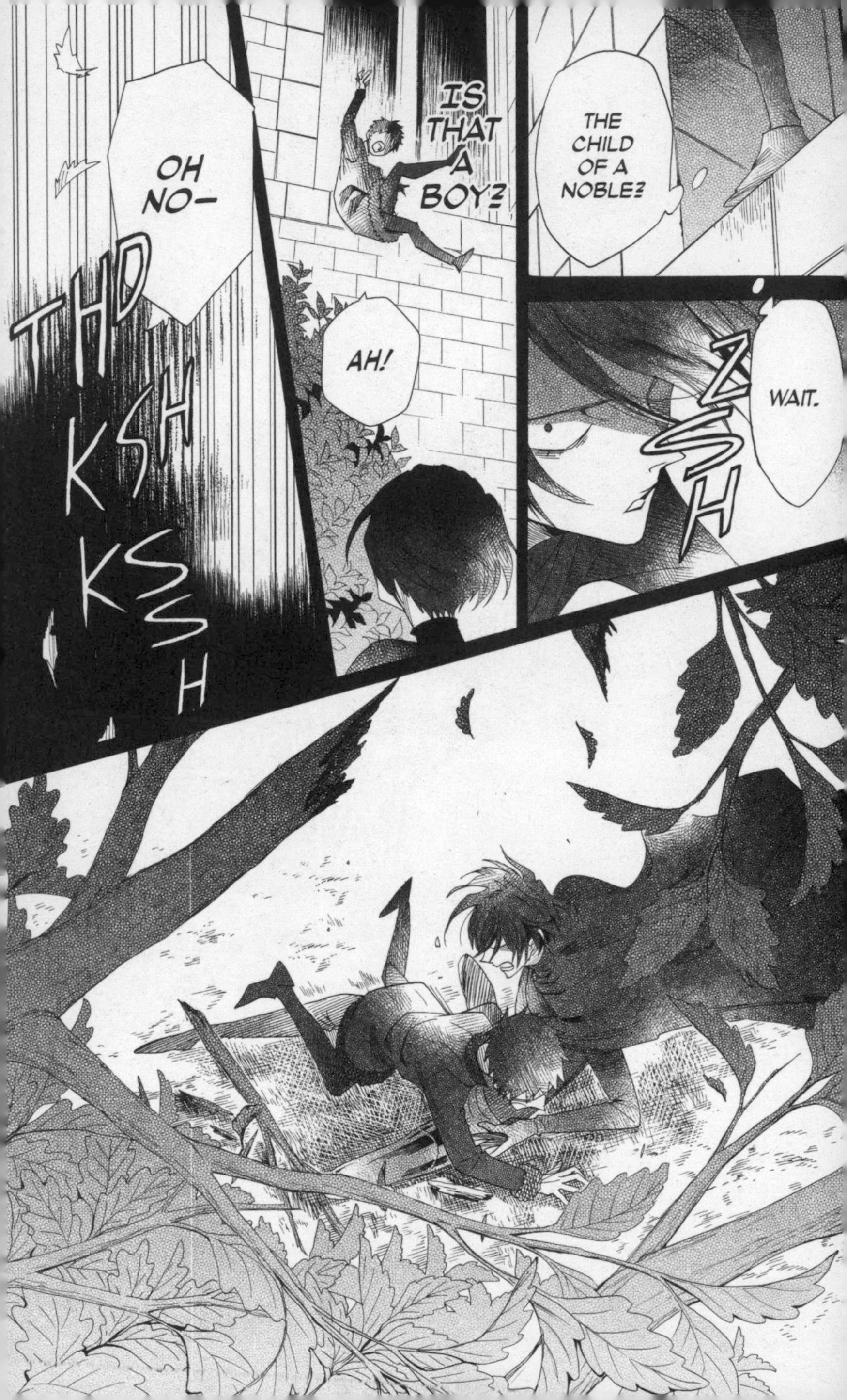
THE CHILD OF A NOBLE?
WAIT.
ZSH
IS THAT A BOY?
AH!
OH NO-
THD
KSH
KSSH

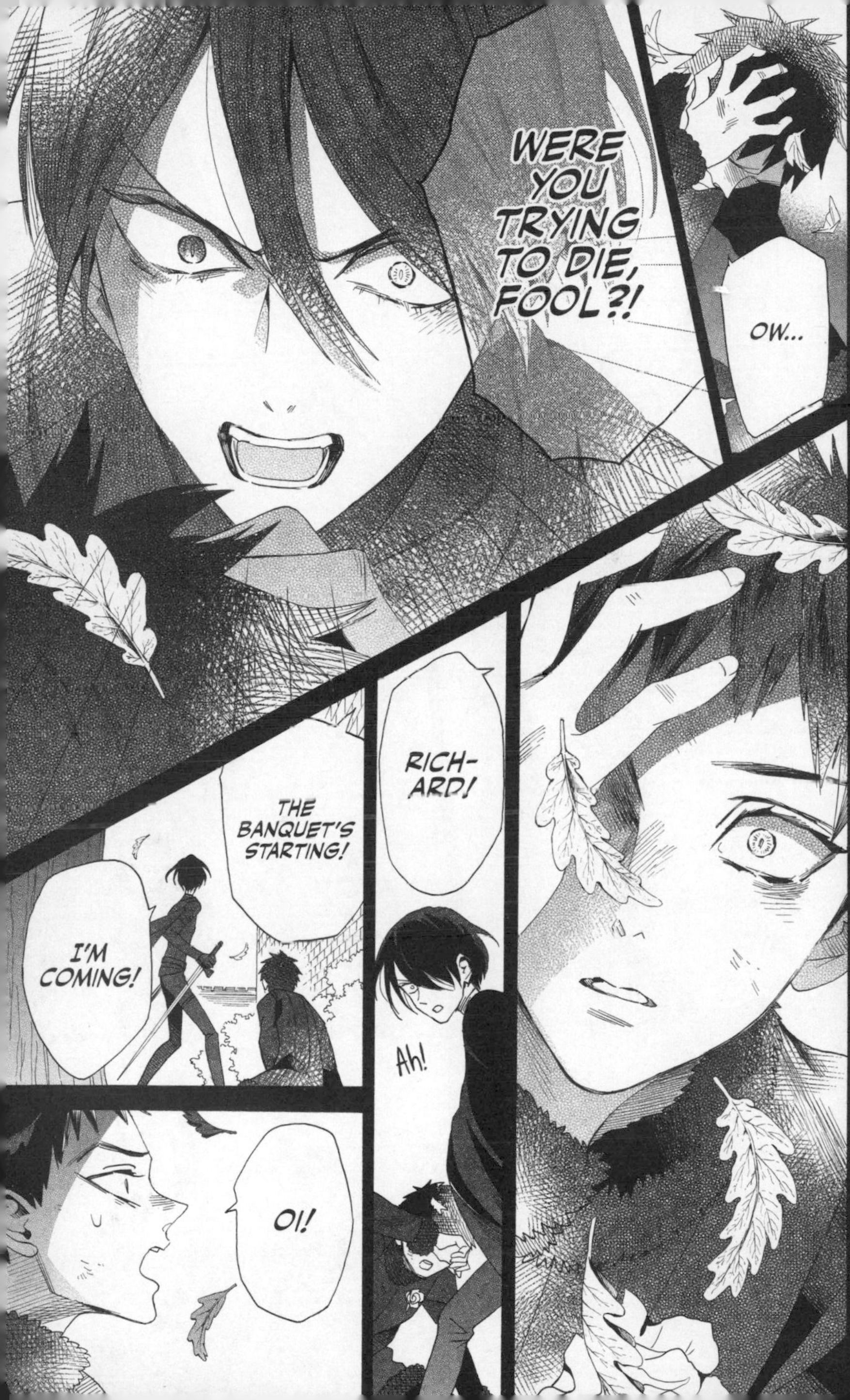
OW...
WERE YOU TRYING TO DIE, FOOL?!
RICH-ARD!
THE BANQUET'S STARTING!
I'M COMING!
Ah!
OI!

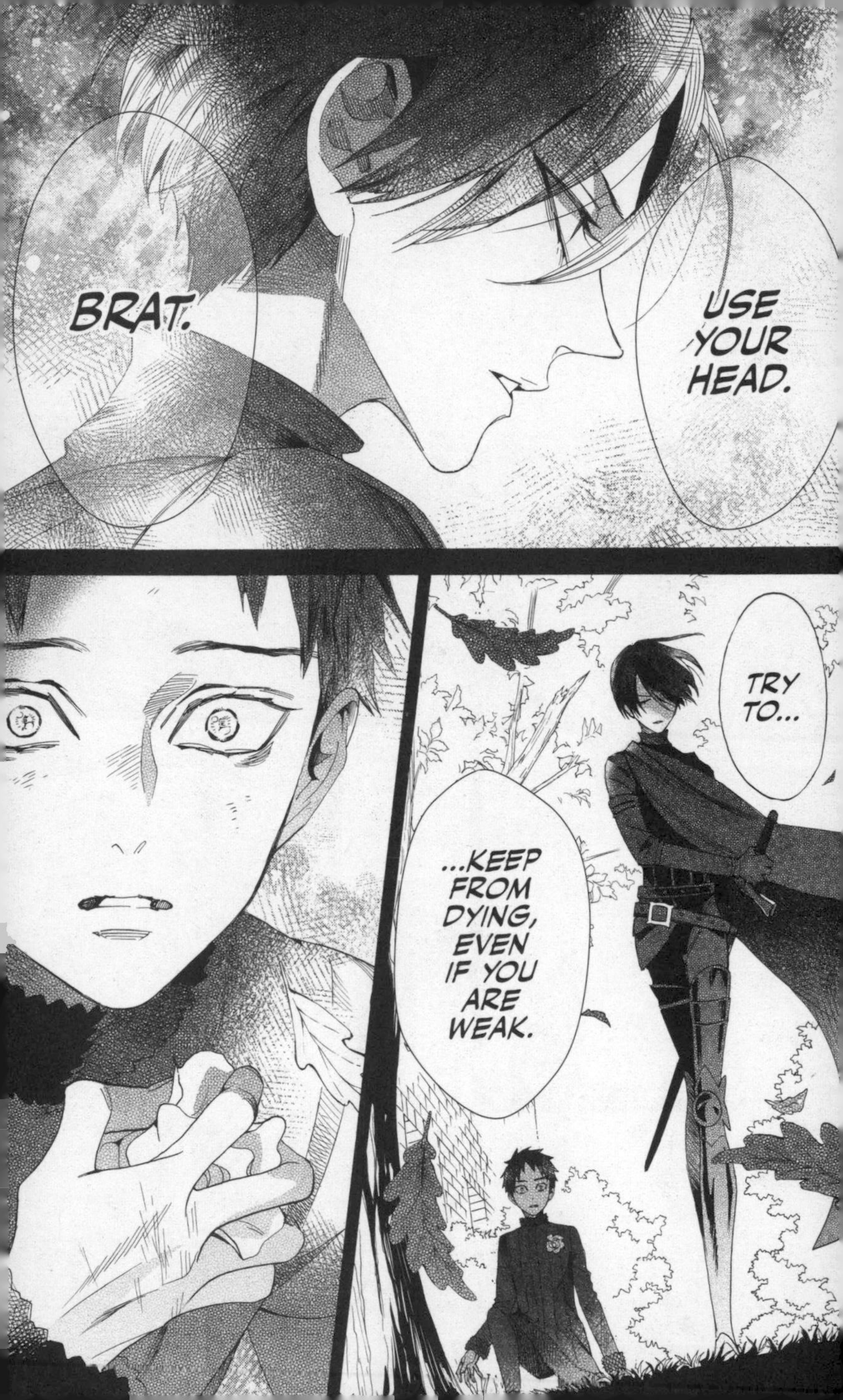
USE YOUR HEAD.
BRAT.
TRY TO...
...KEEP FROM DYING, EVEN IF YOU ARE WEAK.

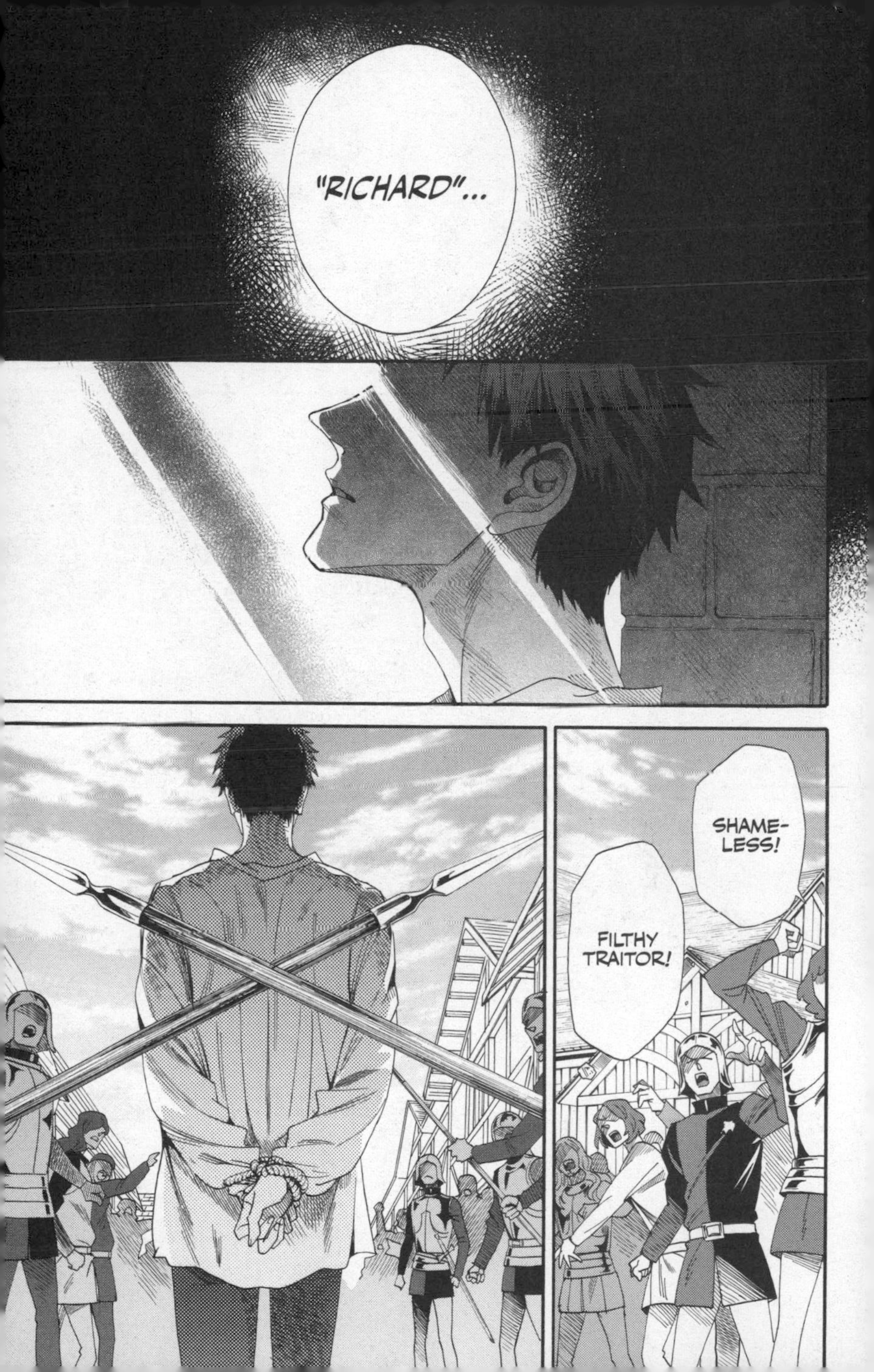
"RICHARD"...
SHAME-LESS!
FILTHY TRAITOR!

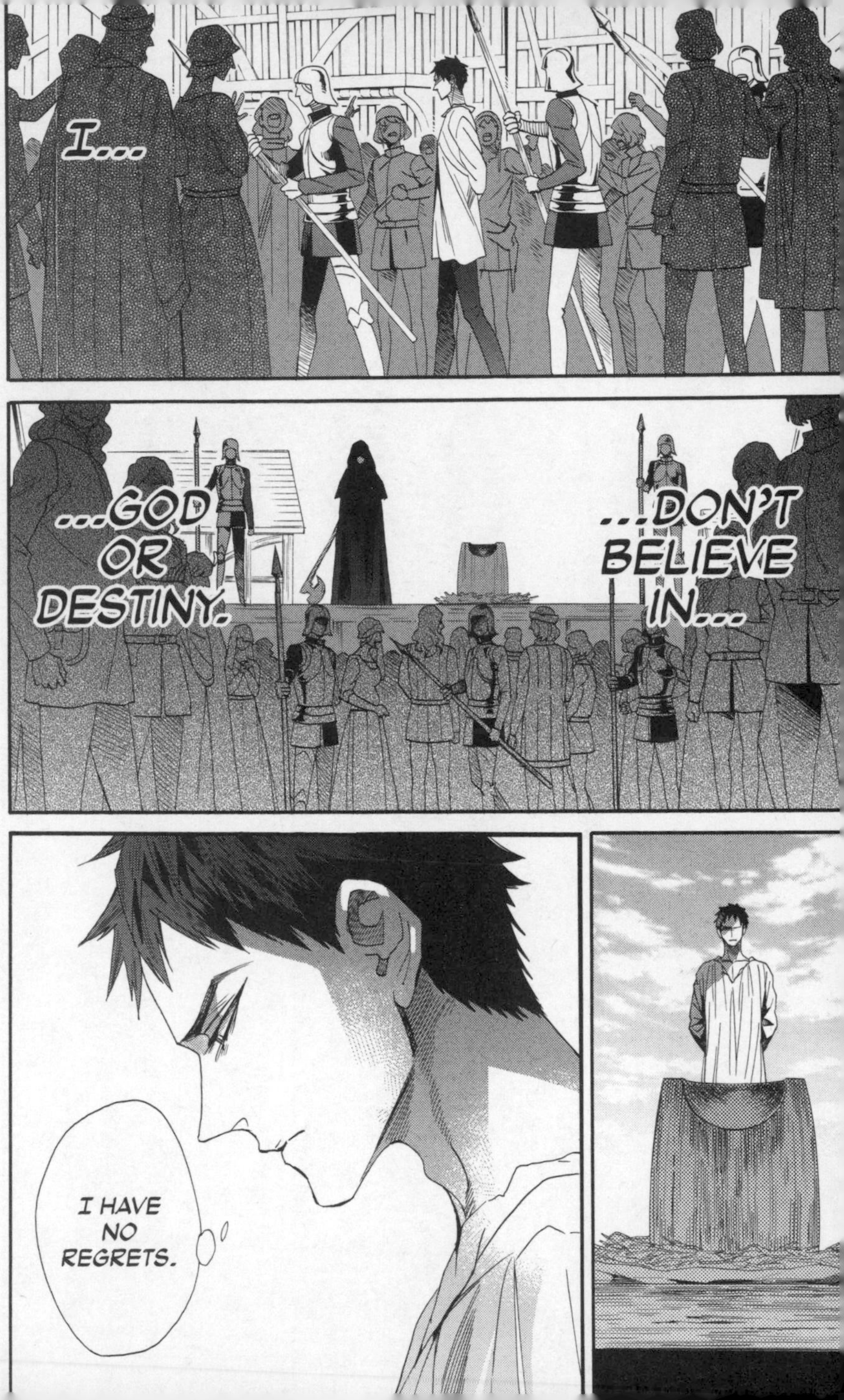
I...
...DON'T BELIEVE IN...
...GOD OR DESTINY.
I HAVE NO REGRETS.

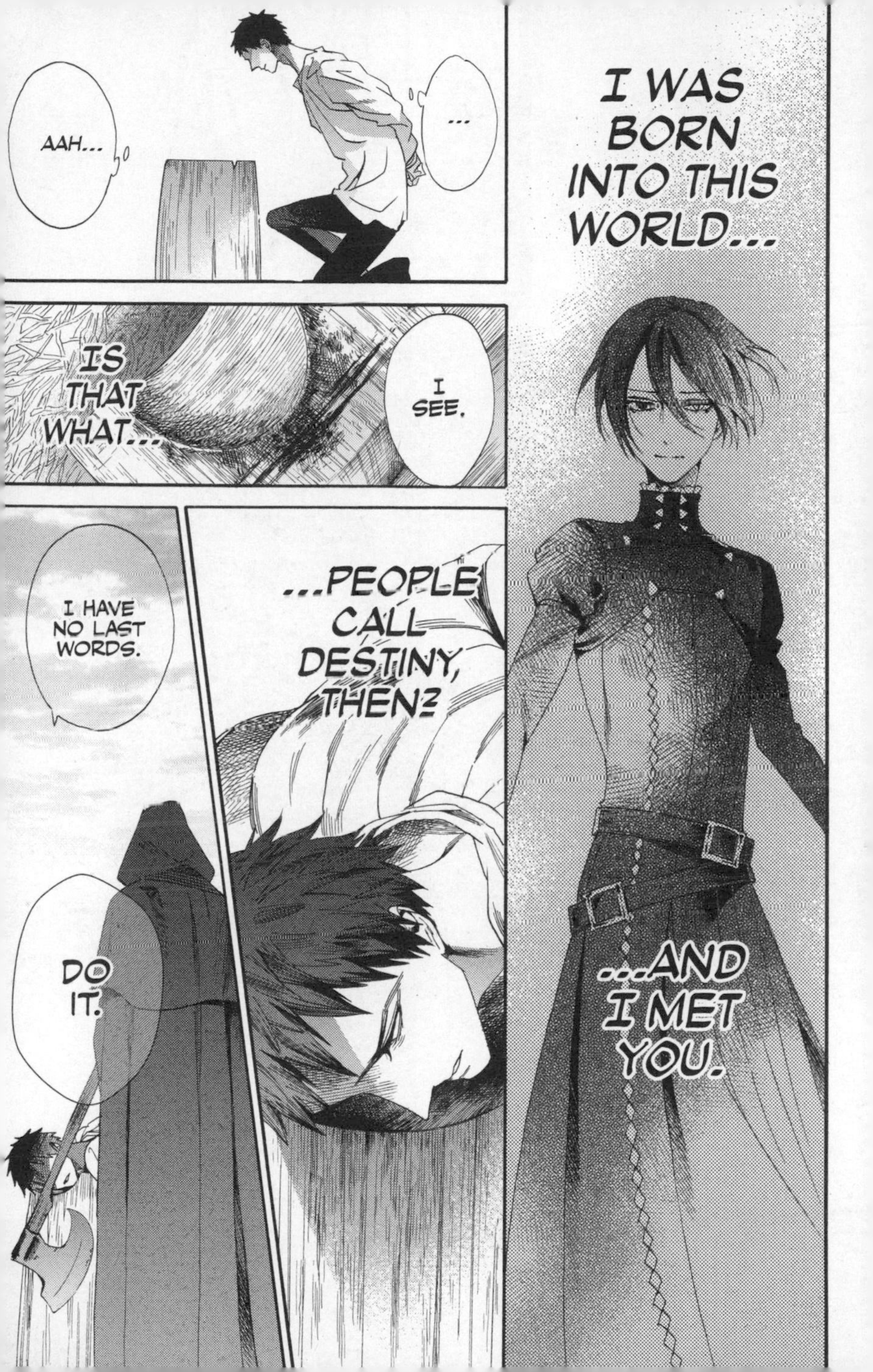
I WAS BORN INTO THIS WORLD...
...AND I MET YOU.
...
AAH...
I SEE.
IS THAT WHAT...
...PEOPLE CALL DESTINY, THEN?
I HAVE NO LAST WORDS.
DO IT.

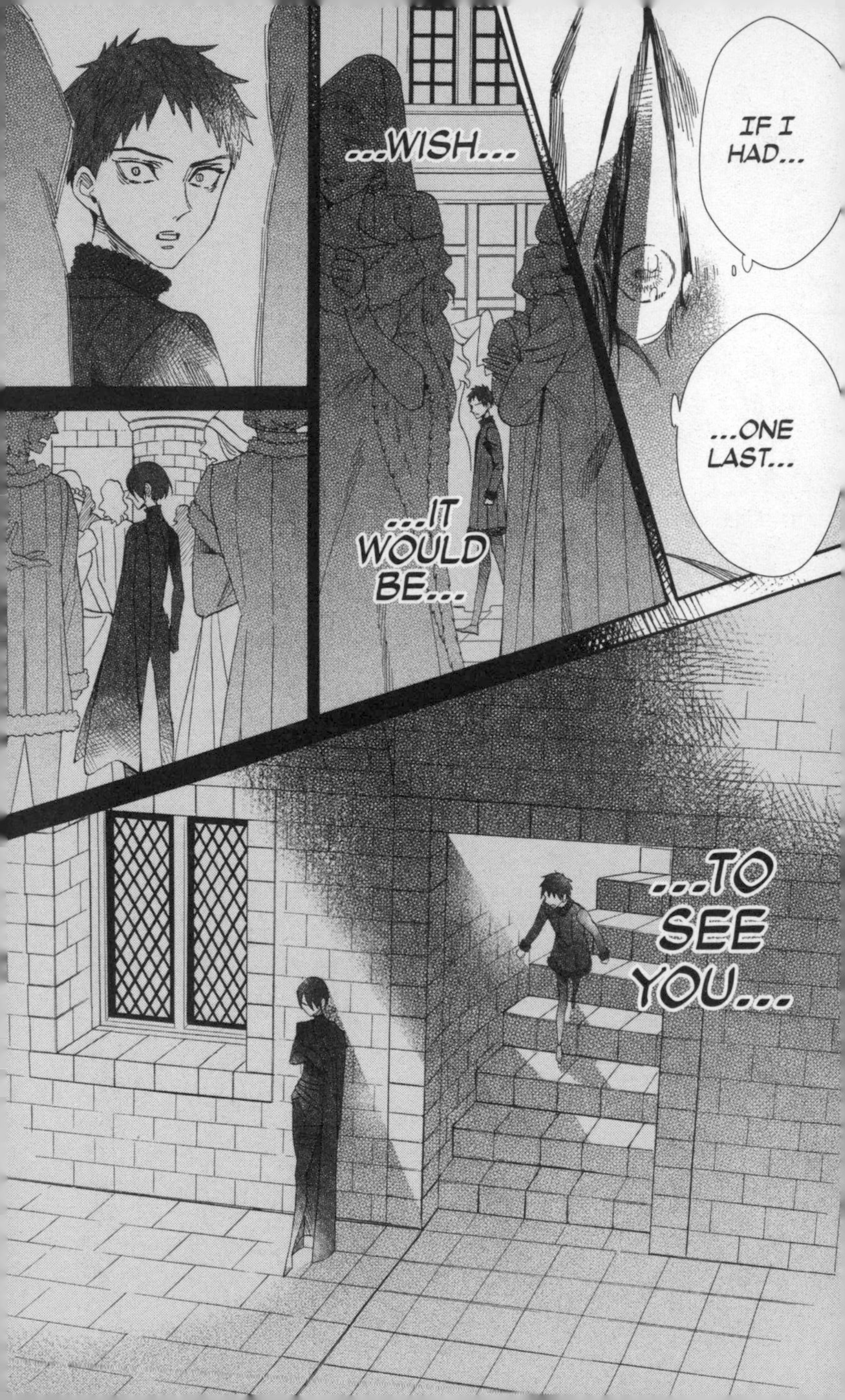
IF I HAD...
...ONE LAST...
...WISH...
...IT WOULD BE...
...TO SEE YOU...

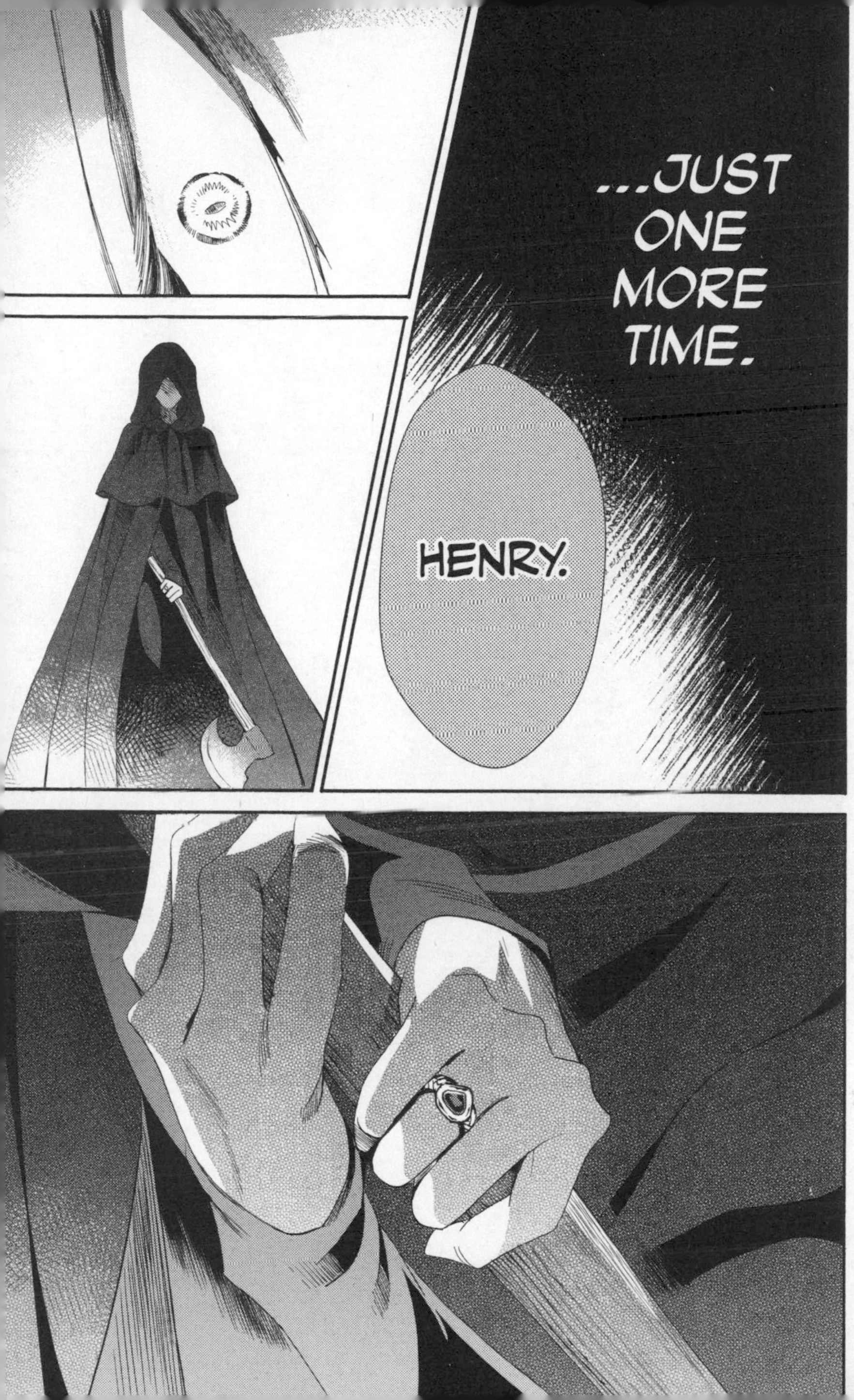
...JUST ONE MORE TIME.
HENRY.

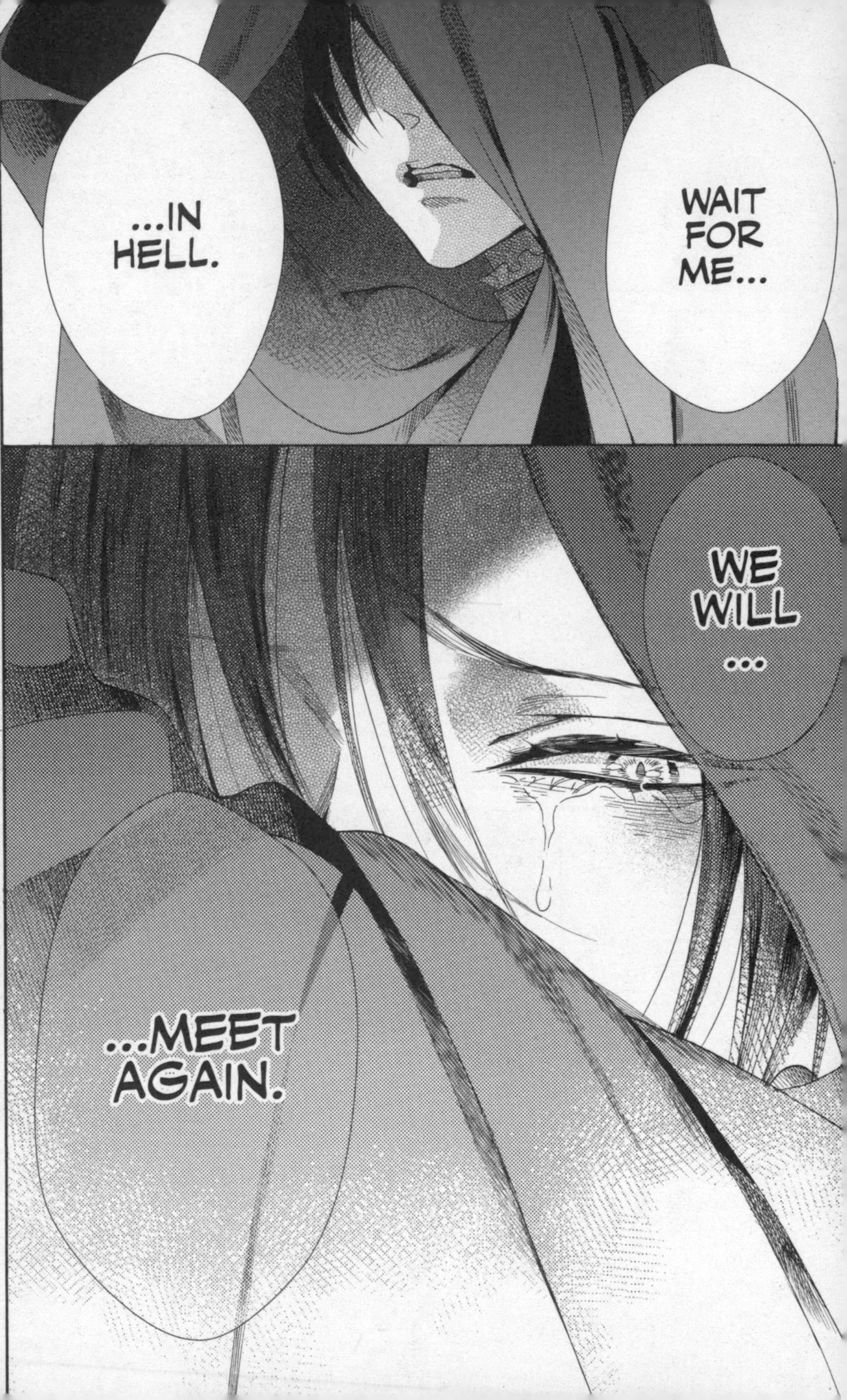
WAIT FOR ME...
...IN HELL.
WE WILL ...
...MEET AGAIN.

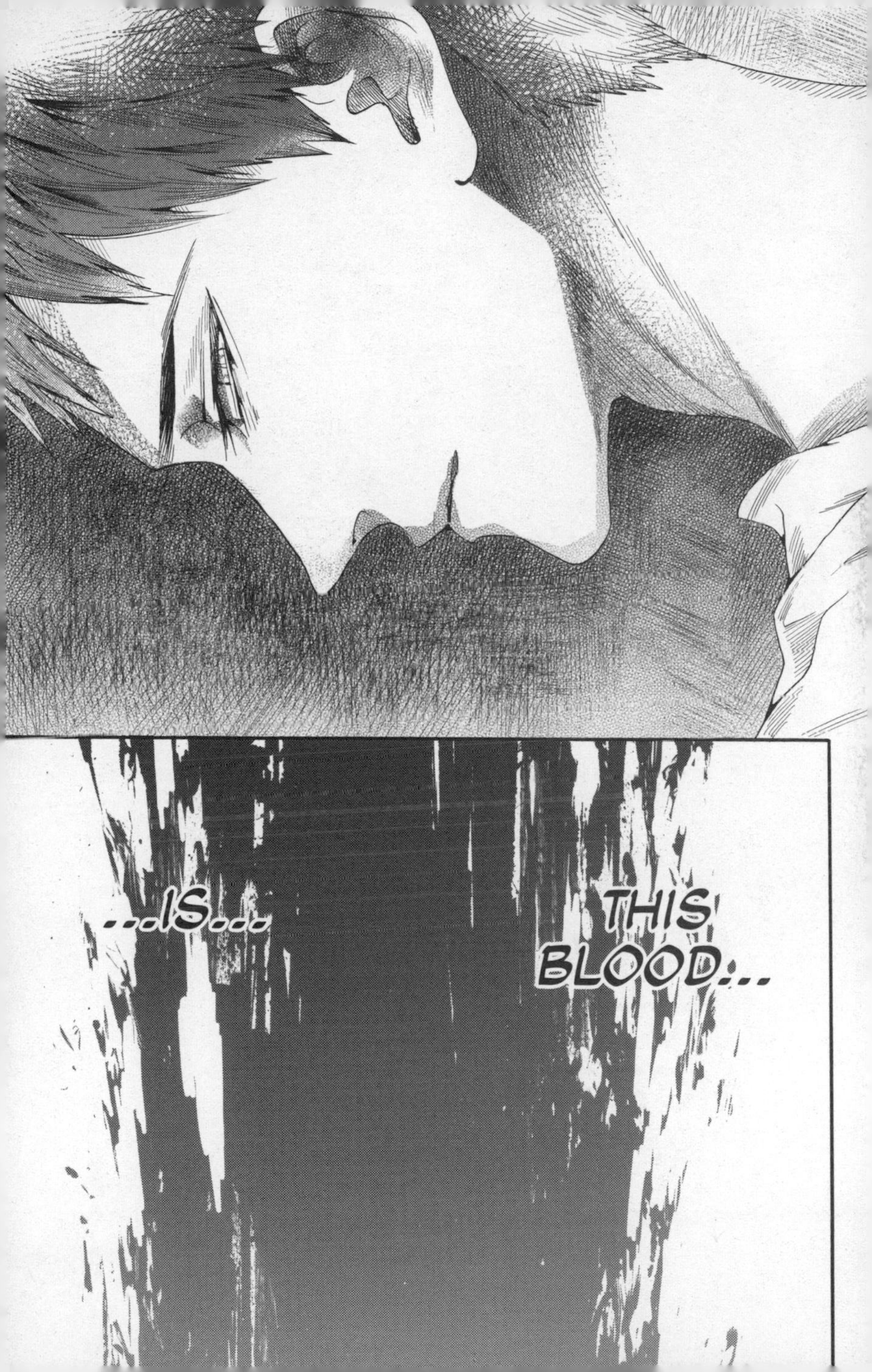
THIS BLOOD...
...IS...

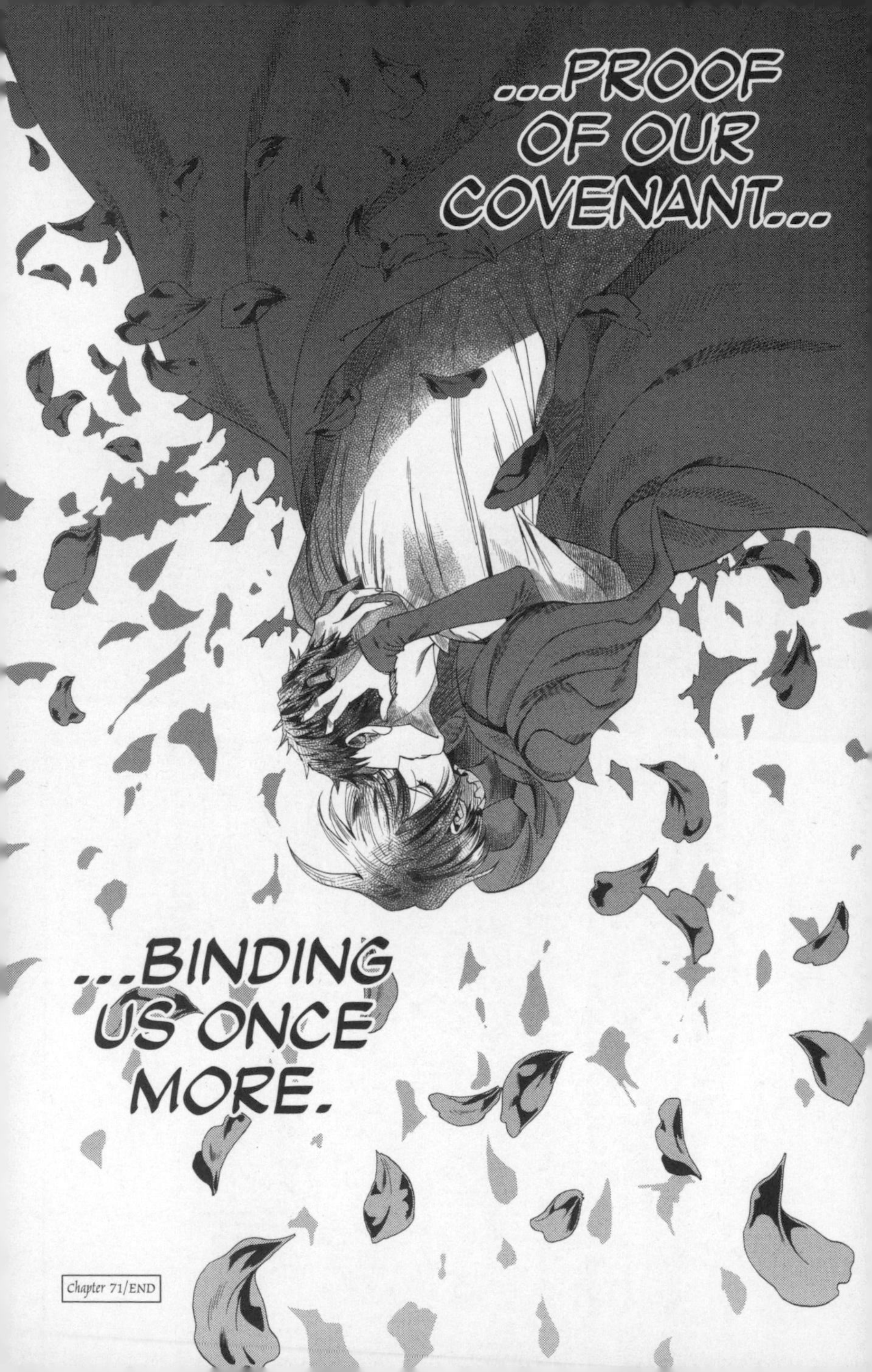
...PROOF OF OUR COVENANT...
...BINDING US ONCE MORE.
Chapter 71/END

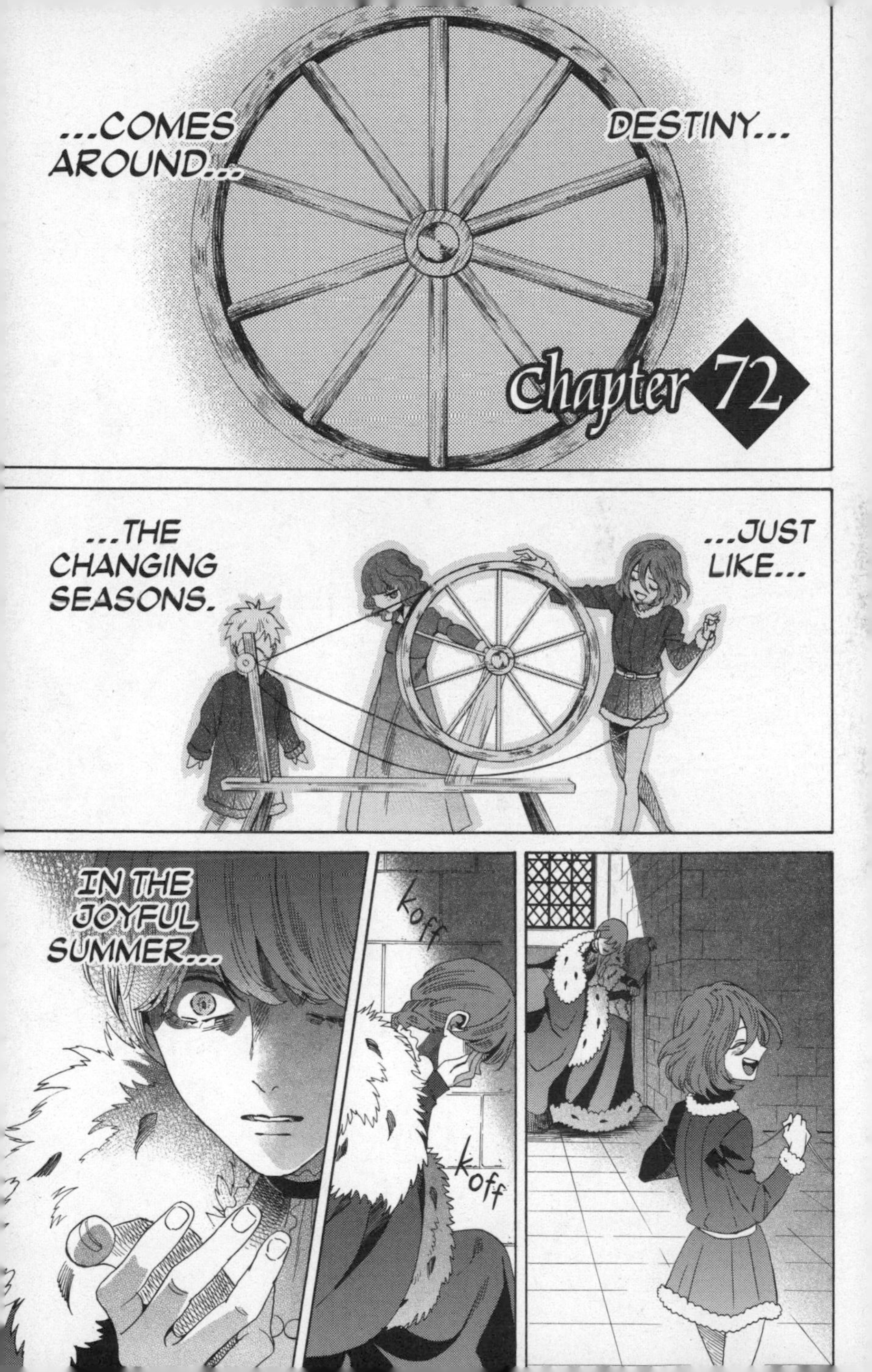
DESTINY...
...COMES AROUND...
Chapter 72
...JUST LIKE...
...THE CHANGING SEASONS.
koff
koff
IN THE JOYFUL SUMMER...

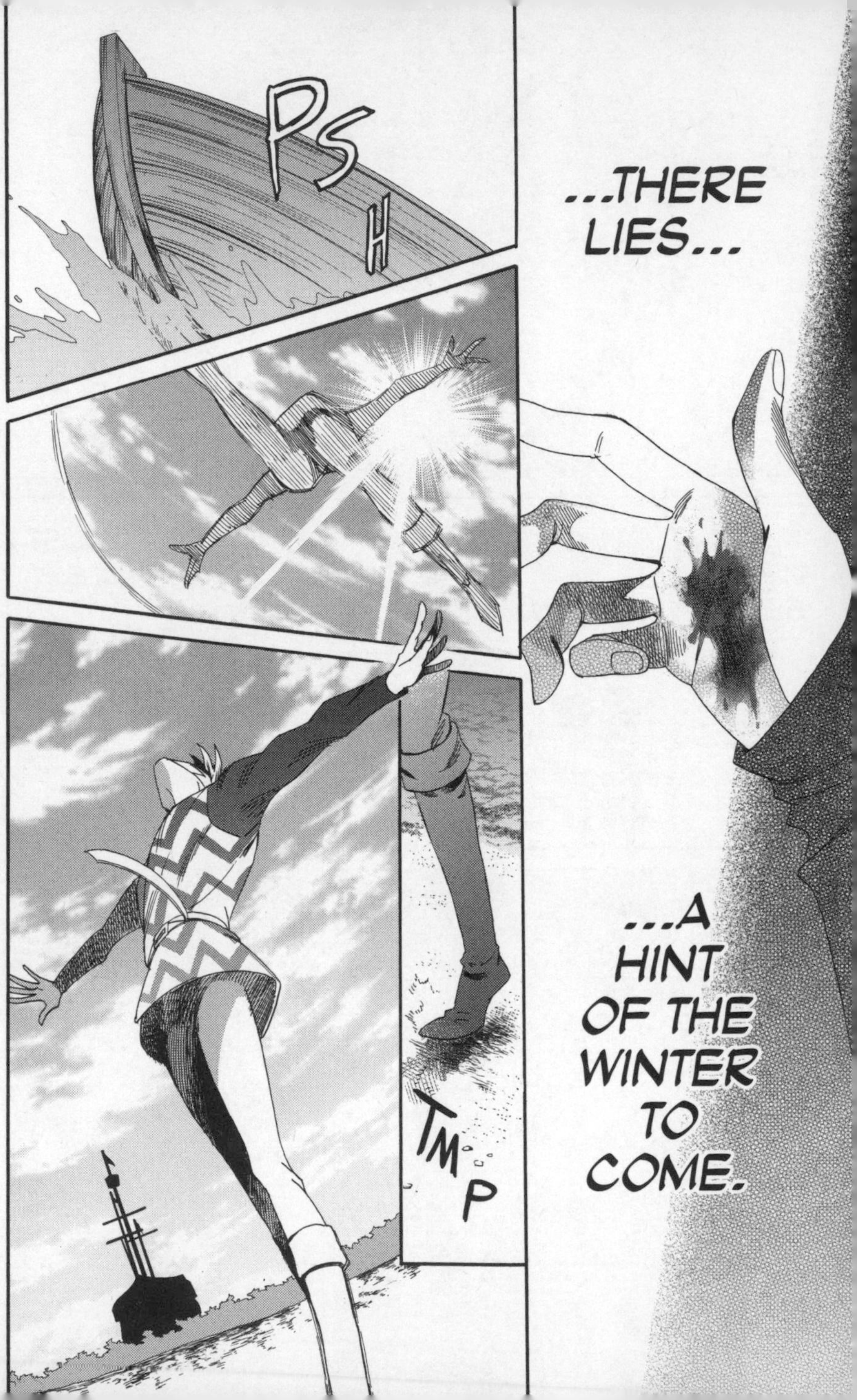
...THERE LIES...
...A HINT OF THE WINTER TO COME.
PSH
TMP

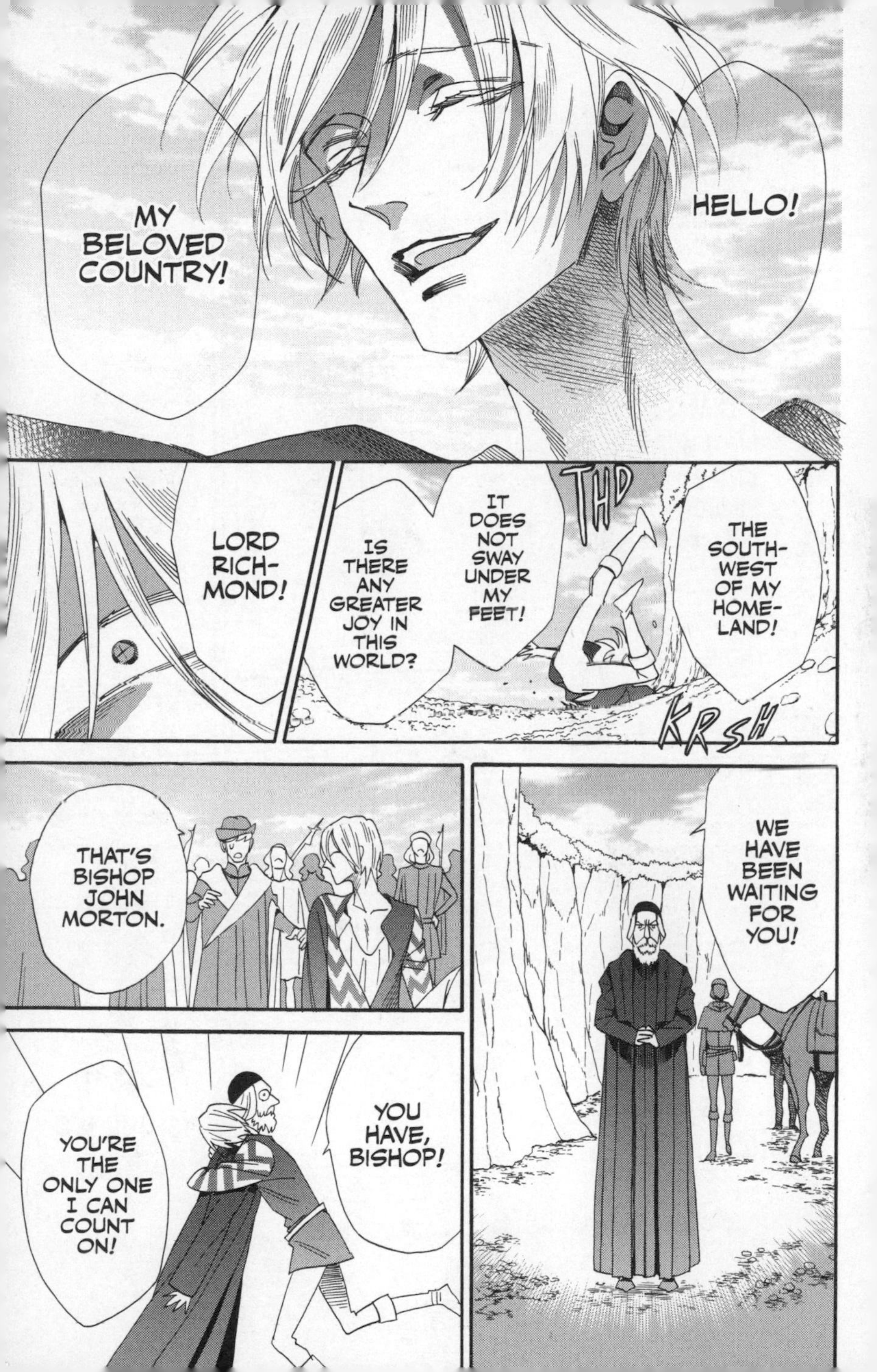
HELLO!
MY BELOVED COUNTRY!
THD
THE SOUTH-WEST OF MY HOME-LAND!
IT DOES NOT SWAY UNDER MY FEET!
IS THERE ANY GREATER JOY IN THIS WORLD?
KRSH
LORD RICH-MOND!
WE HAVE BEEN WAITING FOR YOU!
THAT'S BISHOP JOHN MORTON.
YOU HAVE, BISHOP!
YOU'RE THE ONLY ONE I CAN COUNT ON!

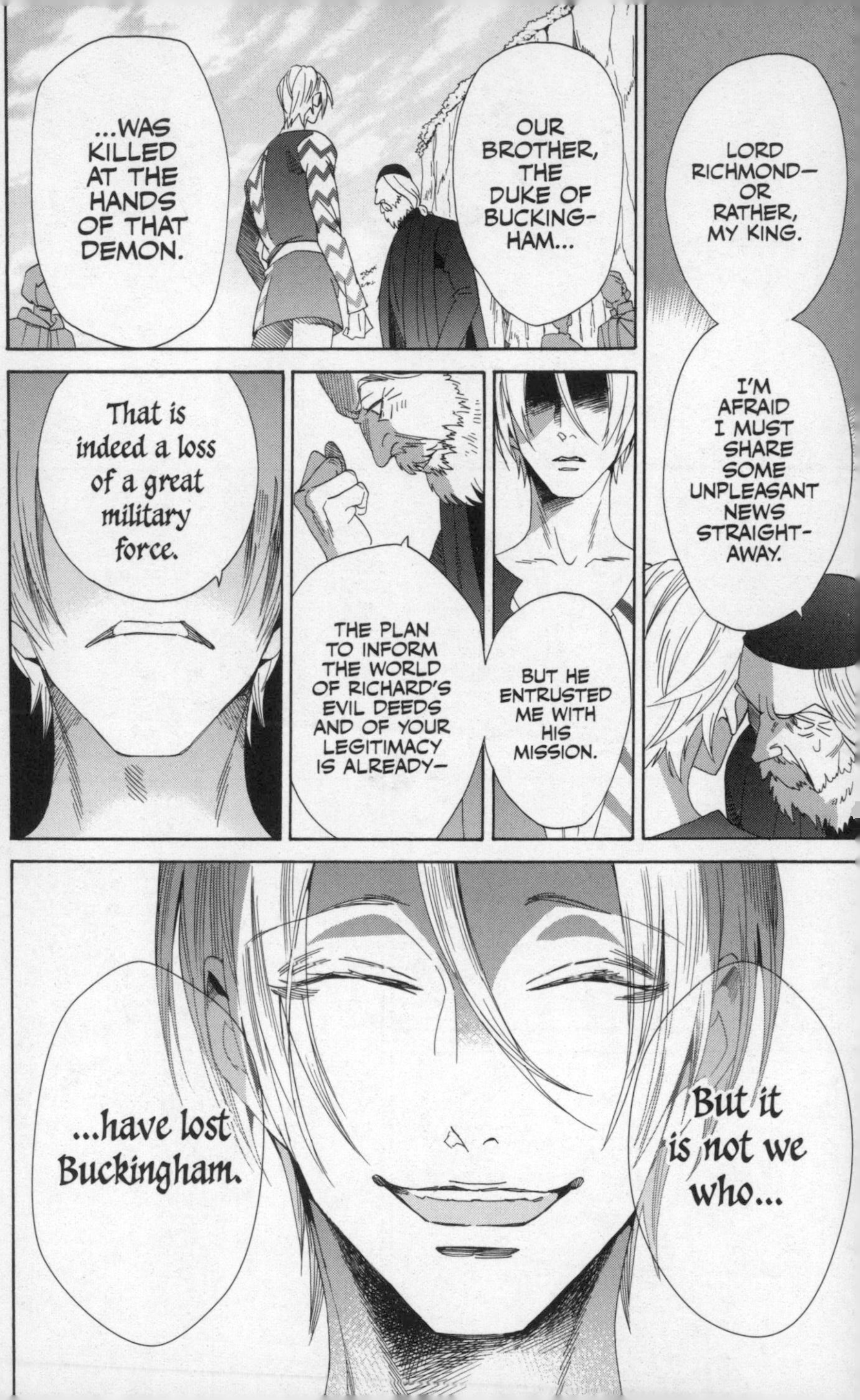
LORD RICHMOND— OR RATHER, MY KING.
I'M AFRAID I MUST SHARE SOME UNPLEASANT NEWS STRAIGHT-AWAY.
OUR BROTHER, THE DUKE OF BUCKING-HAM...
...WAS KILLED AT THE HANDS OF THAT DEMON.
BUT HE ENTRUSTED ME WITH HIS MISSION.
THE PLAN TO INFORM THE WORLD OF RICHARD'S EVIL DEEDS AND OF YOUR LEGITIMACY IS ALREADY—
That is indeed a loss of a great military force.
But it is not we who...
...have lost Buckingham.

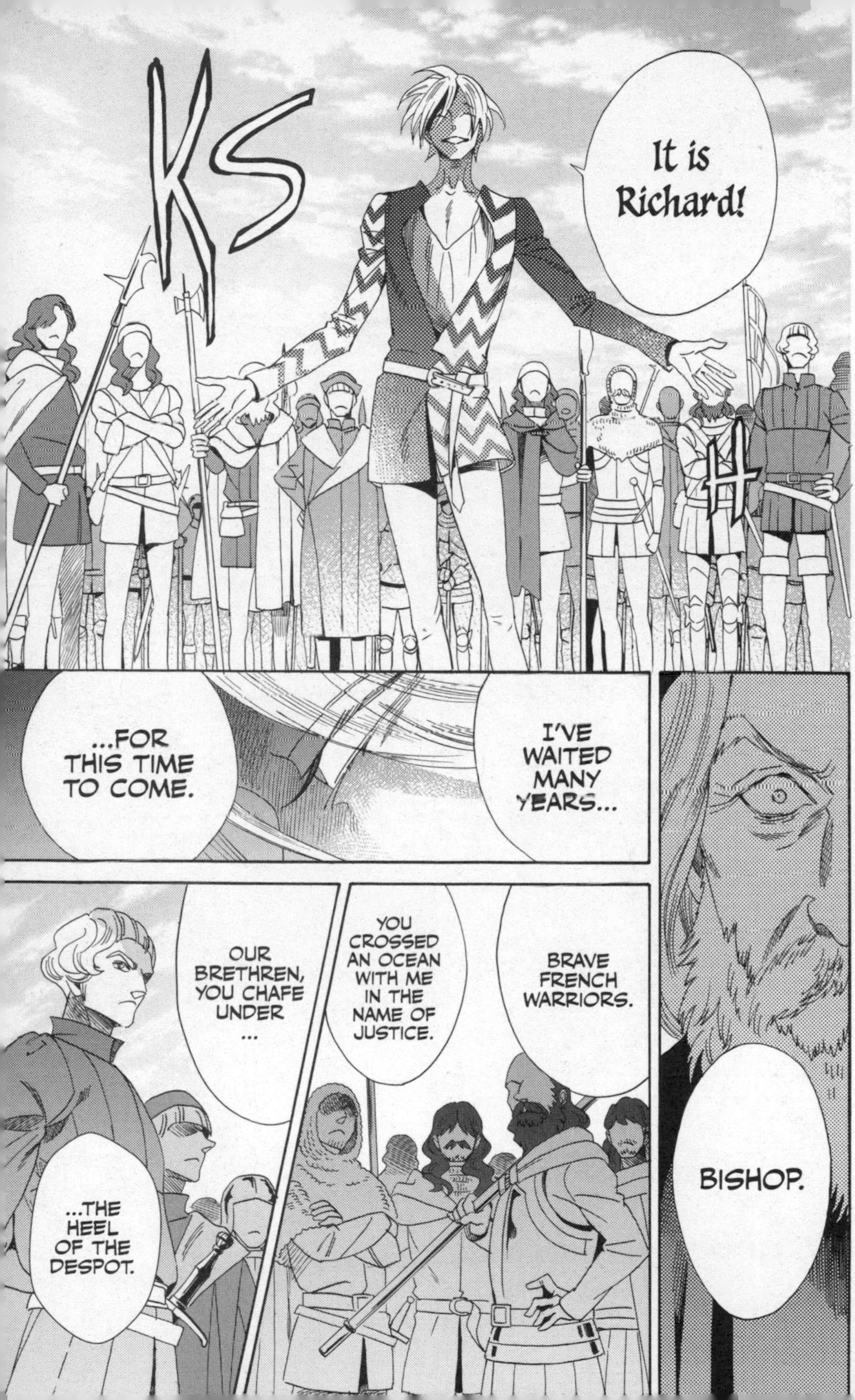
It is Richard!
KS
BISHOP.
I'VE WAITED MANY YEARS...
...FOR THIS TIME TO COME.
BRAVE FRENCH WARRIORS.
YOU CROSSED AN OCEAN WITH ME IN THE NAME OF JUSTICE.
OUR BRETHREN, YOU CHAFE UNDER ...
...THE HEEL OF THE DESPOT.

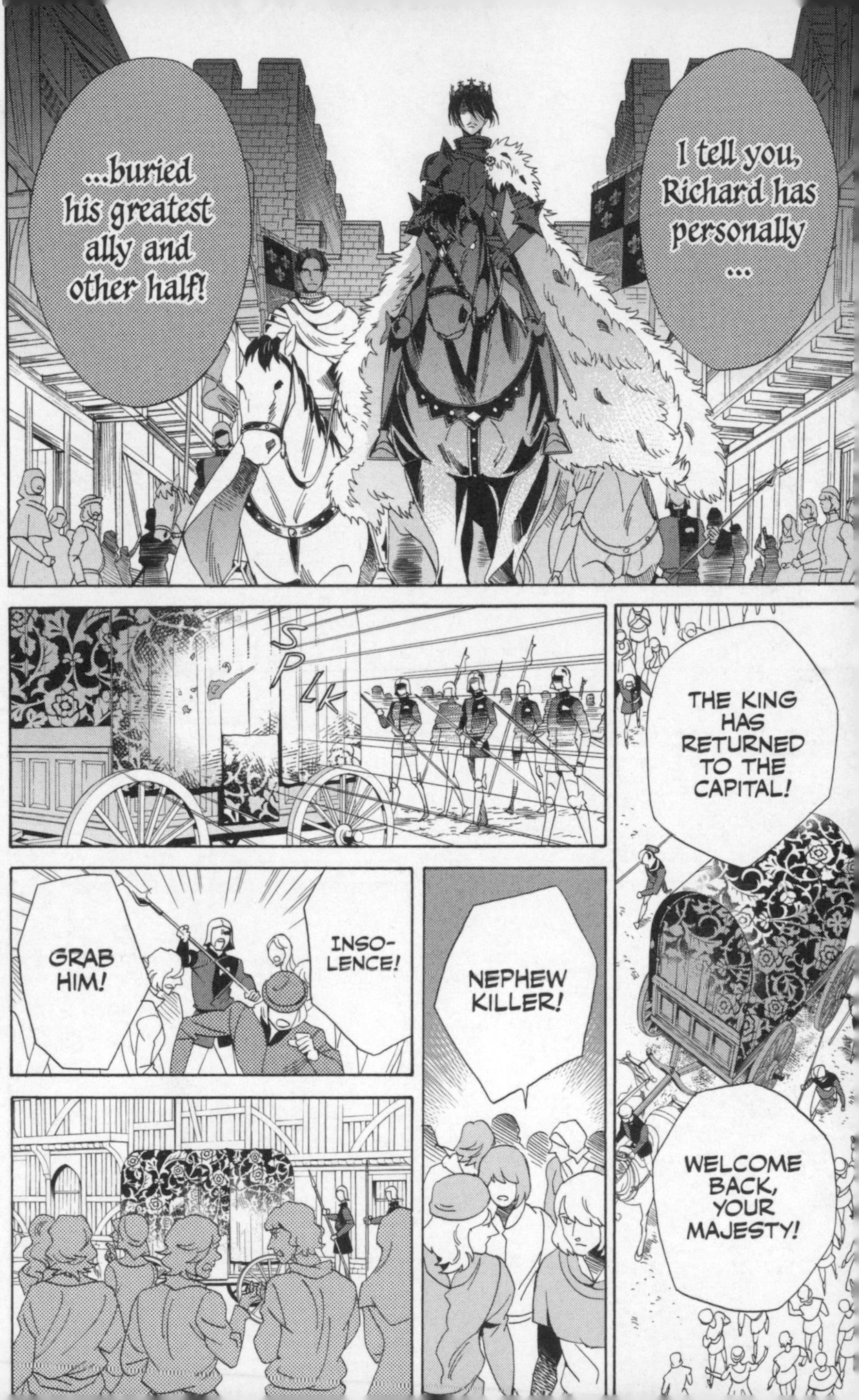
I tell you, Richard has personally ...
...buried his greatest ally and other half!
THE KING HAS RETURNED TO THE CAPITAL!
WELCOME BACK, YOUR MAJESTY!
SPLK
NEPHEW KILLER!
INSO-LENCE!
GRAB HIM!

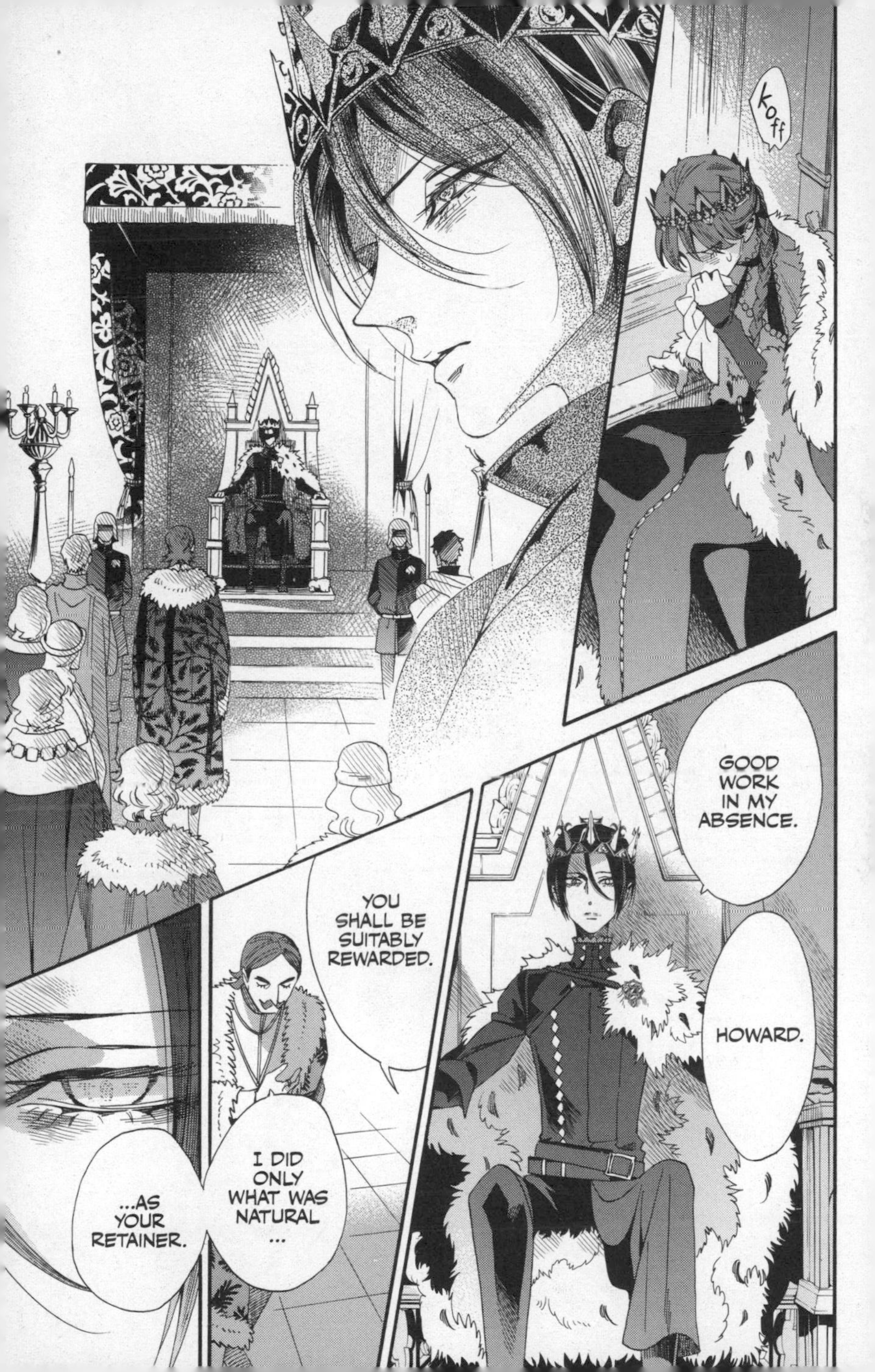
koff
GOOD WORK IN MY ABSENCE.
HOWARD.
YOU SHALL BE SUITABLY REWARDED.
I DID ONLY WHAT WAS NATURAL ...
...AS YOUR RETAINER.

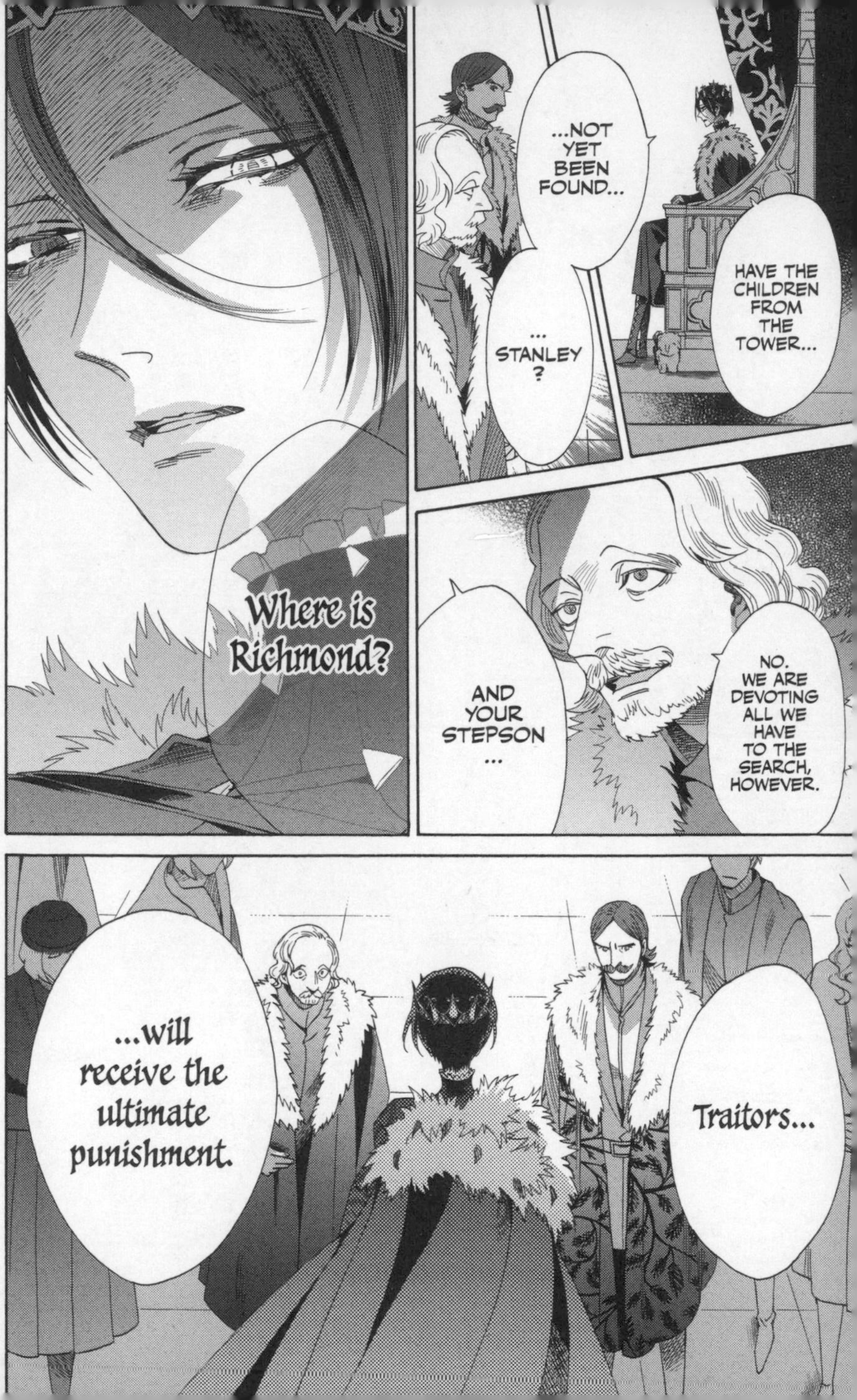
HAVE THE CHILDREN FROM THE TOWER...
...NOT YET BEEN FOUND...
...STANLEY?
NO. WE ARE DEVOTING ALL WE HAVE TO THE SEARCH, HOWEVER.
AND YOUR STEPSON...
Where is Richmond?
Traitors...
...will receive the ultimate punishment.

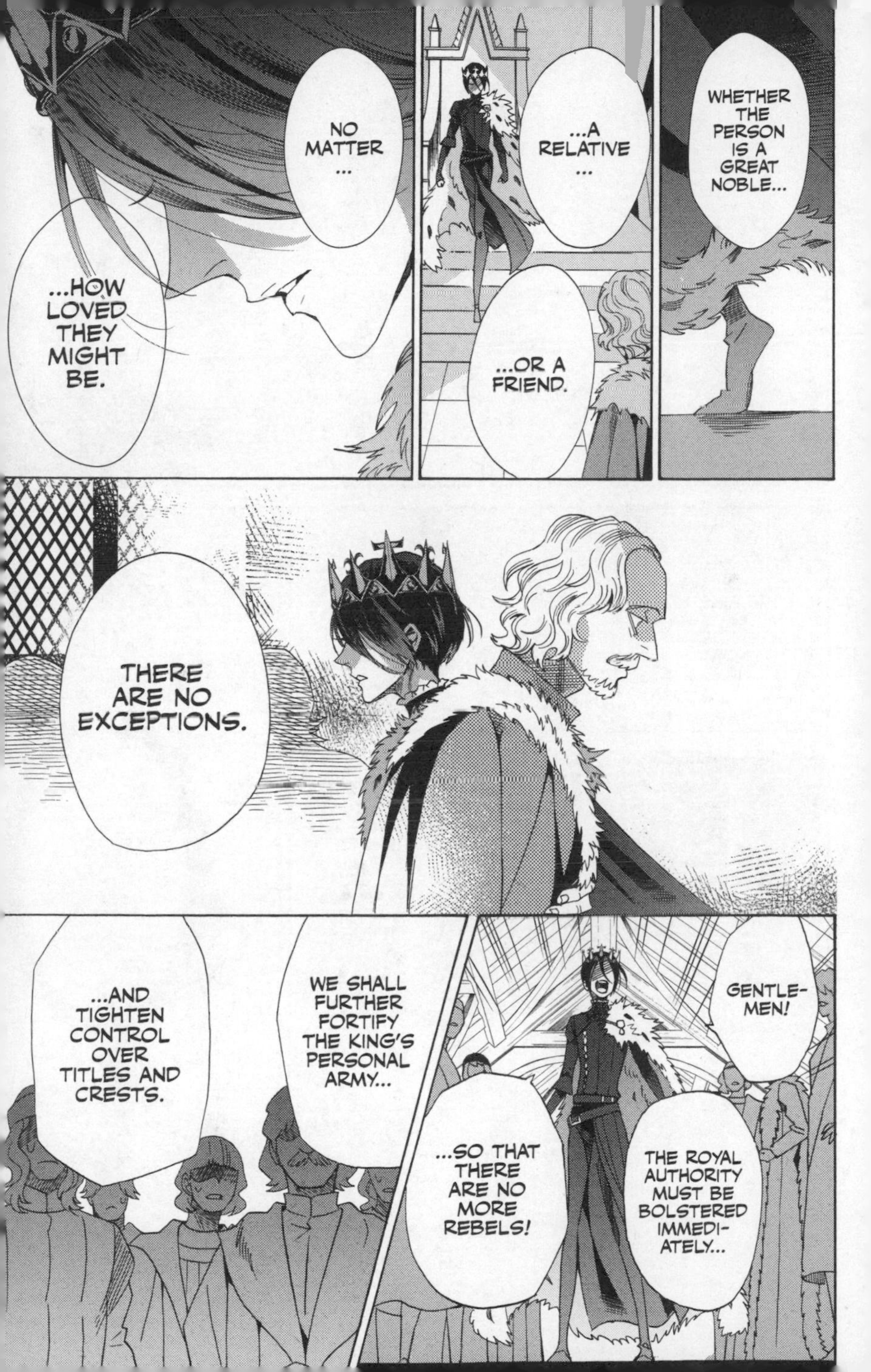
WHETHER THE PERSON IS A GREAT NOBLE...
...A RELATIVE ...
...OR A FRIEND.
NO MATTER ...
...HOW LOVED THEY MIGHT BE.
THERE ARE NO EXCEPTIONS.
GENTLE-MEN!
THE ROYAL AUTHORITY MUST BE BOLSTERED IMMEDI-ATELY...
...SO THAT THERE ARE NO MORE REBELS!
WE SHALL FURTHER FORTIFY THE KING'S PERSONAL ARMY...
...AND TIGHTEN CONTROL OVER TITLES AND CRESTS.

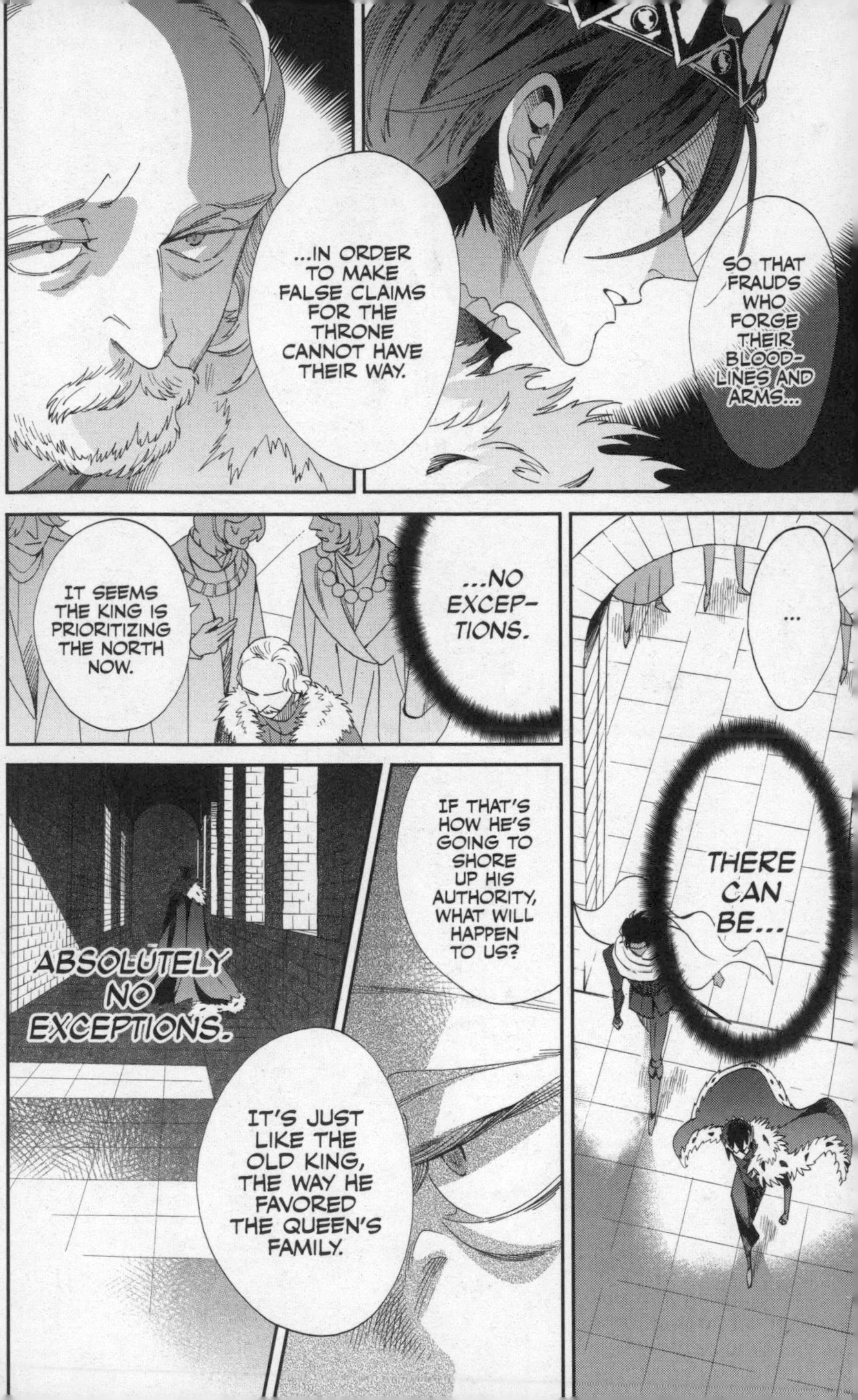
SO THAT FRAUDS WHO FORGE THEIR BLOODLINES AND ARMS...
...IN ORDER TO MAKE FALSE CLAIMS FOR THE THRONE CANNOT HAVE THEIR WAY.
...
THERE CAN BE...
...NO EXCEPTIONS.
IT SEEMS THE KING IS PRIORITIZING THE NORTH NOW.
IF THAT'S HOW HE'S GOING TO SHORE UP HIS AUTHORITY, WHAT WILL HAPPEN TO US?
IT'S JUST LIKE THE OLD KING, THE WAY HE FAVORED THE QUEEN'S FAMILY.
ABSOLUTELY NO EXCEPTIONS.

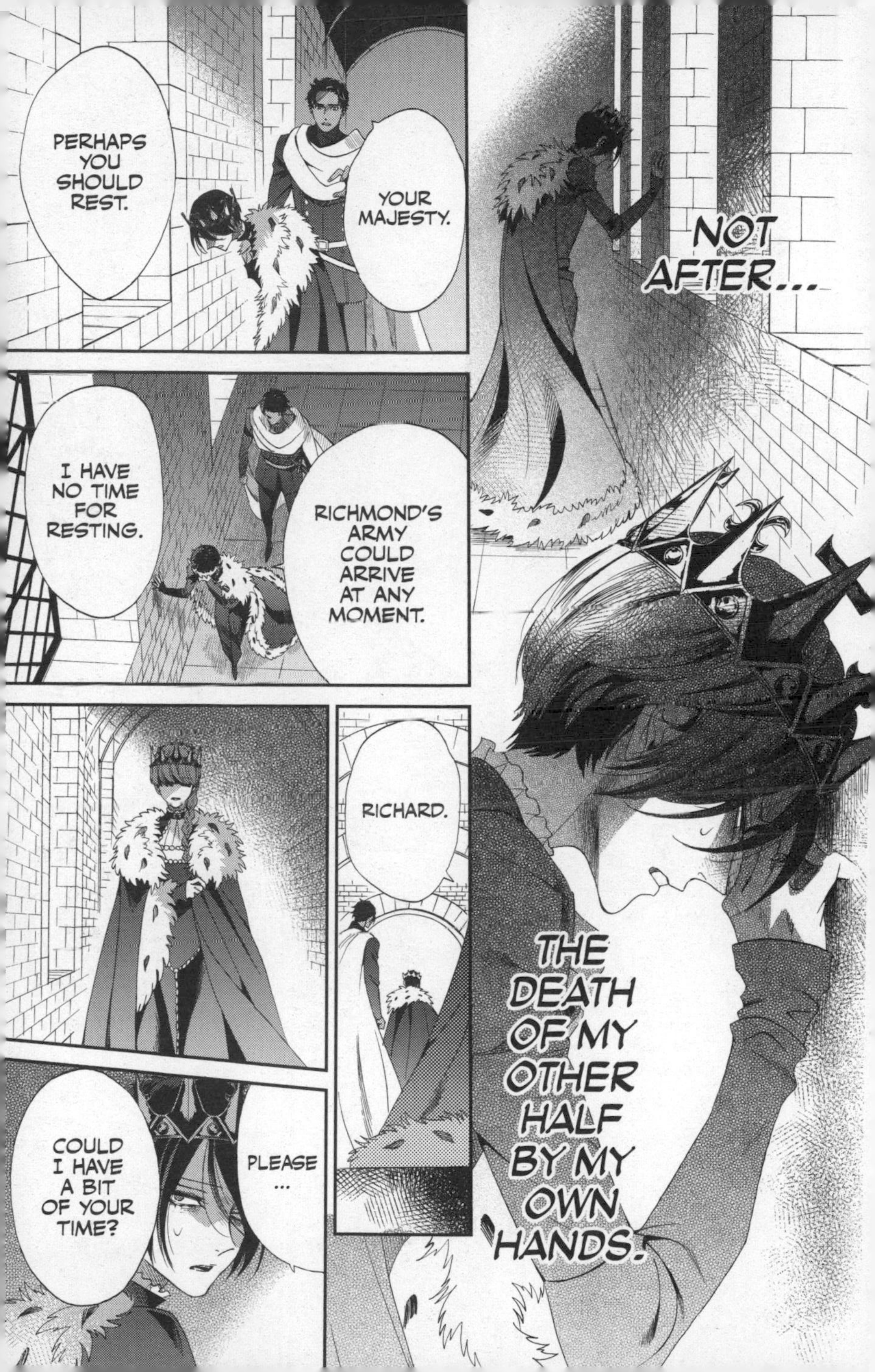
NOT AFTER...
THE DEATH OF MY OTHER HALF BY MY OWN HANDS.
YOUR MAJESTY.
PERHAPS YOU SHOULD REST.
RICHMOND'S ARMY COULD ARRIVE AT ANY MOMENT.
I HAVE NO TIME FOR RESTING.
RICHARD.
PLEASE ...
COULD I HAVE A BIT OF YOUR TIME?

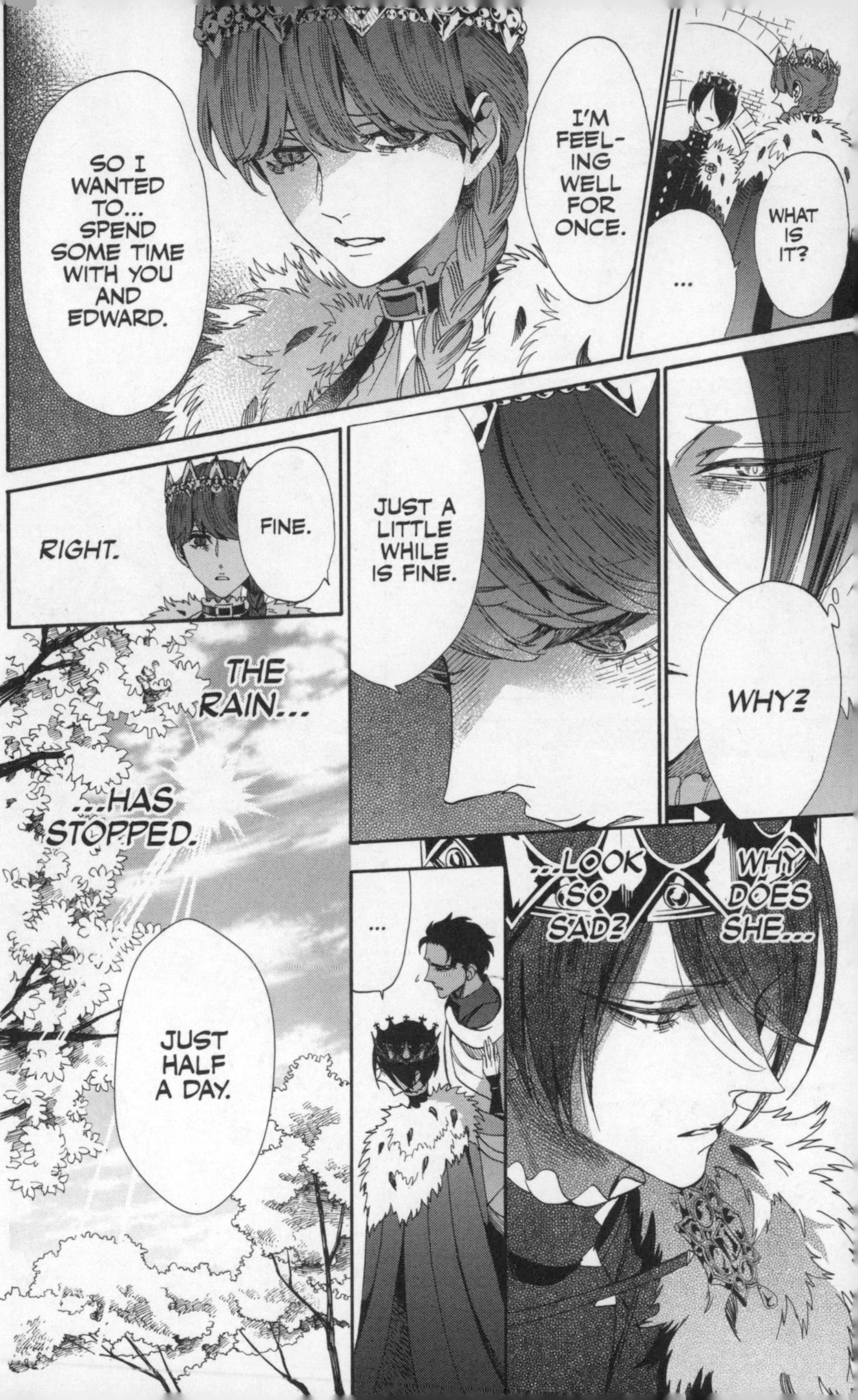
WHAT IS IT?
...
I'M FEEL-ING WELL FOR ONCE.
SO I WANTED TO... SPEND SOME TIME WITH YOU AND EDWARD.
WHY?
JUST A LITTLE WHILE IS FINE.
FINE.
RIGHT.
WHY DOES SHE...
...LOOK SO SAD?
...
THE RAIN...
...HAS STOPPED.
JUST HALF A DAY.

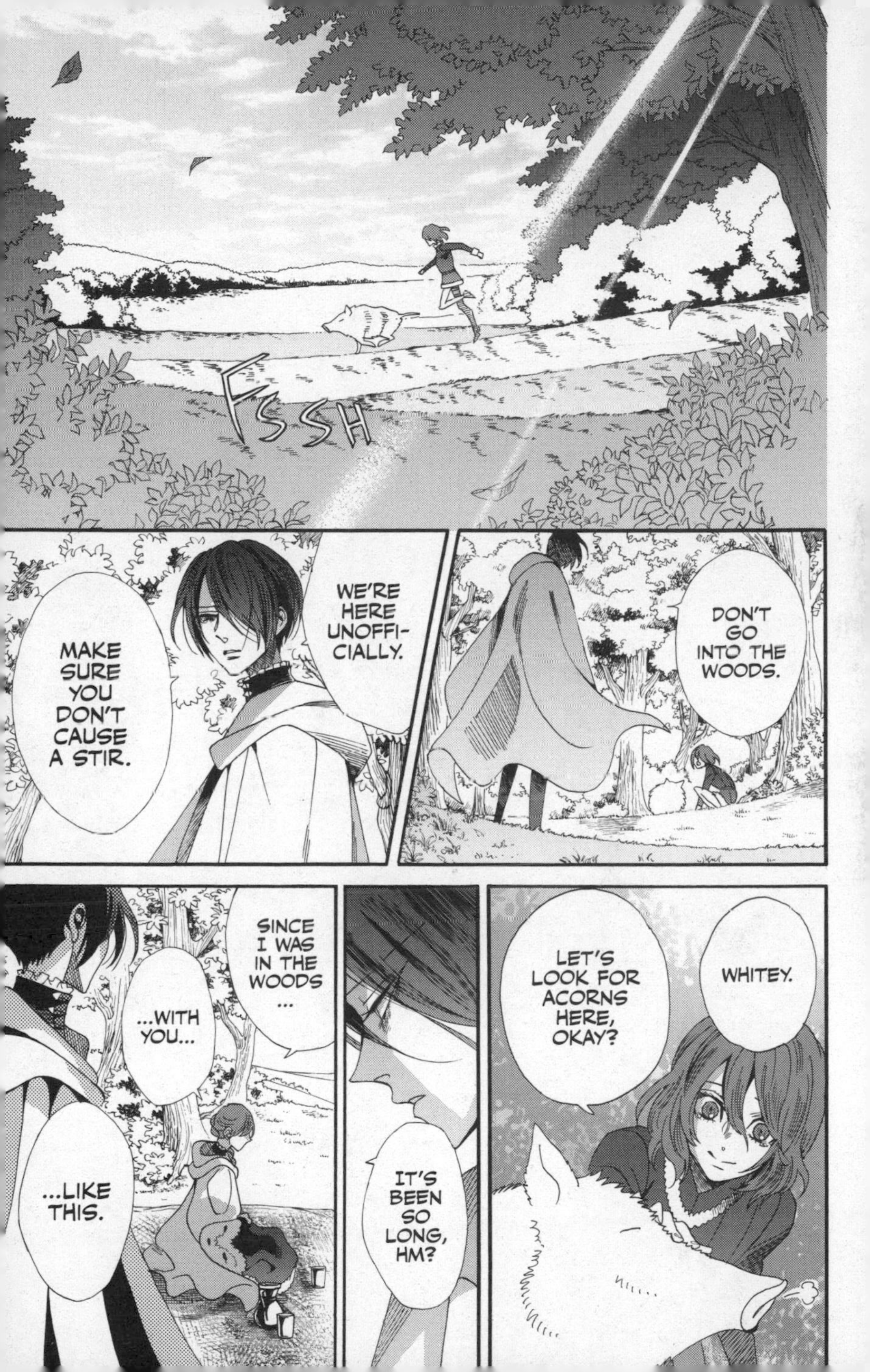
FSSH
DON'T GO INTO THE WOODS.
WE'RE HERE UNOFFICIALLY.
MAKE SURE YOU DON'T CAUSE A STIR.
WHITEY.
LET'S LOOK FOR ACORNS HERE, OKAY?
IT'S BEEN SO LONG, HM?
SINCE I WAS IN THE WOODS...
...WITH YOU...
...LIKE THIS.

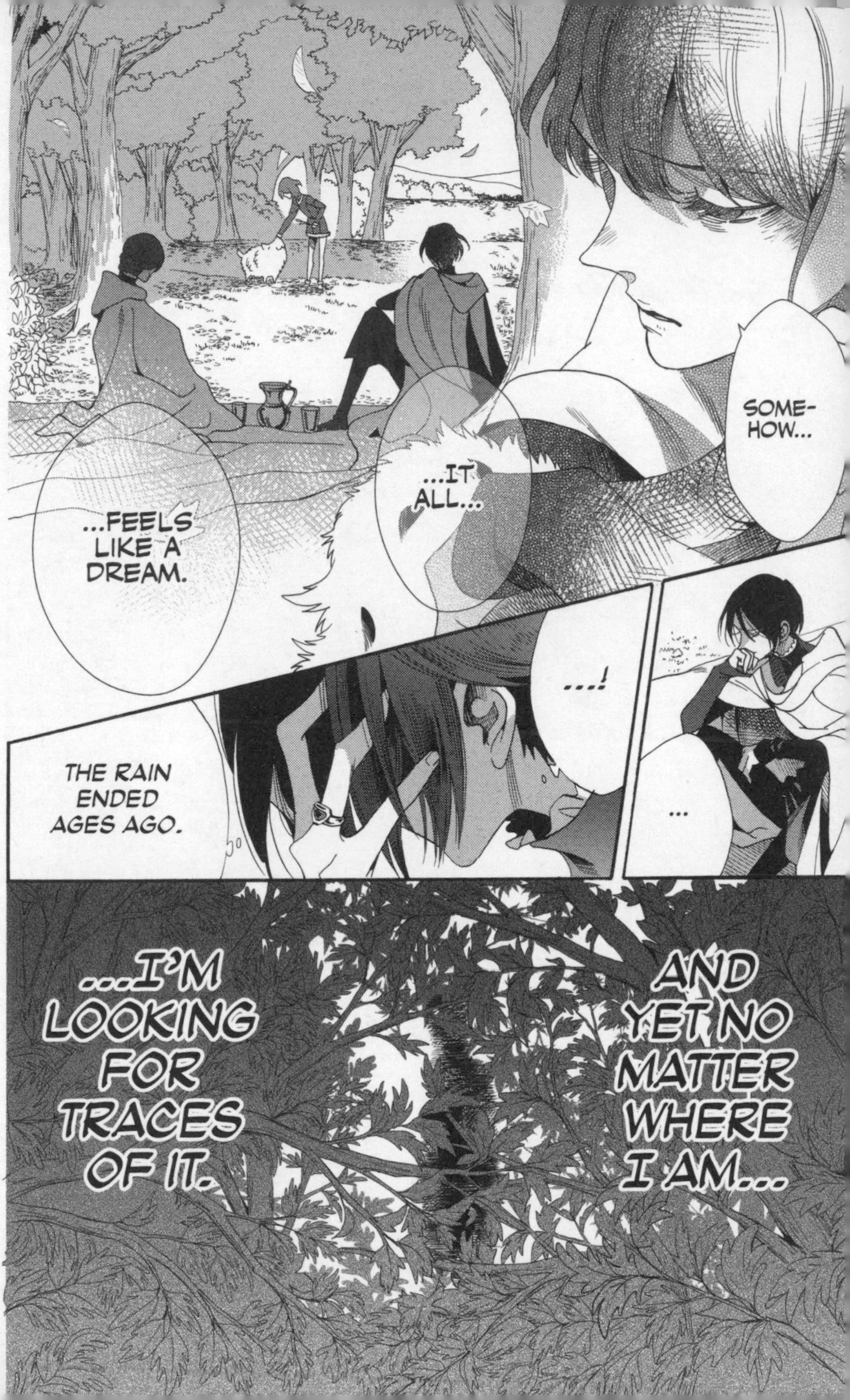
SOME-HOW...
...IT ALL...
...FEELS LIKE A DREAM.
...
...!
THE RAIN ENDED AGES AGO.
AND YET NO MATTER WHERE I AM...
...I'M LOOKING FOR TRACES OF IT.

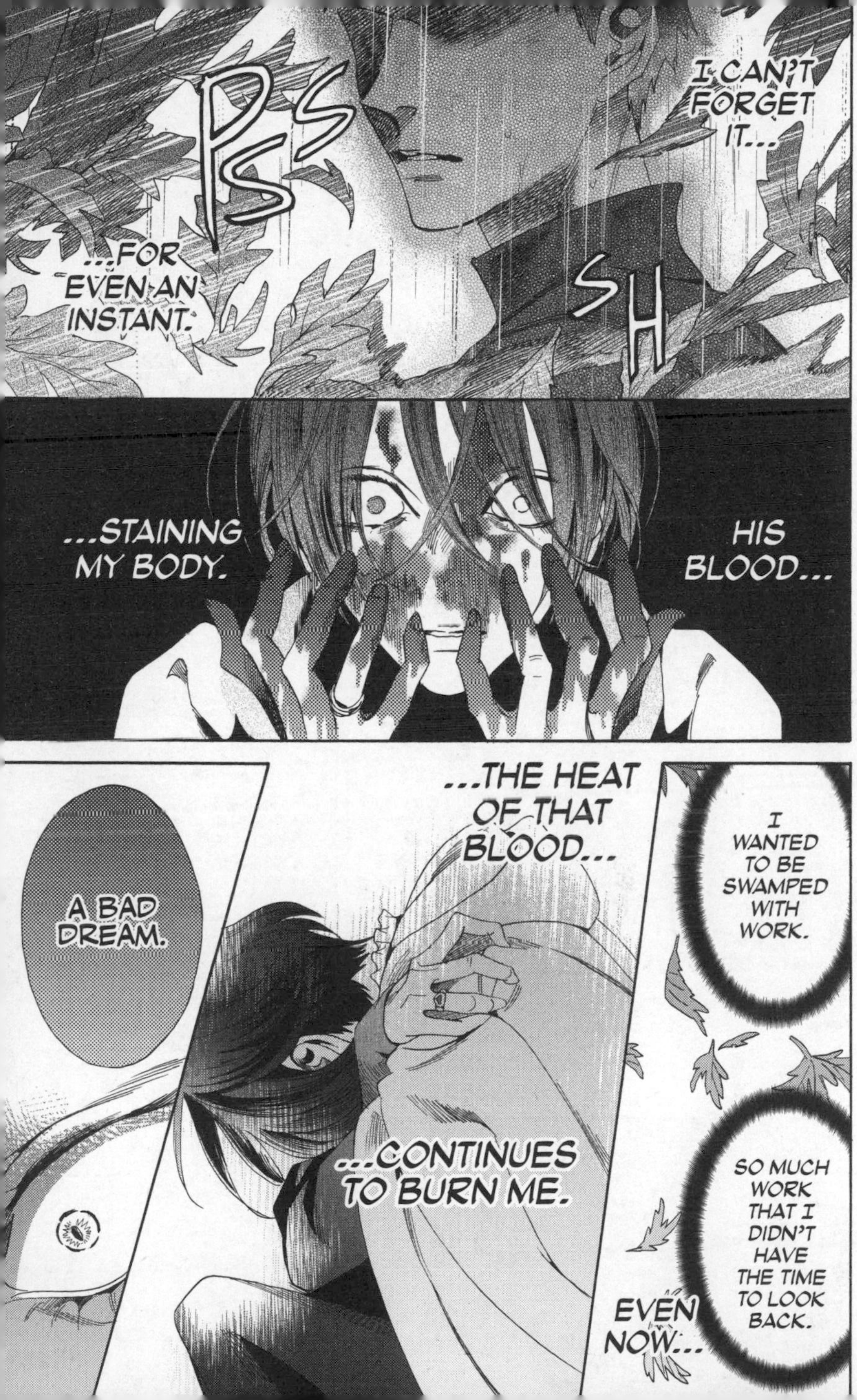
I CAN'T FORGET IT...
PSS
SH
...FOR EVEN AN INSTANT.
HIS BLOOD...
...STAINING MY BODY.
I WANTED TO BE SWAMPED WITH WORK.
SO MUCH WORK THAT I DIDN'T HAVE THE TIME TO LOOK BACK.
EVEN NOW...
...THE HEAT OF THAT BLOOD...
...CONTINUES TO BURN ME.
A BAD DREAM.

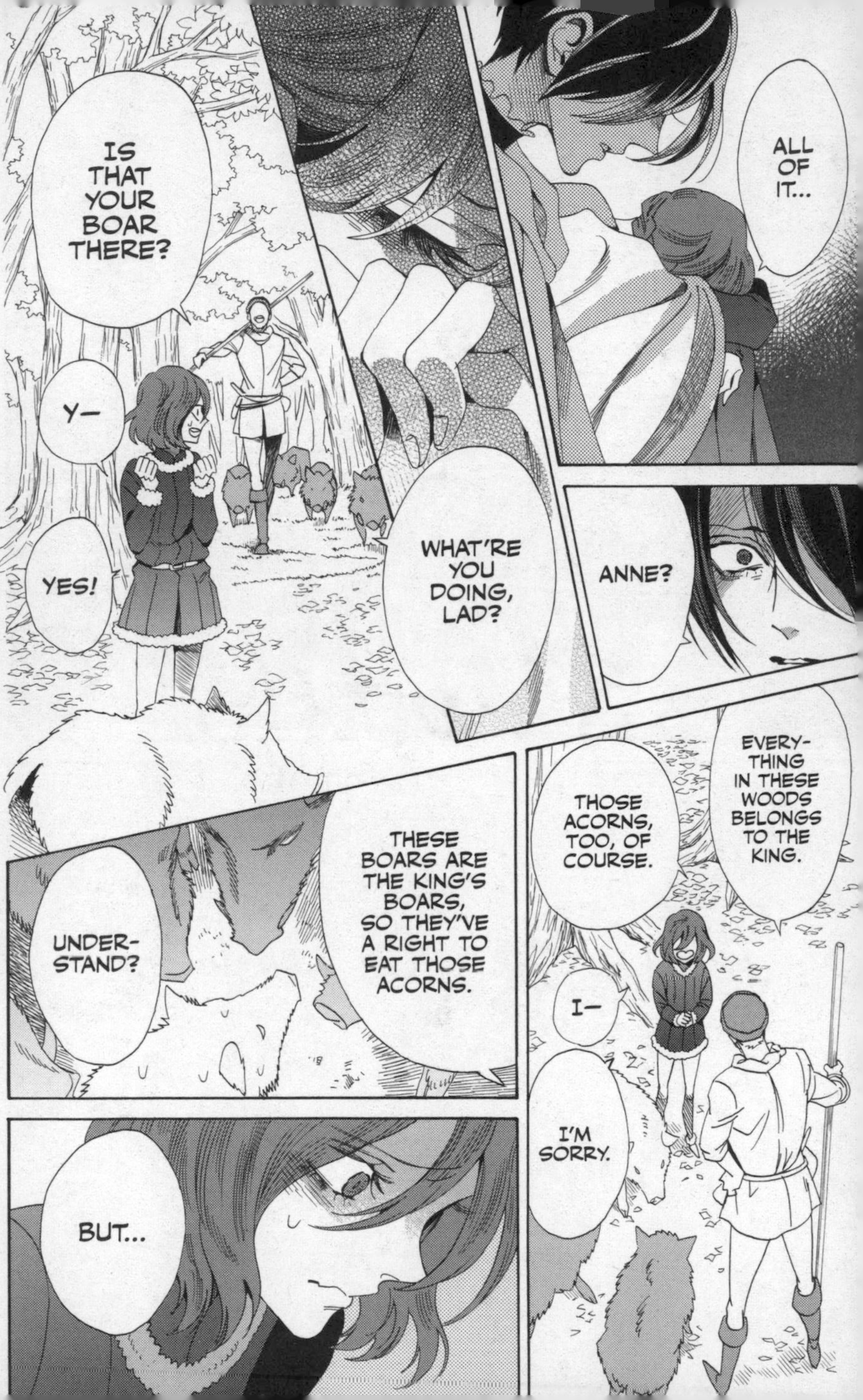
ALL OF IT...
ANNE?
WHAT'RE YOU DOING, LAD?
IS THAT YOUR BOAR THERE?
Y—
YES!
EVERYTHING IN THESE WOODS BELONGS TO THE KING.
THOSE ACORNS, TOO, OF COURSE.
I—
I'M SORRY.
THESE BOARS ARE THE KING'S BOARS, SO THEY'VE A RIGHT TO EAT THOSE ACORNS.
UNDERSTAND?
BUT...

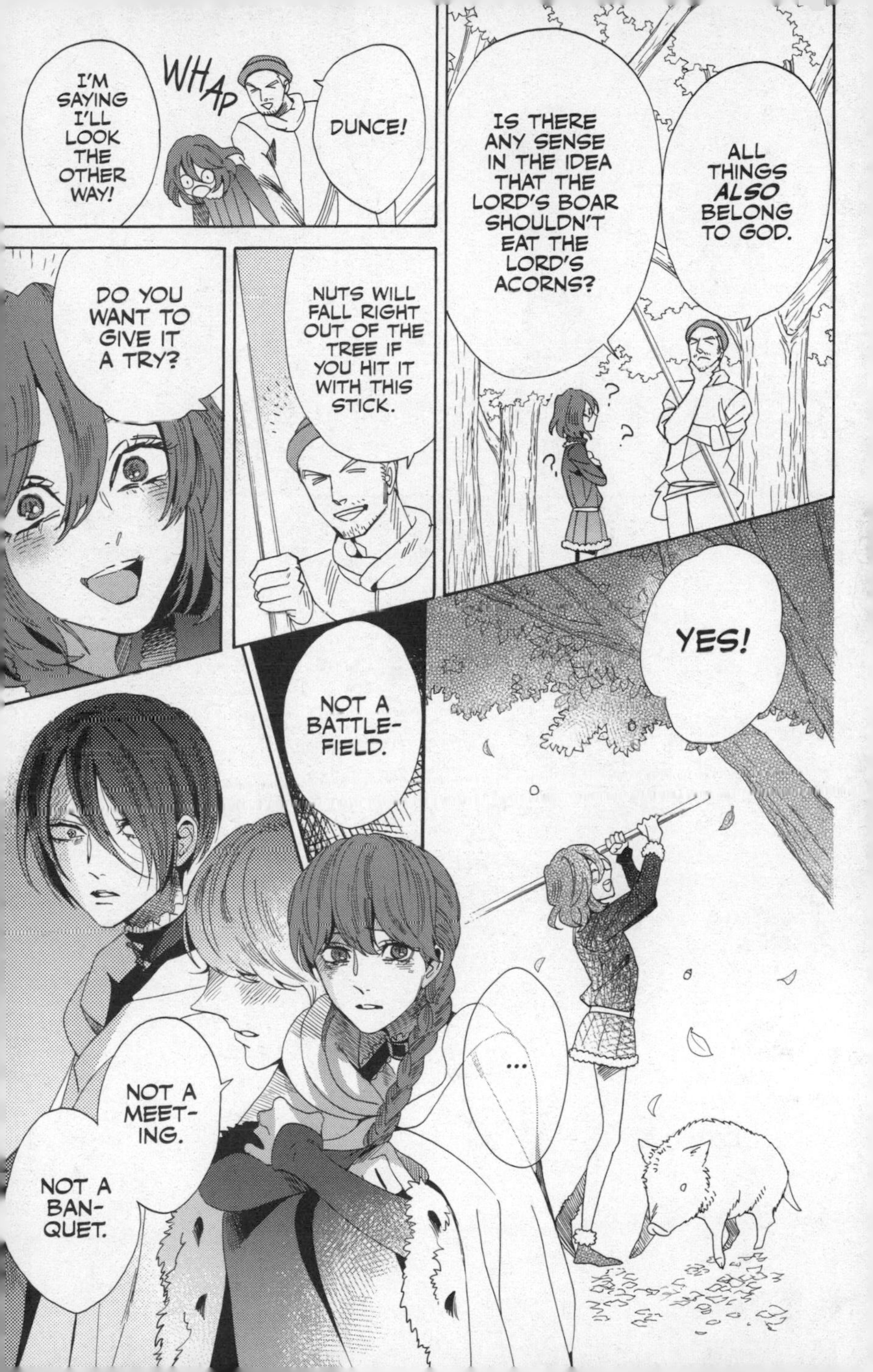
ALL THINGS *ALSO* BELONG TO GOD.
IS THERE ANY SENSE IN THE IDEA THAT THE LORD'S BOAR SHOULDN'T EAT THE LORD'S ACORNS?
? ? ?
DUNCE!
WHAP
I'M SAYING I'LL LOOK THE OTHER WAY!
NUTS WILL FALL RIGHT OUT OF THE TREE IF YOU HIT IT WITH THIS STICK.
DO YOU WANT TO GIVE IT A TRY?
YES!
NOT A BATTLE-FIELD.
...
NOT A MEET-ING.
NOT A BAN-QUET.

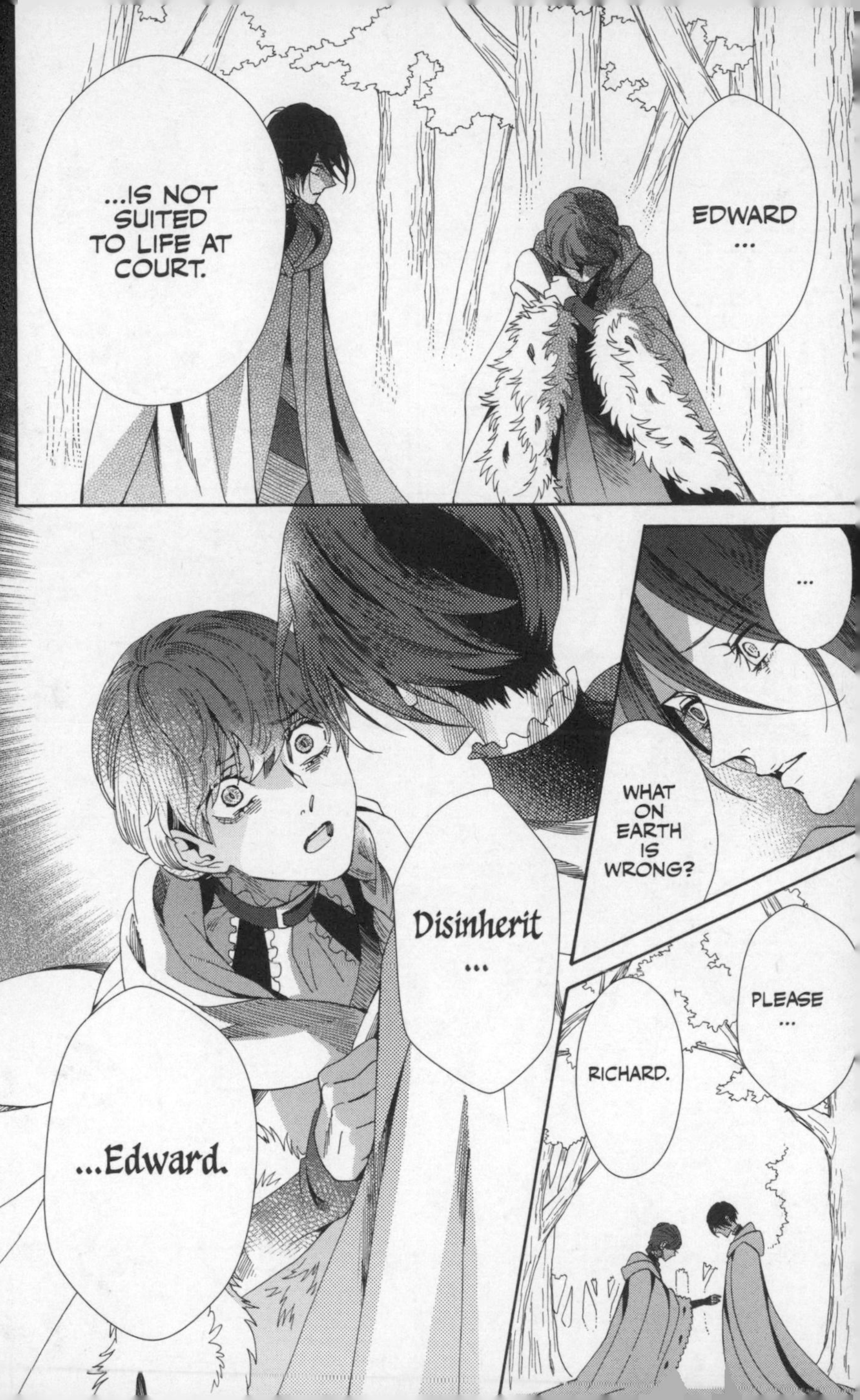
EDWARD ...
...IS NOT SUITED TO LIFE AT COURT.
...
WHAT ON EARTH IS WRONG?
Disinherit ...
PLEASE ...
RICHARD.
...Edward.

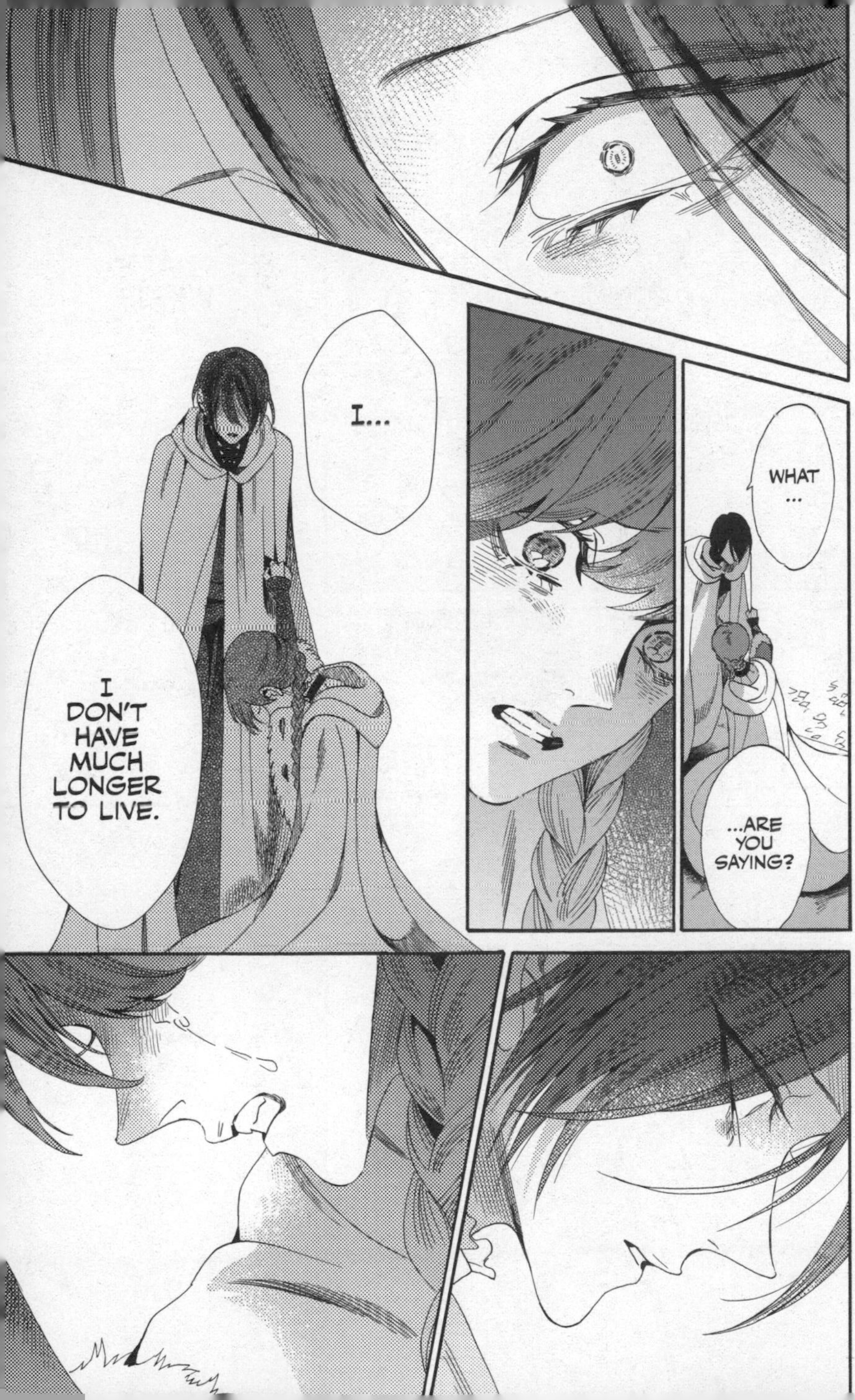
WHAT ...
...ARE YOU SAYING?
I...
I DON'T HAVE MUCH LONGER TO LIVE.

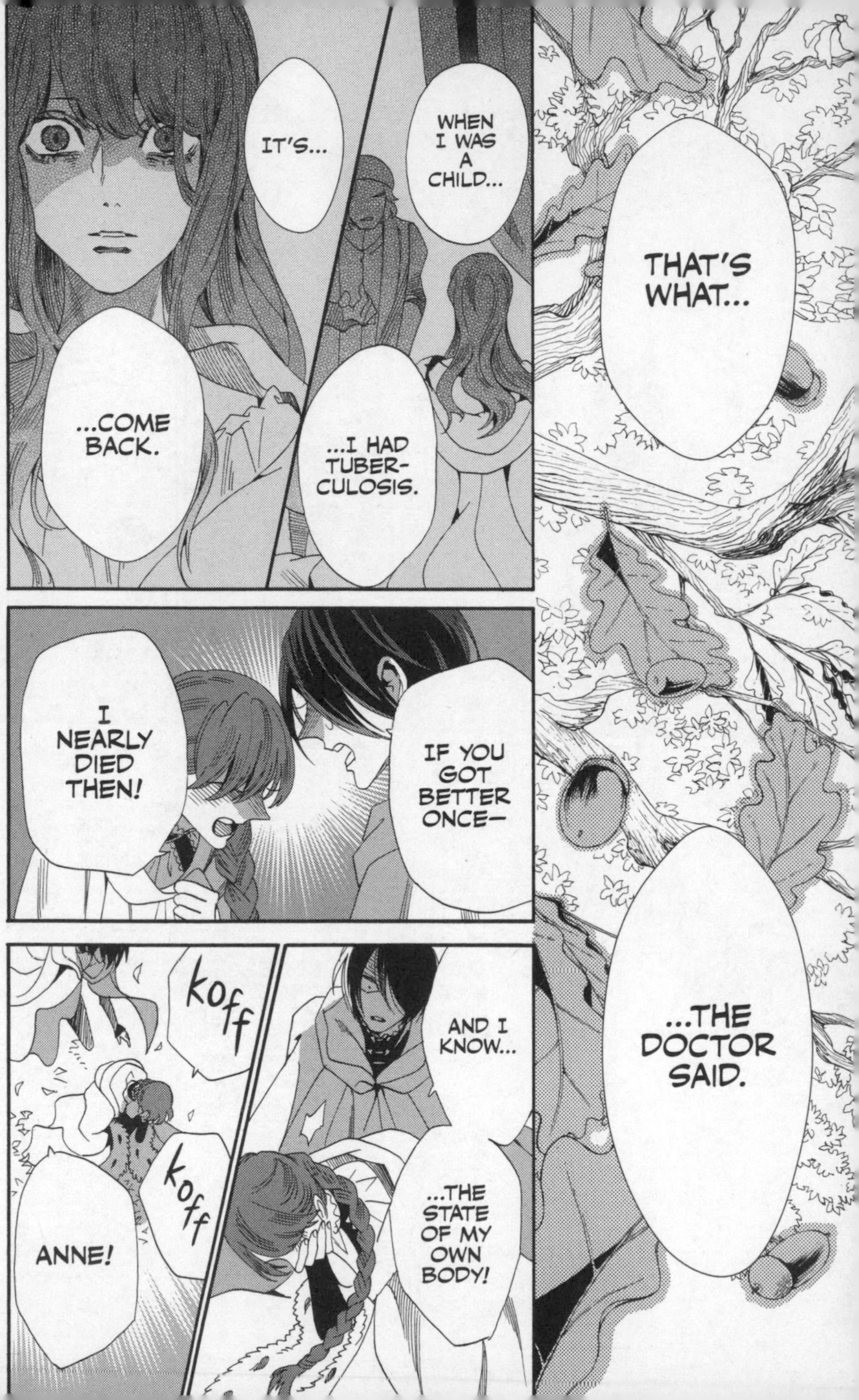
THAT'S WHAT...
...THE DOCTOR SAID.
WHEN I WAS A CHILD...
...I HAD TUBER-CULOSIS.
IT'S...
...COME BACK.
IF YOU GOT BETTER ONCE—
I NEARLY DIED THEN!
AND I KNOW...
...THE STATE OF MY OWN BODY!
koff
koff
ANNE!

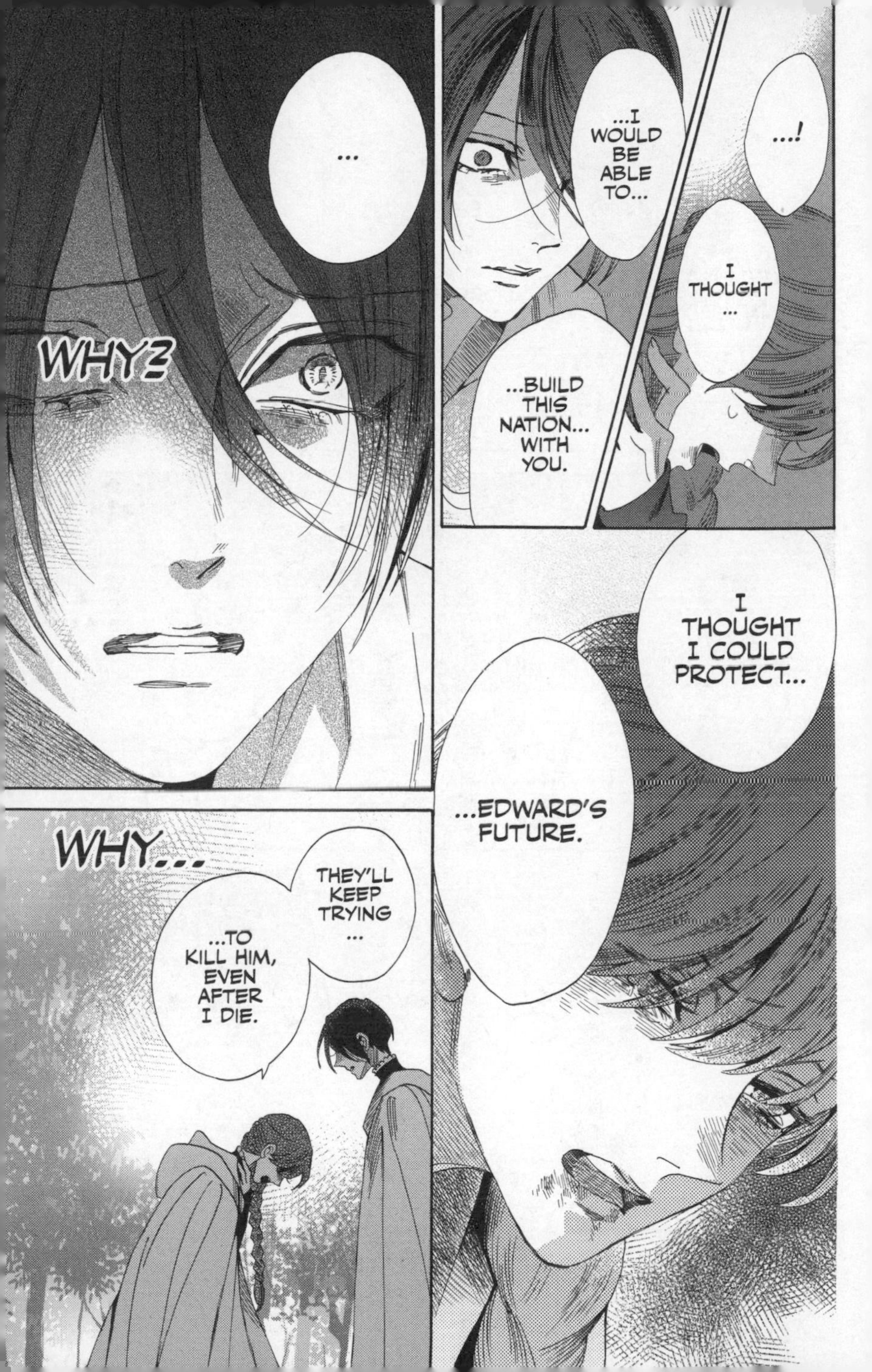
...!
I THOUGHT ...
...I WOULD BE ABLE TO...
...BUILD THIS NATION... WITH YOU.
...
WHY?
I THOUGHT I COULD PROTECT...
...EDWARD'S FUTURE.
WHY...
THEY'LL KEEP TRYING ...
...TO KILL HIM, EVEN AFTER I DIE.

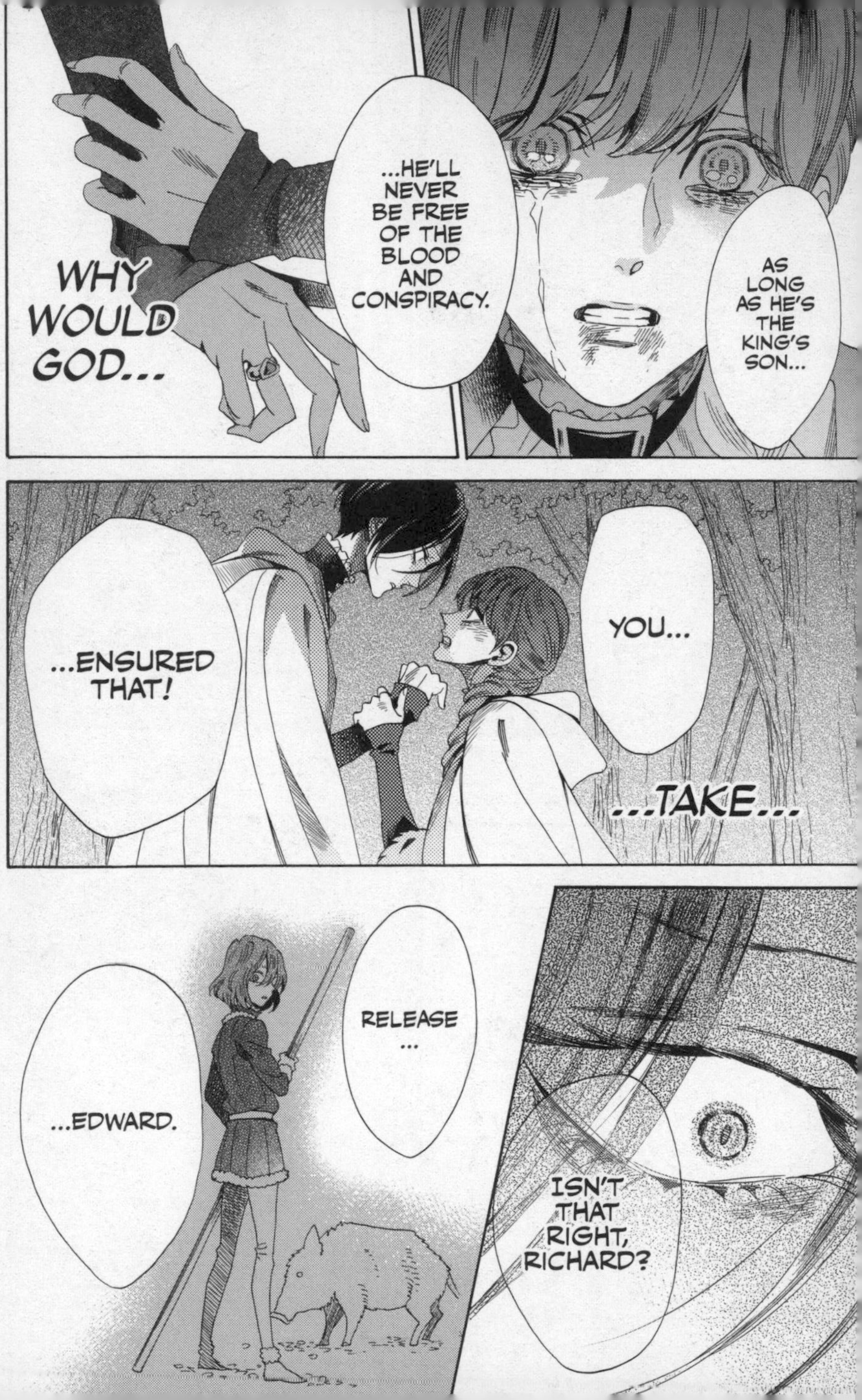
AS LONG AS HE'S THE KING'S SON...
...HE'LL NEVER BE FREE OF THE BLOOD AND CONSPIRACY.
WHY WOULD GOD...
YOU...
...TAKE...
...ENSURED THAT!
ISN'T THAT RIGHT, RICHARD?
RELEASE ...
...EDWARD.

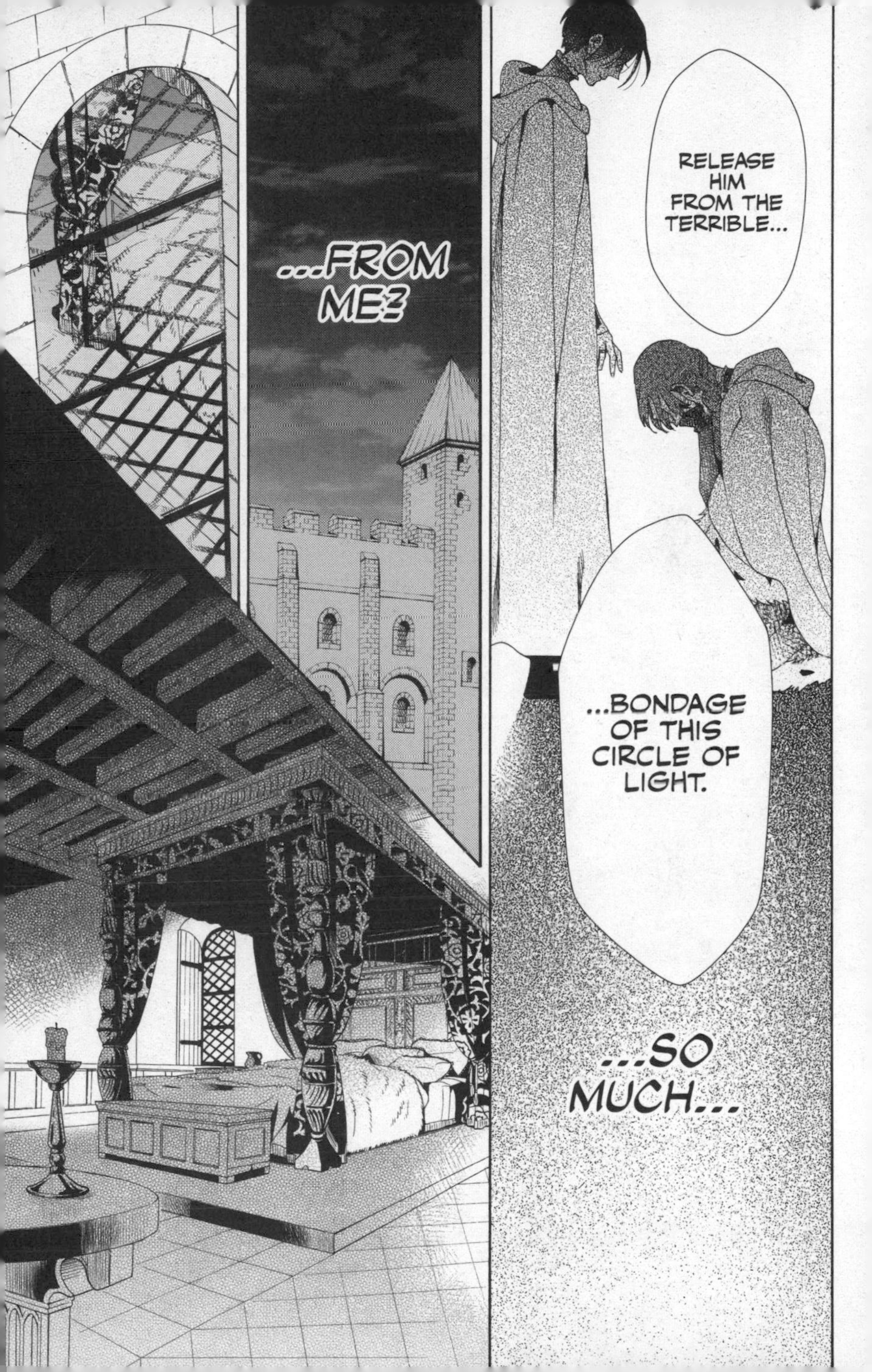
RELEASE HIM FROM THE TERRIBLE...
...BONDAGE OF THIS CIRCLE OF LIGHT.
...SO MUCH...
...FROM ME?

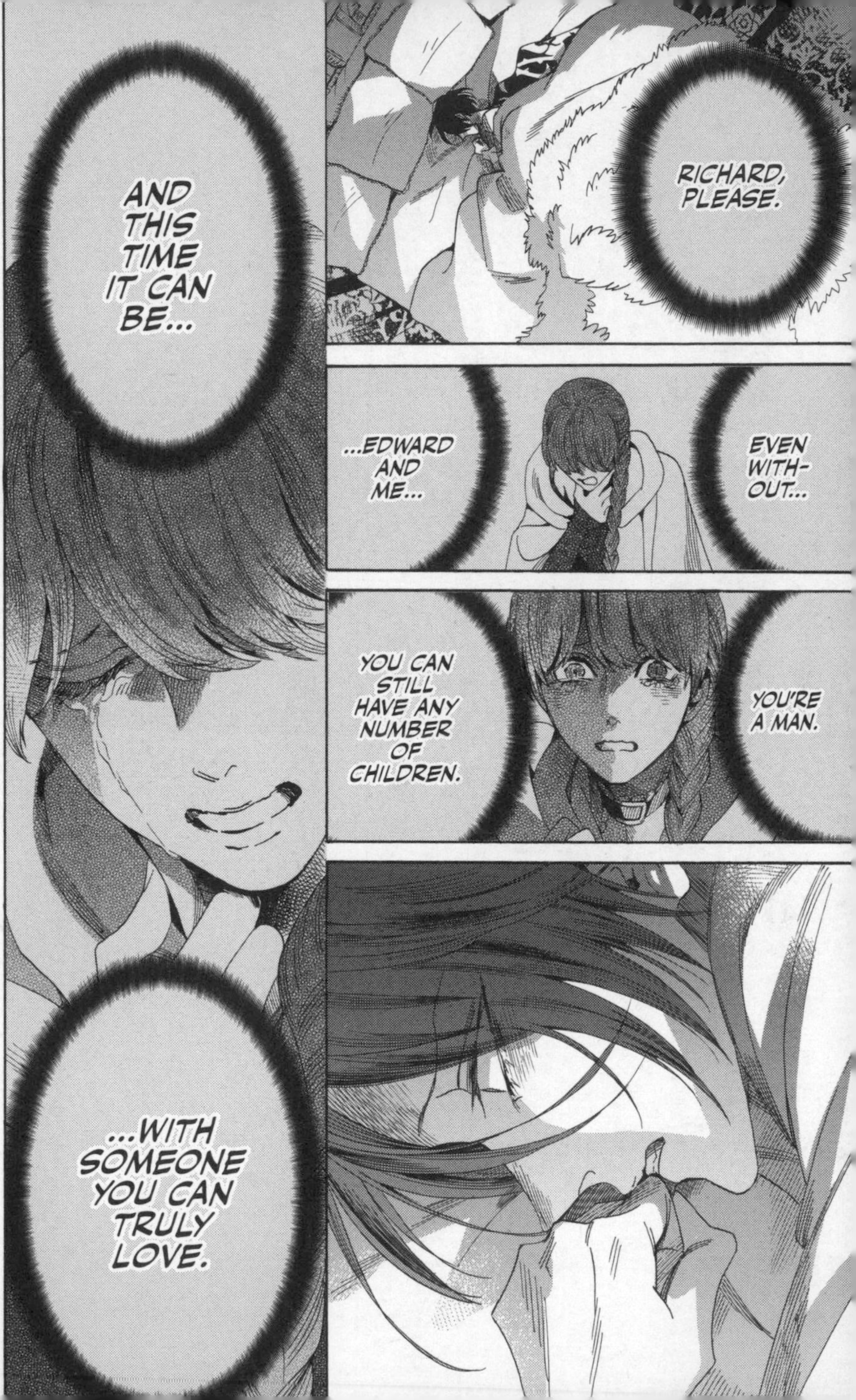
RICHARD, PLEASE.
EVEN WITH-OUT...
...EDWARD AND ME...
YOU'RE A MAN.
YOU CAN STILL HAVE ANY NUMBER OF CHILDREN.
AND THIS TIME IT CAN BE...
...WITH SOMEONE YOU CAN TRULY LOVE.

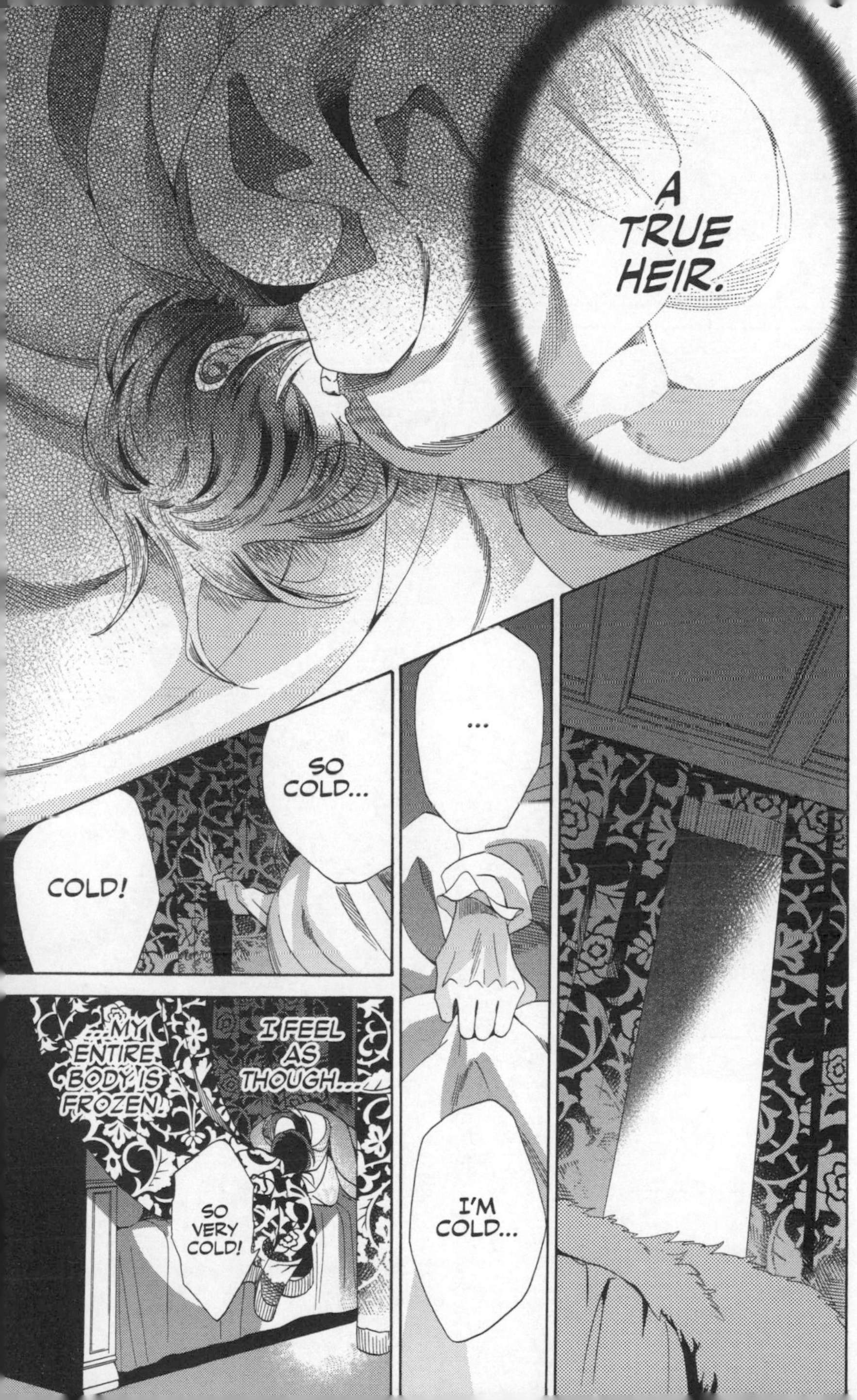
A TRUE HEIR.
...
I'M COLD...
SO COLD...
COLD!
I FEEL AS THOUGH...
...MY ENTIRE BODY IS FROZEN.
SO VERY COLD!

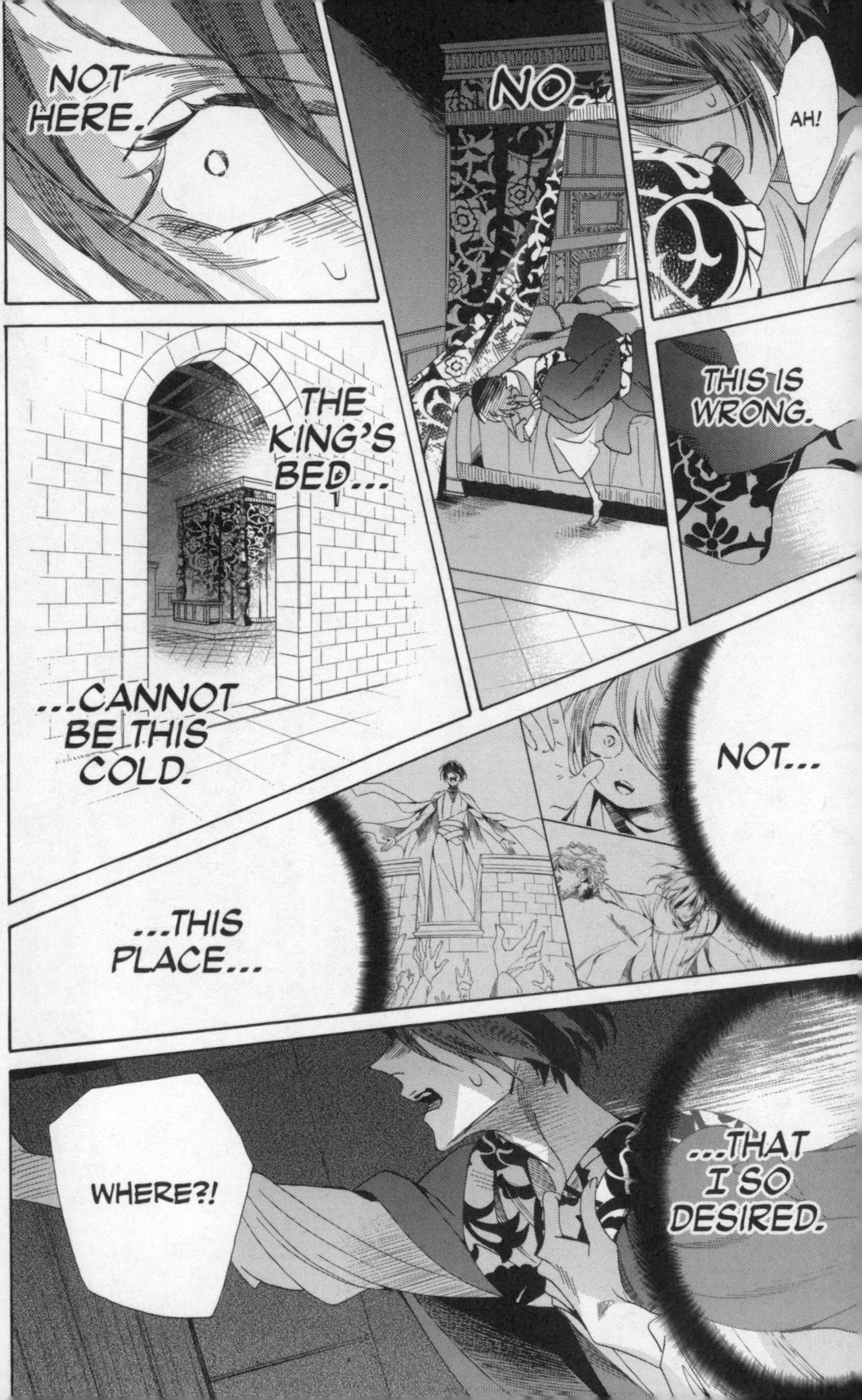
AH!
NO...
NOT HERE.
THIS IS WRONG.
THE KING'S BED...
...CANNOT BE THIS COLD.
NOT...
...THIS PLACE...
...THAT I SO DESIRED.
WHERE?!

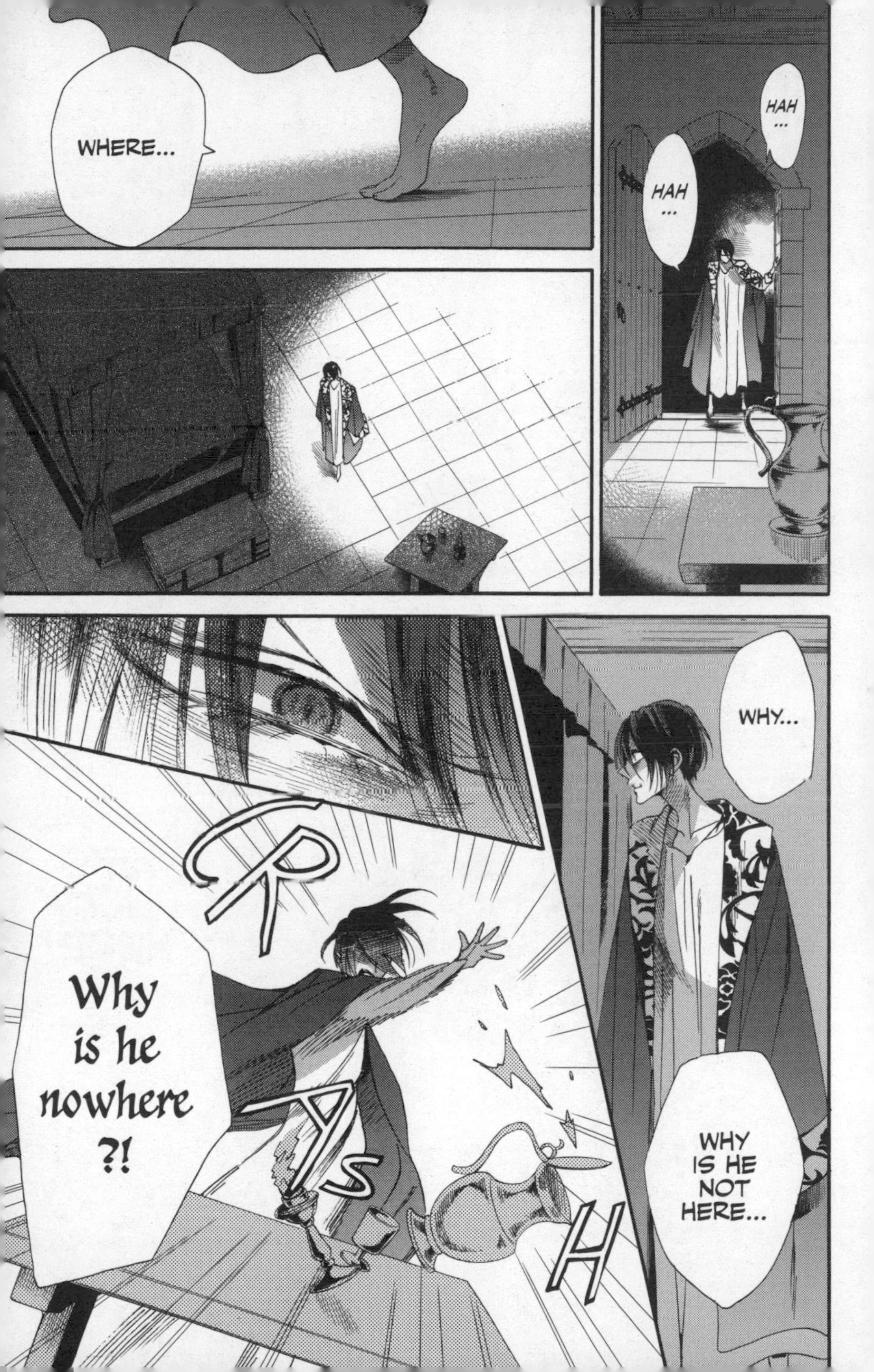
HAH...
HAH...
WHERE...
WHY...
WHY IS HE NOT HERE...
CRASH
Why is he nowhere?!

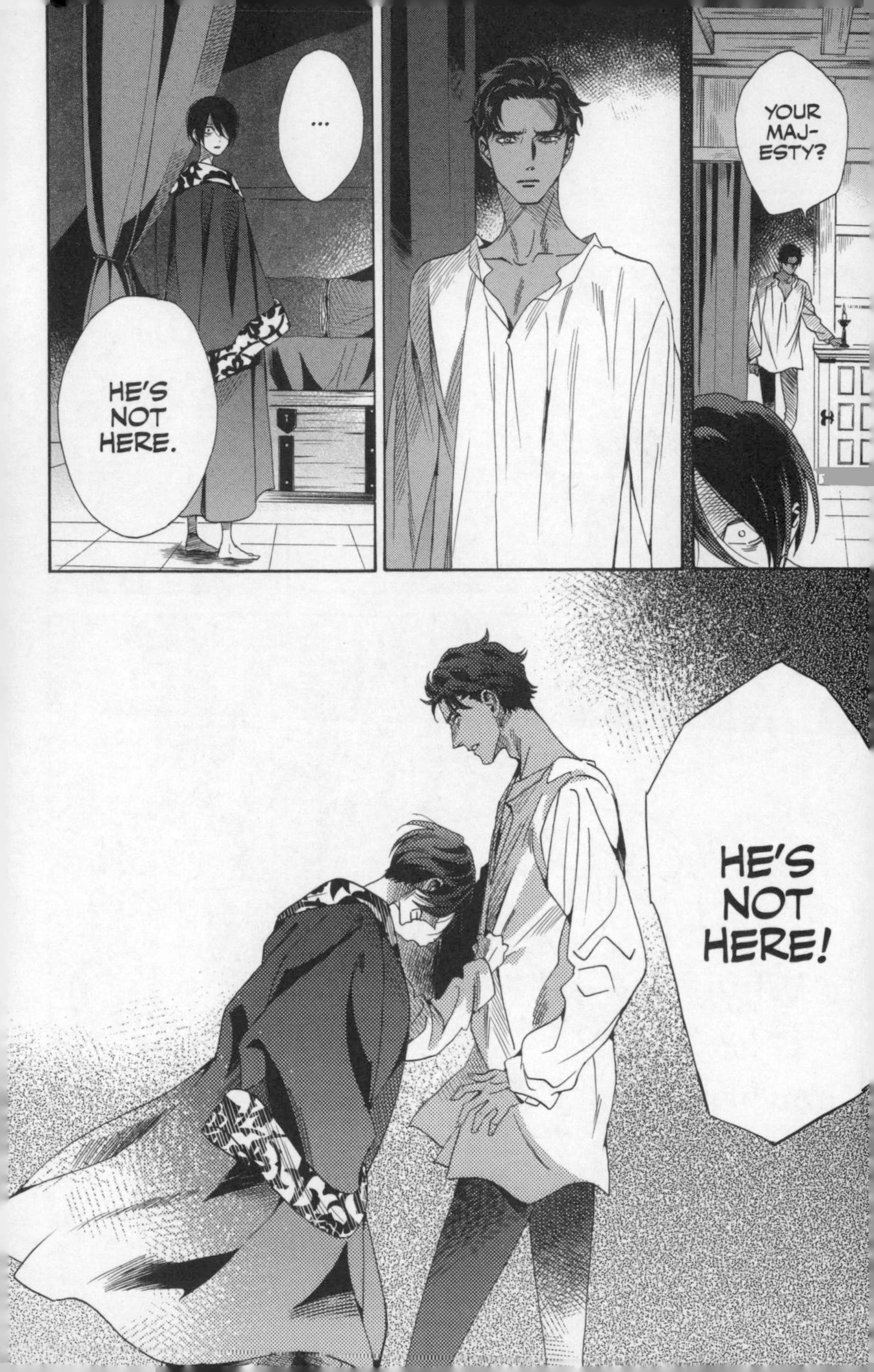
YOUR MAJ-ESTY?
...
HE'S NOT HERE.
HE'S NOT HERE!

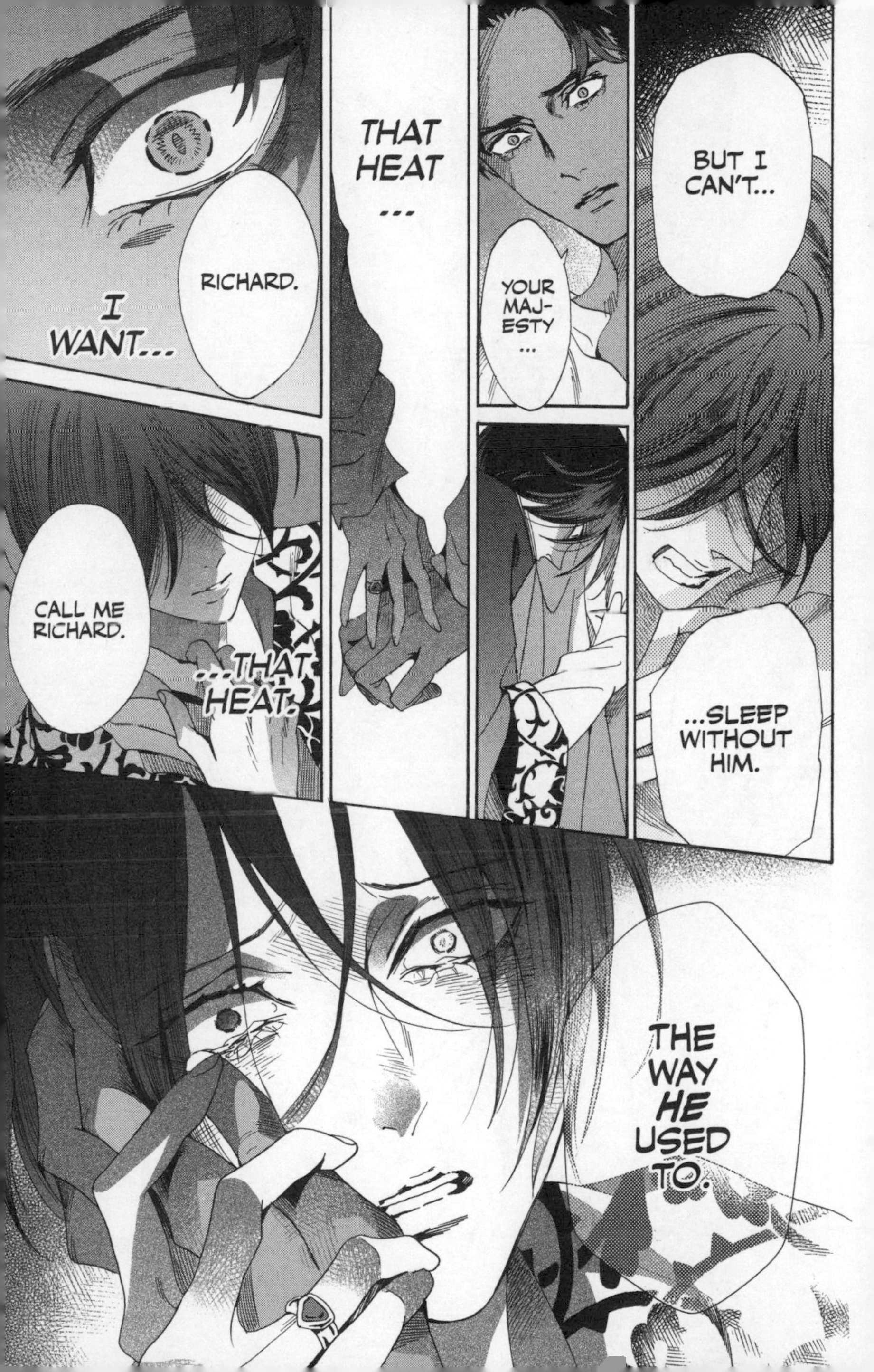
BUT I CAN'T...
...SLEEP WITHOUT HIM.
YOUR MAJESTY...
THAT HEAT...
RICHARD.
I WANT...
CALL ME RICHARD.
...THAT HEAT.
THE WAY *HE* USED TO.

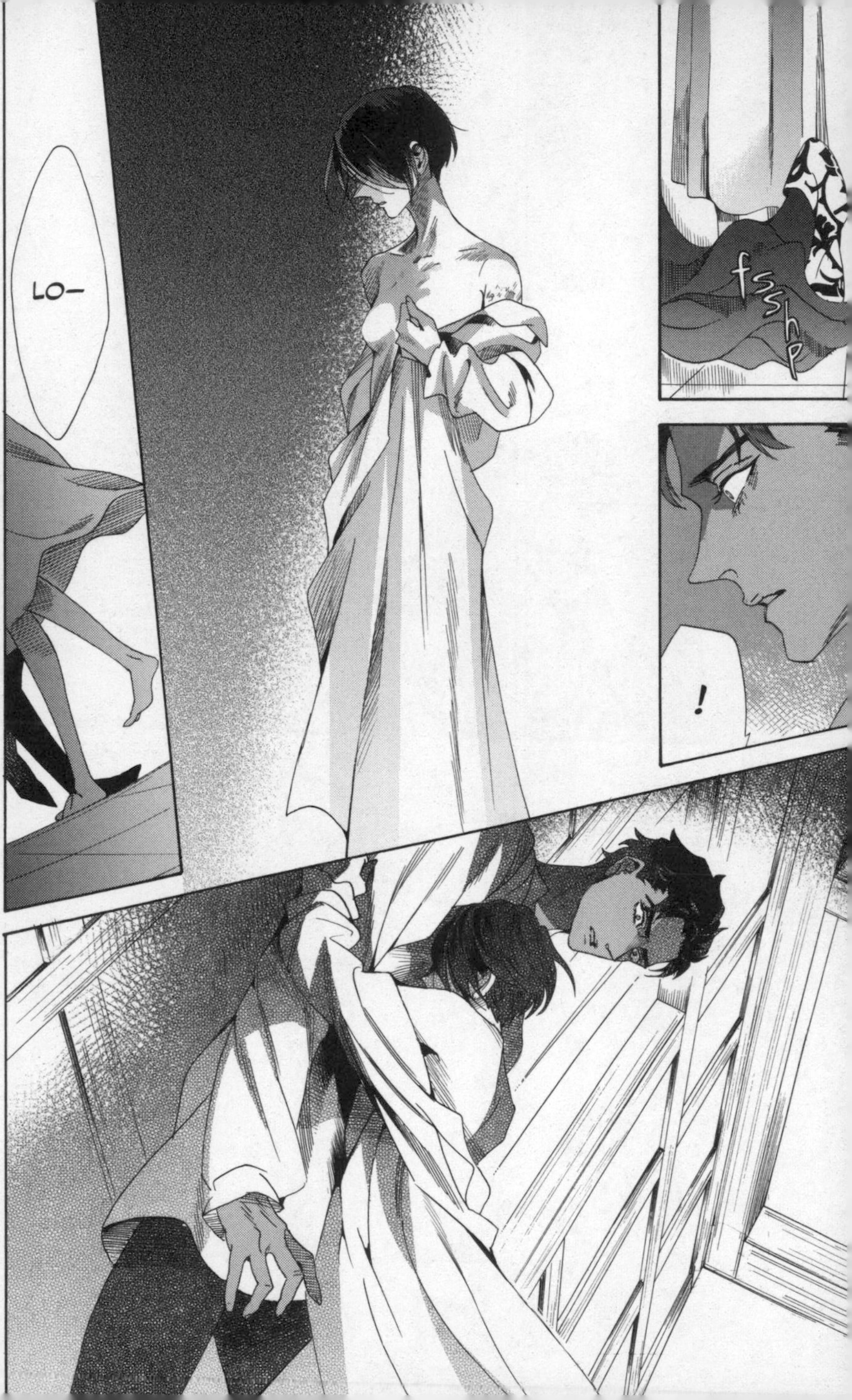
fsshp
!
LO—

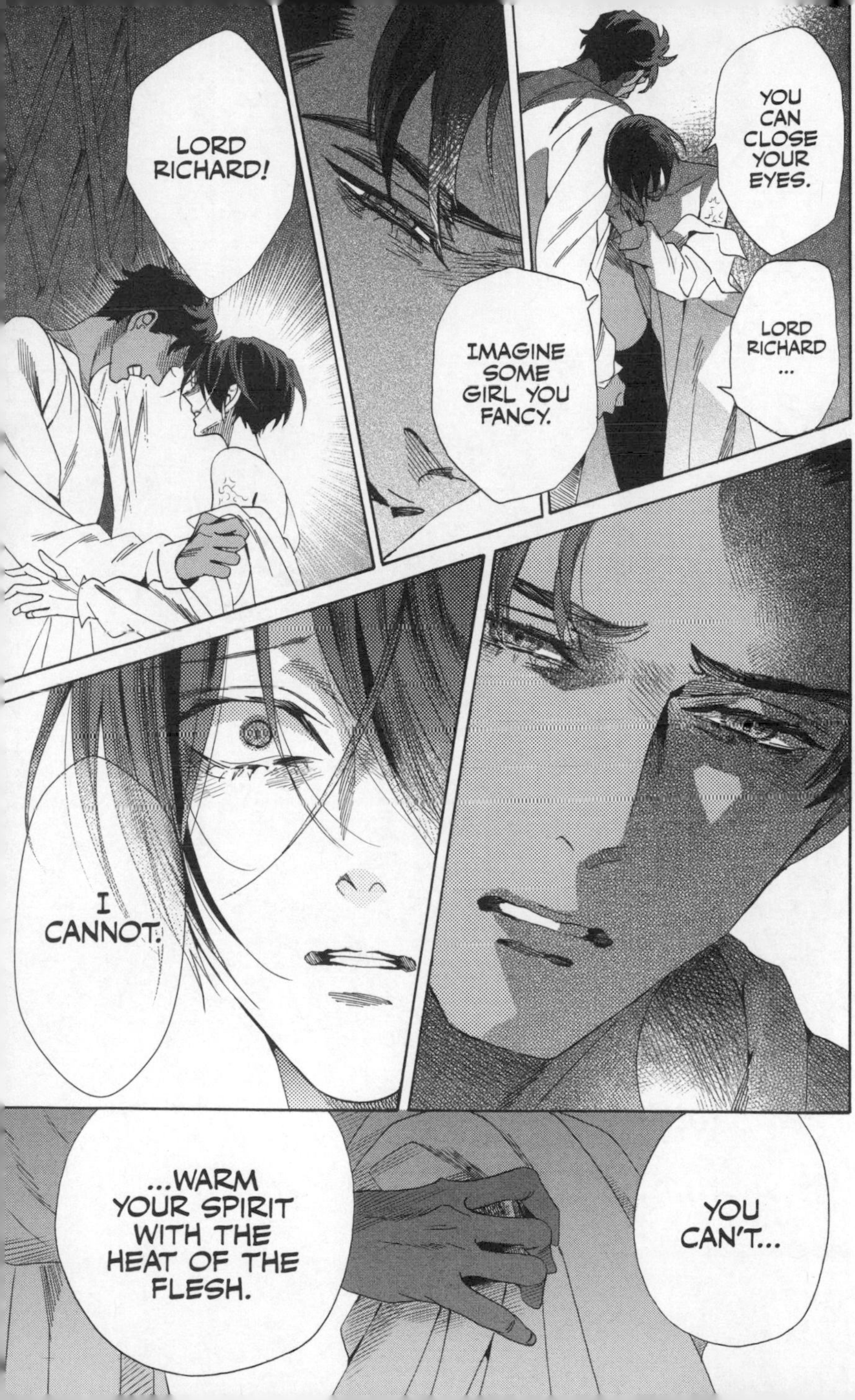
YOU CAN CLOSE YOUR EYES.
LORD RICHARD ...
IMAGINE SOME GIRL YOU FANCY.
LORD RICHARD!
I CANNOT.
YOU CAN'T...
...WARM YOUR SPIRIT WITH THE HEAT OF THE FLESH.

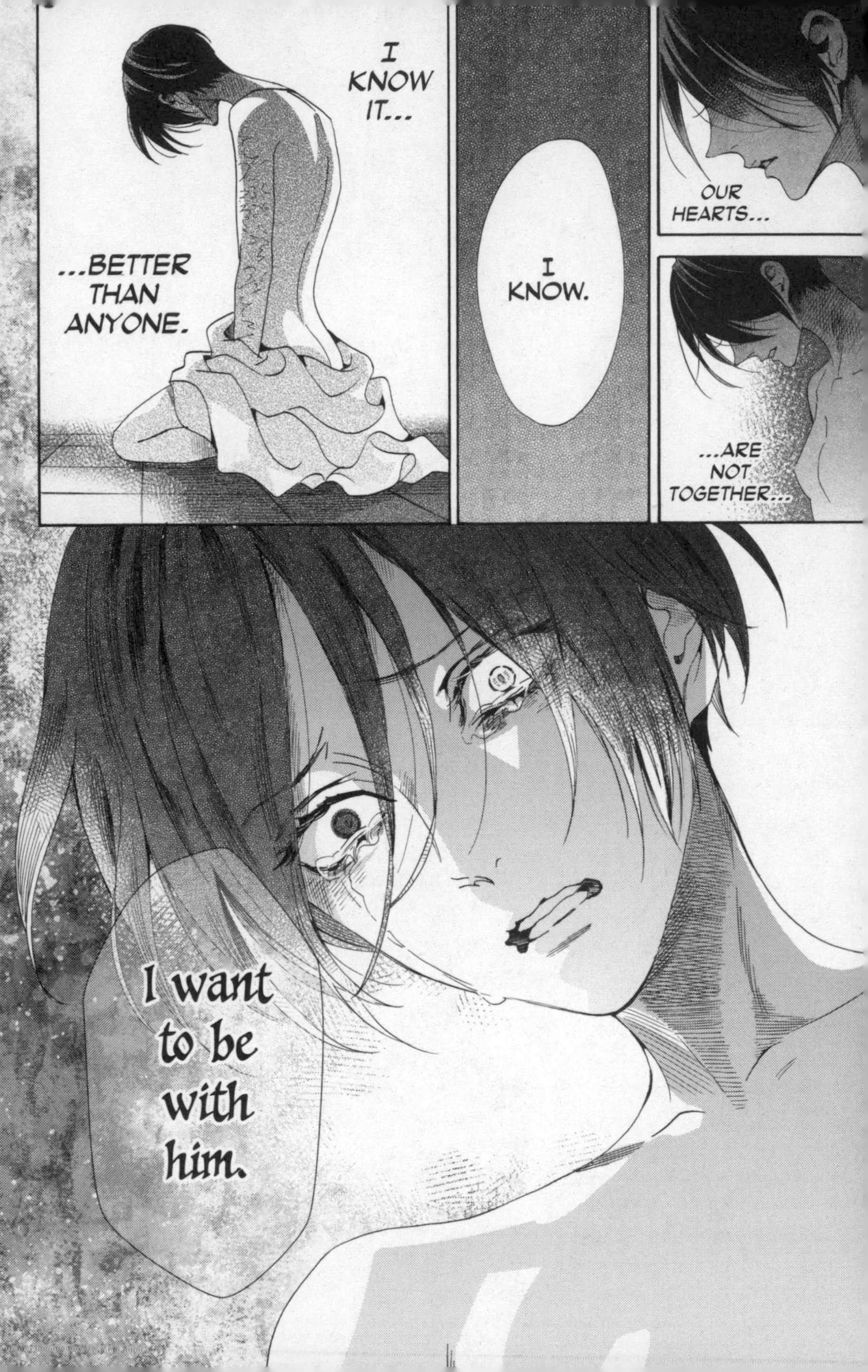
OUR HEARTS...
...ARE NOT TOGETHER...
I KNOW.
I KNOW IT...
...BETTER THAN ANYONE.
I want to be with him.

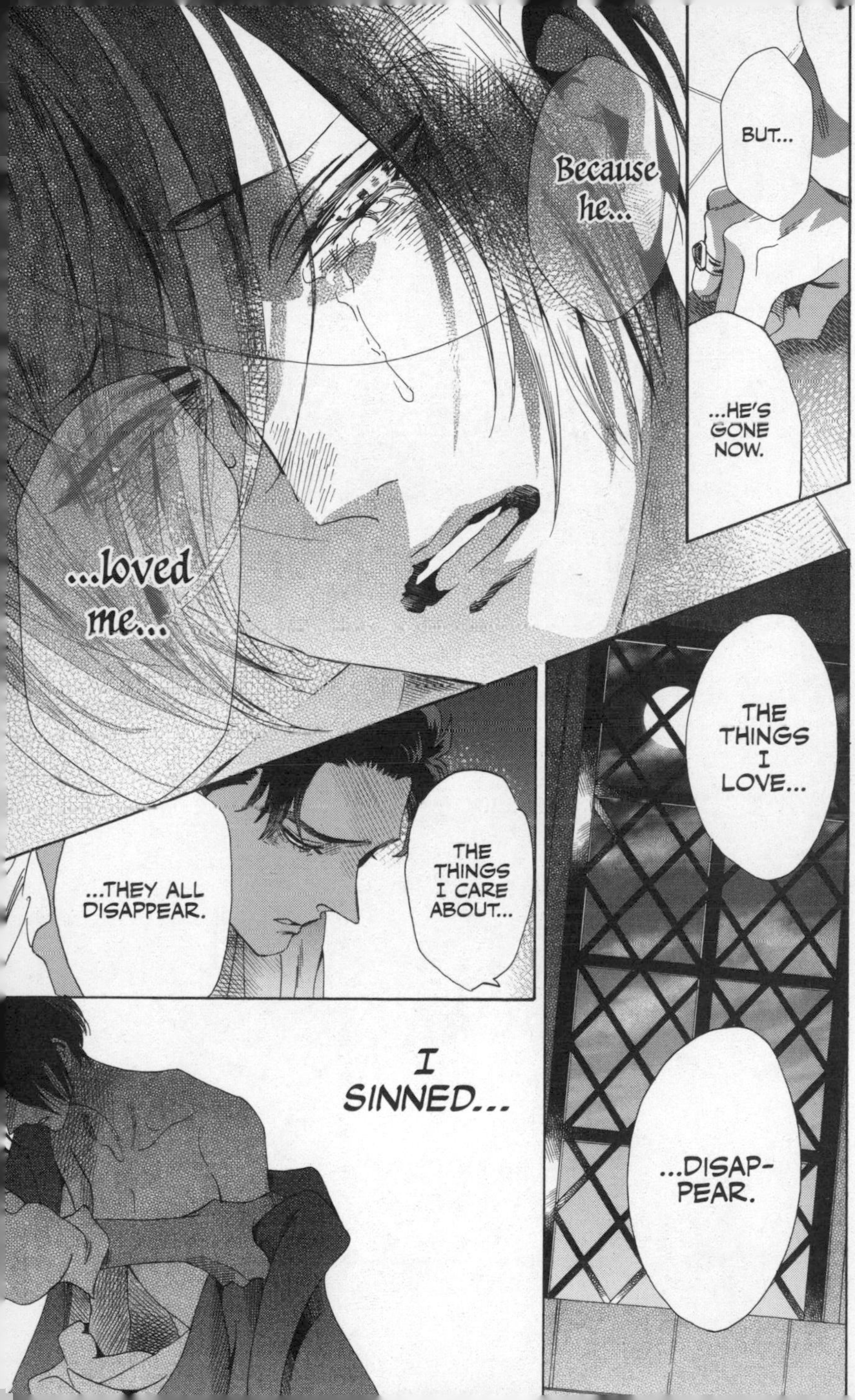
BUT...
...HE'S GONE NOW.
Because he...
...loved me...
THE THINGS I LOVE...
...DISAP-PEAR.
THE THINGS I CARE ABOUT...
...THEY ALL DISAPPEAR.
I SINNED...

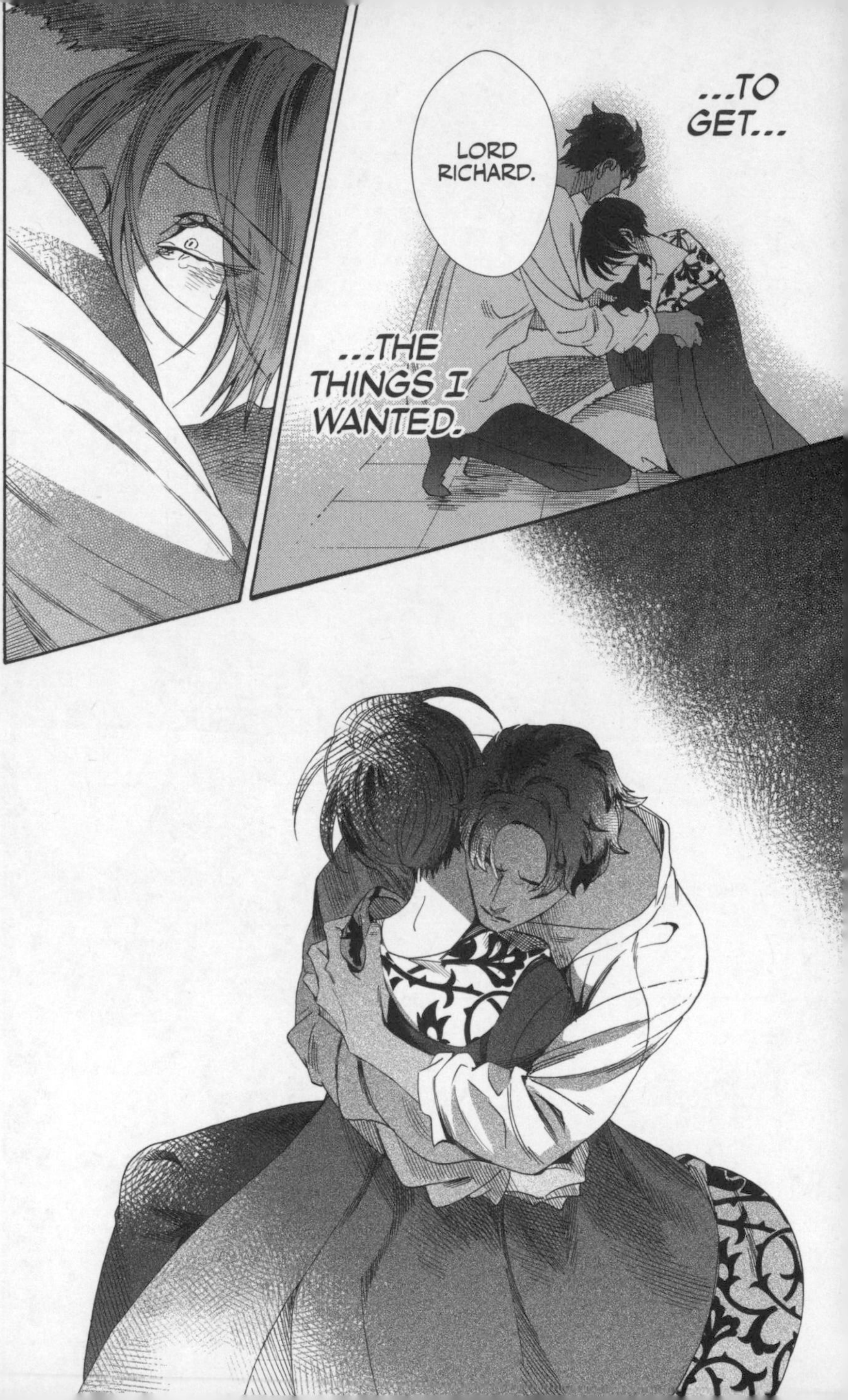
...TO GET...
LORD RICHARD.
...THE THINGS I WANTED.

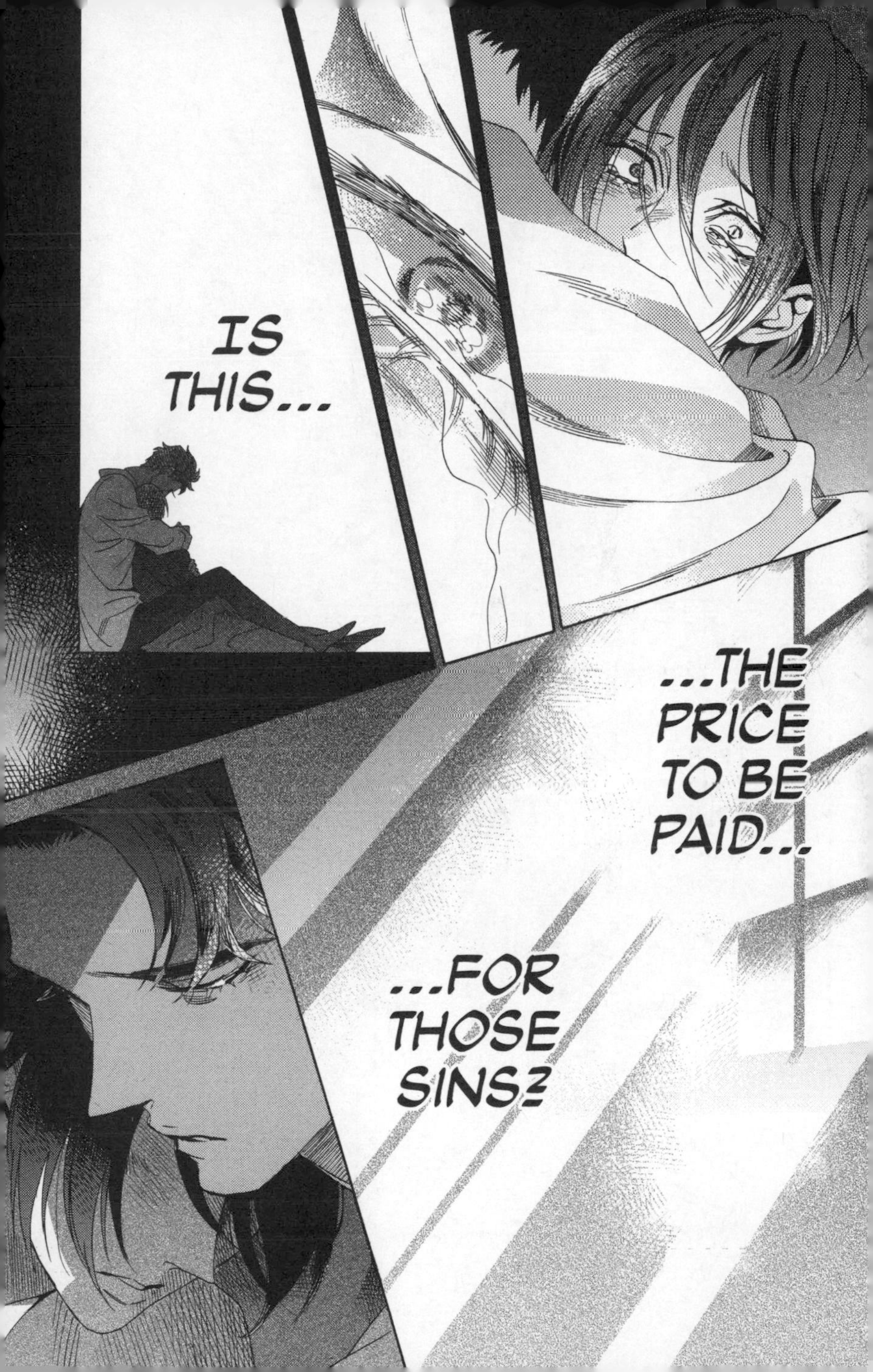
IS THIS...
...THE PRICE TO BE PAID...
...FOR THOSE SINS?

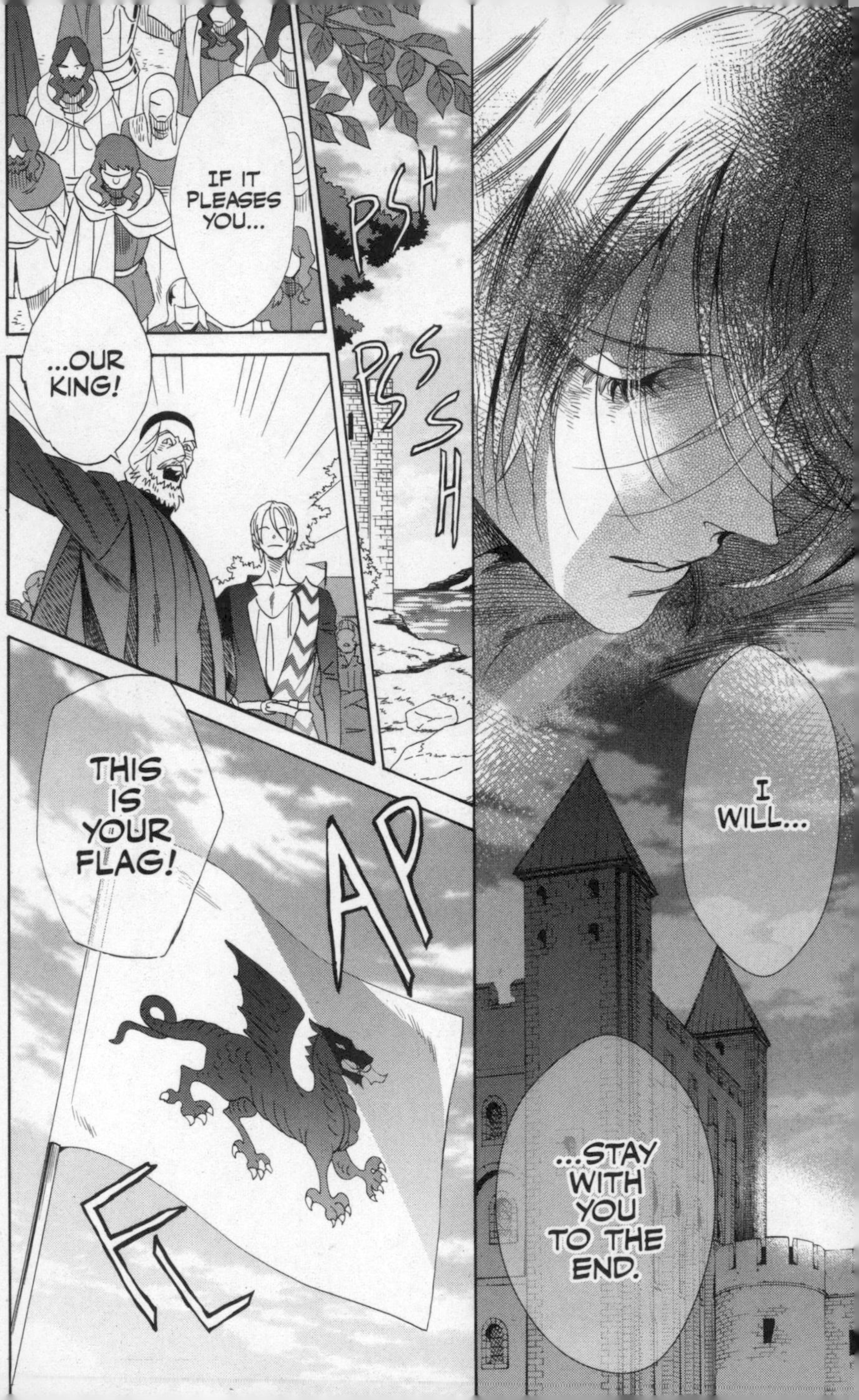
I WILL...
...STAY WITH YOU TO THE END.
IF IT PLEASES YOU...
...OUR KING!
PSH
PSSH
THIS IS YOUR FLAG!
FLAP

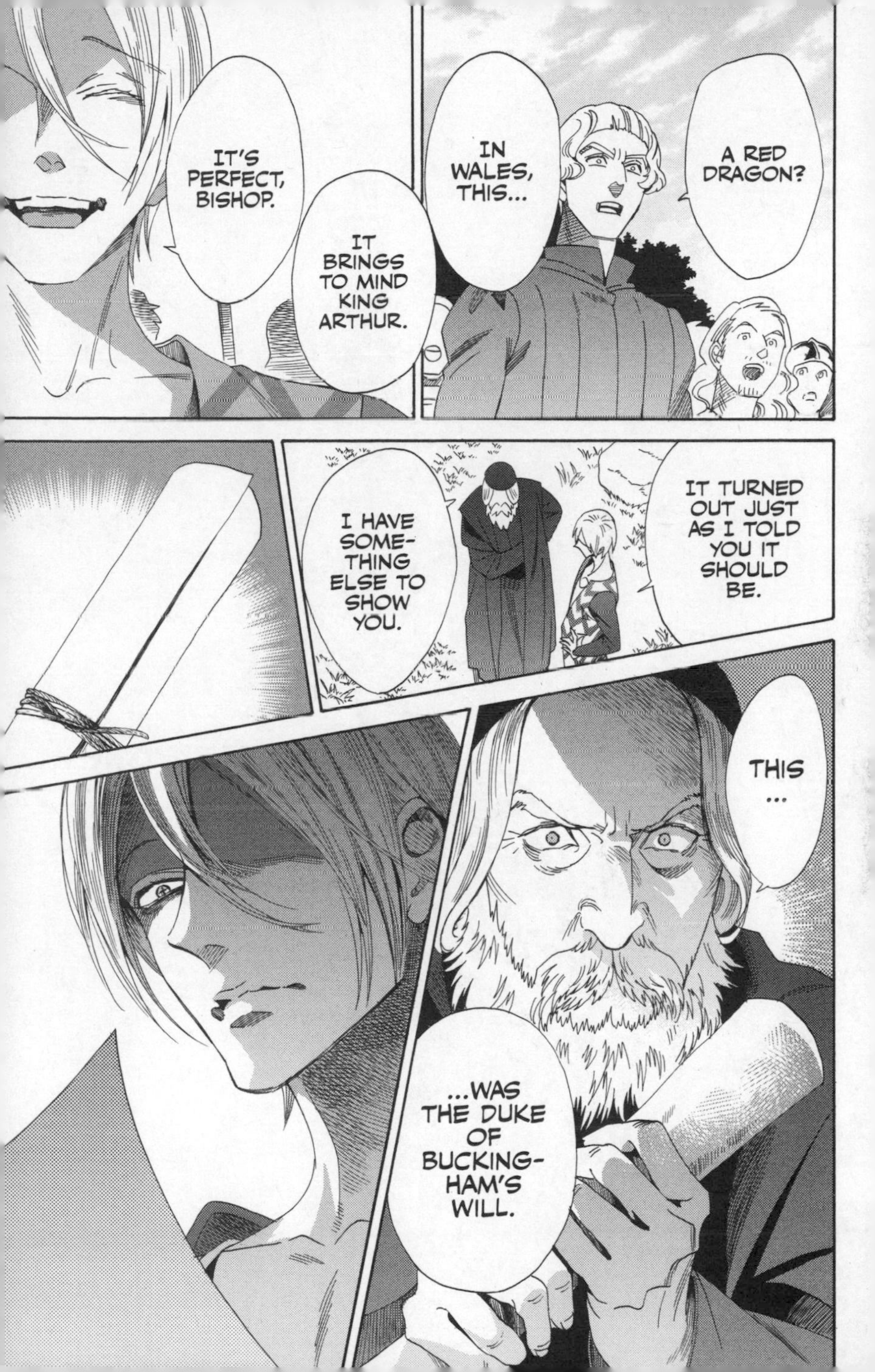
A RED DRAGON?
IN WALES, THIS...
IT'S PERFECT, BISHOP.
IT BRINGS TO MIND KING ARTHUR.
IT TURNED OUT JUST AS I TOLD YOU IT SHOULD BE.
I HAVE SOME-THING ELSE TO SHOW YOU.
THIS ...
...WAS THE DUKE OF BUCKING-HAM'S WILL.

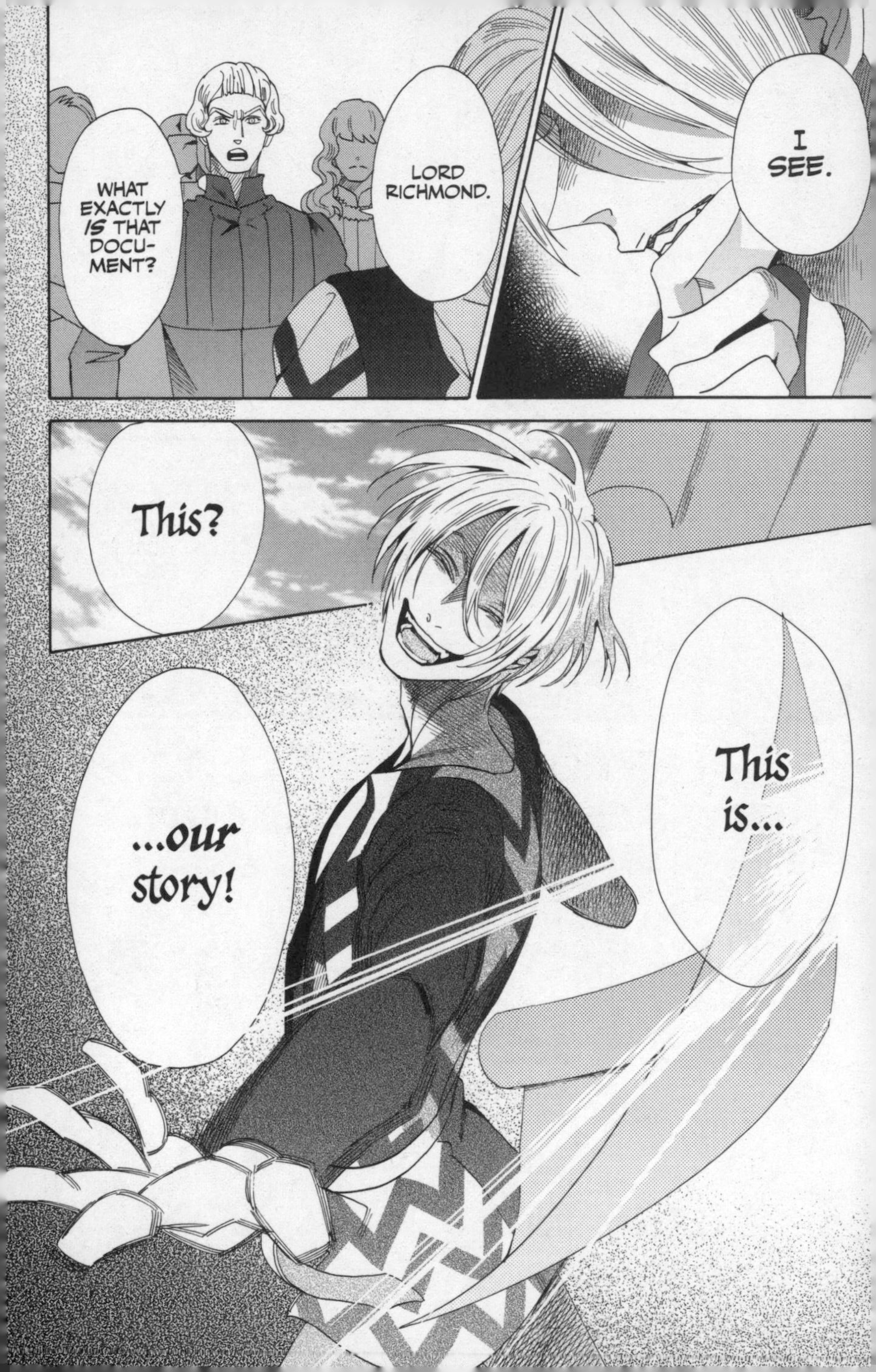
I SEE.
LORD RICHMOND.
WHAT EXACTLY *IS* THAT DOCUMENT?
This?
This is...
...our story!

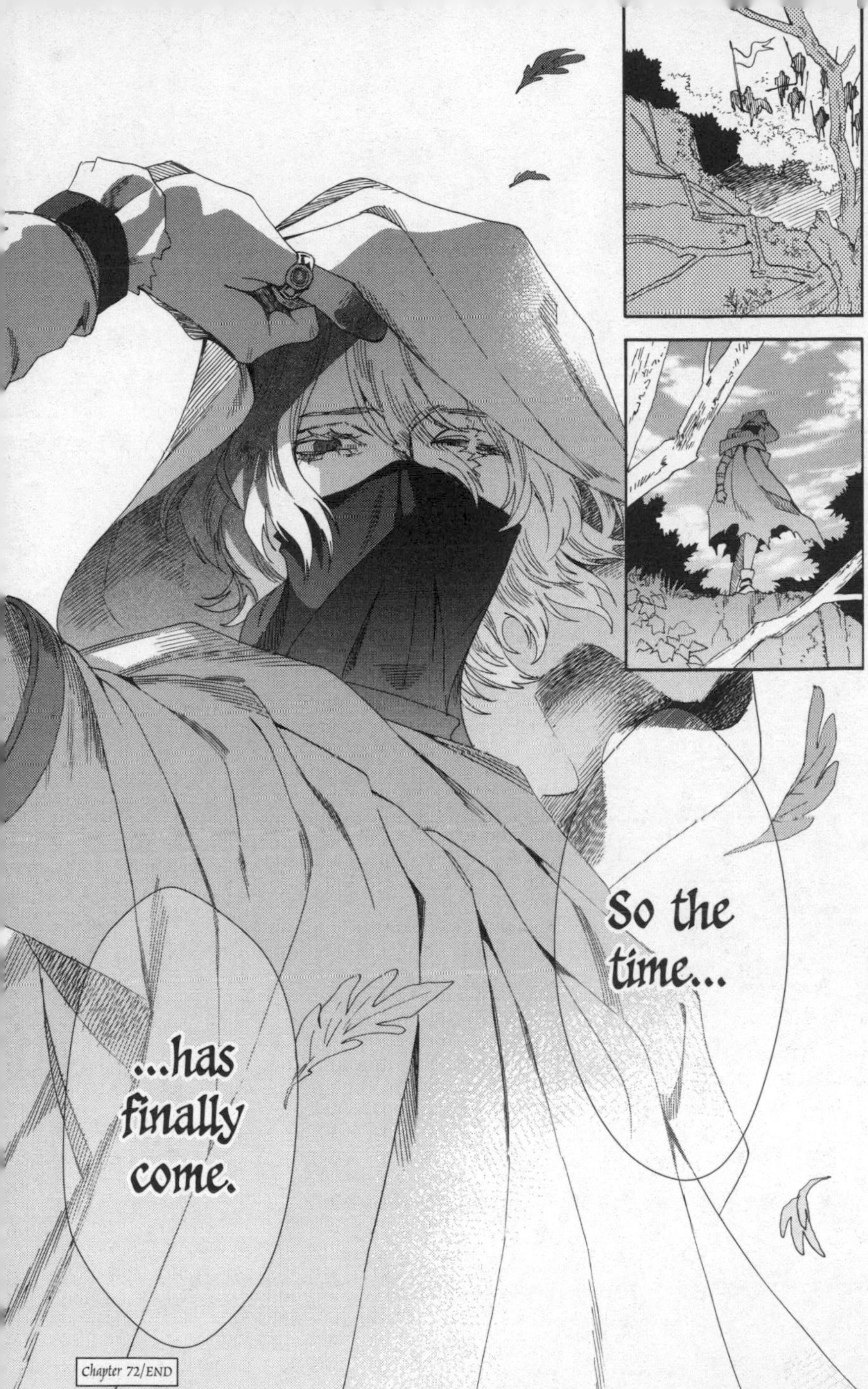
So the time...
...has finally come.
Chapter 72/END

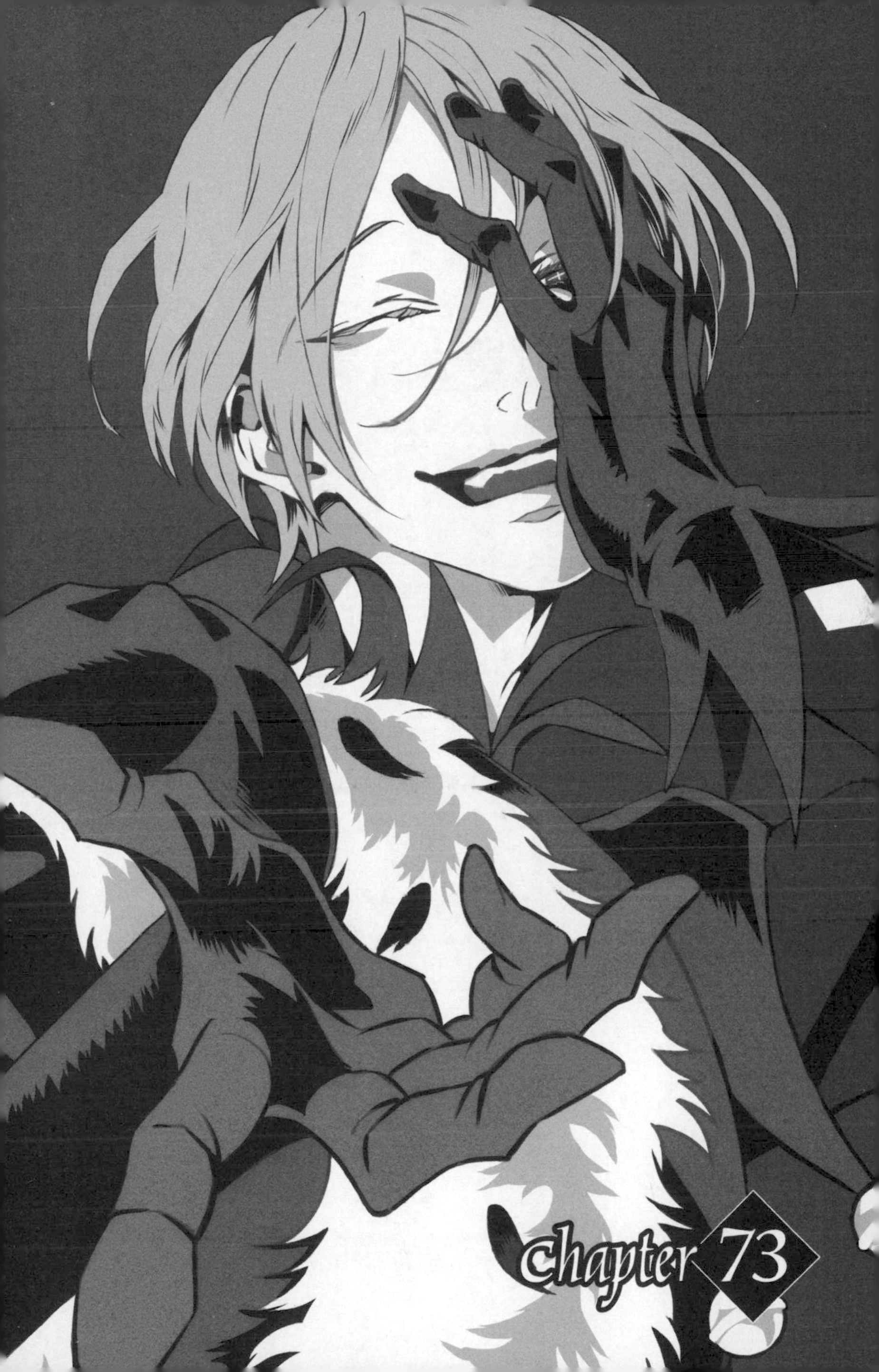
chapter 73

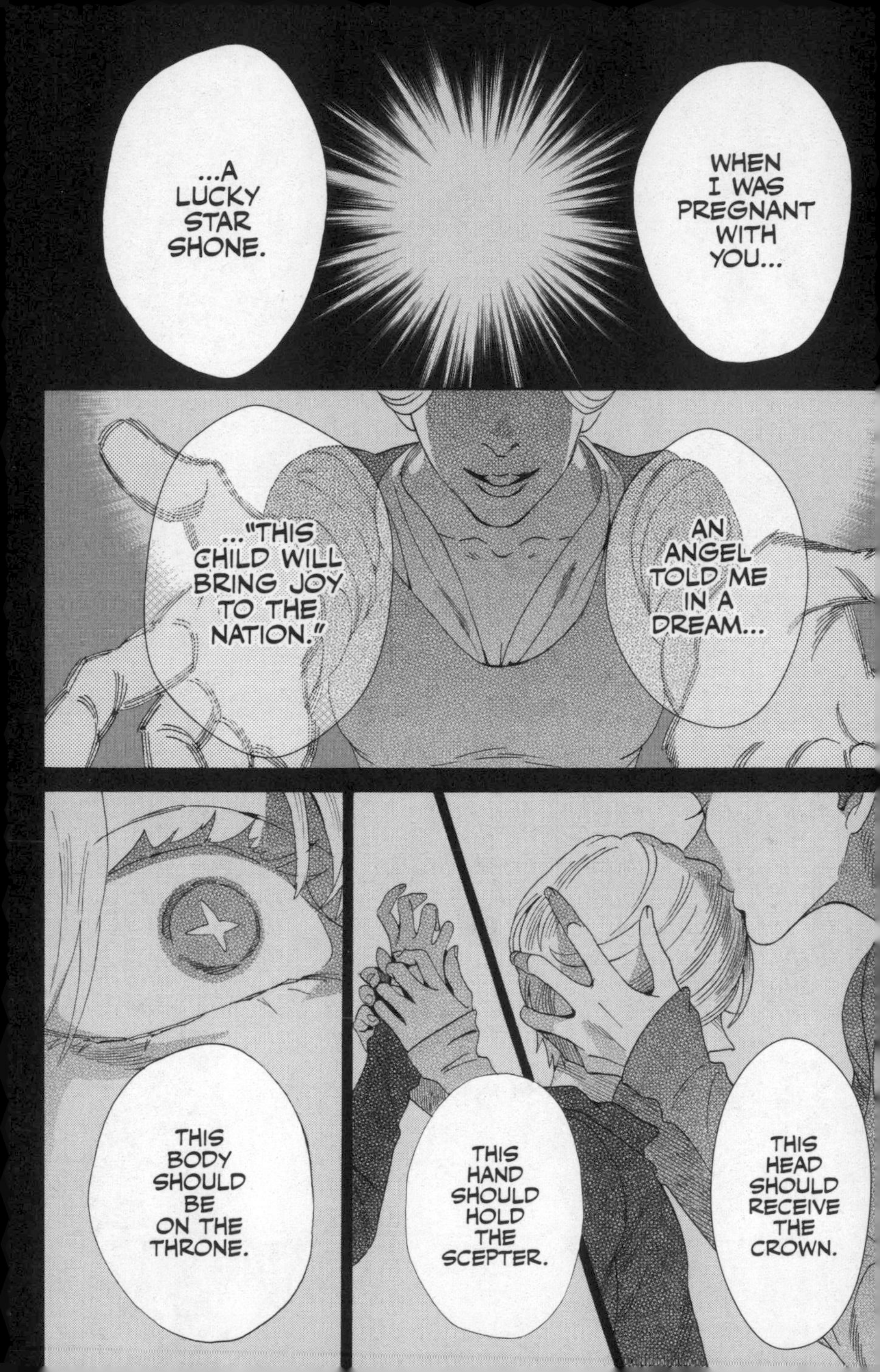
WHEN I WAS PREGNANT WITH YOU...
...A LUCKY STAR SHONE.
AN ANGEL TOLD ME IN A DREAM...
..."THIS CHILD WILL BRING JOY TO THE NATION."
THIS HEAD SHOULD RECEIVE THE CROWN.
THIS HAND SHOULD HOLD THE SCEPTER.
THIS BODY SHOULD BE ON THE THRONE.

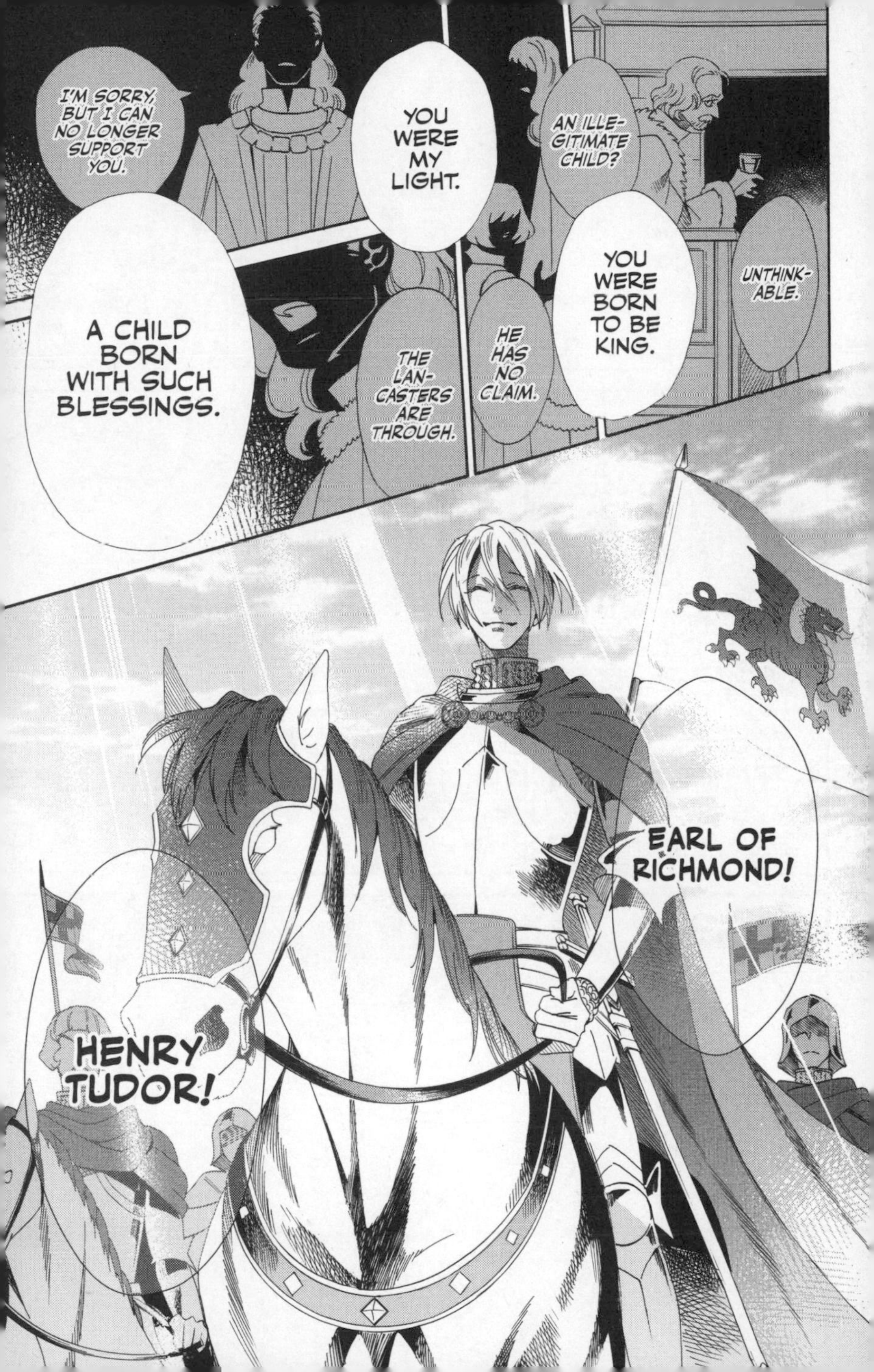
AN ILLE-GITIMATE CHILD?
UNTHINK-ABLE.
YOU WERE BORN TO BE KING.
HE HAS NO CLAIM.
YOU WERE MY LIGHT.
THE LAN-CASTERS ARE THROUGH.
I'M SORRY, BUT I CAN NO LONGER SUPPORT YOU.
A CHILD BORN WITH SUCH BLESSINGS.
EARL OF RICHMOND!
HENRY TUDOR!

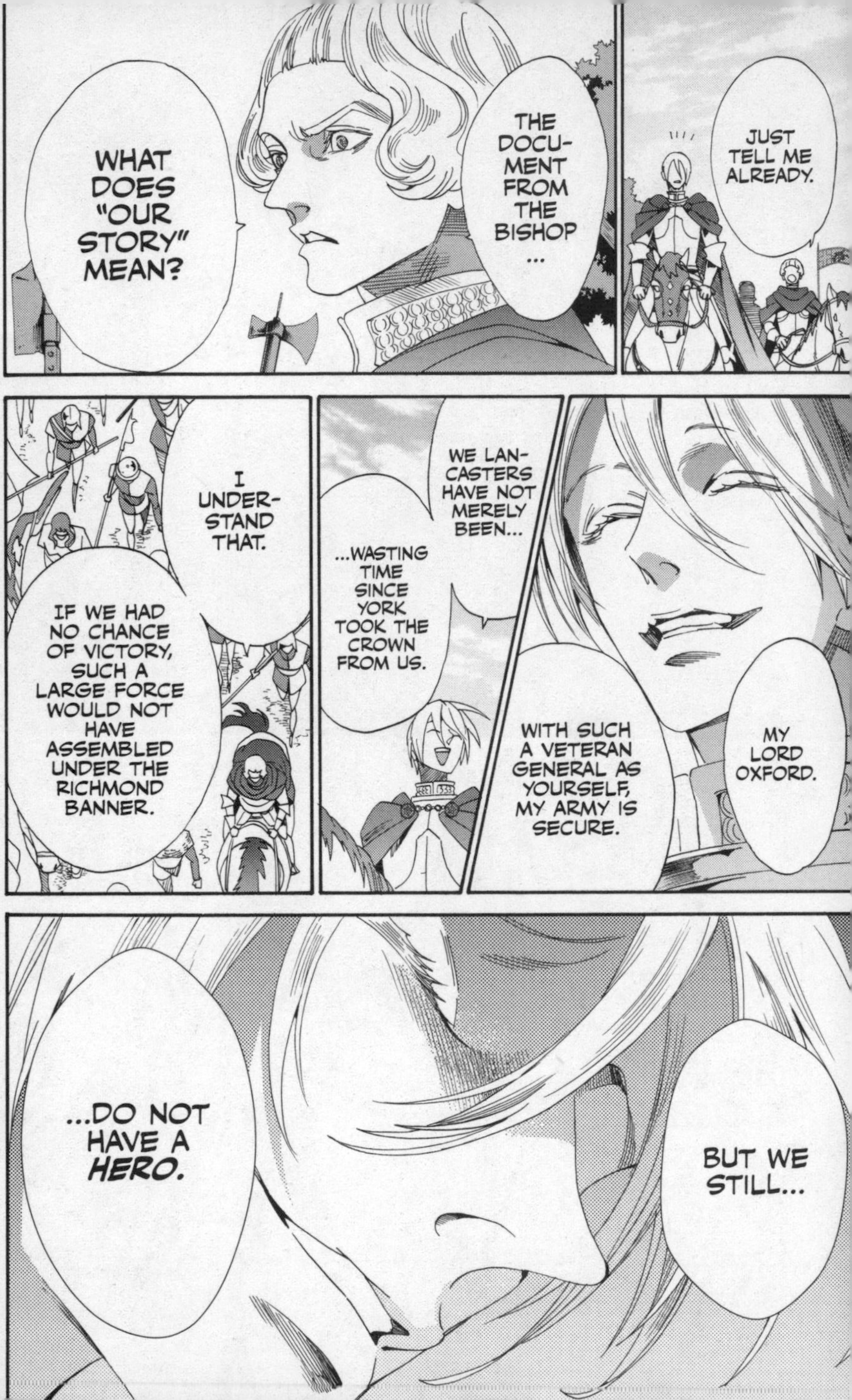
JUST TELL ME ALREADY.
THE DOCUMENT FROM THE BISHOP...
WHAT DOES "OUR STORY" MEAN?
MY LORD OXFORD.
WITH SUCH A VETERAN GENERAL AS YOURSELF, MY ARMY IS SECURE.
WE LANCASTERS HAVE NOT MERELY BEEN...
...WASTING TIME SINCE YORK TOOK THE CROWN FROM US.
I UNDERSTAND THAT.
IF WE HAD NO CHANCE OF VICTORY, SUCH A LARGE FORCE WOULD NOT HAVE ASSEMBLED UNDER THE RICHMOND BANNER.
BUT WE STILL...
...DO NOT HAVE A ***HERO.***

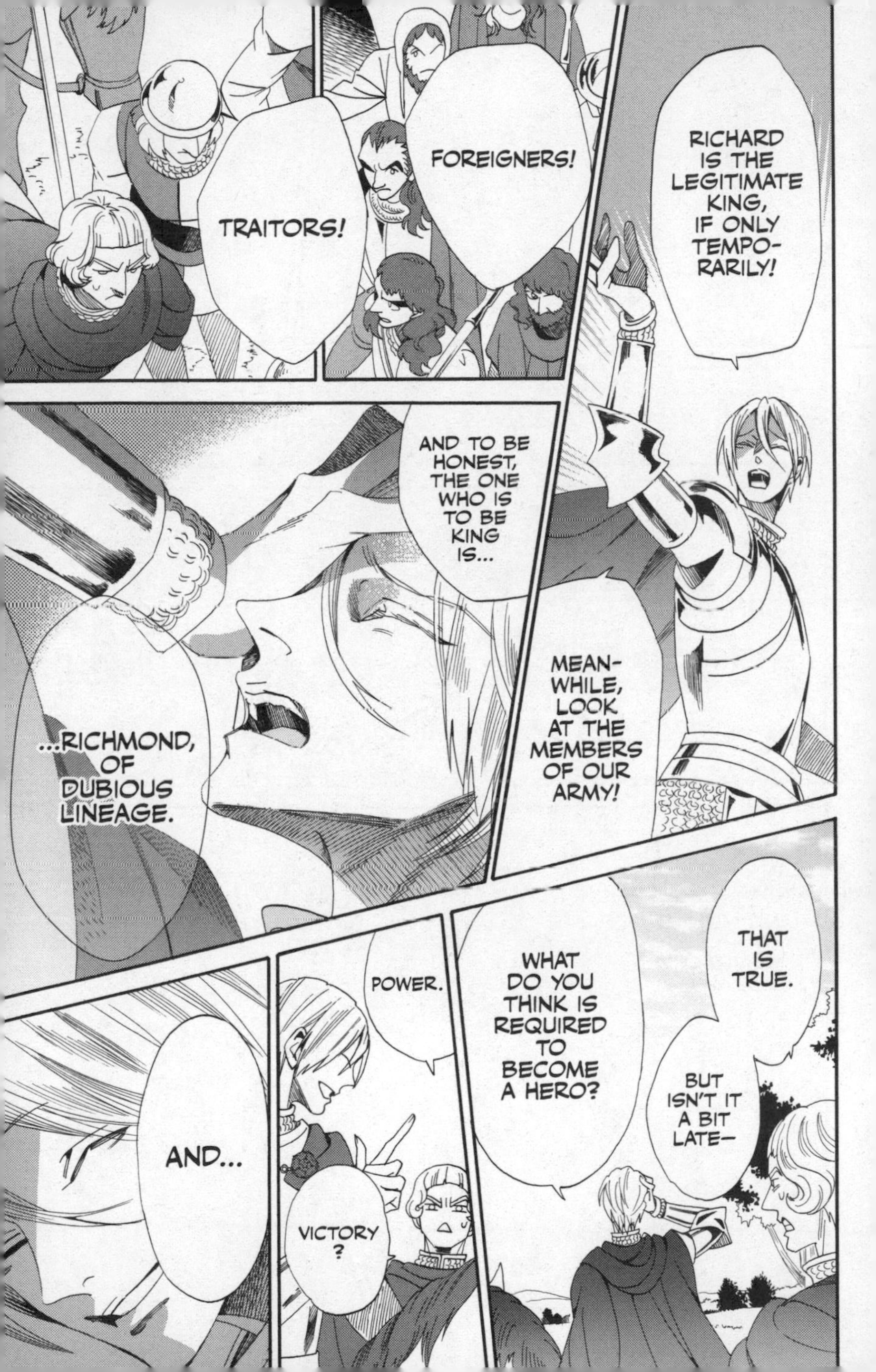
RICHARD IS THE LEGITIMATE KING, IF ONLY TEMPO-RARILY!
MEAN-WHILE, LOOK AT THE MEMBERS OF OUR ARMY!
FOREIGNERS!
TRAITORS!
AND TO BE HONEST, THE ONE WHO IS TO BE KING IS...
...RICHMOND, OF DUBIOUS LINEAGE.
THAT IS TRUE.
BUT ISN'T IT A BIT LATE—
WHAT DO YOU THINK IS REQUIRED TO BECOME A HERO?
POWER.
VICTORY?
AND...

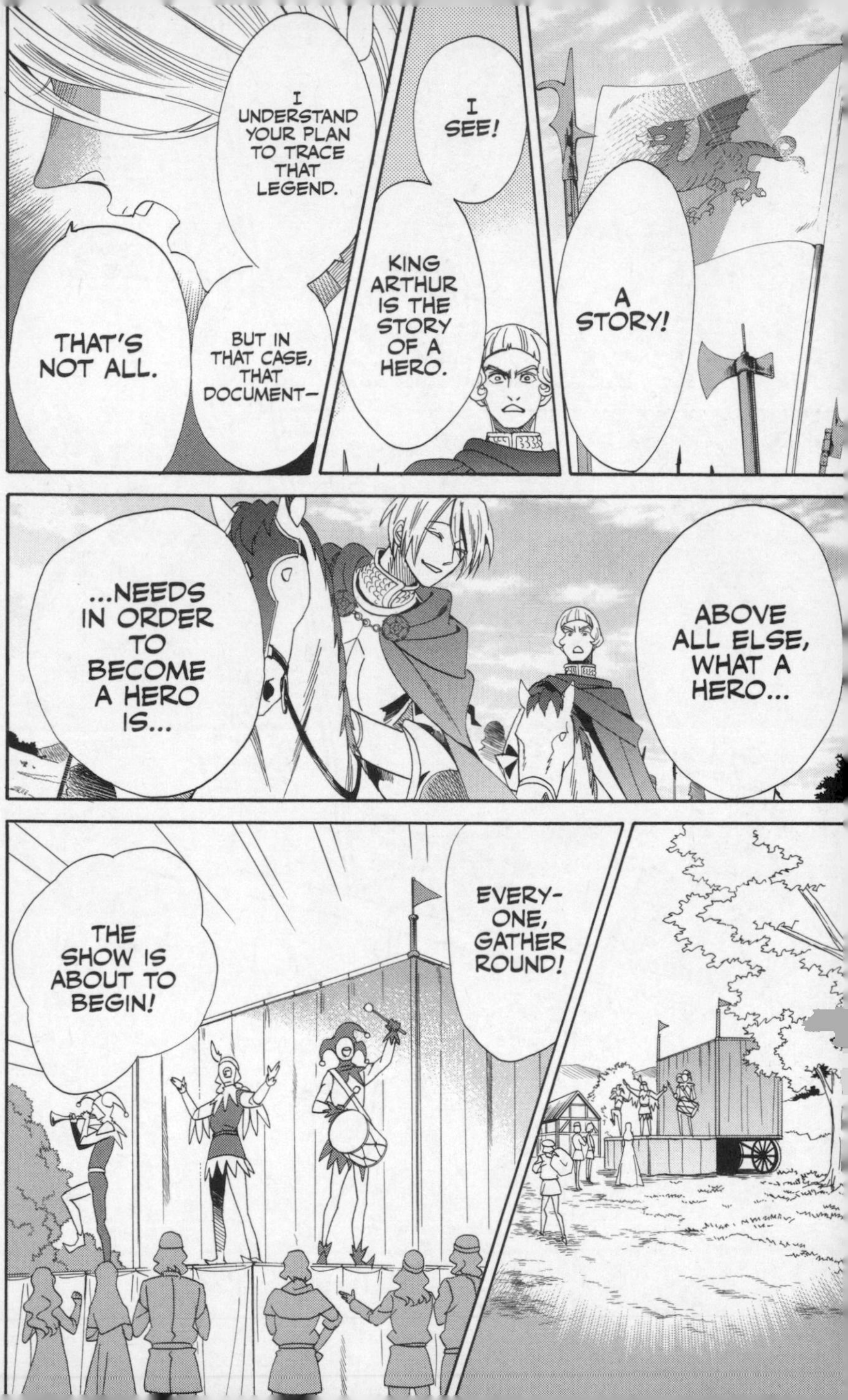
A STORY!
I SEE!
KING ARTHUR IS THE STORY OF A HERO.
I UNDERSTAND YOUR PLAN TO TRACE THAT LEGEND.
BUT IN THAT CASE, THAT DOCUMENT—
THAT'S NOT ALL.
ABOVE ALL ELSE, WHAT A HERO...
...NEEDS IN ORDER TO BECOME A HERO IS...
EVERY-ONE, GATHER ROUND!
THE SHOW IS ABOUT TO BEGIN!

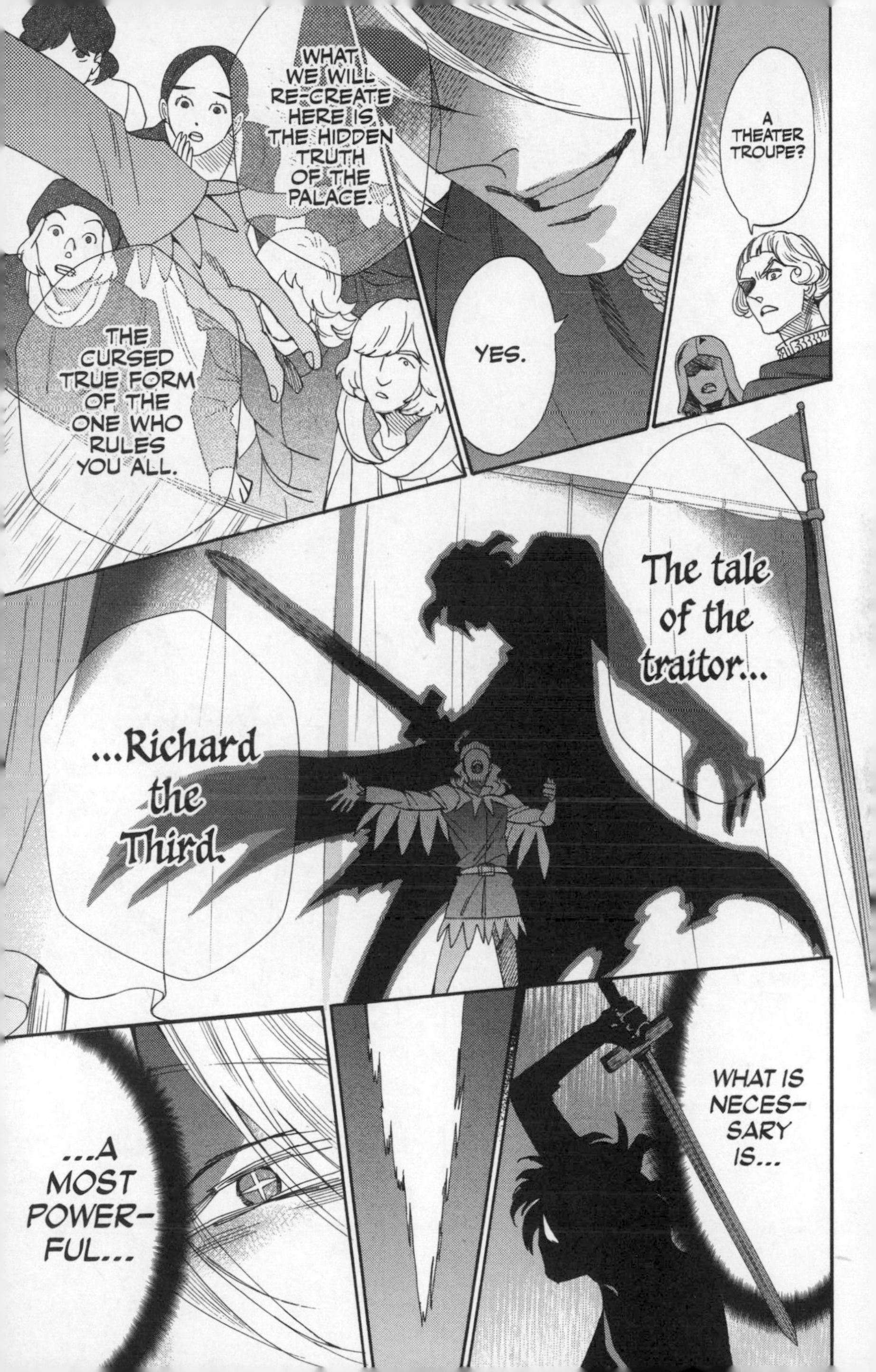
A THEATER TROUPE?
YES.
WHAT WE WILL RE-CREATE HERE IS THE HIDDEN TRUTH OF THE PALACE.
THE CURSED TRUE FORM OF THE ONE WHO RULES YOU ALL.
The tale of the traitor...
...Richard the Third.
WHAT IS NECESSARY IS...
...A MOST POWERFUL...

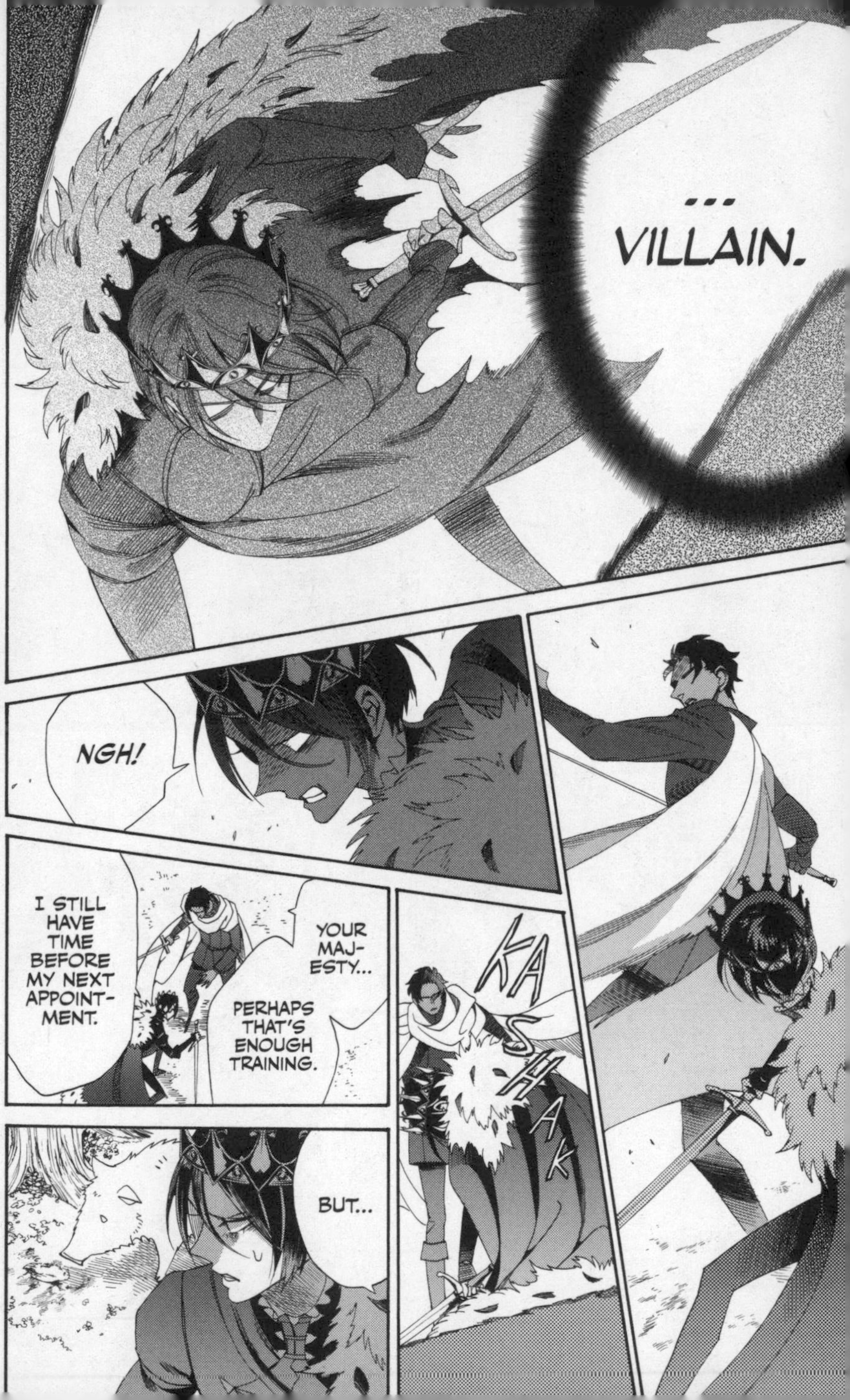
...VILLAIN.
NGH!
KASHAK
YOUR MAJESTY...
PERHAPS THAT'S ENOUGH TRAINING.
I STILL HAVE TIME BEFORE MY NEXT APPOINTMENT.
BUT...

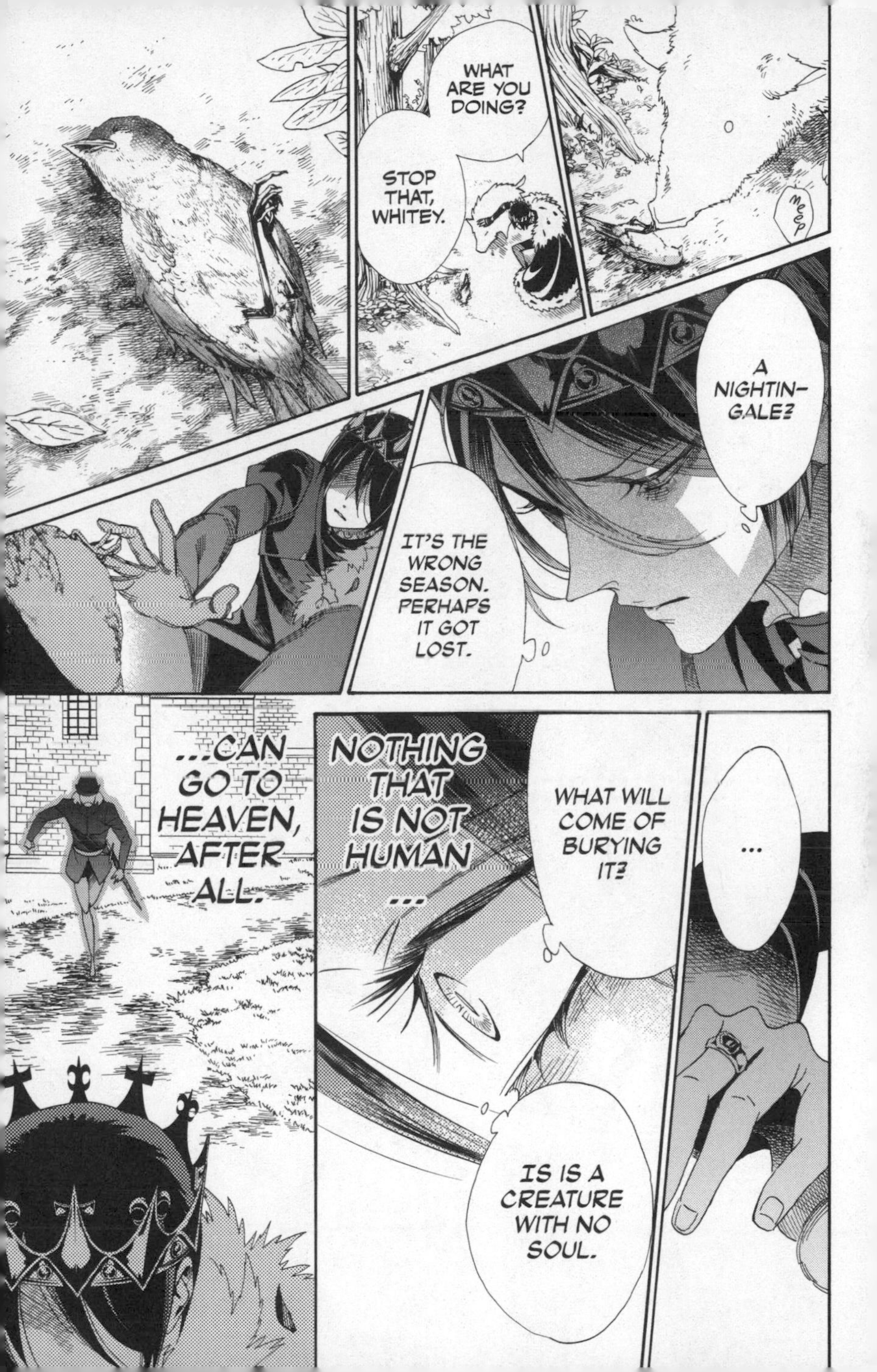
meep
WHAT ARE YOU DOING?
STOP THAT, WHITEY.
A NIGHTIN-GALE?
IT'S THE WRONG SEASON. PERHAPS IT GOT LOST.
...
WHAT WILL COME OF BURYING IT?
IS IS A CREATURE WITH NO SOUL.
NOTHING THAT IS NOT HUMAN ...
...CAN GO TO HEAVEN, AFTER ALL.

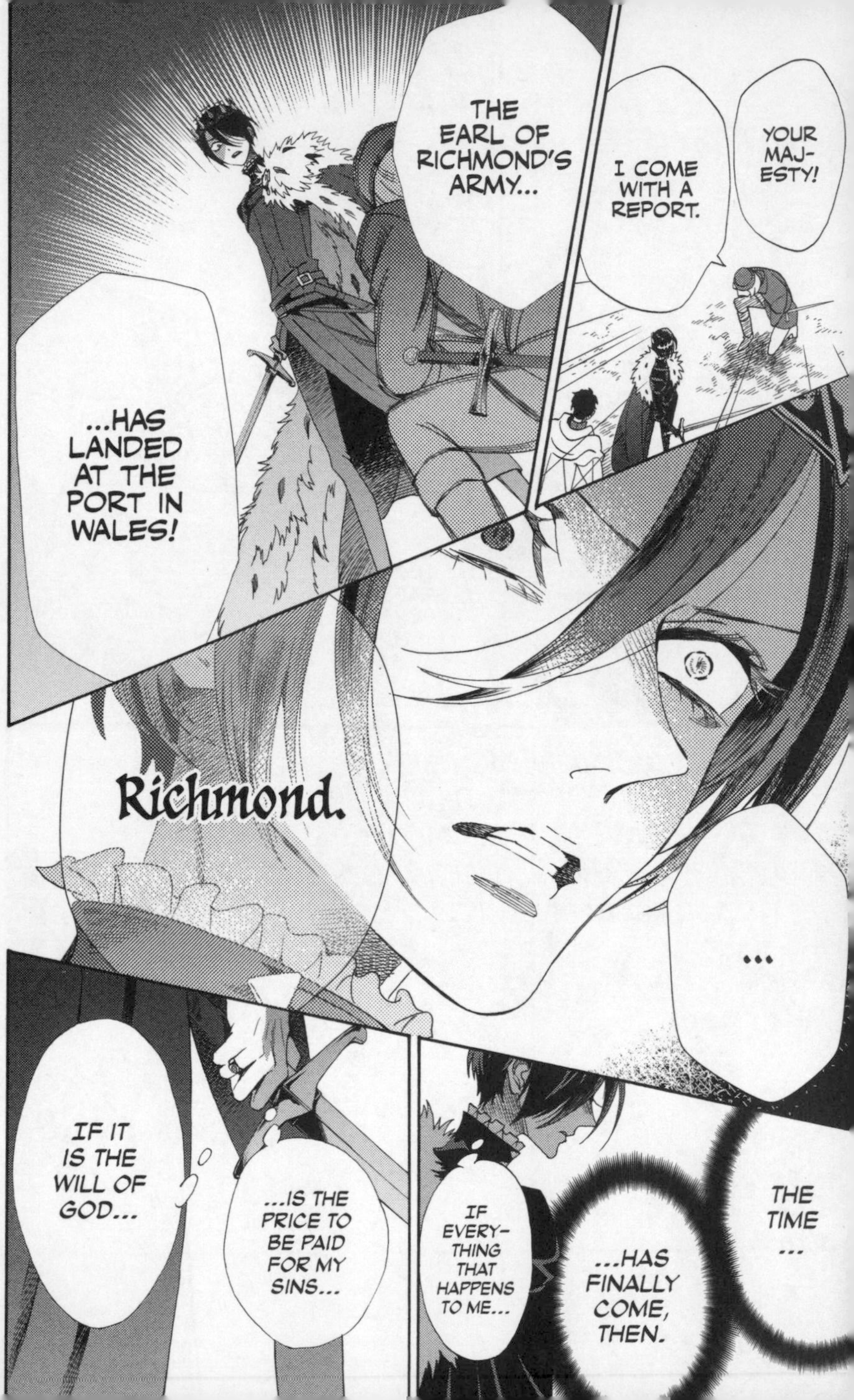
YOUR MAJ-ESTY!
I COME WITH A REPORT.
THE EARL OF RICHMOND'S ARMY...
...HAS LANDED AT THE PORT IN WALES!
...
Richmond.
THE TIME...
...HAS FINALLY COME, THEN.
IF EVERY-THING THAT HAPPENS TO ME...
...IS THE PRICE TO BE PAID FOR MY SINS...
IF IT IS THE WILL OF GOD...

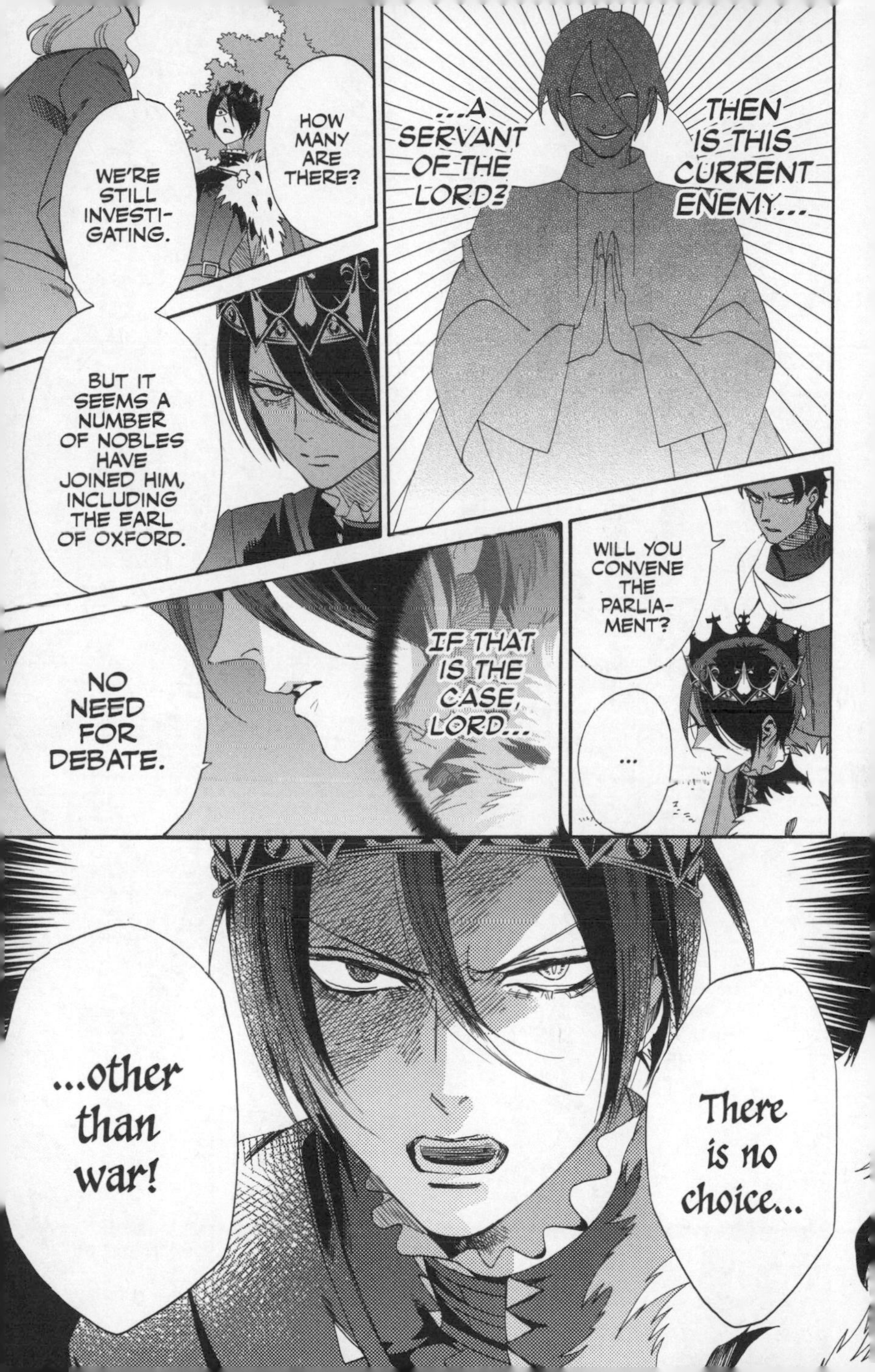
THEN IS THIS CURRENT ENEMY...
...A SERVANT OF THE LORD?
HOW MANY ARE THERE?
WE'RE STILL INVESTIGATING.
BUT IT SEEMS A NUMBER OF NOBLES HAVE JOINED HIM, INCLUDING THE EARL OF OXFORD.
WILL YOU CONVENE THE PARLIAMENT?
...
IF THAT IS THE CASE, LORD...
NO NEED FOR DEBATE.
There is no choice...
...other than war!

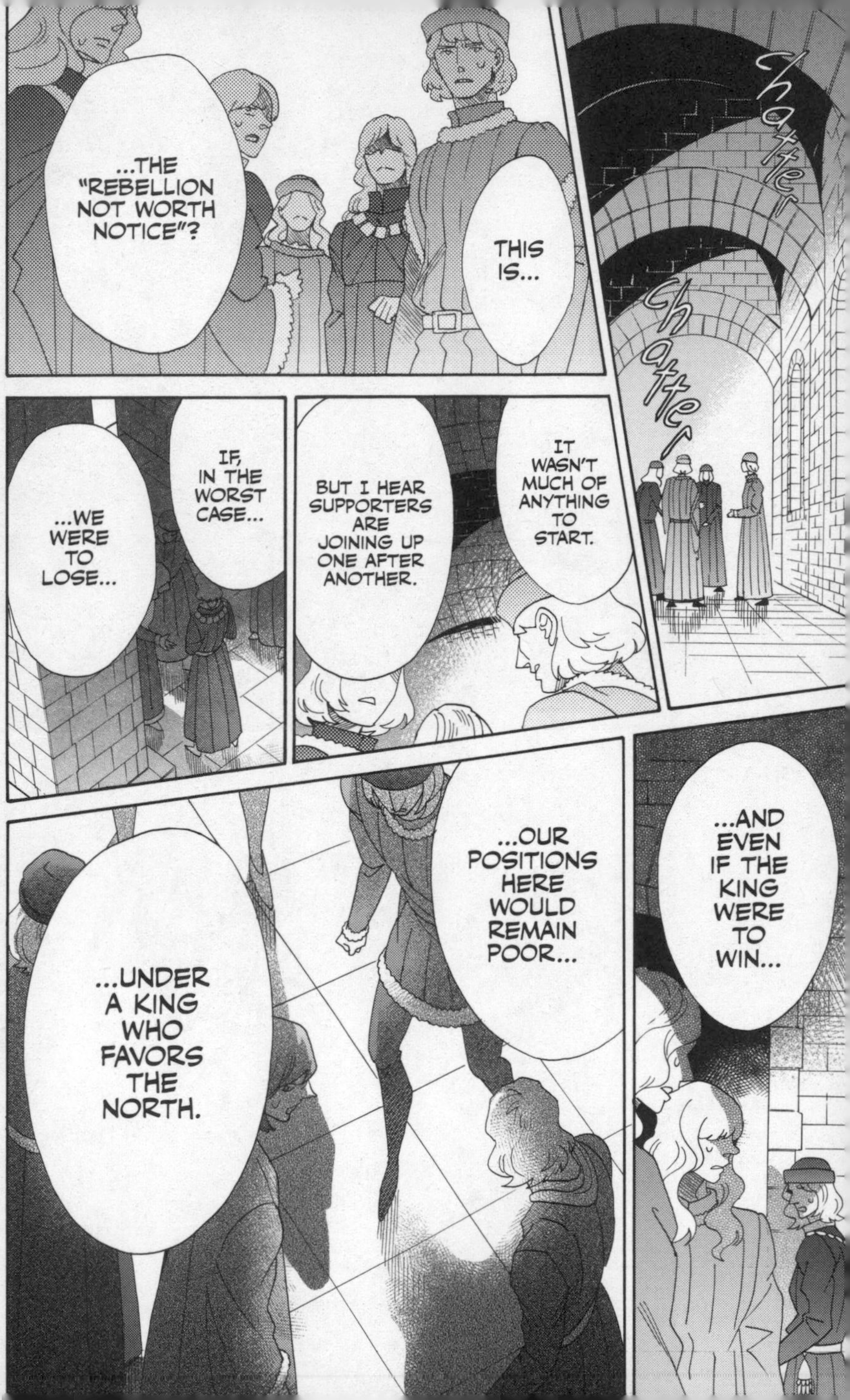
chatter
chatter
THIS IS...
...THE "REBELLION NOT WORTH NOTICE"?
IT WASN'T MUCH OF ANYTHING TO START.
BUT I HEAR SUPPORTERS ARE JOINING UP ONE AFTER ANOTHER.
IF, IN THE WORST CASE...
...WE WERE TO LOSE...
...AND EVEN IF THE KING WERE TO WIN...
...OUR POSITIONS HERE WOULD REMAIN POOR...
...UNDER A KING WHO FAVORS THE NORTH.

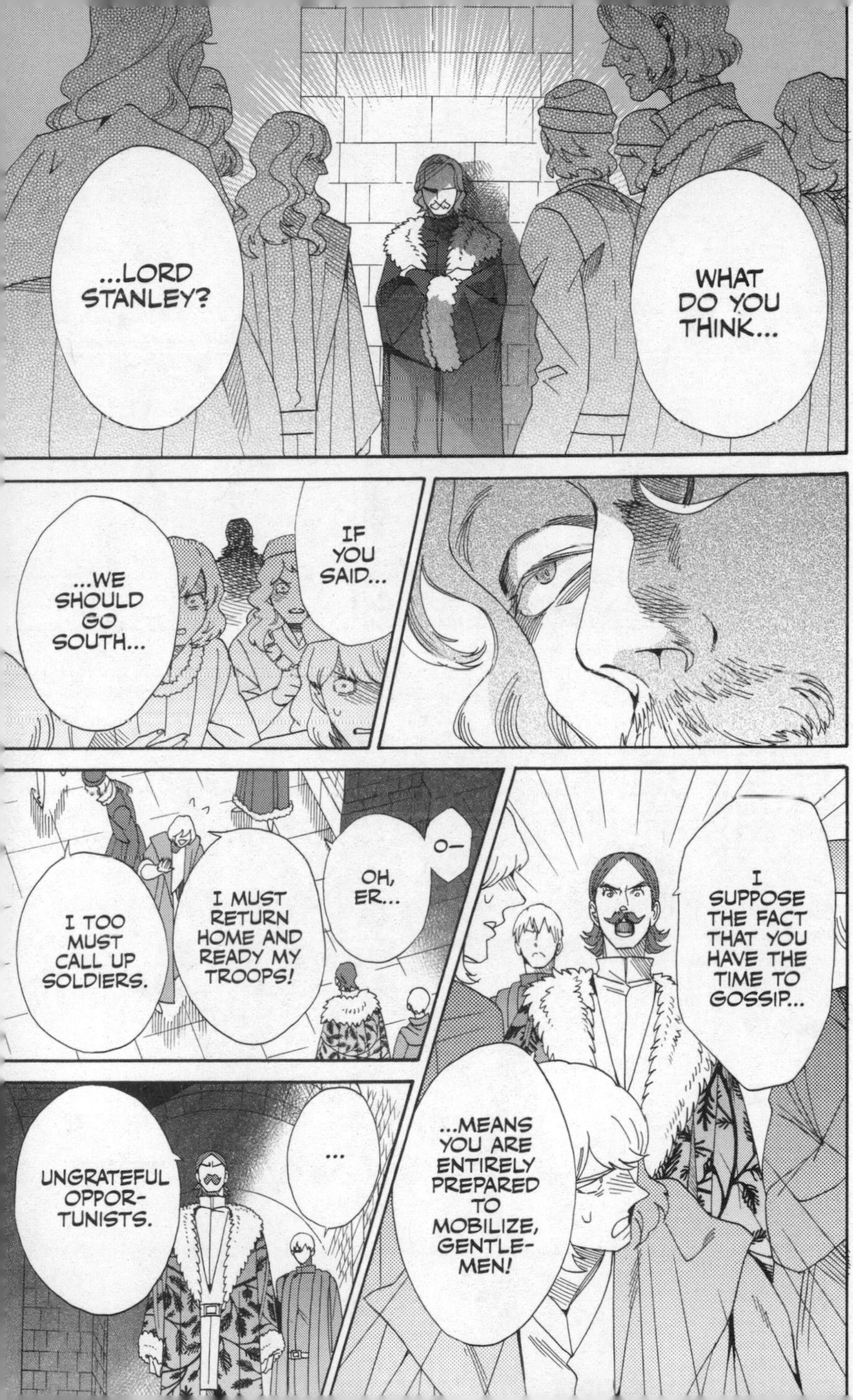
WHAT DO YOU THINK...
...LORD STANLEY?
IF YOU SAID...
...WE SHOULD GO SOUTH...
I SUPPOSE THE FACT THAT YOU HAVE THE TIME TO GOSSIP...
...MEANS YOU ARE ENTIRELY PREPARED TO MOBILIZE, GENTLEMEN!
O—
OH, ER...
I MUST RETURN HOME AND READY MY TROOPS!
I TOO MUST CALL UP SOLDIERS.
...
UNGRATEFUL OPPOR-TUNISTS.

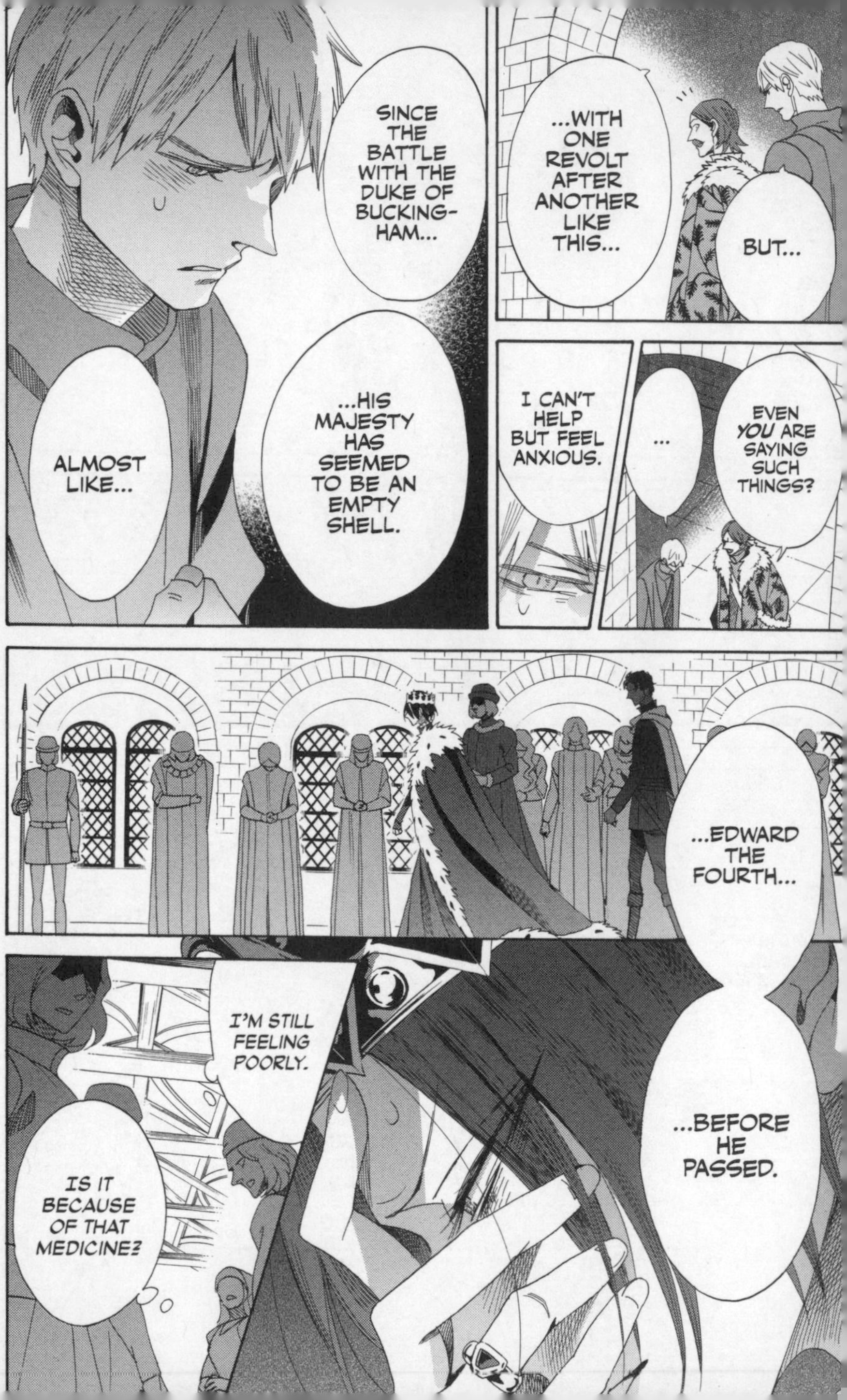
BUT...
...WITH ONE REVOLT AFTER ANOTHER LIKE THIS...
EVEN *YOU* ARE SAYING SUCH THINGS?
...
I CAN'T HELP BUT FEEL ANXIOUS.
SINCE THE BATTLE WITH THE DUKE OF BUCKING-HAM...
...HIS MAJESTY HAS SEEMED TO BE AN EMPTY SHELL.
ALMOST LIKE...
...EDWARD THE FOURTH...
...BEFORE HE PASSED.
I'M STILL FEELING POORLY.
IS IT BECAUSE OF THAT MEDICINE?

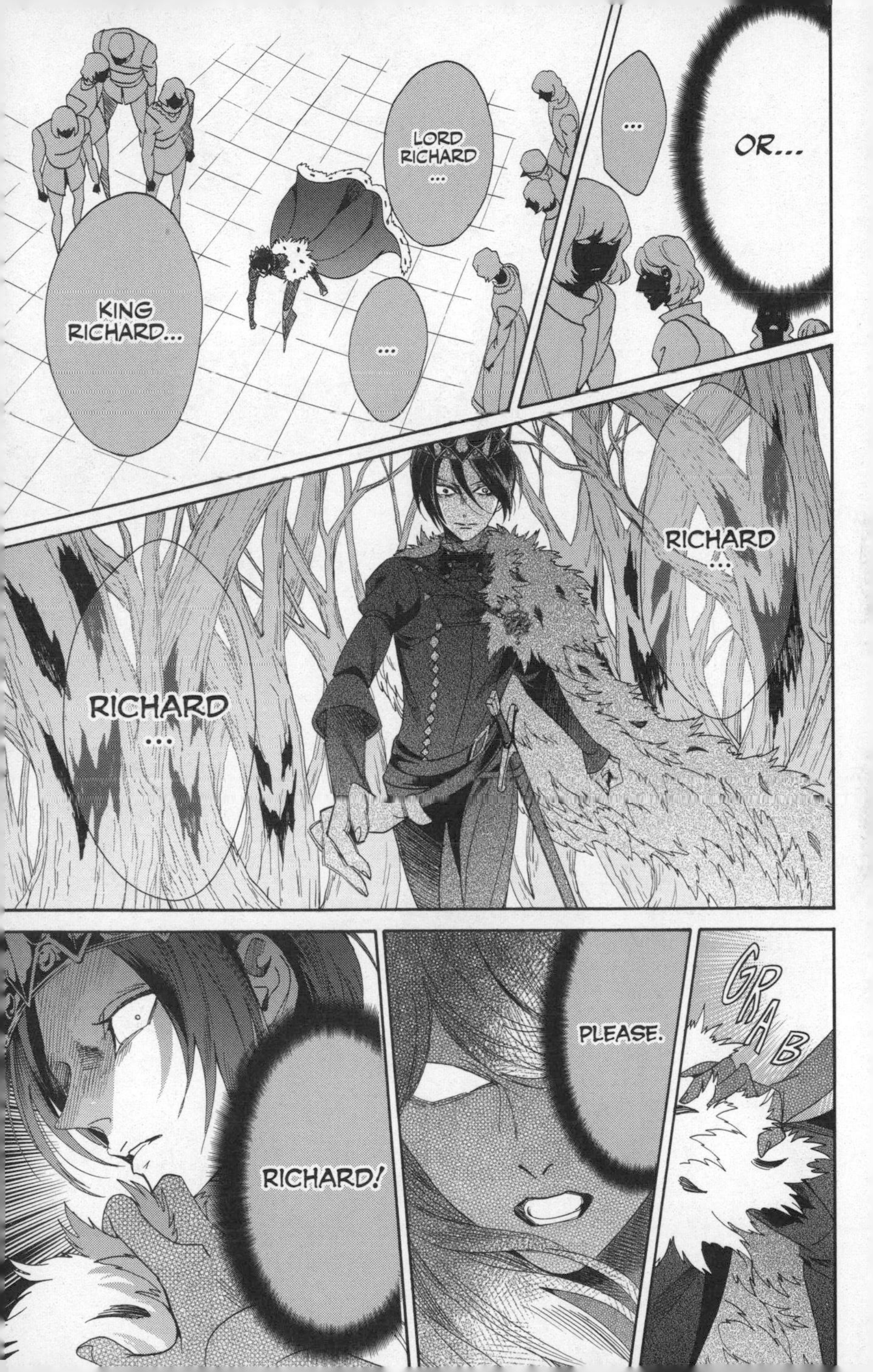
OR...
...
LORD RICHARD ...
...
KING RICHARD...
RICHARD ...
RICHARD ...
GRAB
PLEASE.
RICHARD!

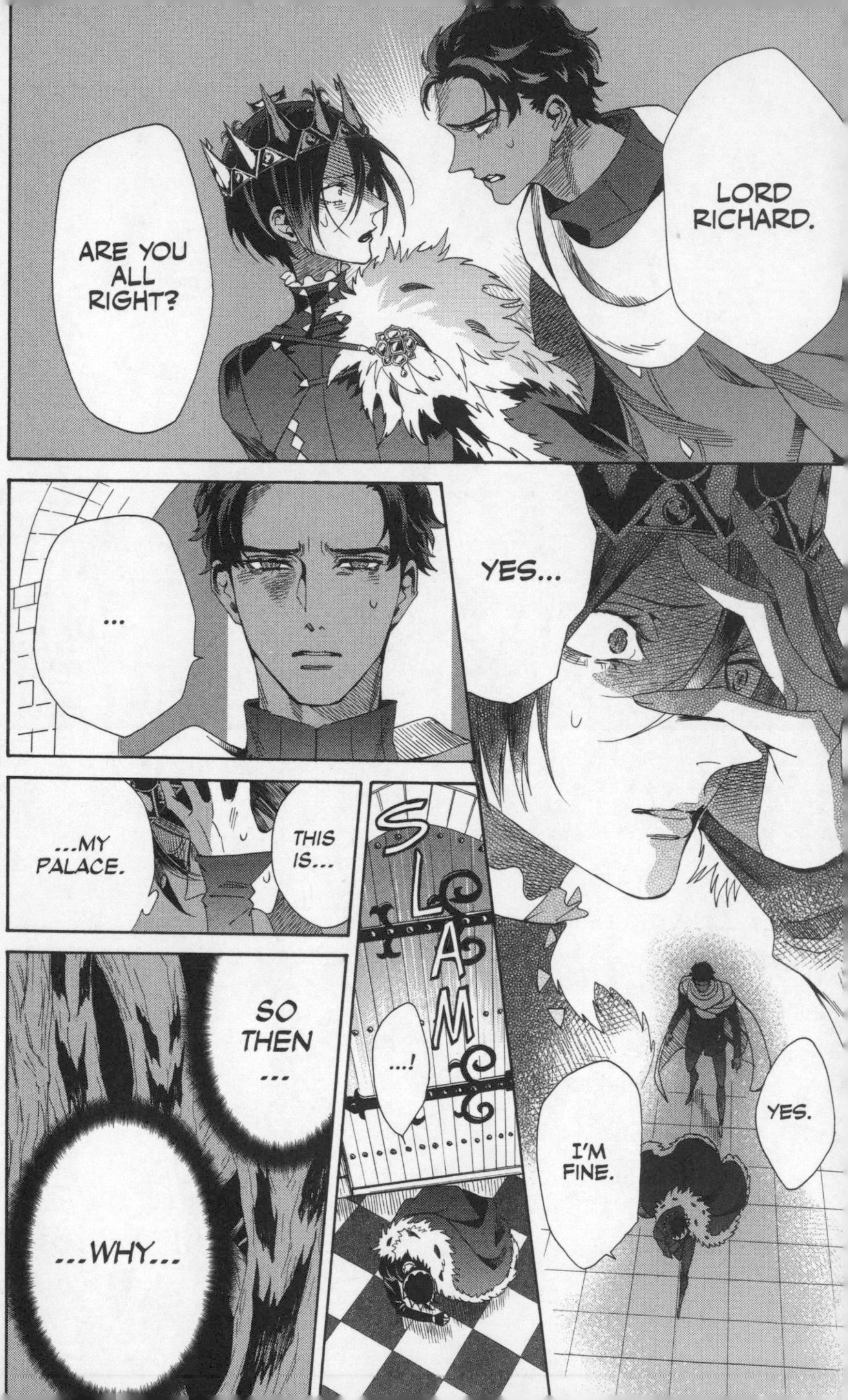
LORD RICHARD.
ARE YOU ALL RIGHT?
YES...
YES.
I'M FINE.
...
SLAM
...!
THIS IS...
...MY PALACE.
SO THEN ...
...WHY...

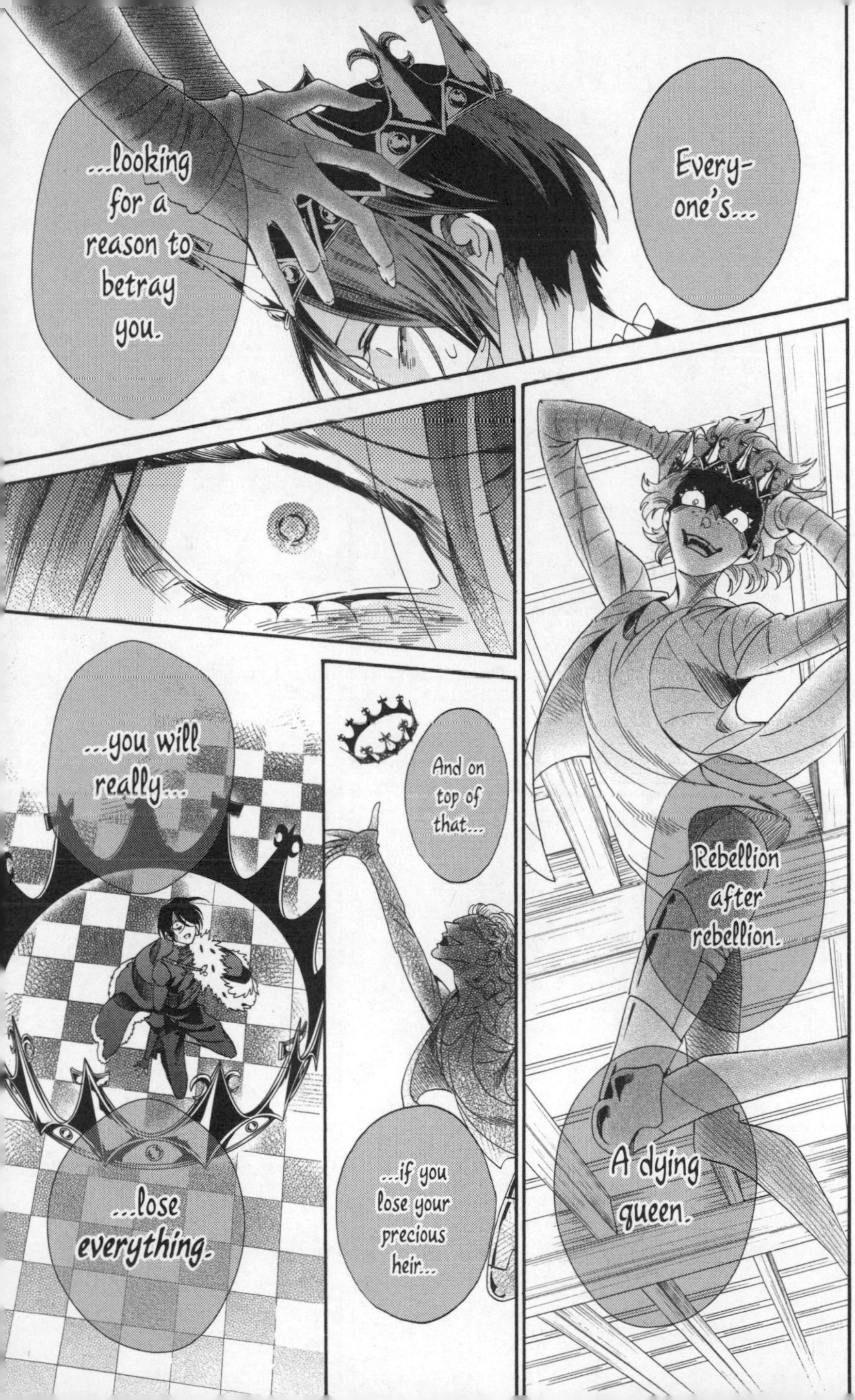
Every-one's...
...looking for a reason to betray you.
Rebellion after rebellion.
A dying queen.
And on top of that...
...if you lose your precious heir...
...you will really...
...lose everything.

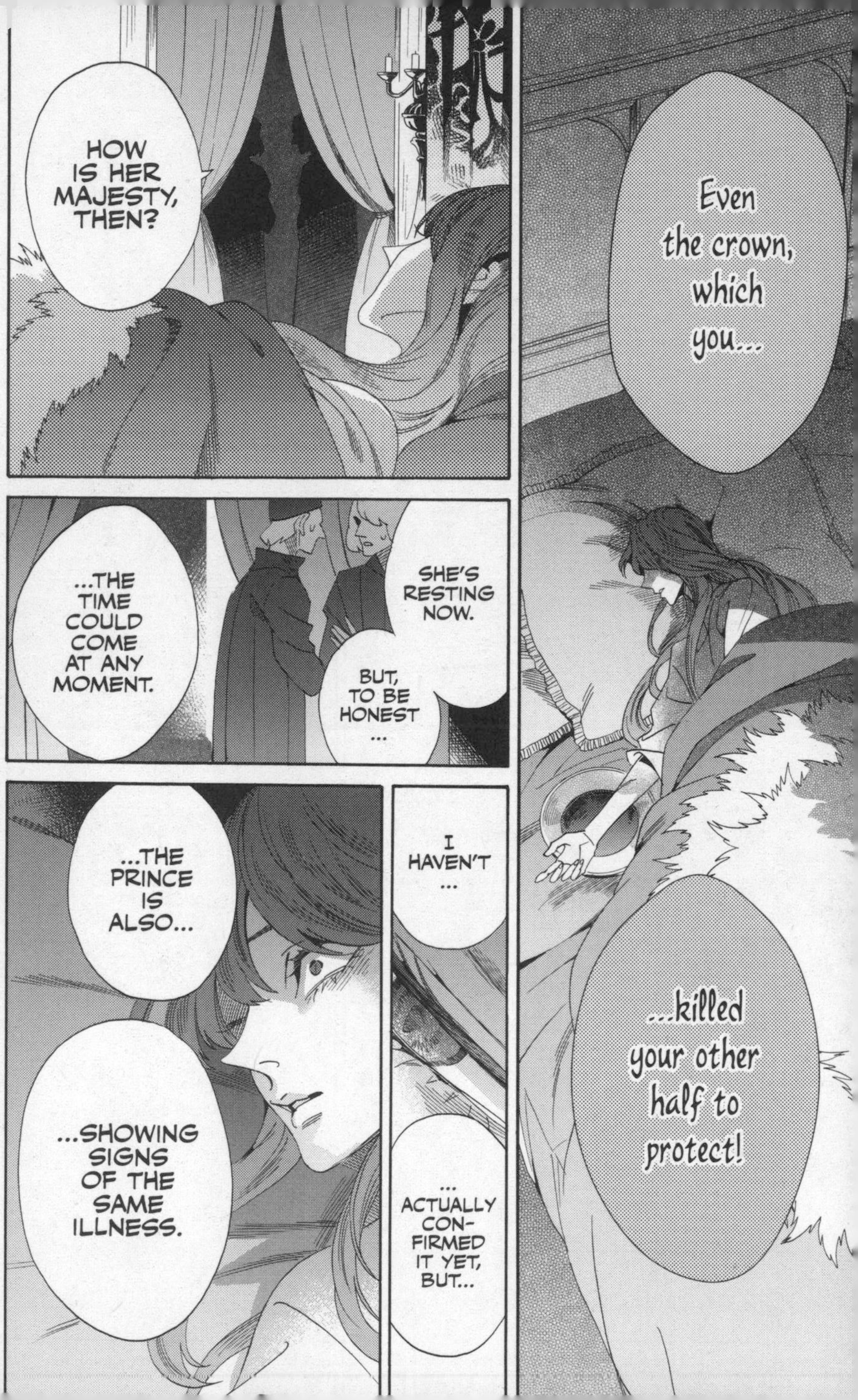
Even the crown, which you...
...killed your other half to protect!
HOW IS HER MAJESTY, THEN?
SHE'S RESTING NOW.
BUT, TO BE HONEST...
...THE TIME COULD COME AT ANY MOMENT.
I HAVEN'T...
...ACTUALLY CON-FIRMED IT YET, BUT...
...THE PRINCE IS ALSO...
...SHOWING SIGNS OF THE SAME ILLNESS.

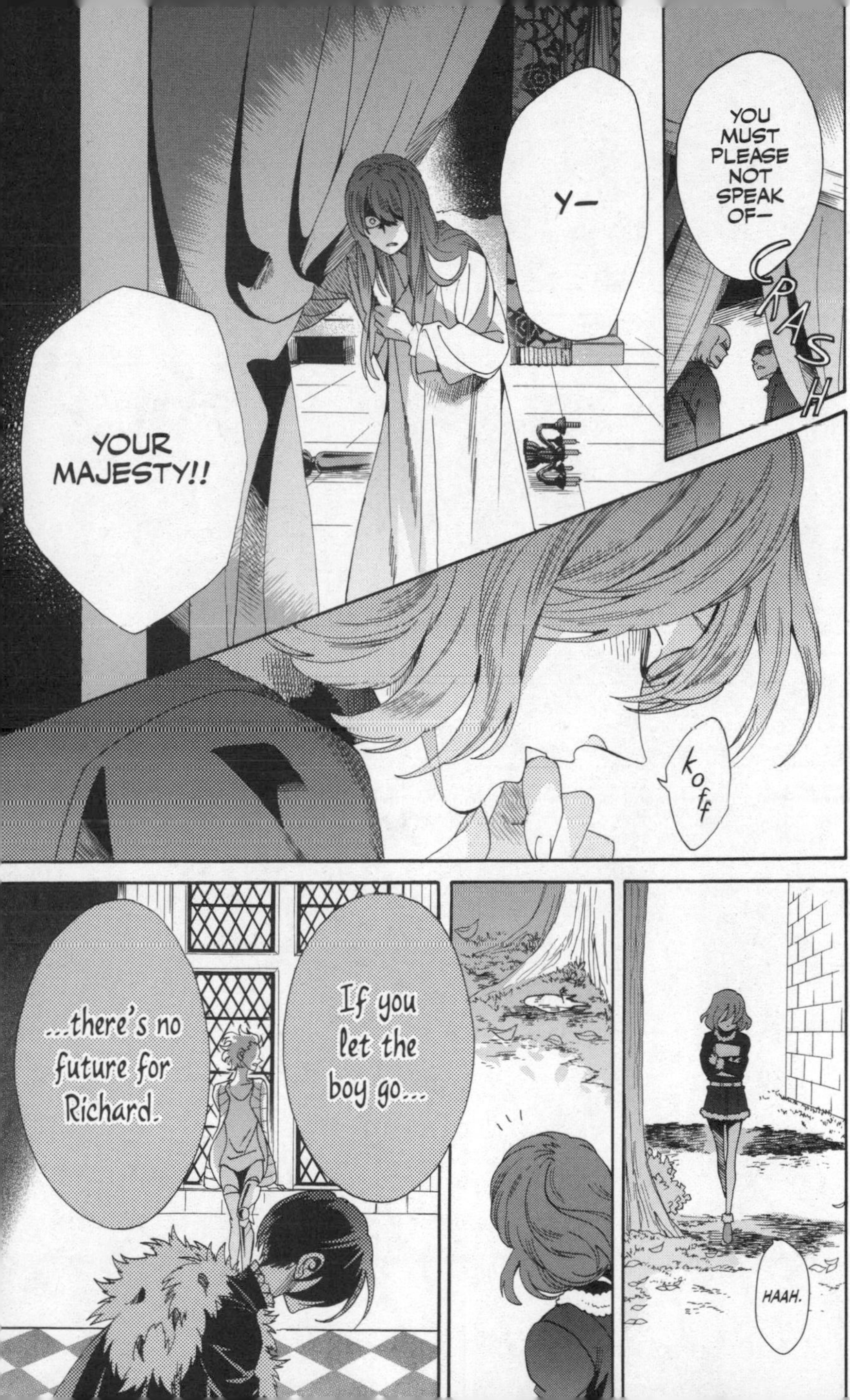
YOU MUST PLEASE NOT SPEAK OF—
CRASH
Y—
YOUR MAJESTY!!
koff
HAAH.
If you let the boy go...
...there's no future for Richard.

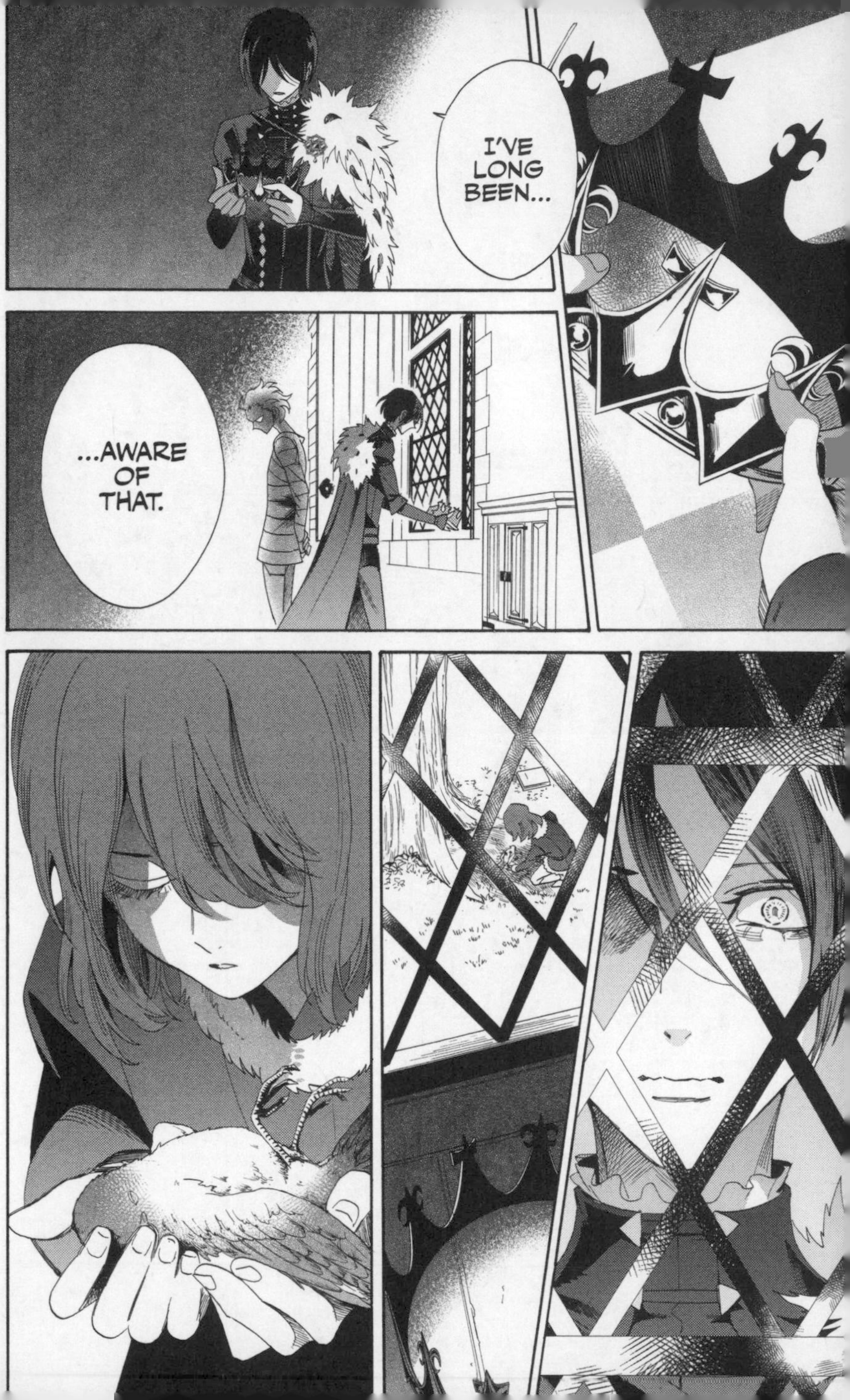
I'VE LONG BEEN...
...AWARE OF THAT.

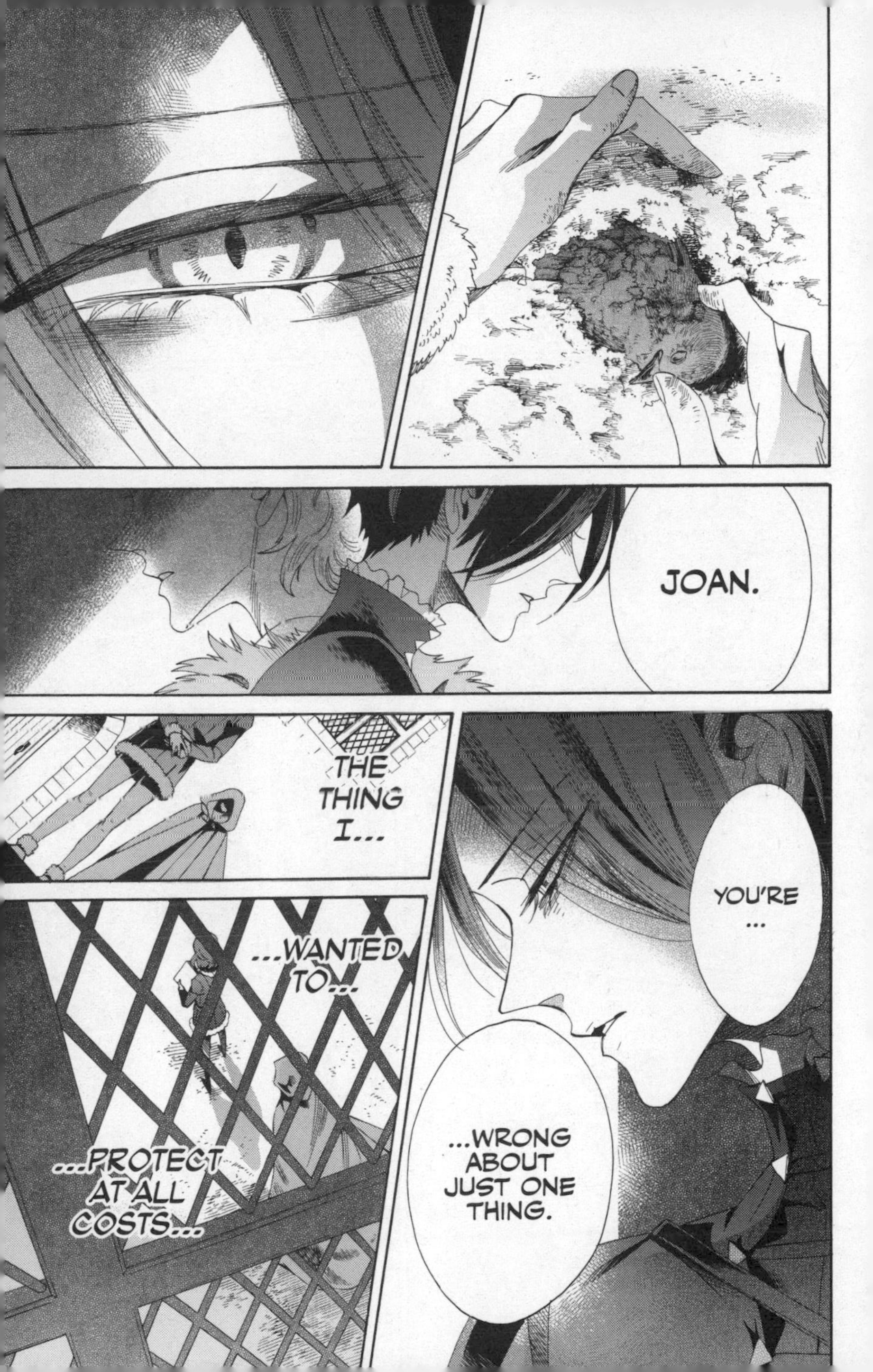
JOAN.
YOU'RE ...
...WRONG ABOUT JUST ONE THING.
THE THING I...
...WANTED TO...
...PROTECT AT ALL COSTS...

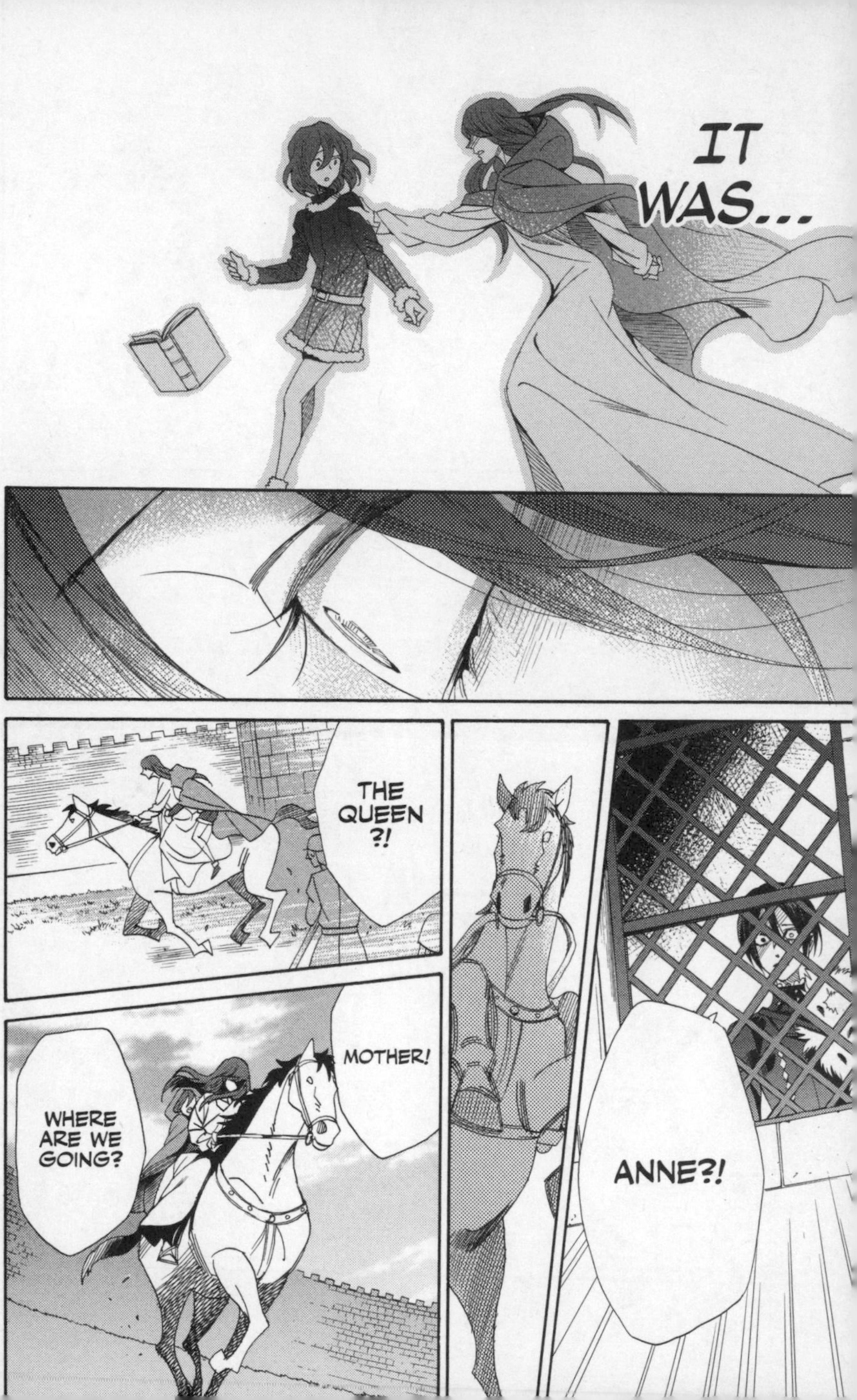
IT WAS...
ANNE?!
THE QUEEN?!
MOTHER!
WHERE ARE WE GOING?

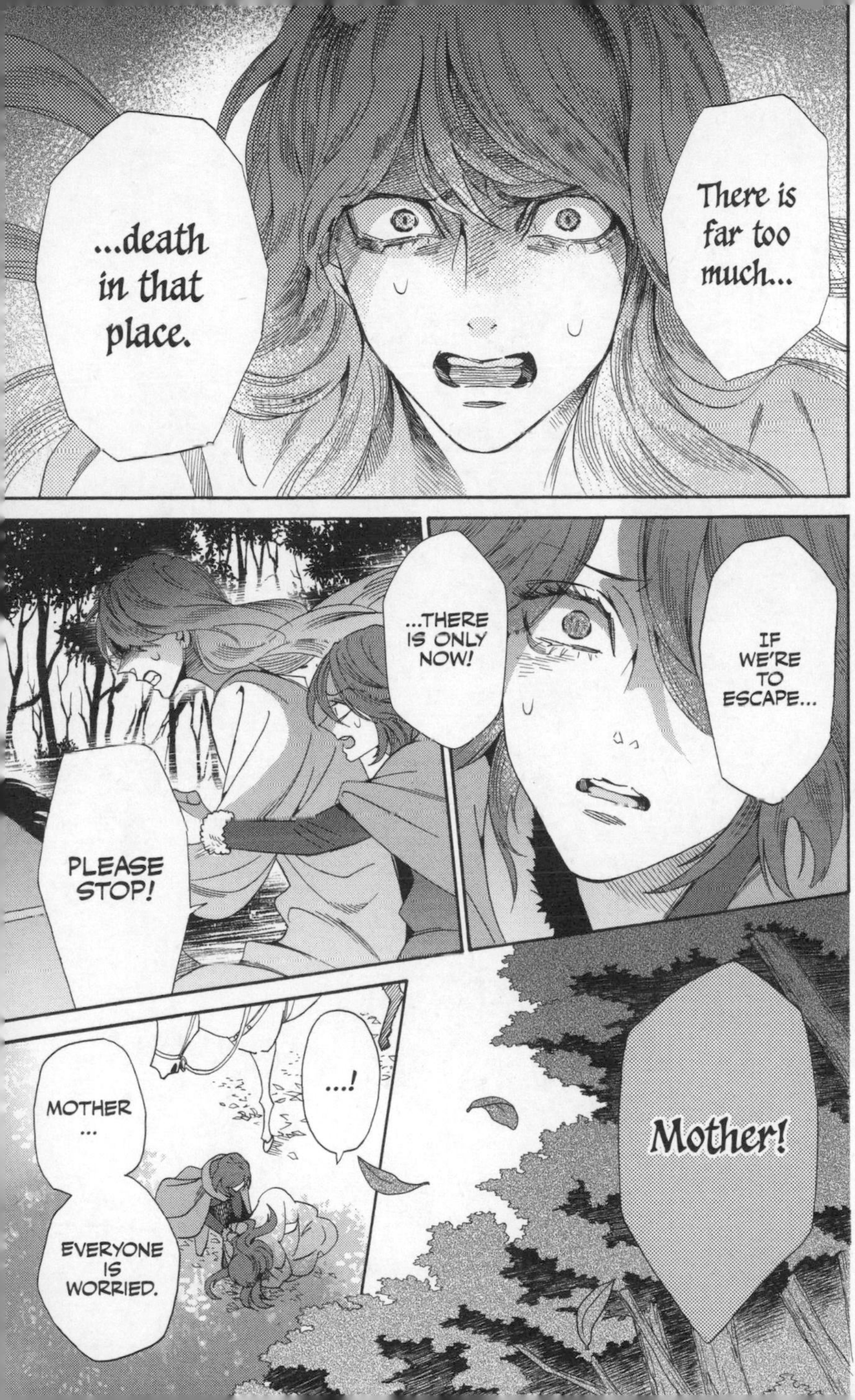
There is far too much...
...death in that place.
IF WE'RE TO ESCAPE...
...THERE IS ONLY NOW!
PLEASE STOP!
Mother!
...!
MOTHER ...
EVERYONE IS WORRIED.

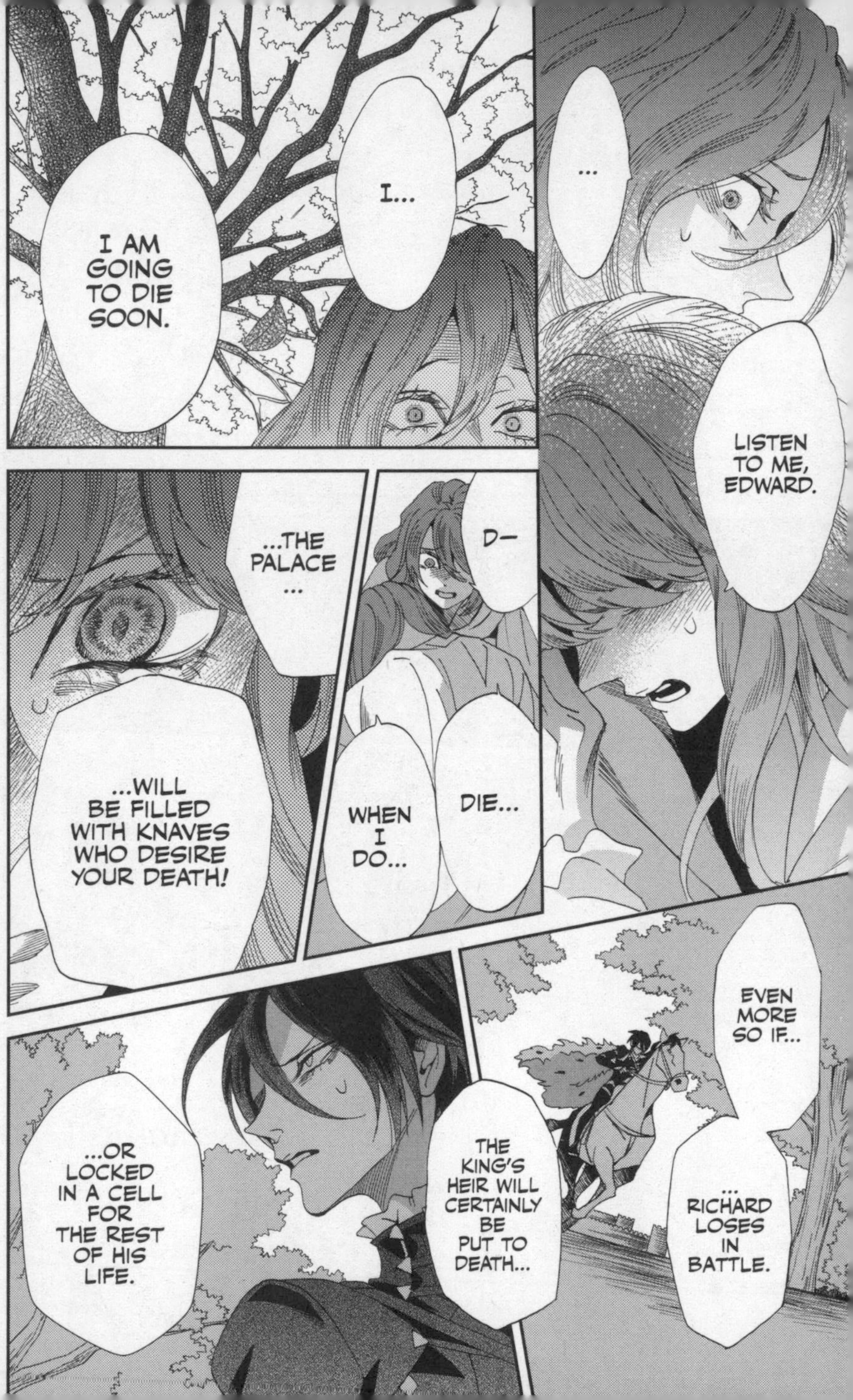
...
LISTEN TO ME, EDWARD.
I...
I AM GOING TO DIE SOON.
D—
DIE...
WHEN I DO...
...THE PALACE ...
...WILL BE FILLED WITH KNAVES WHO DESIRE YOUR DEATH!
EVEN MORE SO IF...
...RICHARD LOSES IN BATTLE.
THE KING'S HEIR WILL CERTAINLY BE PUT TO DEATH...
...OR LOCKED IN A CELL FOR THE REST OF HIS LIFE.

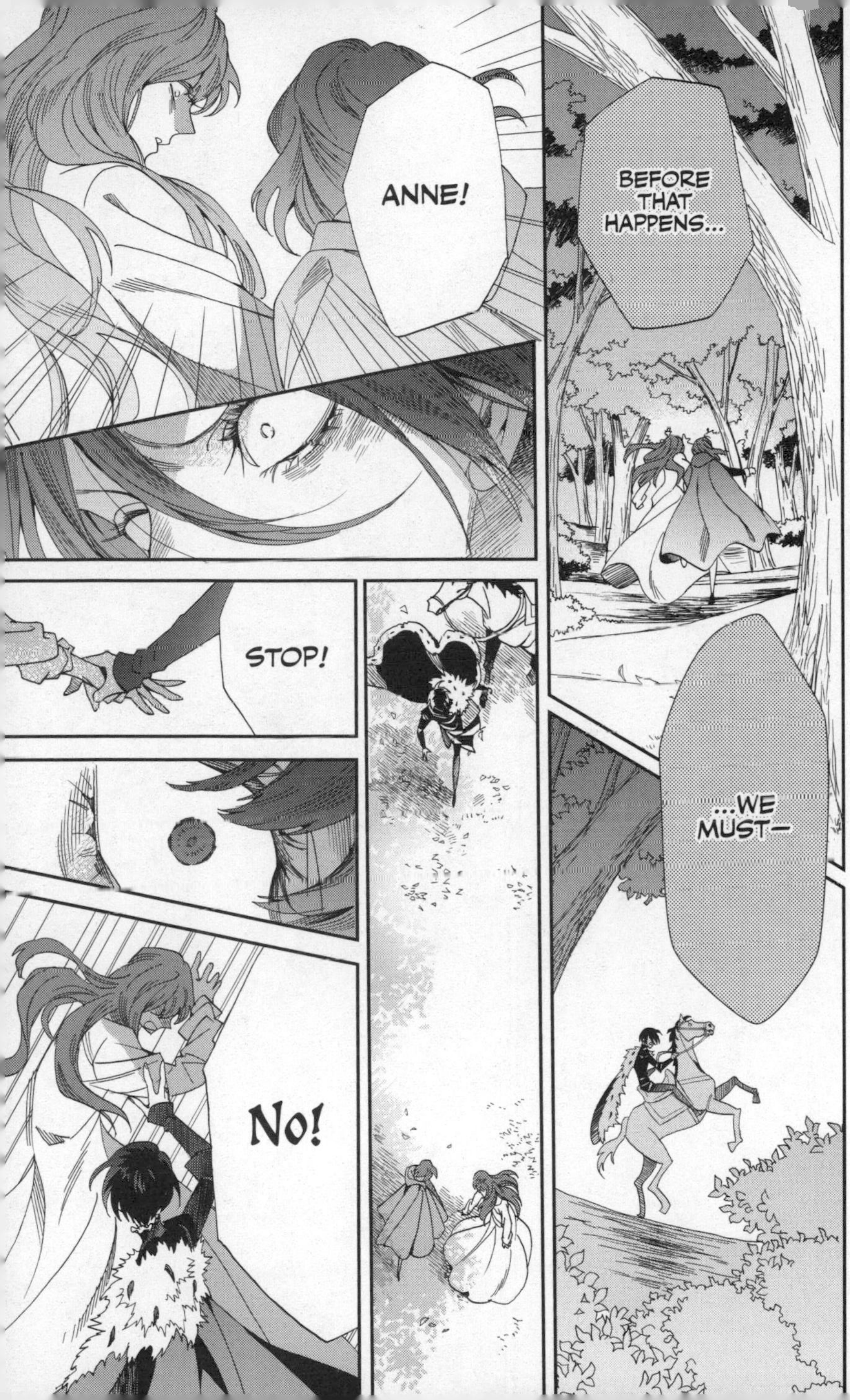
BEFORE THAT HAPPENS...
...WE MUST—
ANNE!
STOP!
No!

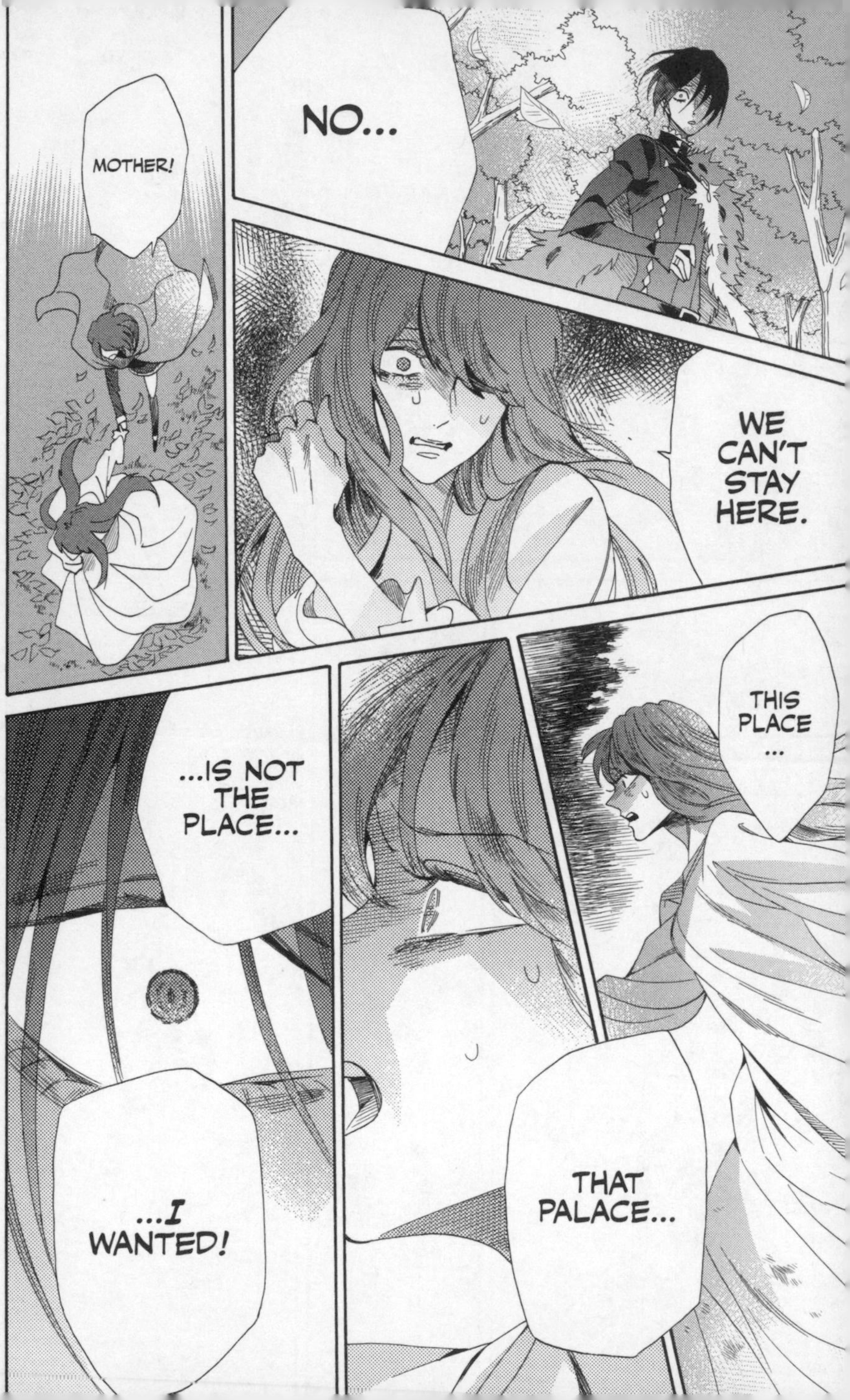
NO...
WE CAN'T STAY HERE.
MOTHER!
THIS PLACE...
THAT PALACE...
...IS NOT THE PLACE...
...I WANTED!

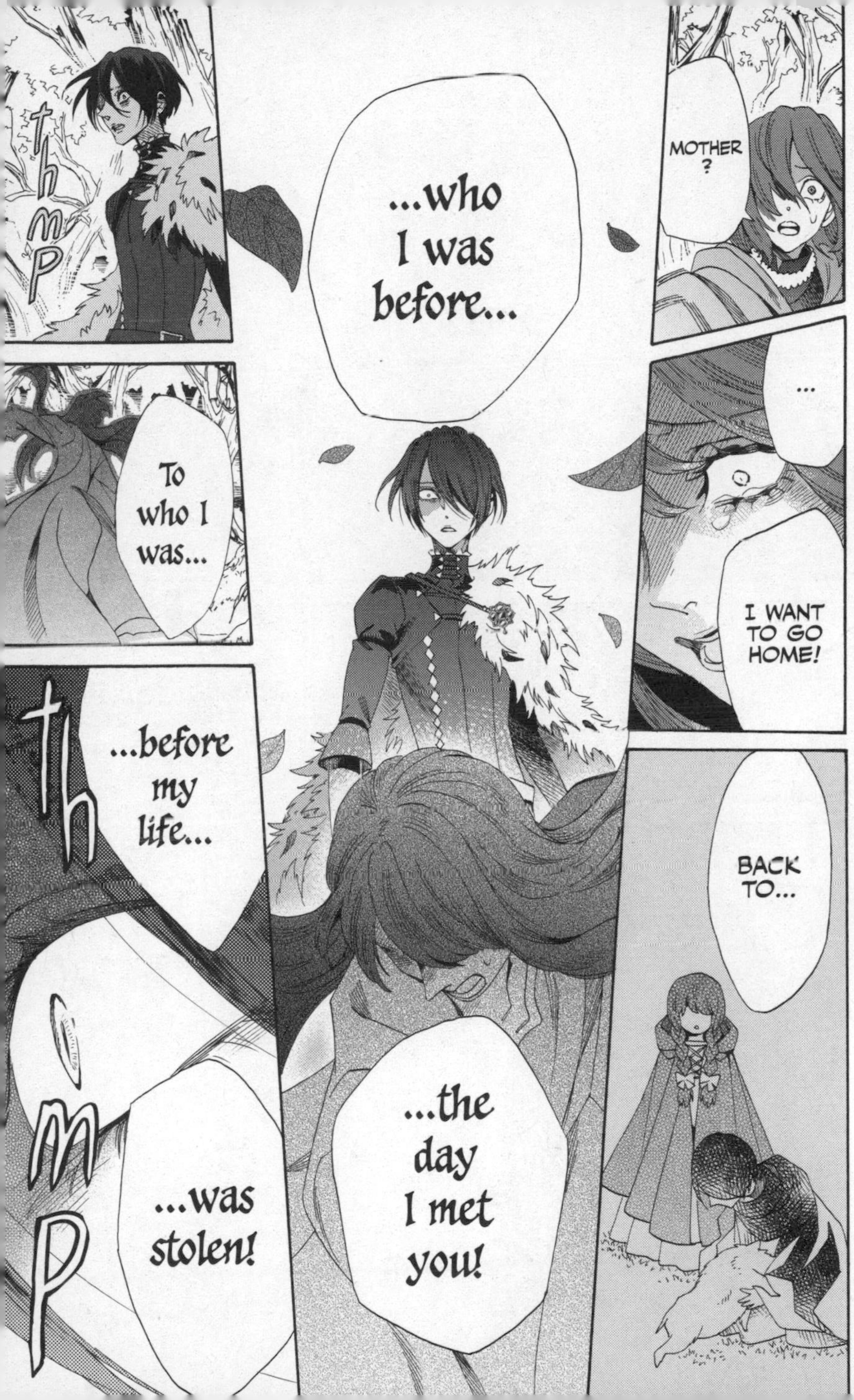
MOTHER?
...
I WANT TO GO HOME!
BACK TO...
...who I was before...
...the day I met you!
thmp
To who I was...
...before my life...
...was stolen!
thmp

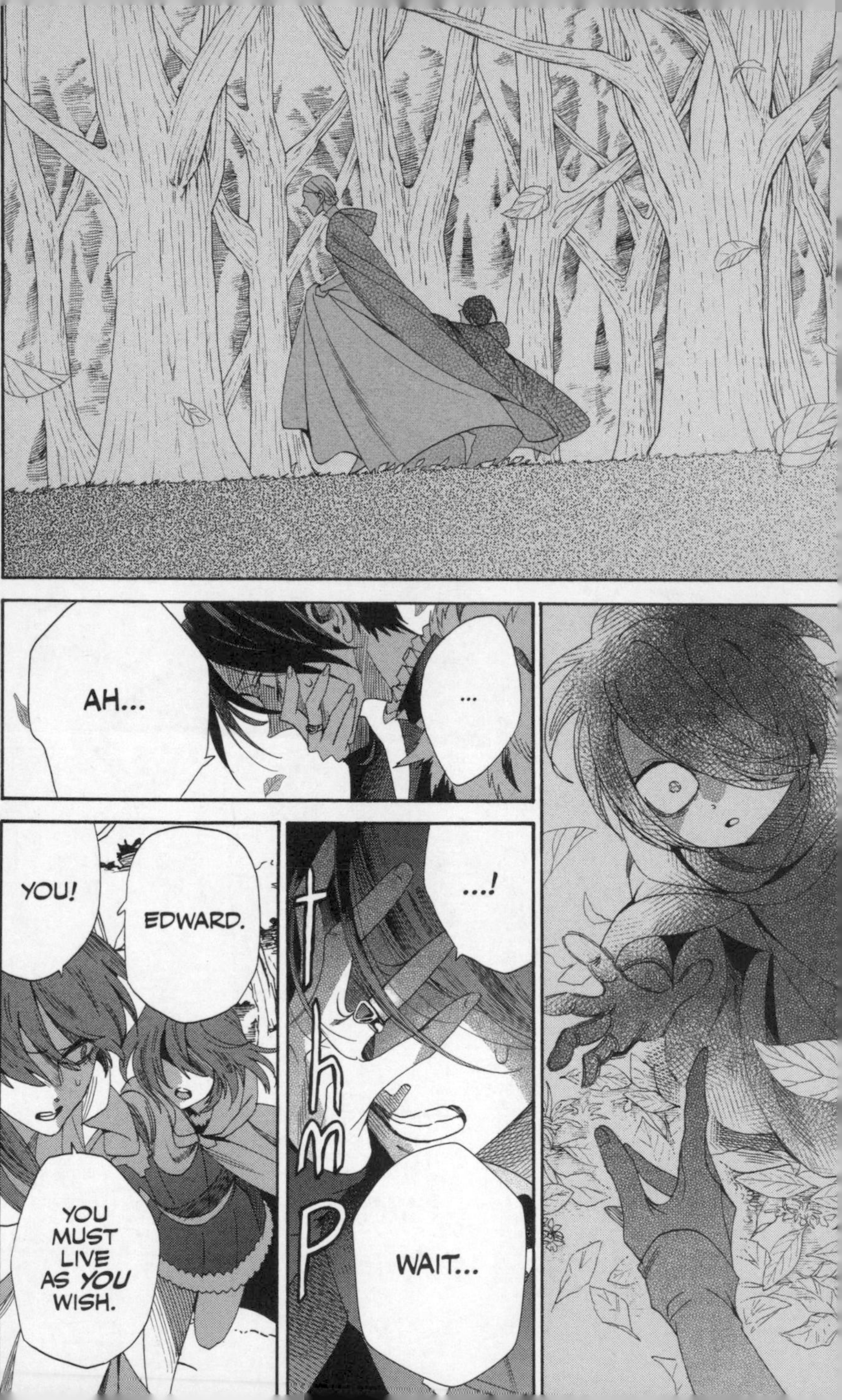
...
AH...
...!
thmp
WAIT...
EDWARD.
YOU!
YOU MUST LIVE AS *YOU* WISH.

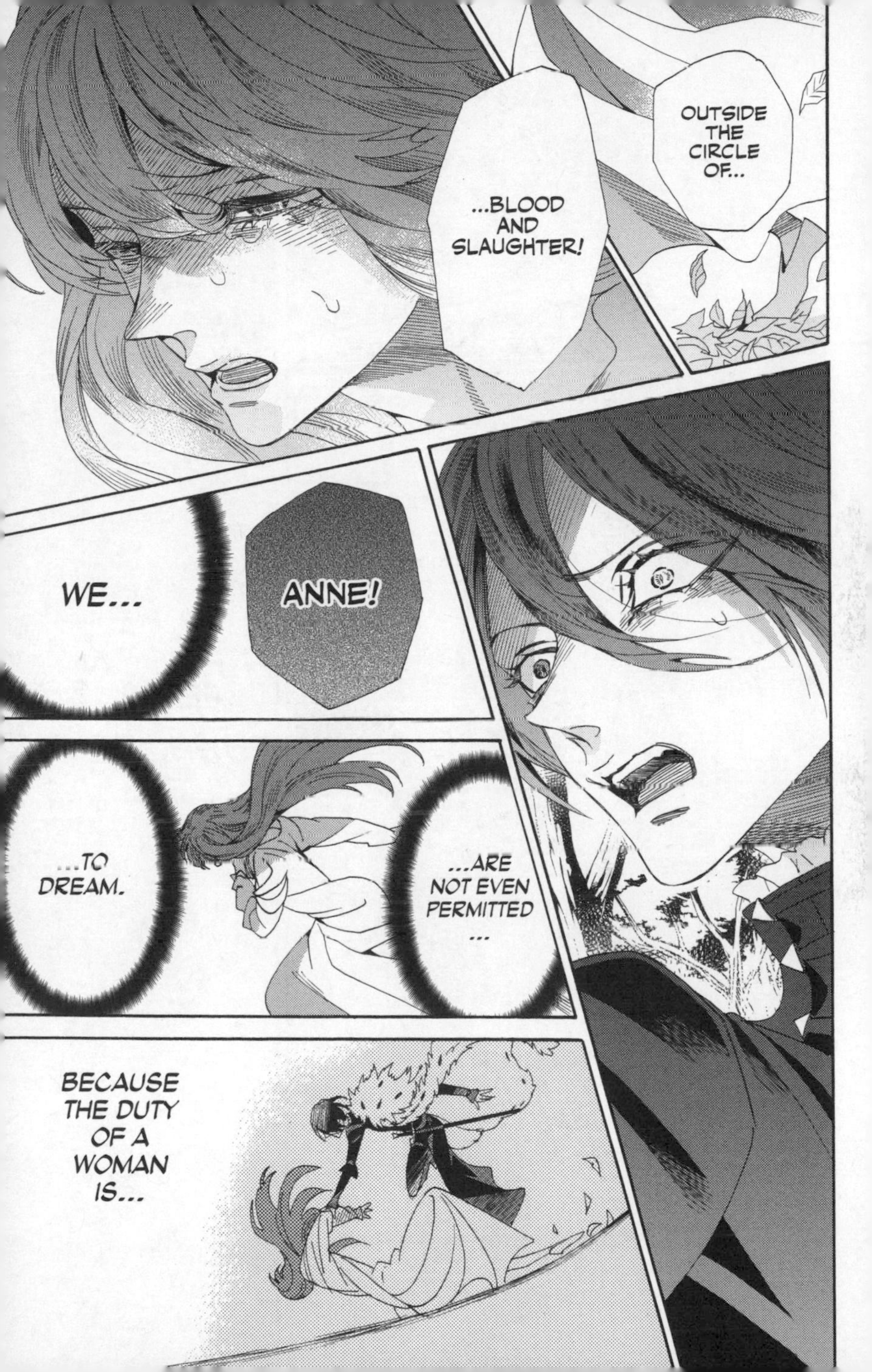
OUTSIDE THE CIRCLE OF...
...BLOOD AND SLAUGHTER!
ANNE!
WE...
...ARE NOT EVEN PERMITTED ...
...TO DREAM.
BECAUSE THE DUTY OF A WOMAN IS...

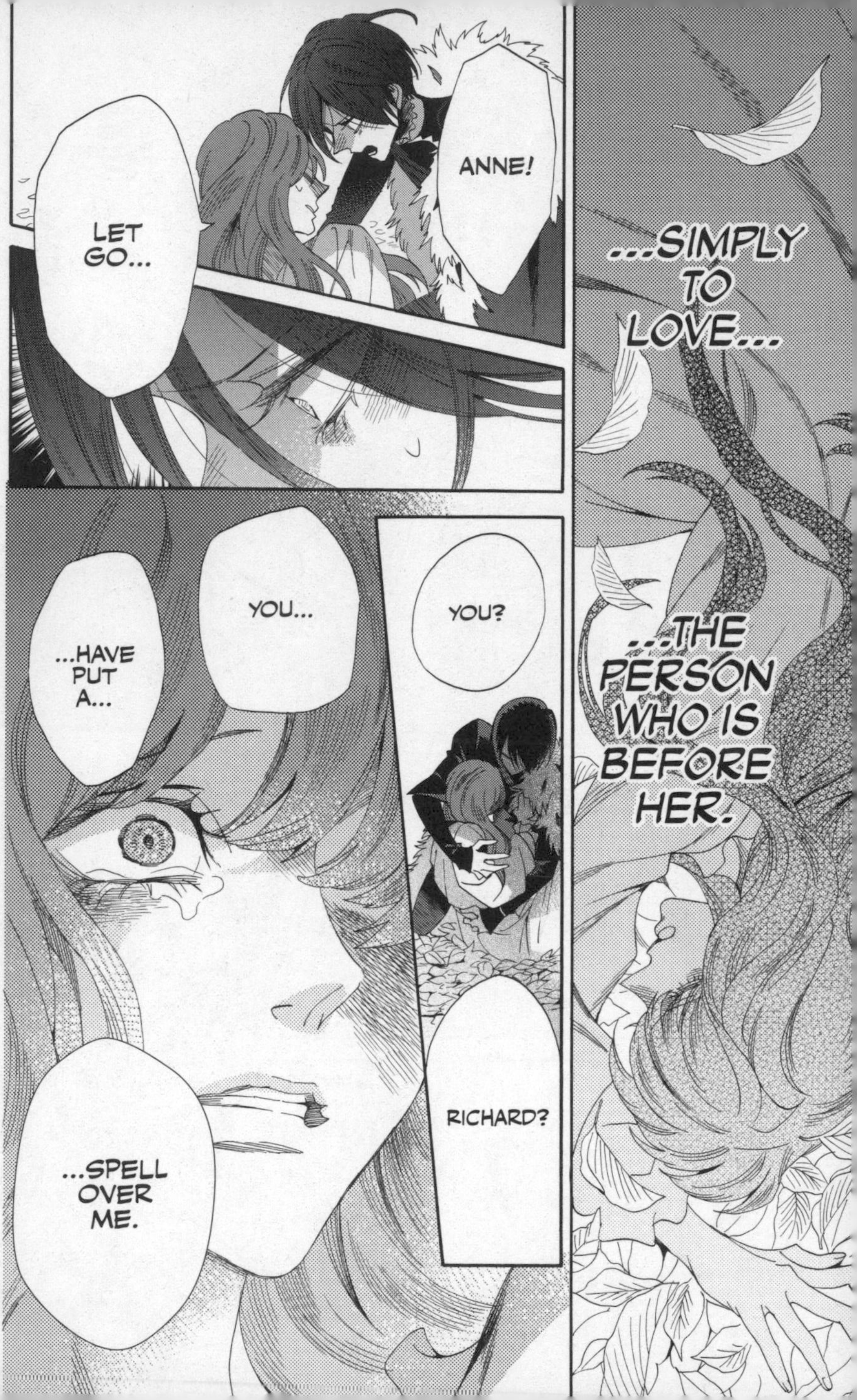
...SIMPLY TO LOVE...
...THE PERSON WHO IS BEFORE HER.
ANNE!
LET GO...
YOU?
RICHARD?
YOU...
...HAVE PUT A...
...SPELL OVER ME.

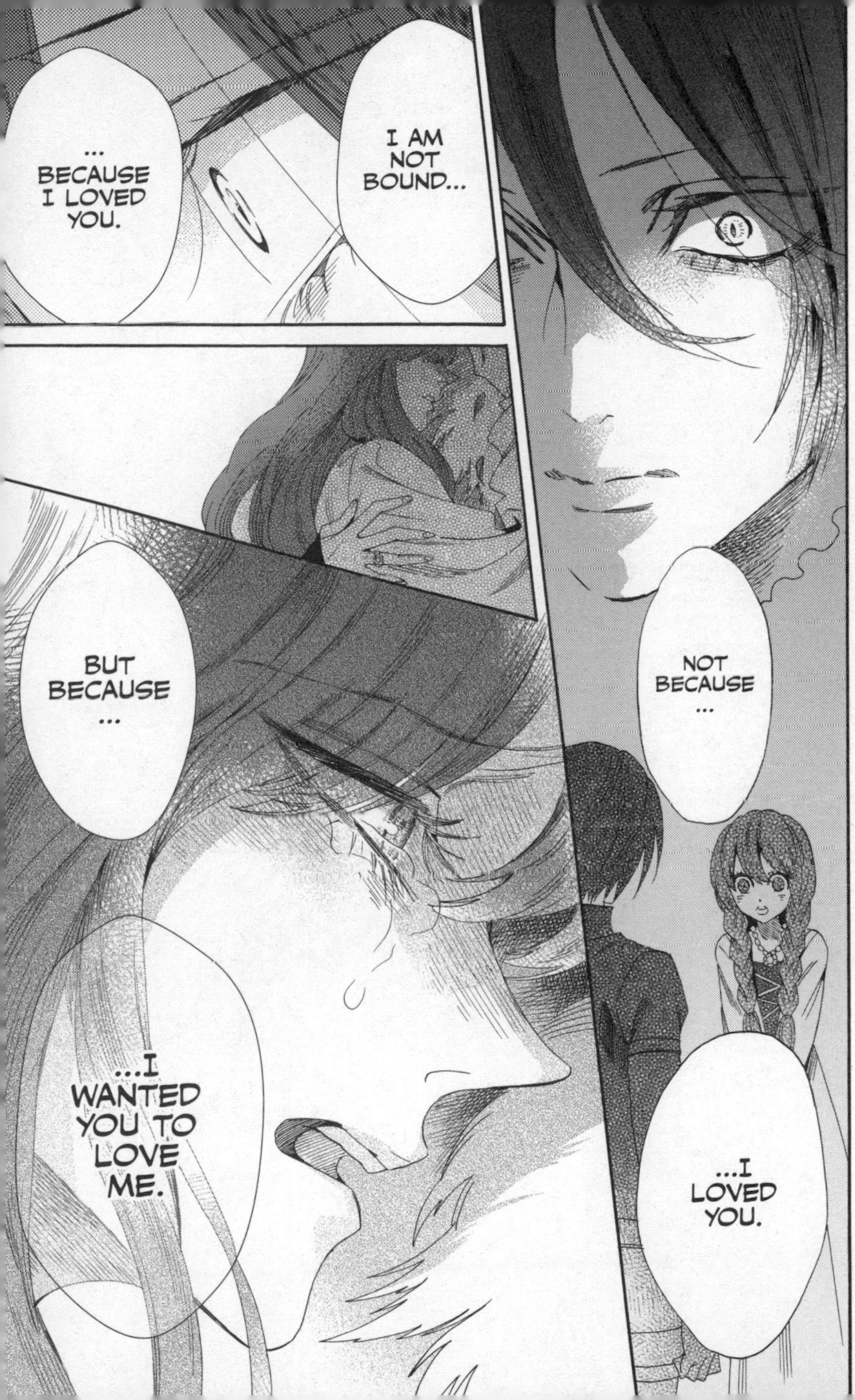
I AM NOT BOUND...
... BECAUSE I LOVED YOU.
NOT BECAUSE ...
...I LOVED YOU.
BUT BECAUSE ...
...I WANTED YOU TO LOVE ME.

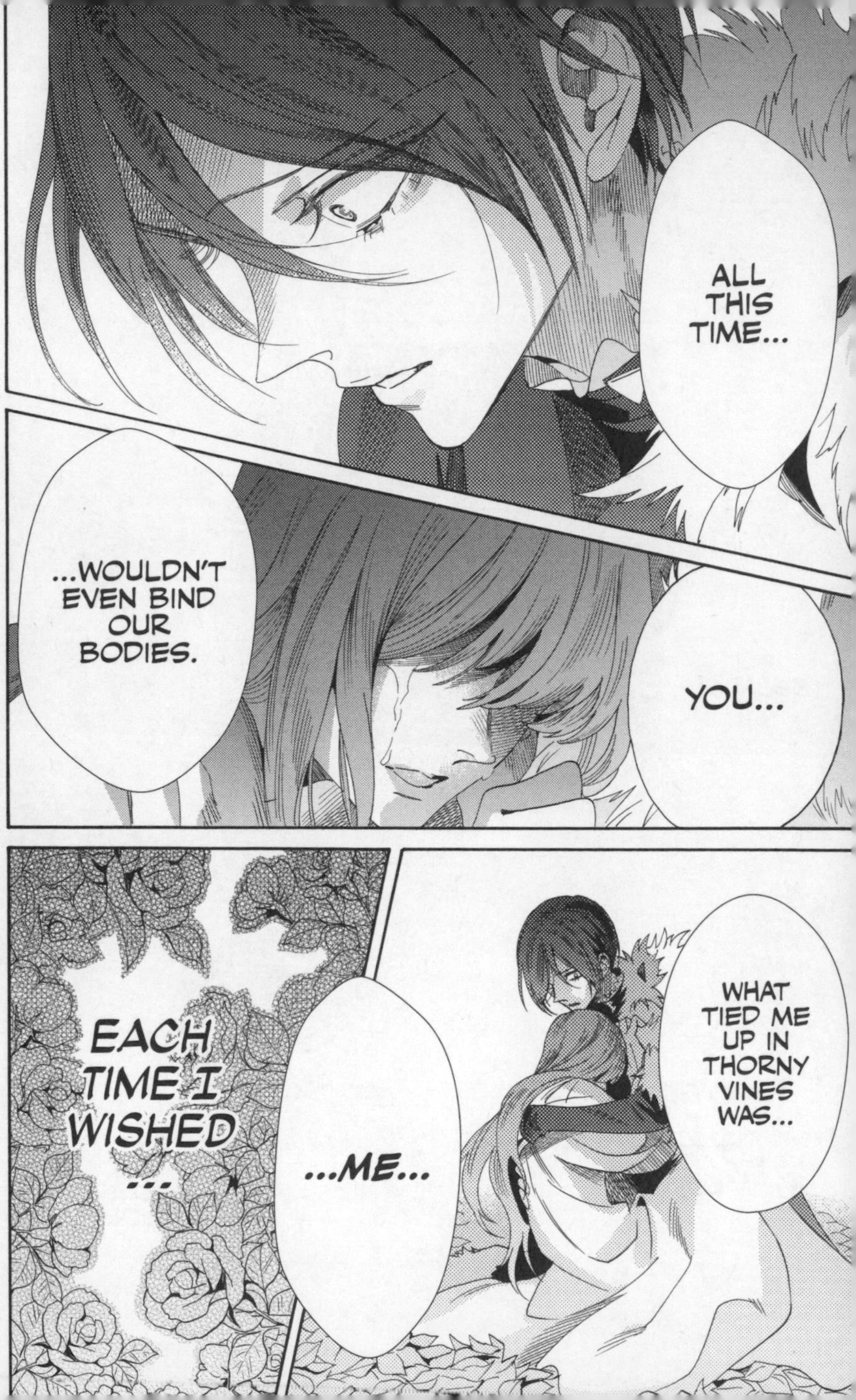
ALL THIS TIME...
YOU...
...WOULDN'T EVEN BIND OUR BODIES.
WHAT TIED ME UP IN THORNY VINES WAS...
...ME...
EACH TIME I WISHED ...

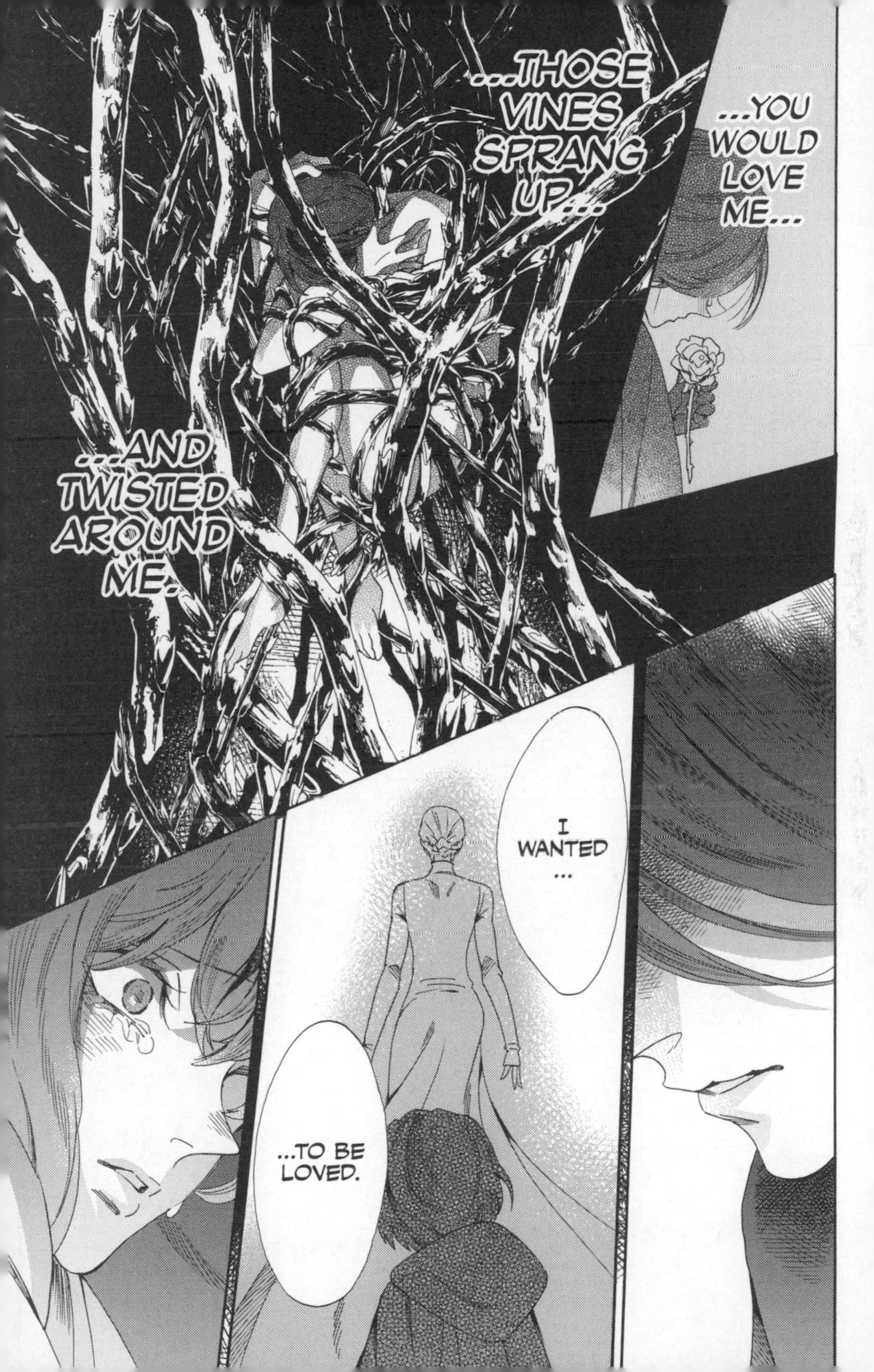
...YOU WOULD LOVE ME...
...THOSE VINES SPRANG UP...
...AND TWISTED AROUND ME.
I WANTED...
...TO BE LOVED.

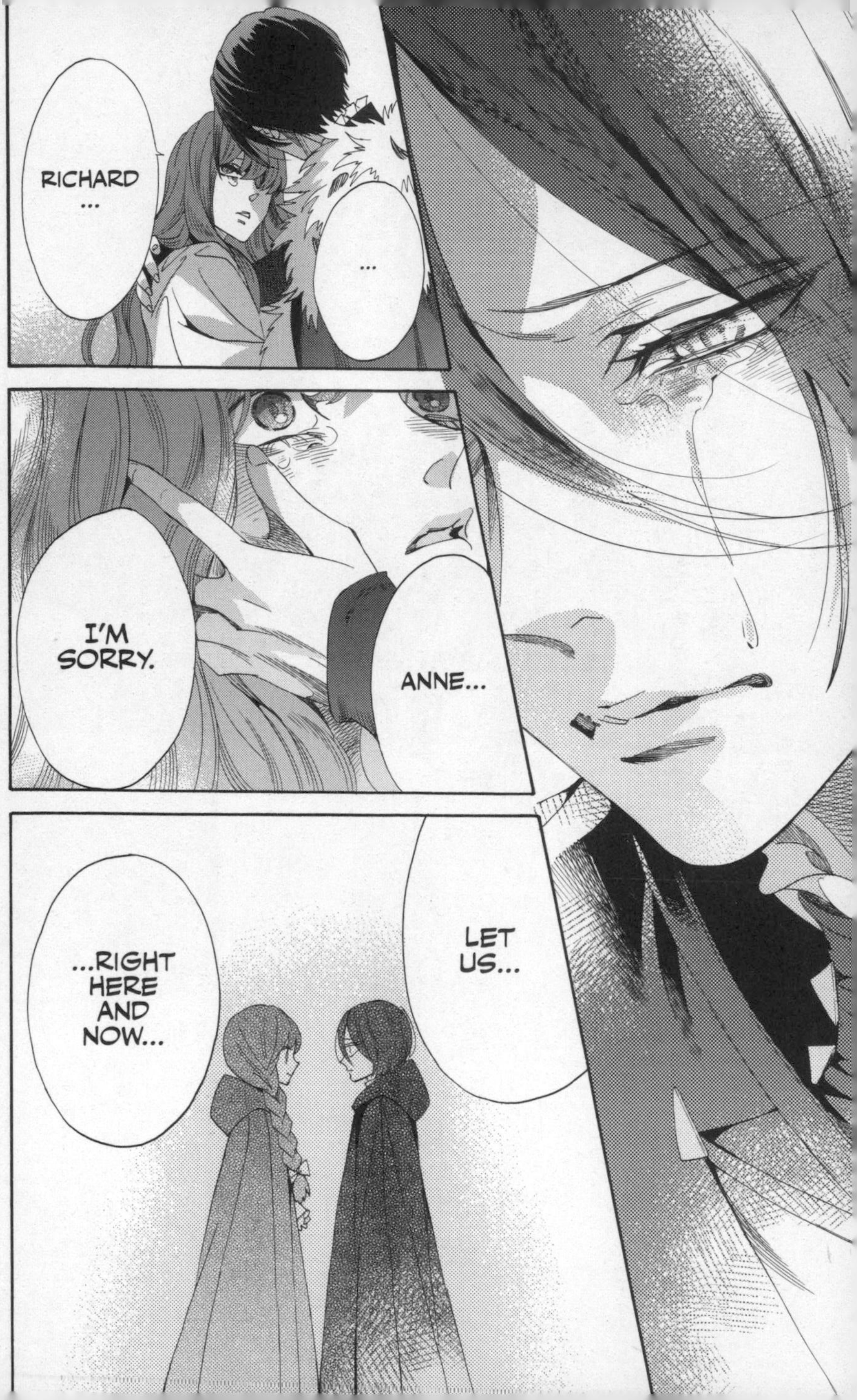
RICHARD ...
...
ANNE...
I'M SORRY.
LET US...
...RIGHT HERE AND NOW...

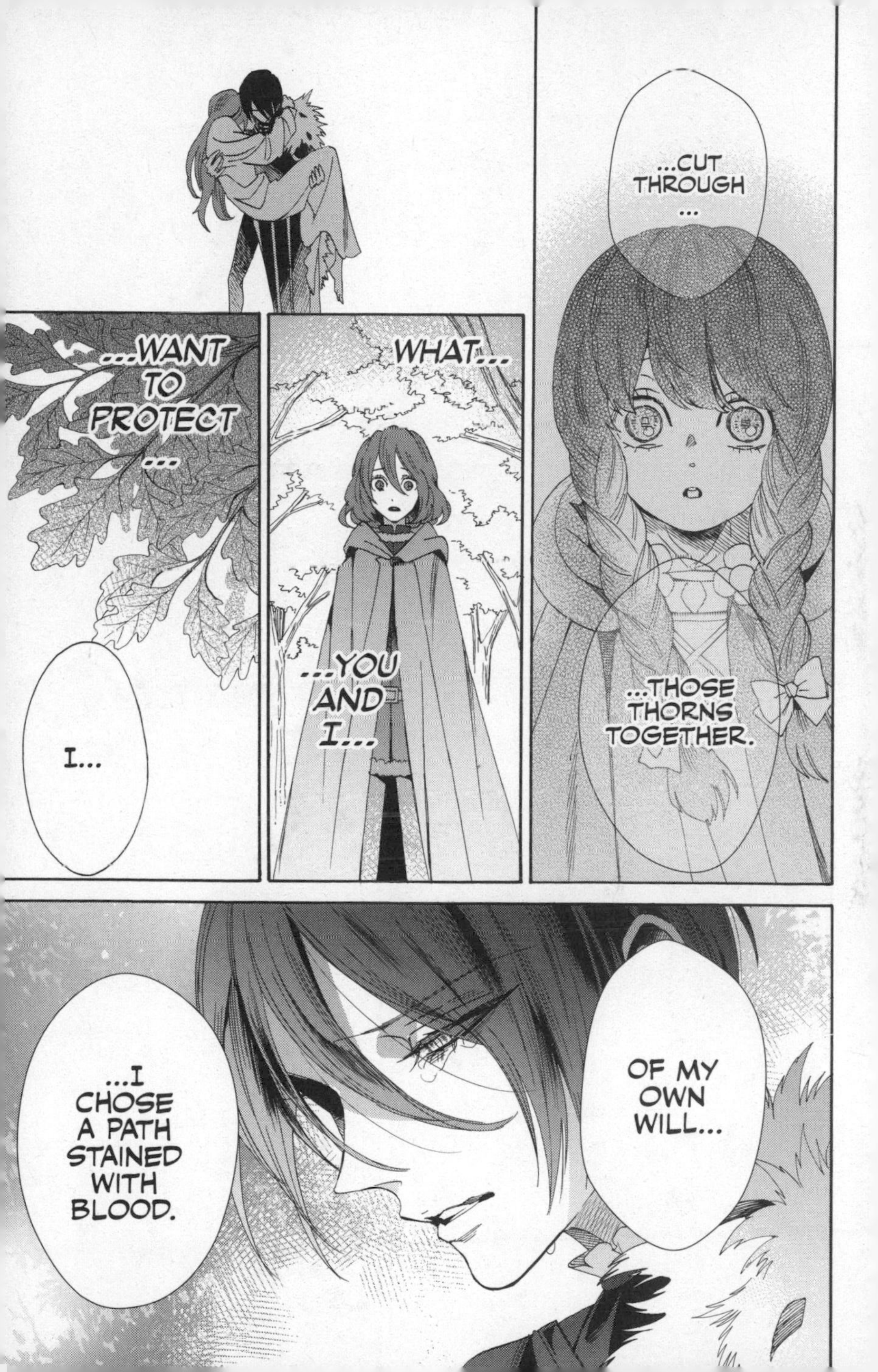
...CUT THROUGH ...
...THOSE THORNS TOGETHER.
WHAT...
...YOU AND I...
...WANT TO PROTECT ...
I...
OF MY OWN WILL...
...I CHOSE A PATH STAINED WITH BLOOD.

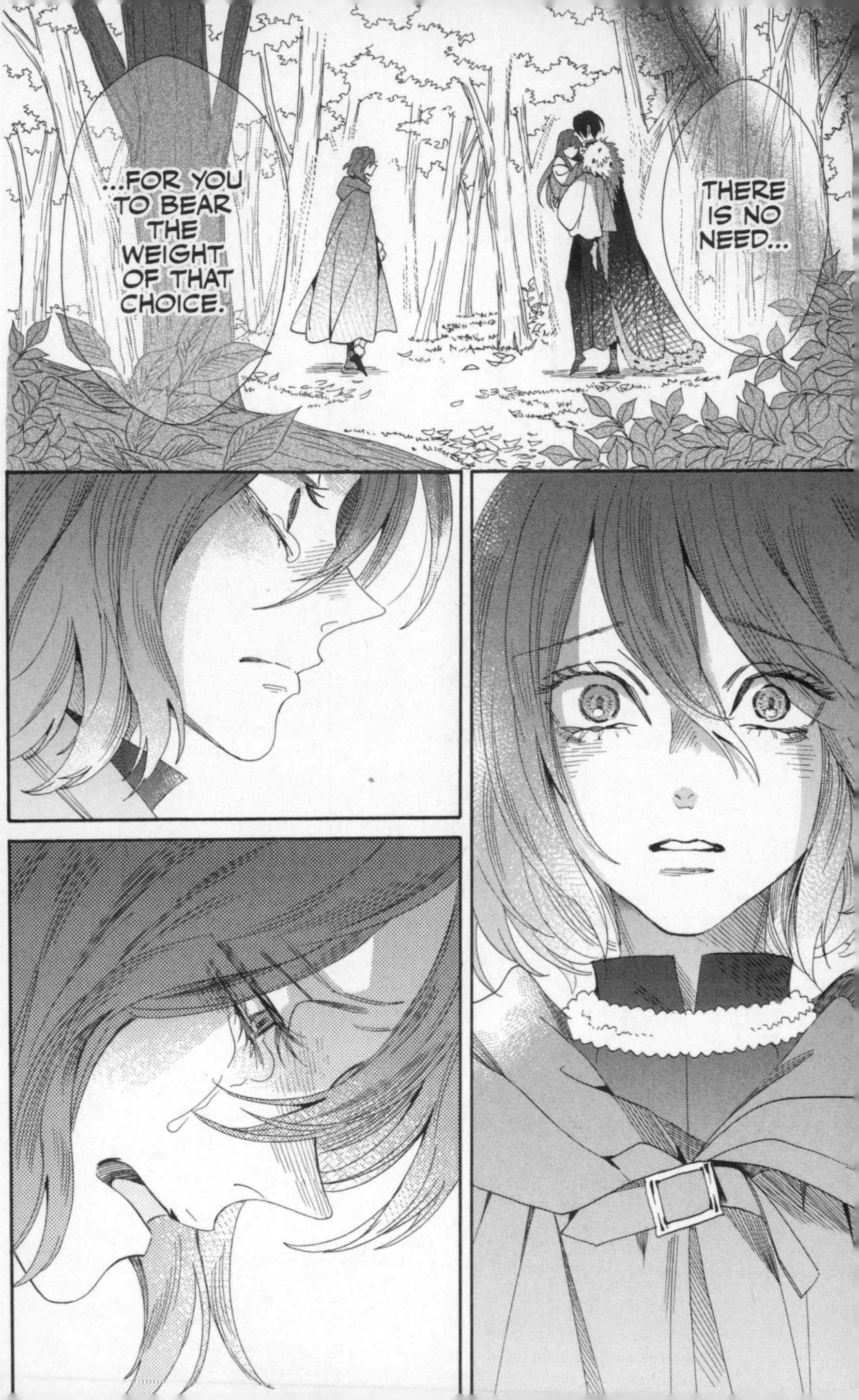
THERE IS NO NEED...
...FOR YOU TO BEAR THE WEIGHT OF THAT CHOICE.

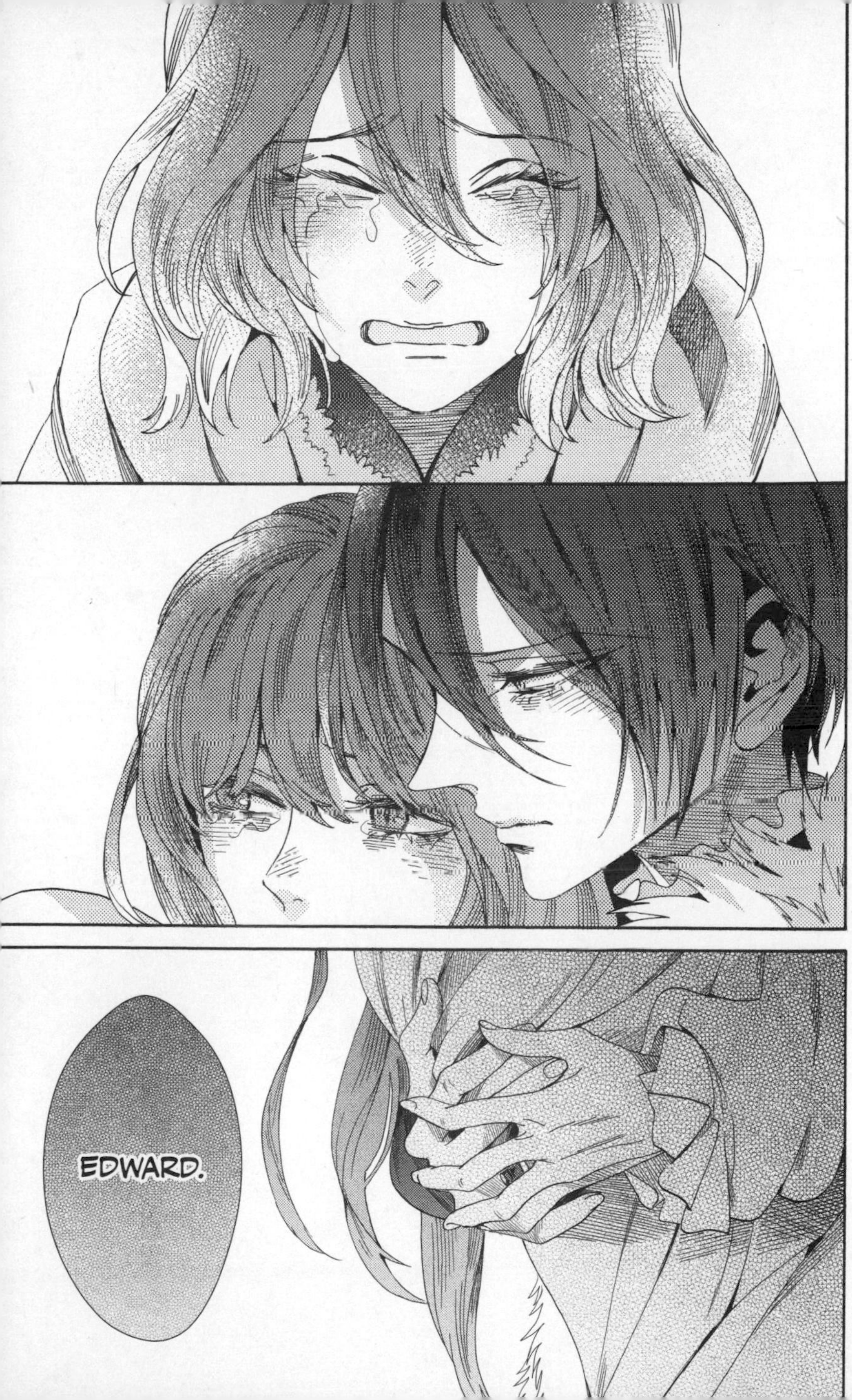
EDWARD.

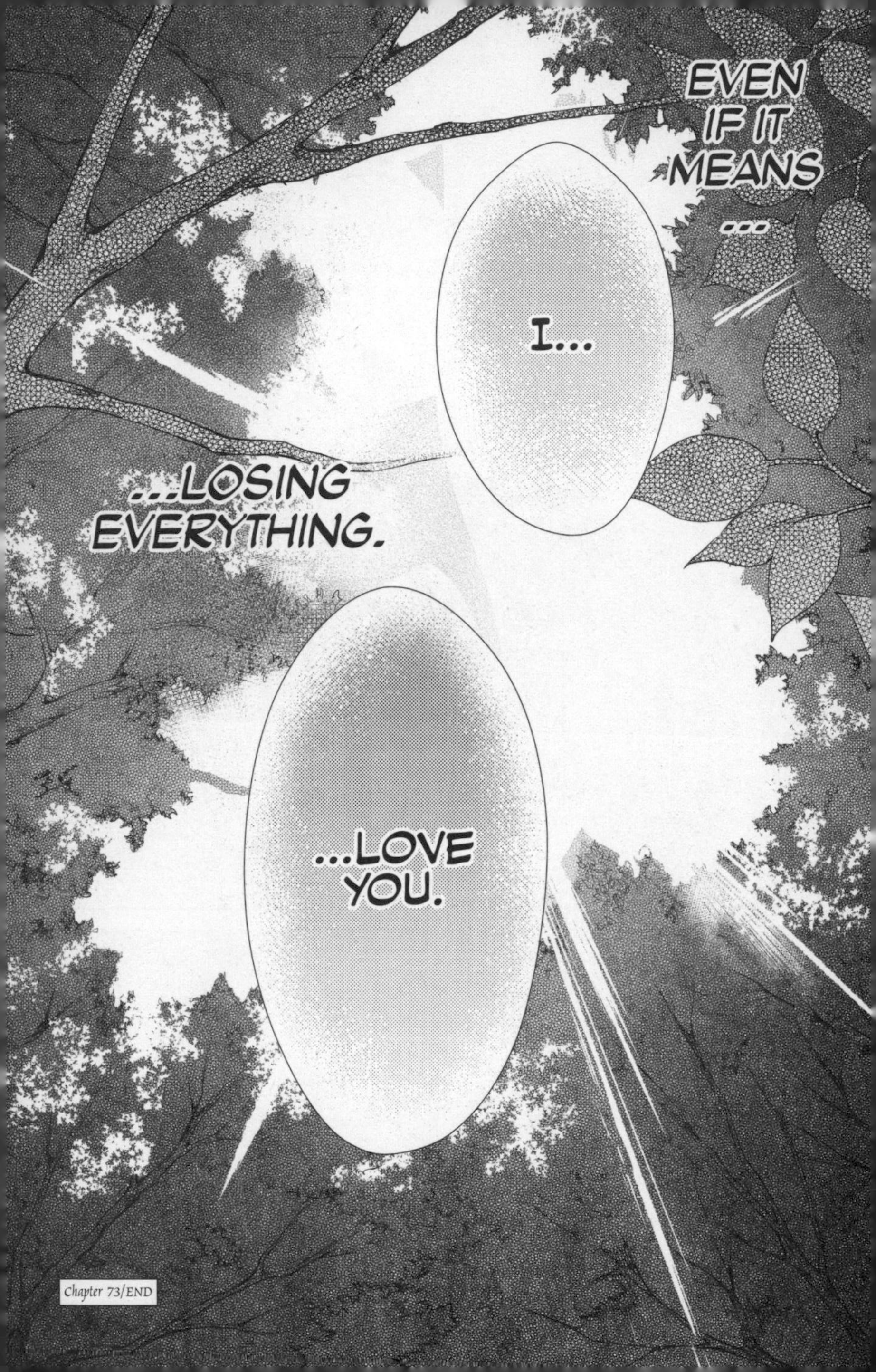
EVEN IF IT MEANS ...
I...
...LOSING EVERYTHING.
...LOVE YOU.
Chapter 73/END

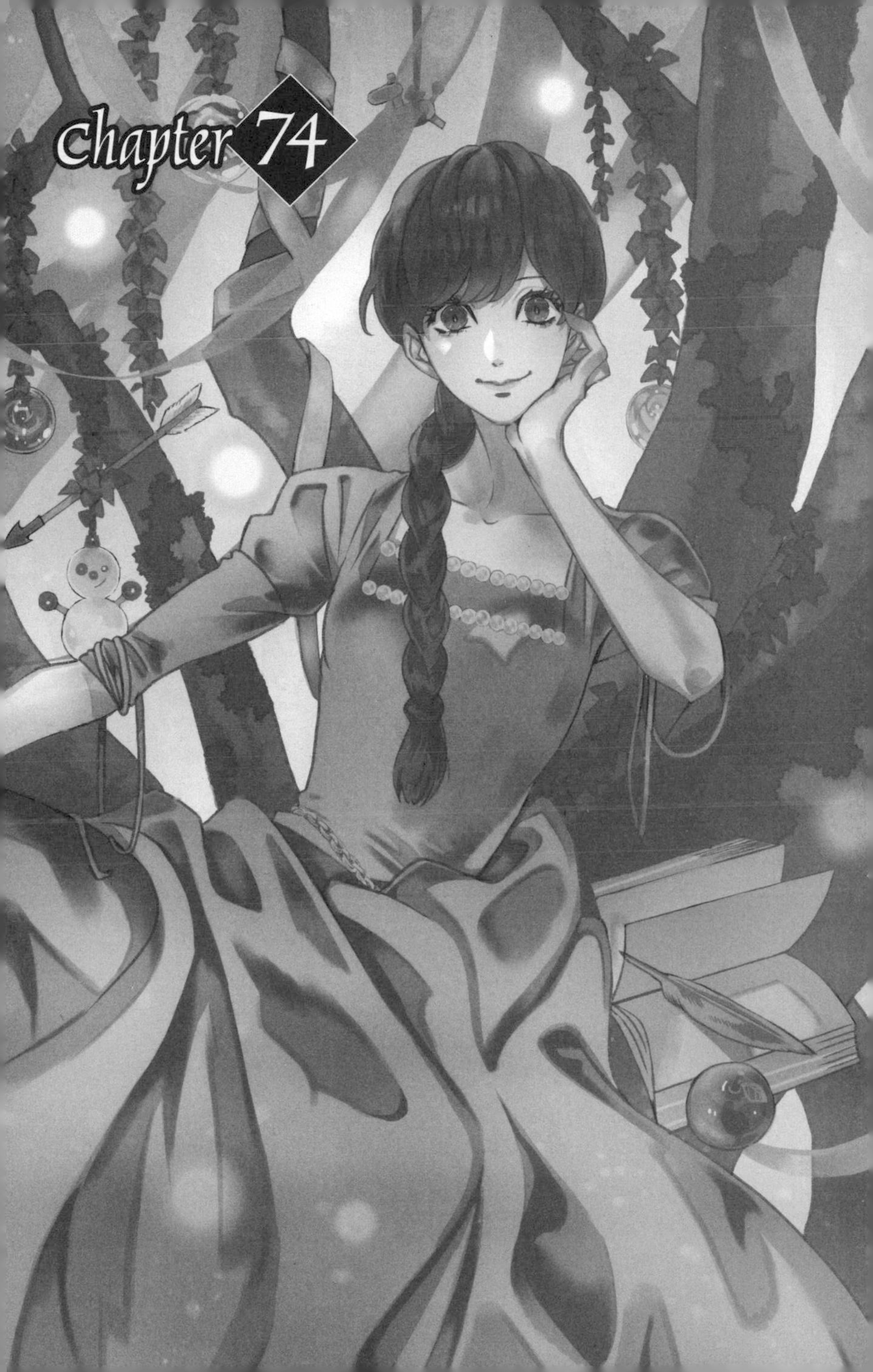
Chapter 74

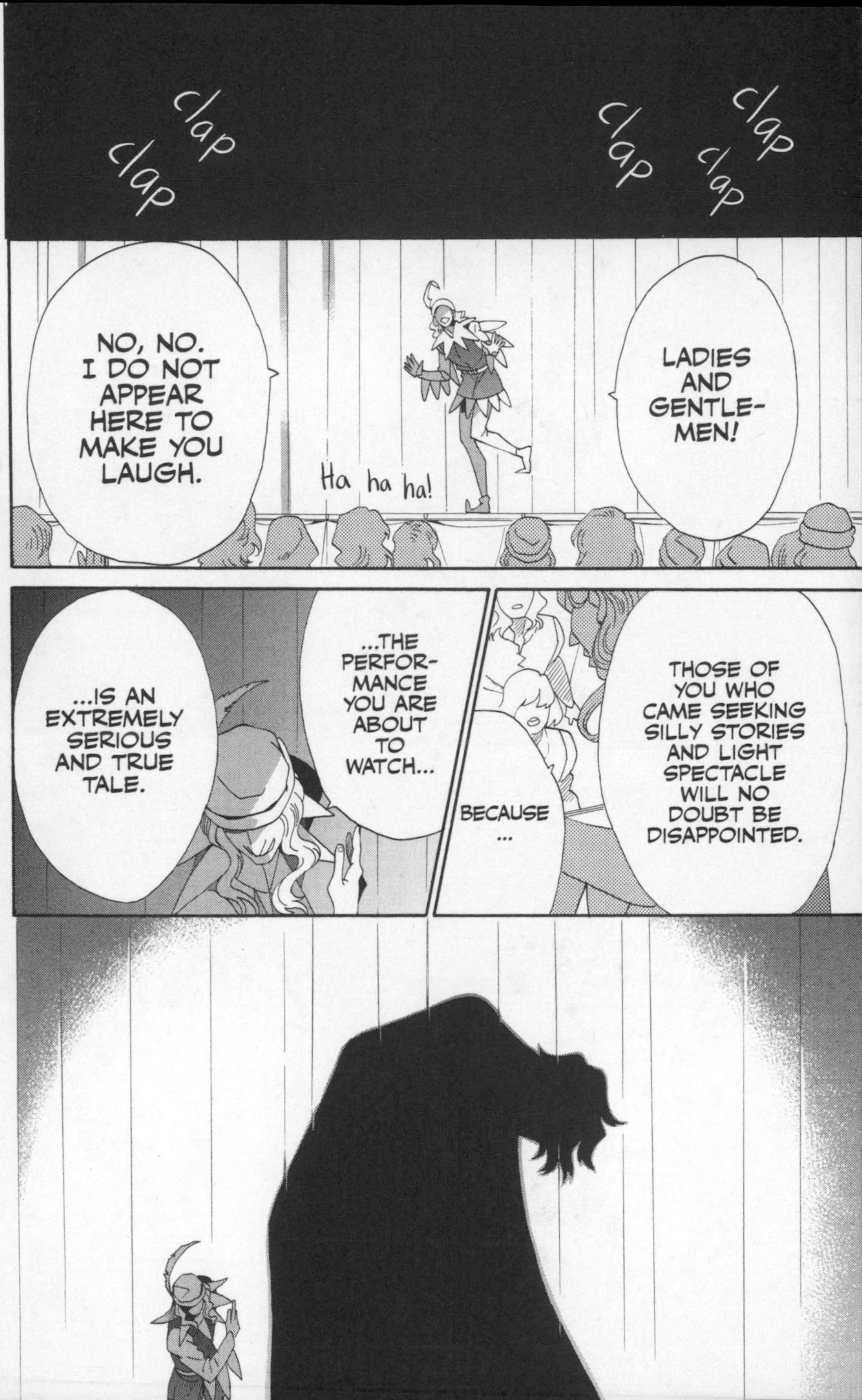
clap clap
clap clap
clap clap
LADIES AND GENTLE-MEN!
Ha ha ha!
NO, NO. I DO NOT APPEAR HERE TO MAKE YOU LAUGH.
THOSE OF YOU WHO CAME SEEKING SILLY STORIES AND LIGHT SPECTACLE WILL NO DOUBT BE DISAPPOINTED.
BECAUSE ...
...THE PERFOR-MANCE YOU ARE ABOUT TO WATCH...
...IS AN EXTREMELY SERIOUS AND TRUE TALE.

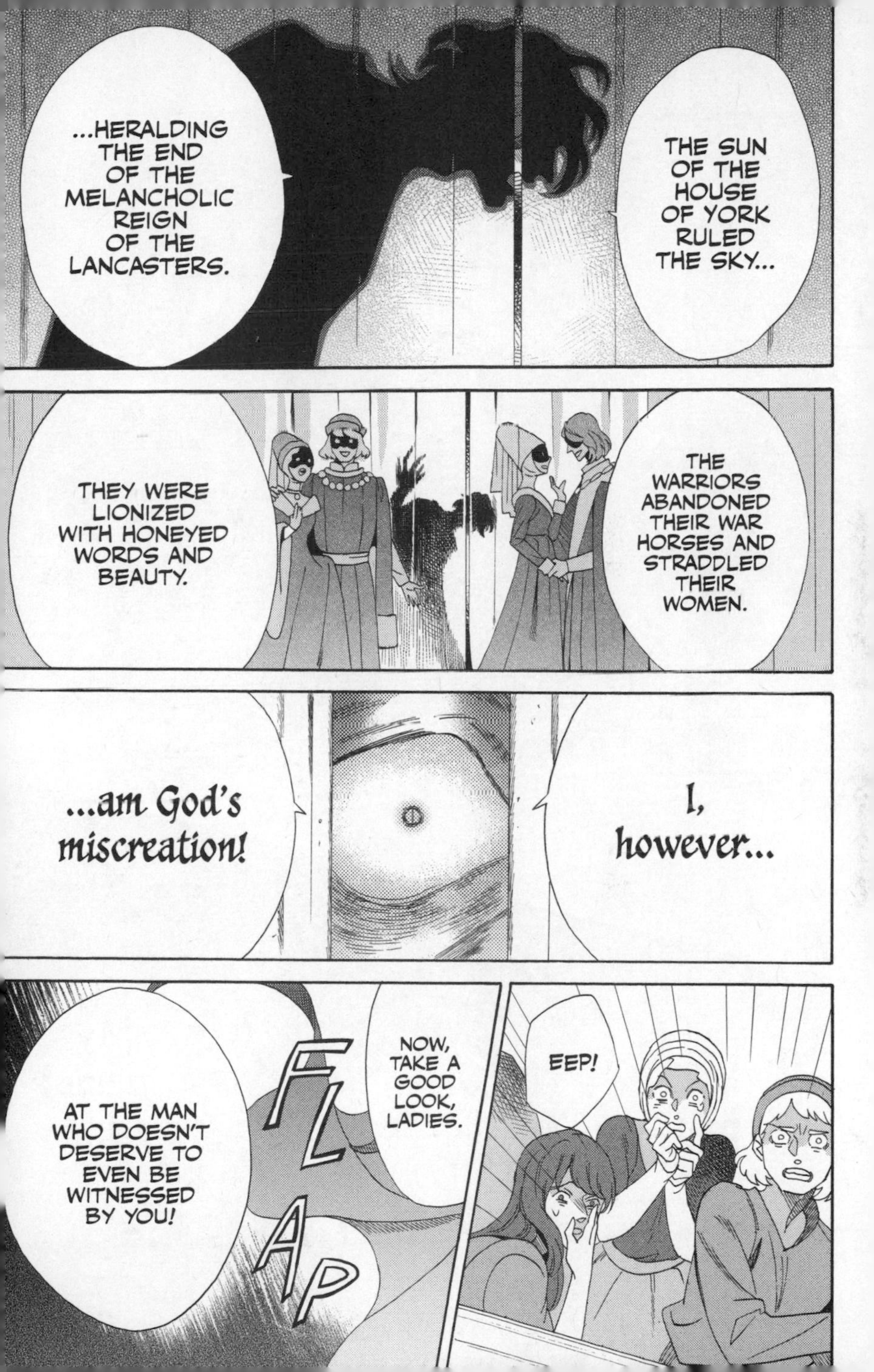
THE SUN OF THE HOUSE OF YORK RULED THE SKY...
...HERALDING THE END OF THE MELANCHOLIC REIGN OF THE LANCASTERS.
THE WARRIORS ABANDONED THEIR WAR HORSES AND STRADDLED THEIR WOMEN.
THEY WERE LIONIZED WITH HONEYED WORDS AND BEAUTY.
I, however...
...am God's miscreation!
EEP!
NOW, TAKE A GOOD LOOK, LADIES.
FLAP
AT THE MAN WHO DOESN'T DESERVE TO EVEN BE WITNESSED BY YOU!

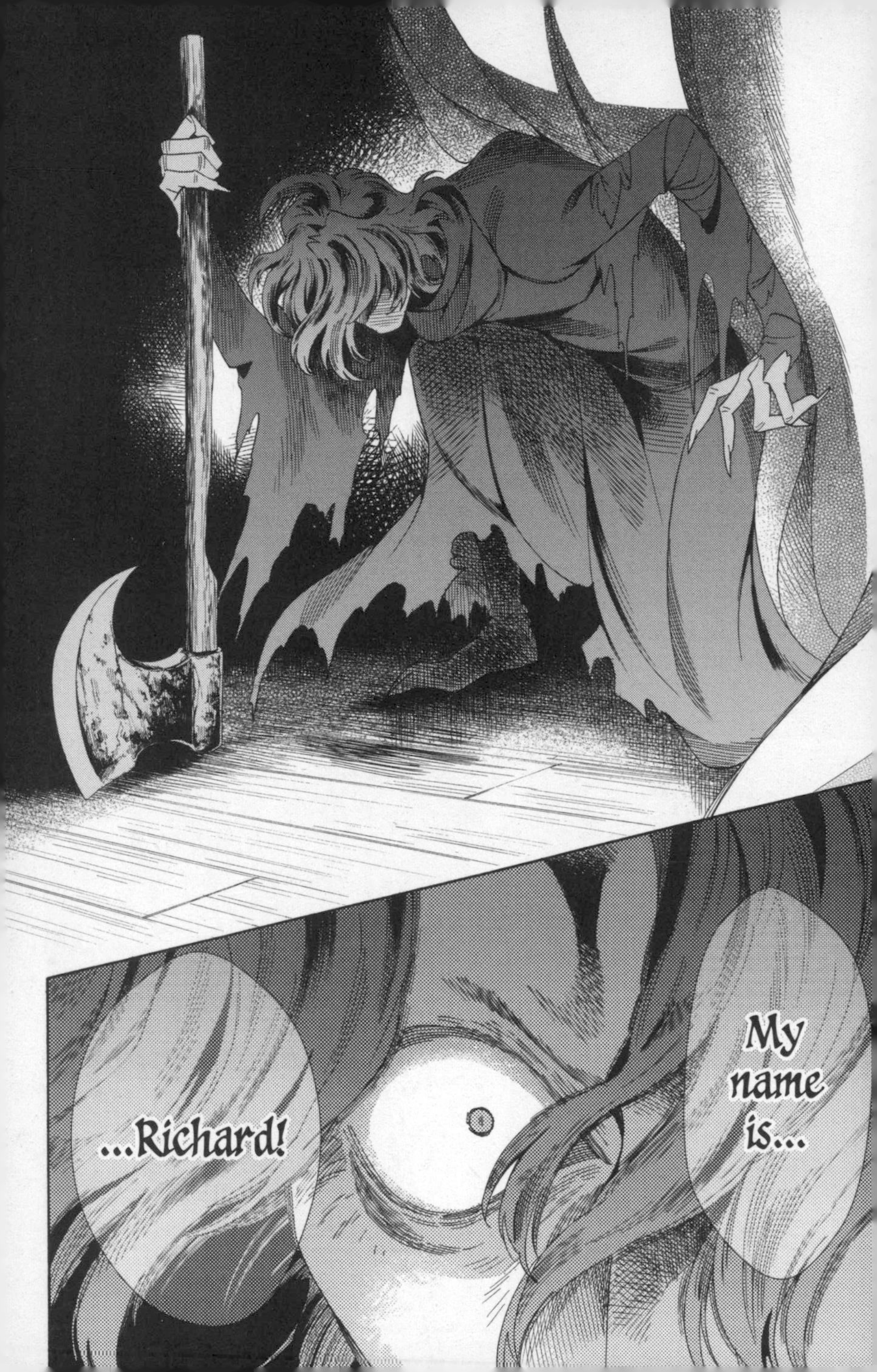
My name is...
...Richard!

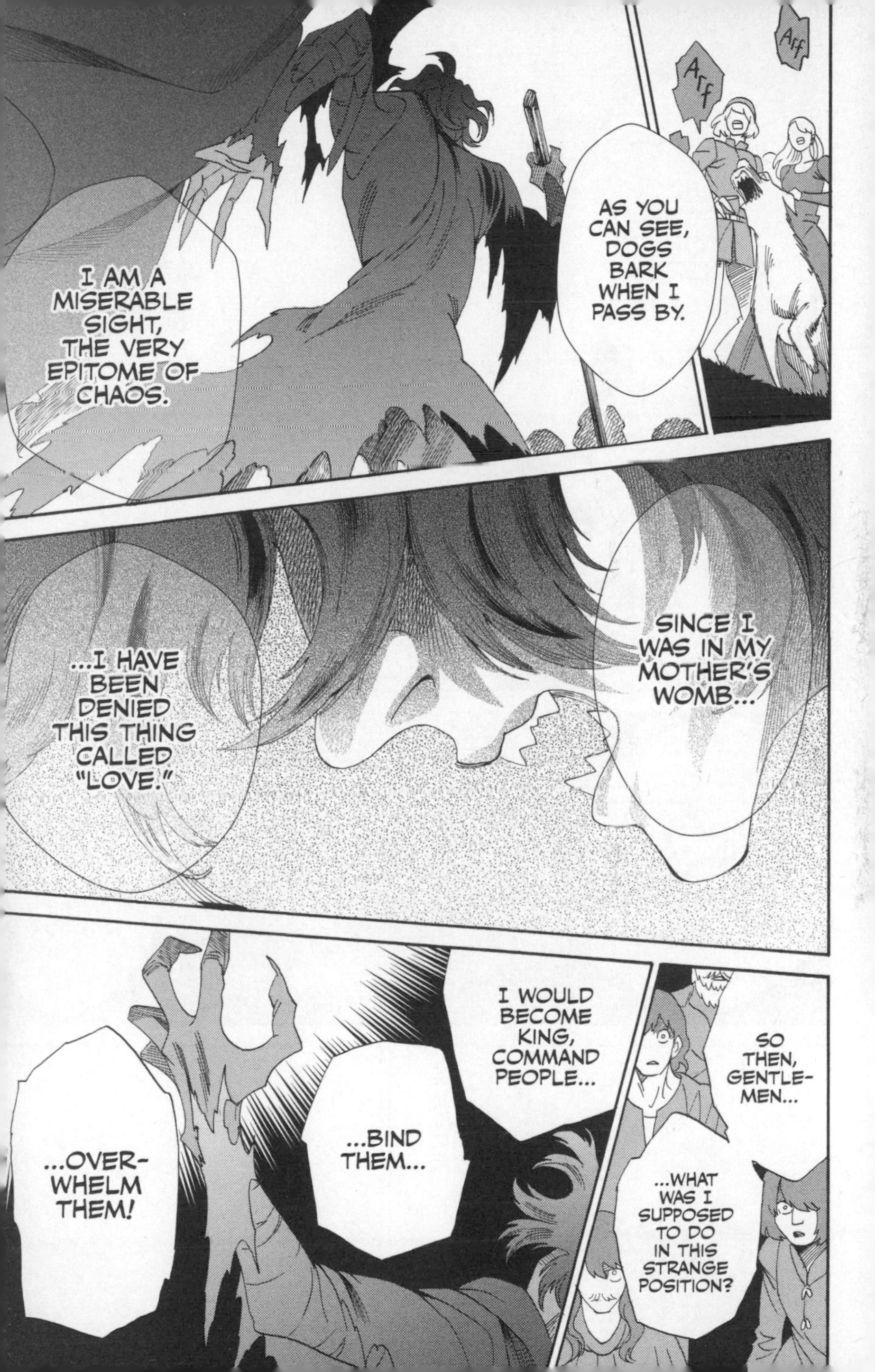
Arf
Arf
AS YOU CAN SEE, DOGS BARK WHEN I PASS BY.
I AM A MISERABLE SIGHT, THE VERY EPITOME OF CHAOS.
SINCE I WAS IN MY MOTHER'S WOMB...
...I HAVE BEEN DENIED THIS THING CALLED "LOVE."
SO THEN, GENTLE-MEN...
...WHAT WAS I SUPPOSED TO DO IN THIS STRANGE POSITION?
I WOULD BECOME KING, COMMAND PEOPLE...
...BIND THEM...
...OVER-WHELM THEM!

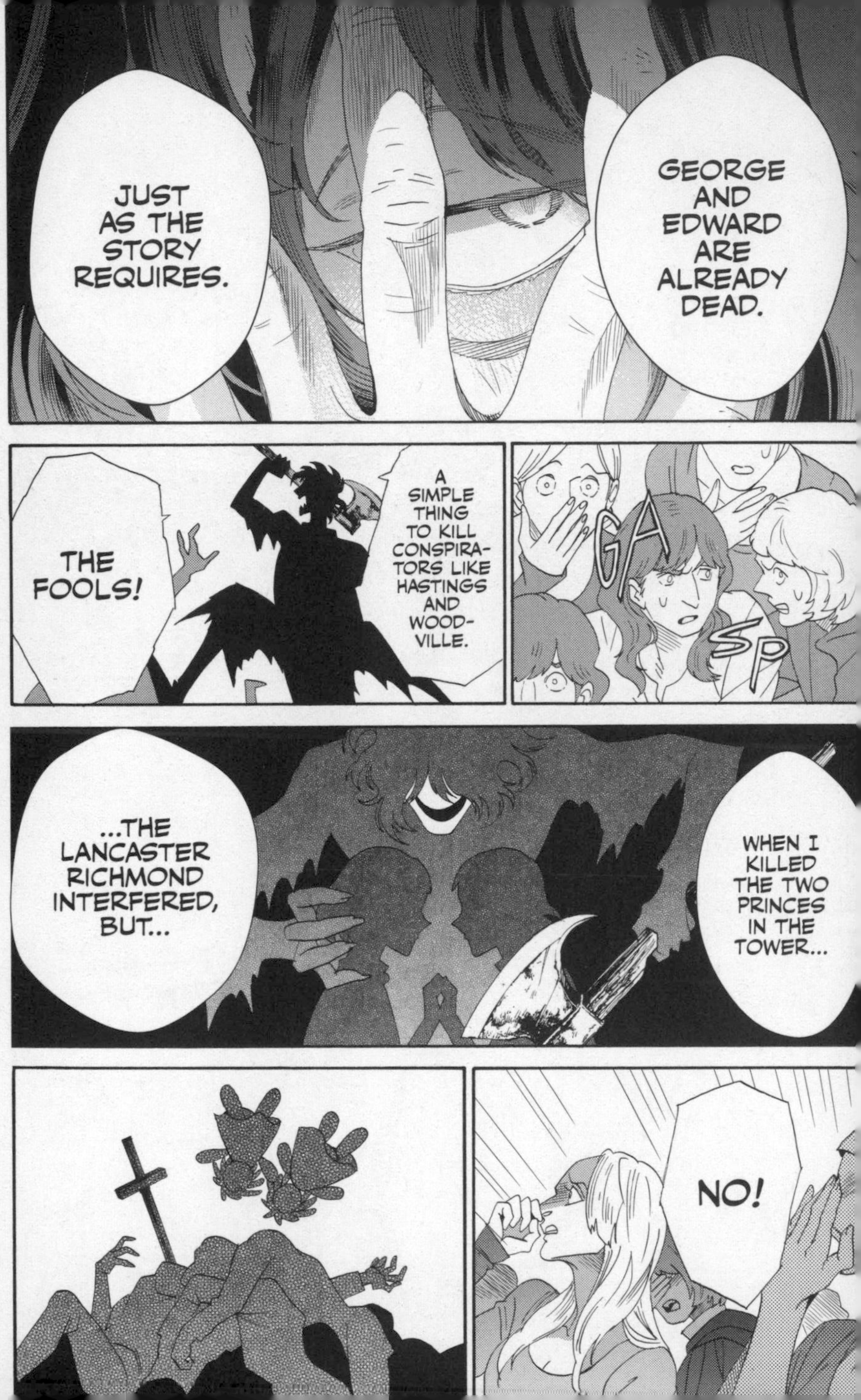
GEORGE AND EDWARD ARE ALREADY DEAD.
JUST AS THE STORY REQUIRES.
GA
SP
A SIMPLE THING TO KILL CONSPIRA-TORS LIKE HASTINGS AND WOOD-VILLE.
THE FOOLS!
WHEN I KILLED THE TWO PRINCES IN THE TOWER...
...THE LANCASTER RICHMOND INTERFERED, BUT...
NO!

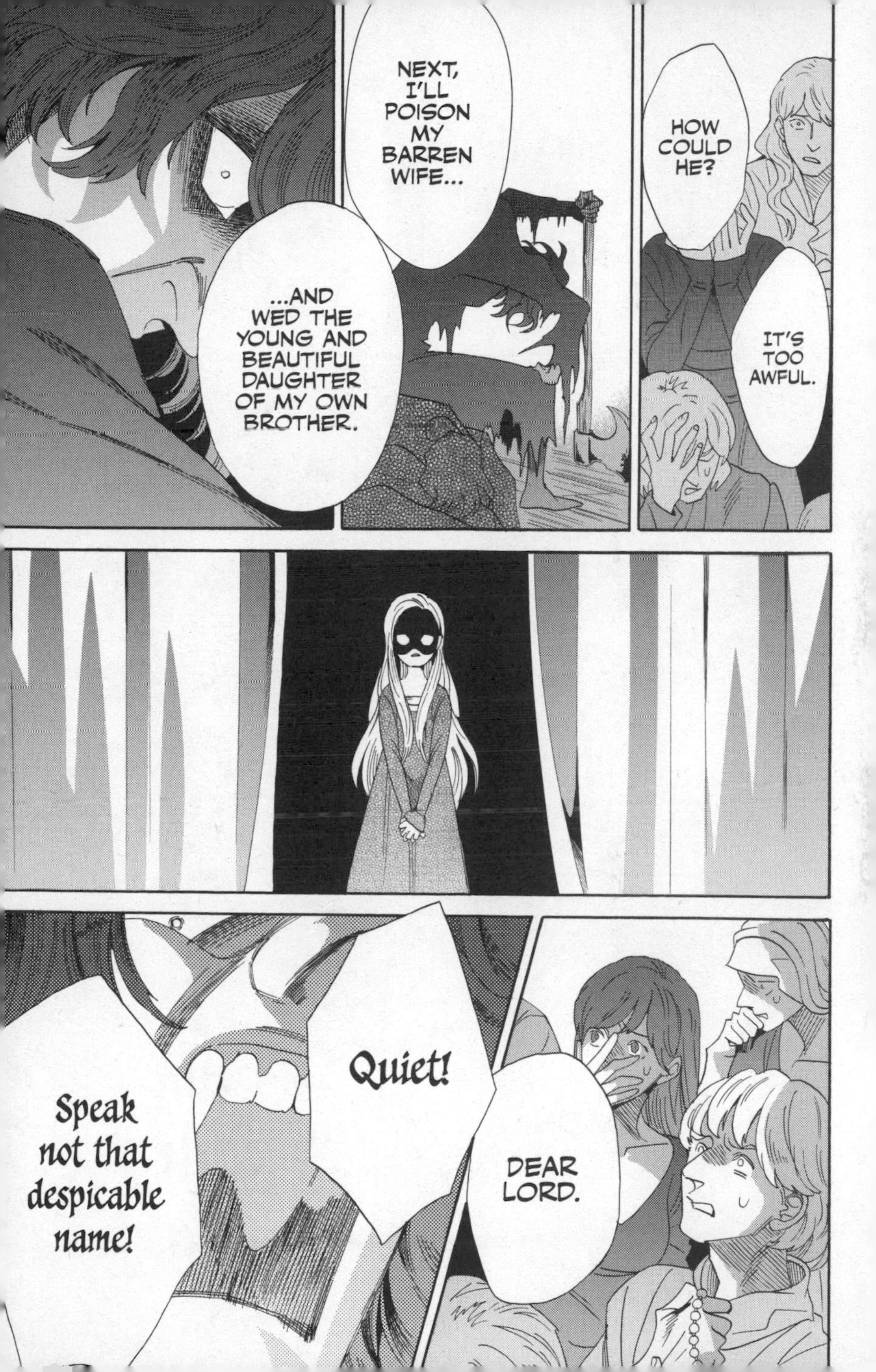
HOW COULD HE?
IT'S TOO AWFUL.
NEXT, I'LL POISON MY BARREN WIFE...
...AND WED THE YOUNG AND BEAUTIFUL DAUGHTER OF MY OWN BROTHER.
DEAR LORD.
Quiet!
Speak not that despicable name!

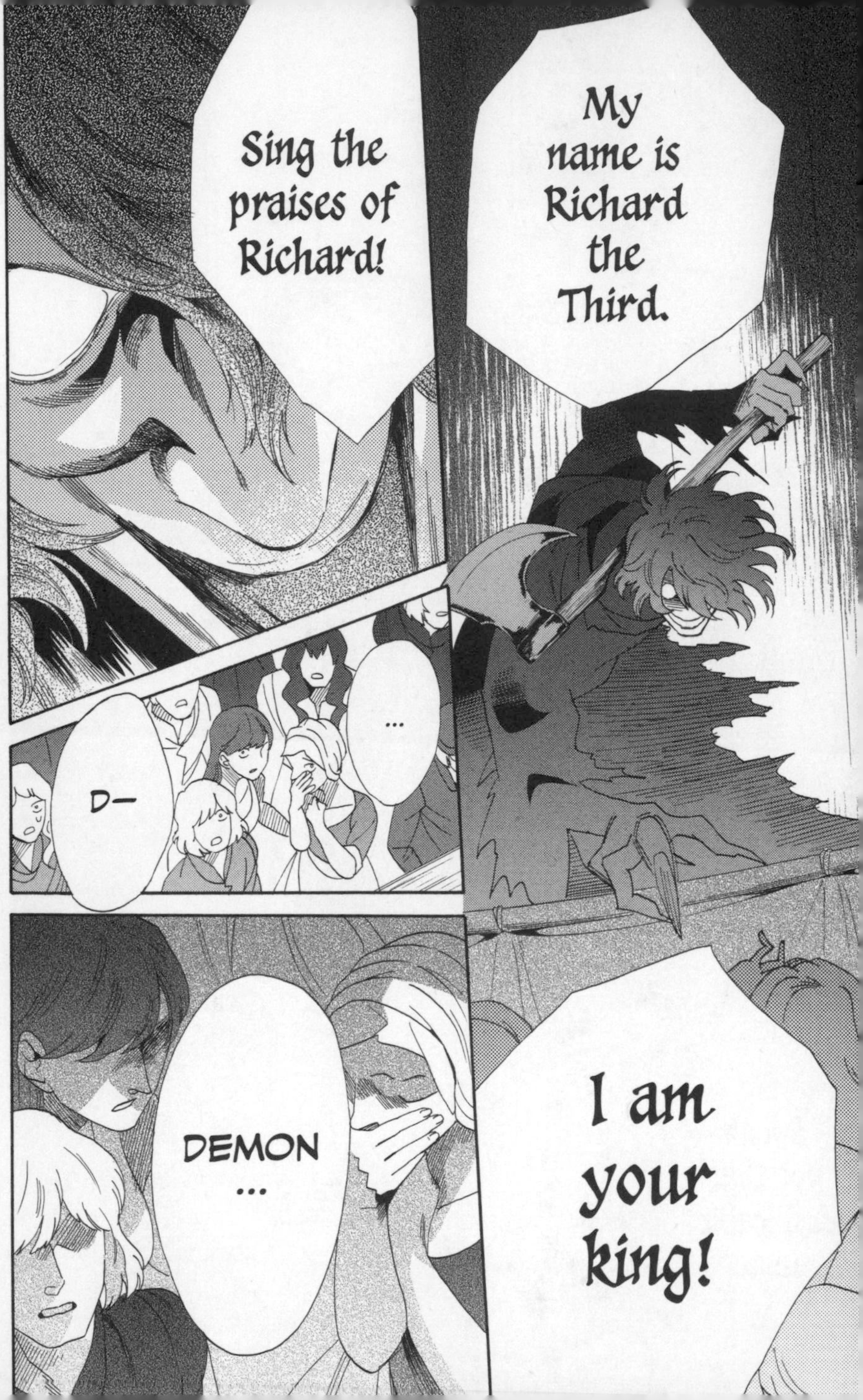
My name is Richard the Third.
Sing the praises of Richard!
...
D—
I am your king!
DEMON ...

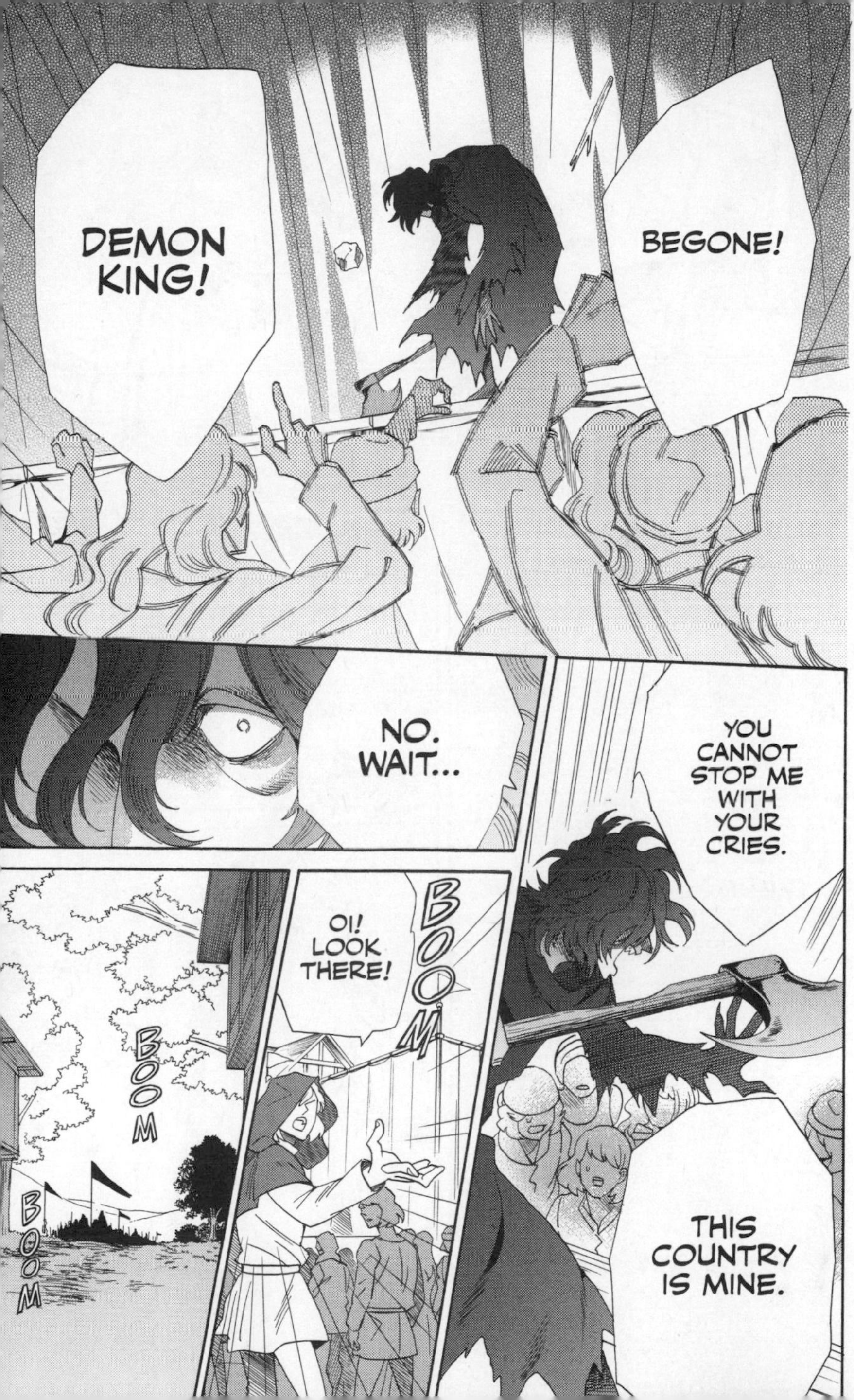
BEGONE!
DEMON KING!
YOU CANNOT STOP ME WITH YOUR CRIES.
THIS COUNTRY IS MINE.
NO. WAIT...
BOOM
OI! LOOK THERE!
BOOM
BOOM
BOOM

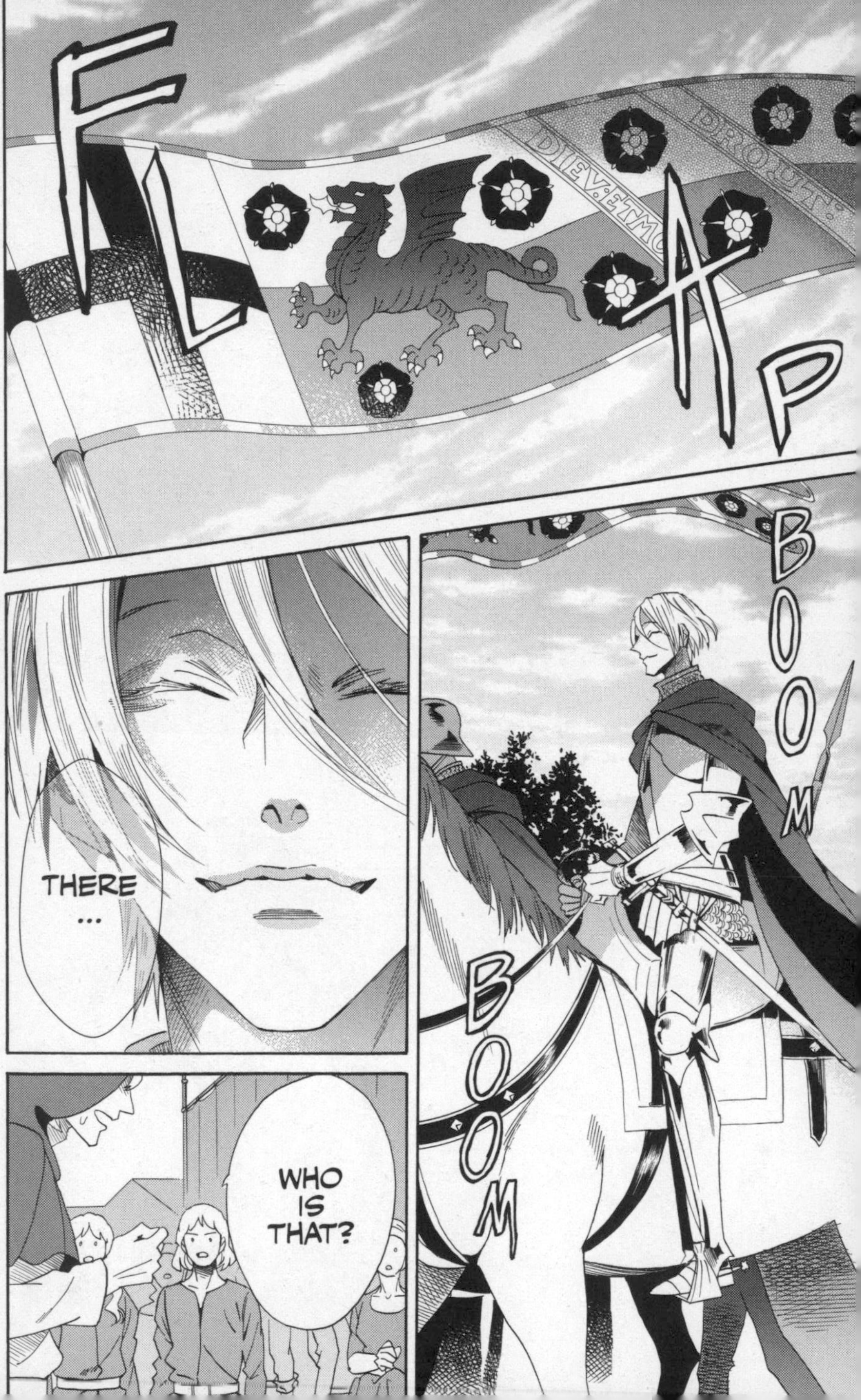
FLAP
BOOM
BOOM
THERE
...
WHO IS THAT?

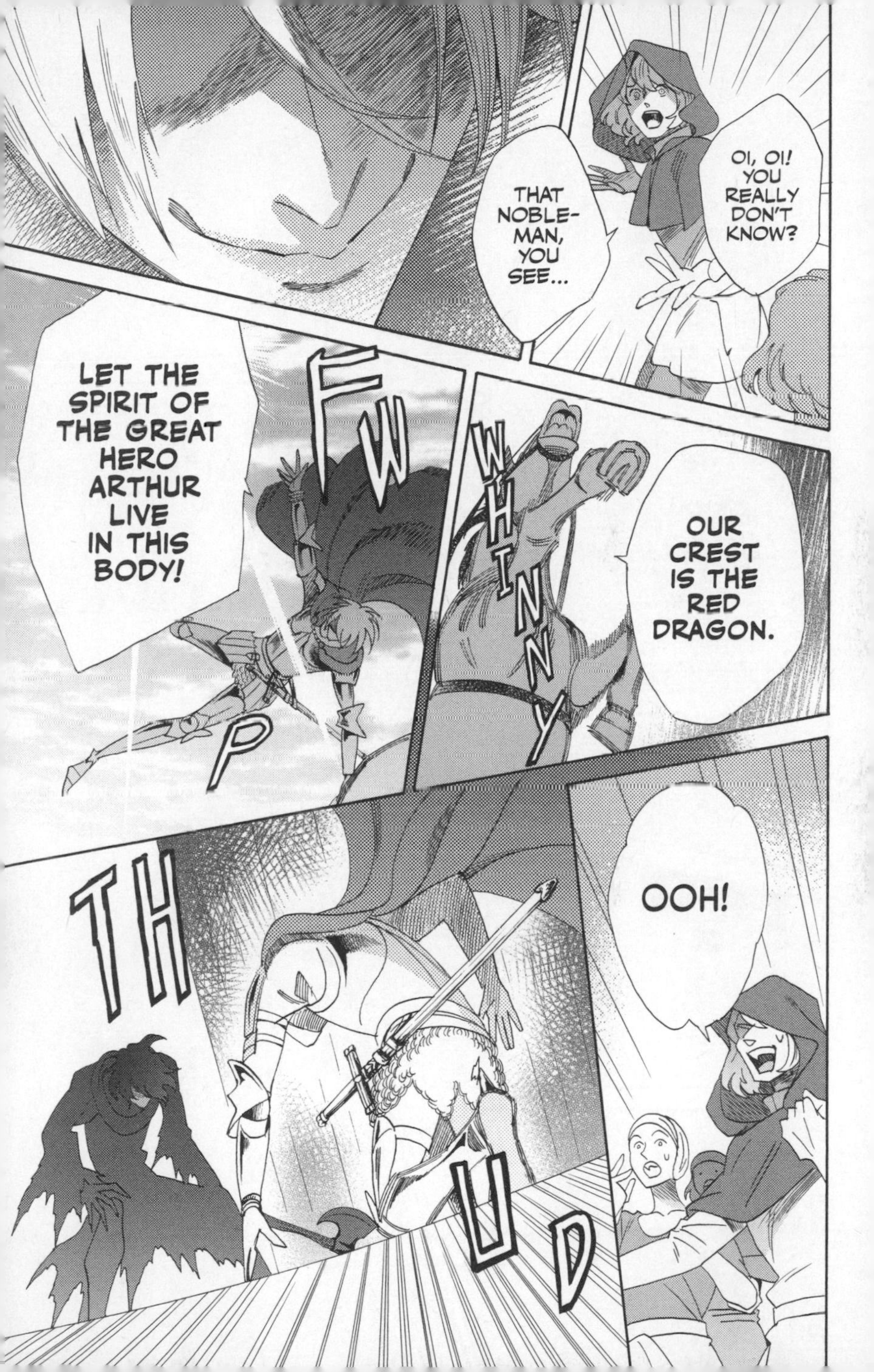
OI, OI! YOU REALLY DON'T KNOW?
THAT NOBLE-MAN, YOU SEE...
OUR CREST IS THE RED DRAGON.
WHINNY
LET THE SPIRIT OF THE GREAT HERO ARTHUR LIVE IN THIS BODY!
FWP
OOH!
THUD

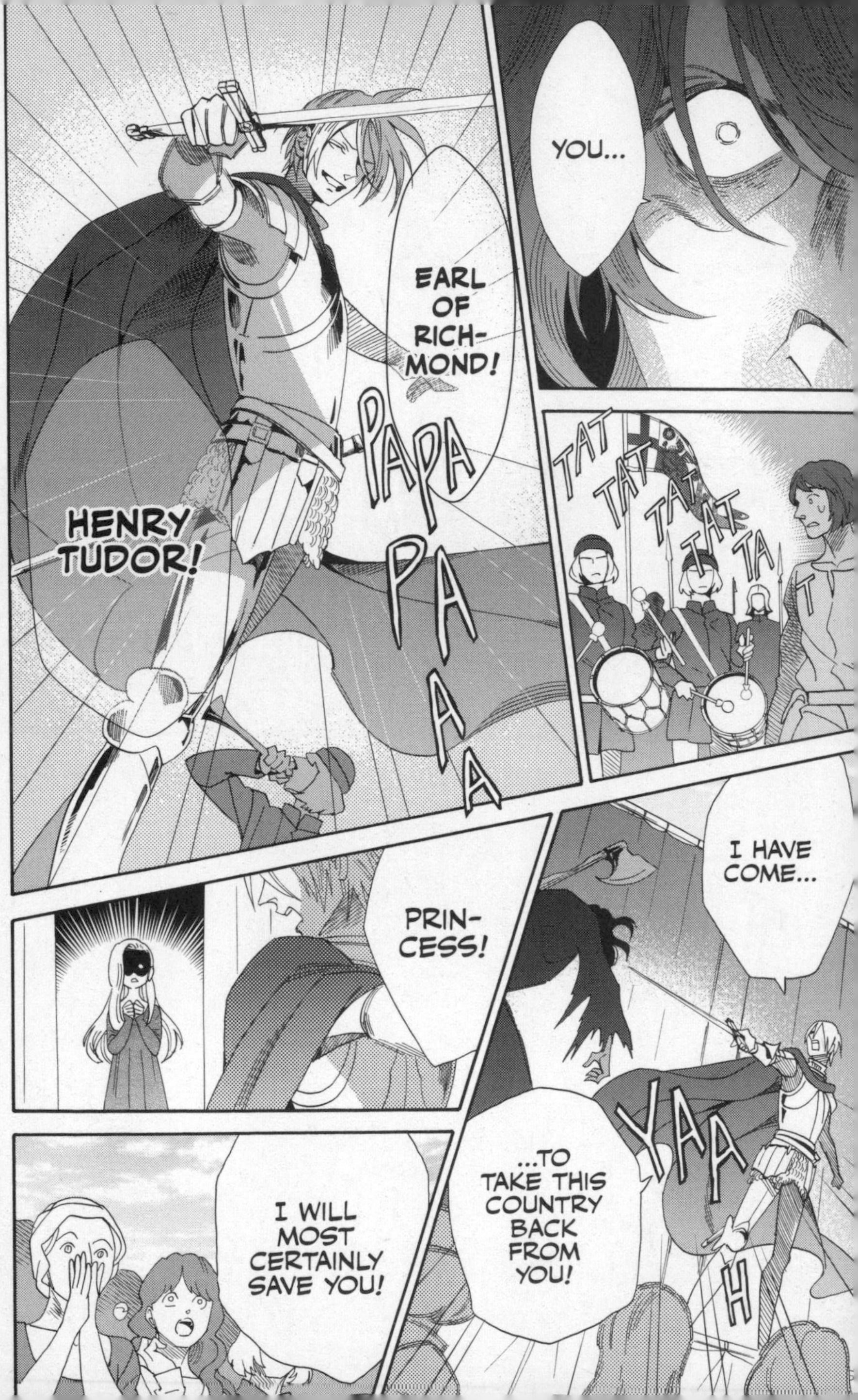
YOU...
TAT TAT TAT TAT TA
EARL OF RICH-MOND!
PAPA PA A A
HENRY TUDOR!
I HAVE COME...
...TO TAKE THIS COUNTRY BACK FROM YOU!
YAAAH
PRIN-CESS!
I WILL MOST CERTAINLY SAVE YOU!

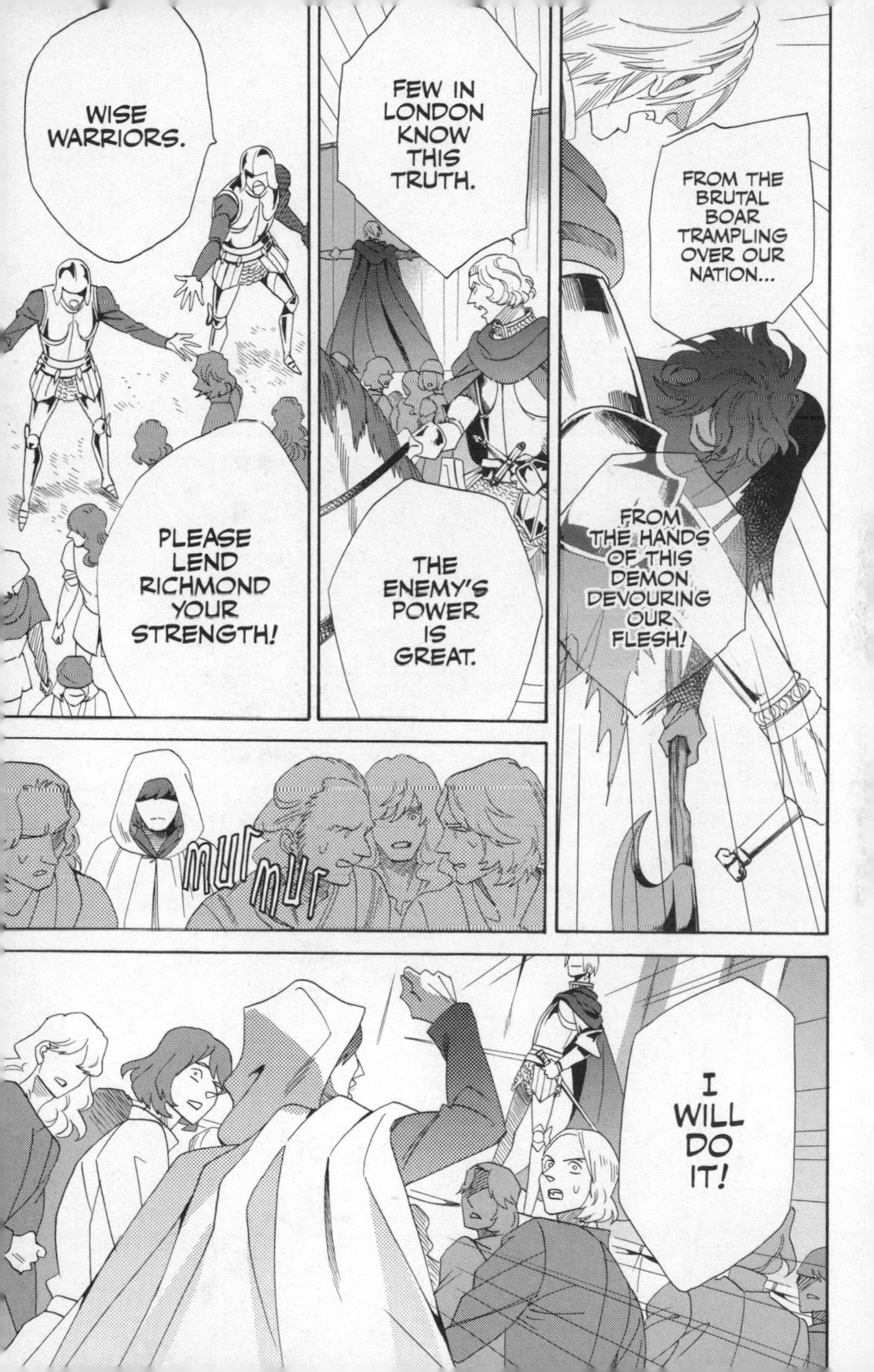
FROM THE BRUTAL BOAR TRAMPLING OVER OUR NATION...
FROM THE HANDS OF THIS DEMON DEVOURING OUR FLESH!
FEW IN LONDON KNOW THIS TRUTH.
THE ENEMY'S POWER IS GREAT.
WISE WARRIORS.
PLEASE LEND RICHMOND YOUR STRENGTH!
MURMUR
I WILL DO IT!

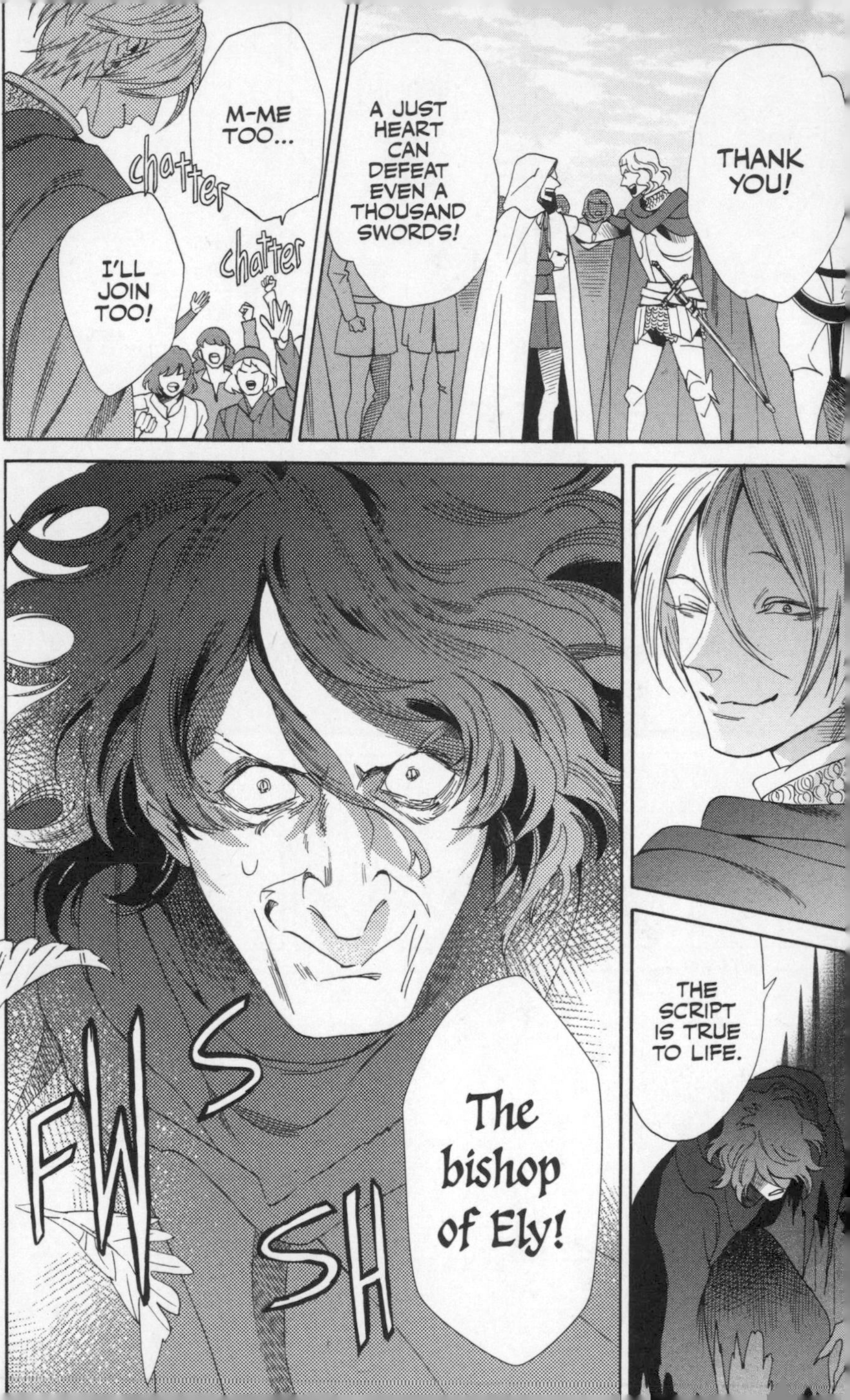
THANK YOU!
A JUST HEART CAN DEFEAT EVEN A THOUSAND SWORDS!
M-ME TOO...
chatter
chatter
I'LL JOIN TOO!
THE SCRIPT IS TRUE TO LIFE.
The bishop of Ely!
FWSSH

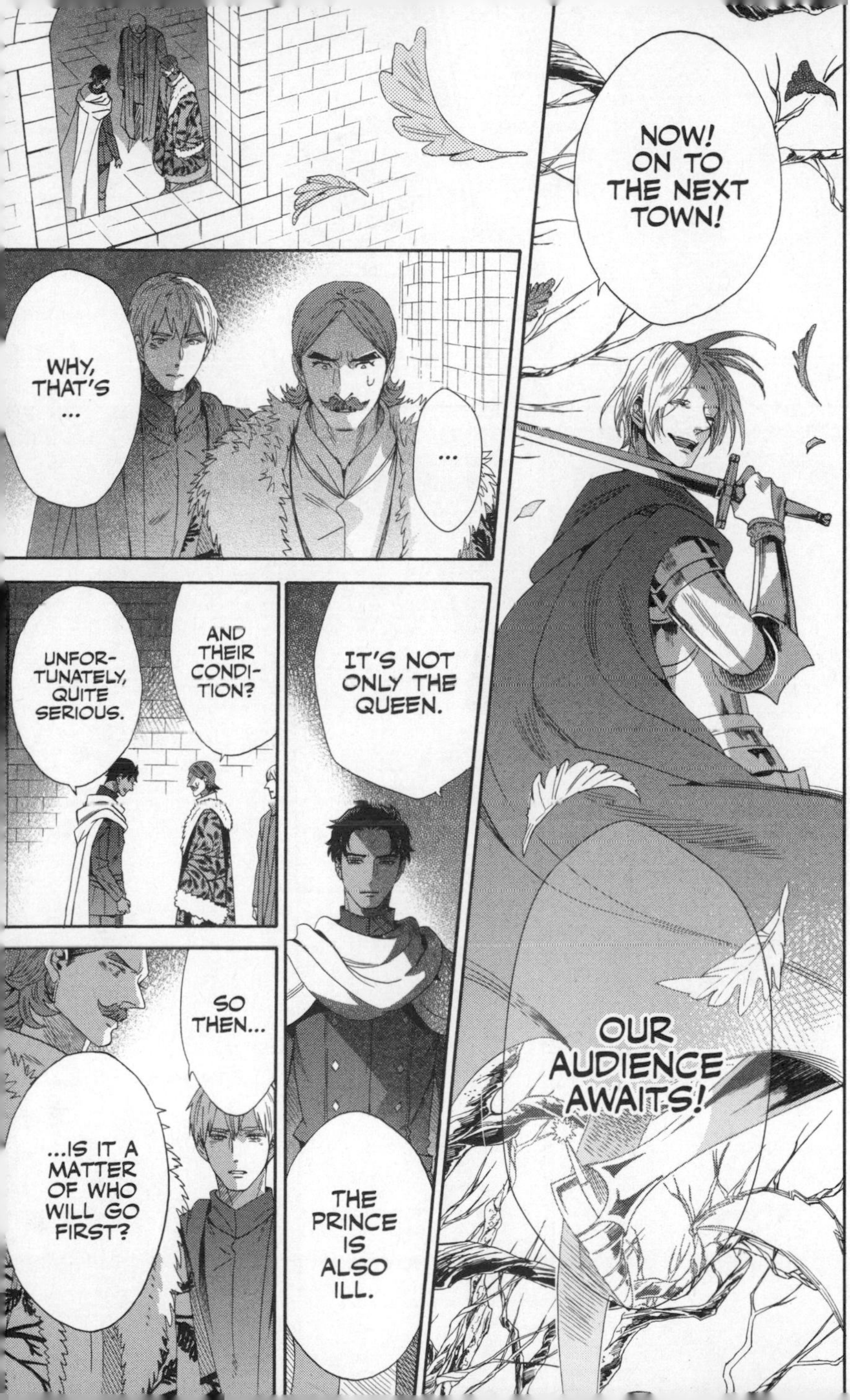
NOW! ON TO THE NEXT TOWN!
OUR AUDIENCE AWAITS!
...
WHY, THAT'S ...
IT'S NOT ONLY THE QUEEN.
THE PRINCE IS ALSO ILL.
AND THEIR CONDITION?
UNFORTUNATELY, QUITE SERIOUS.
SO THEN...
...IS IT A MATTER OF WHO WILL GO FIRST?

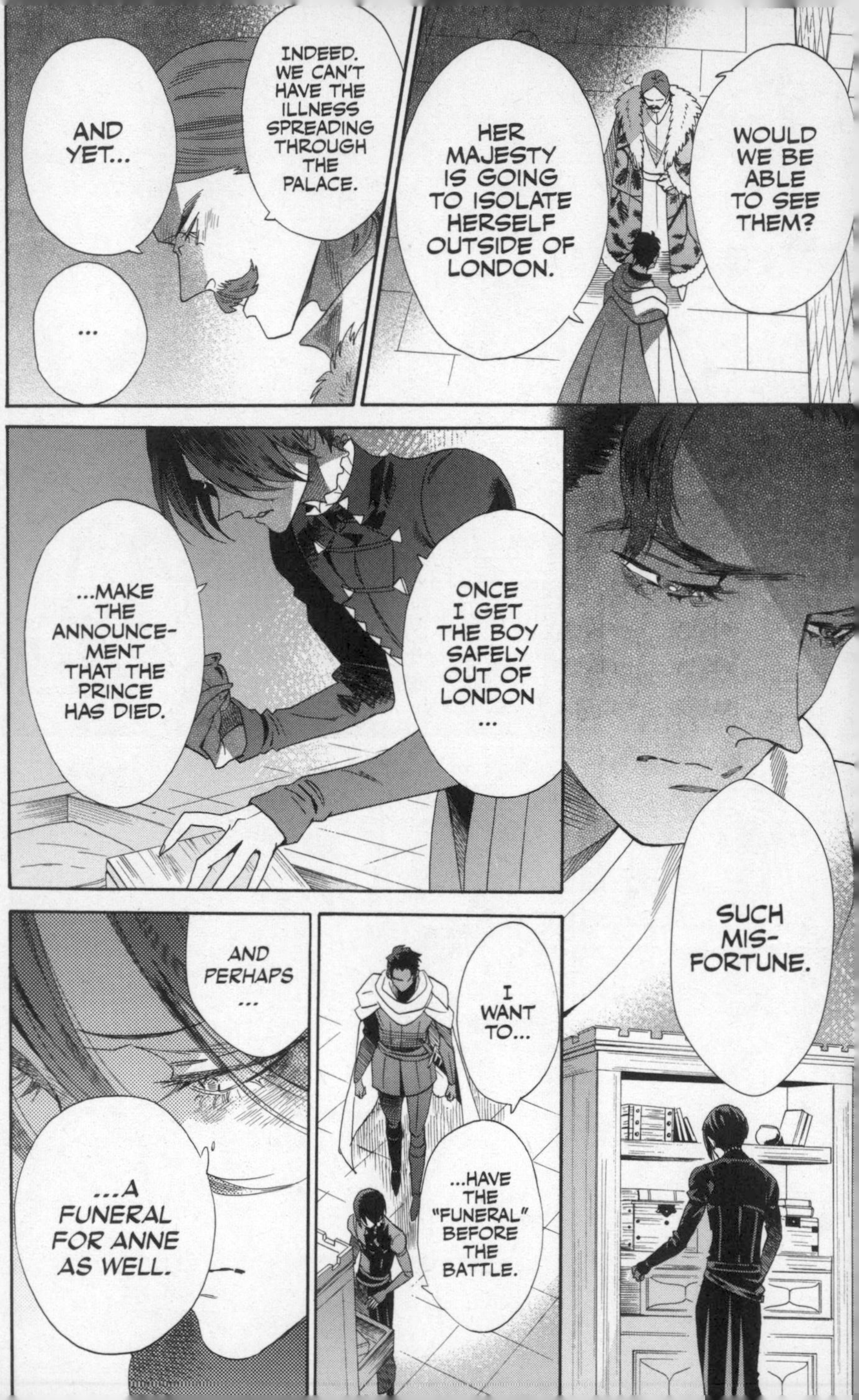
WOULD WE BE ABLE TO SEE THEM?
HER MAJESTY IS GOING TO ISOLATE HERSELF OUTSIDE OF LONDON.
INDEED. WE CAN'T HAVE THE ILLNESS SPREADING THROUGH THE PALACE.
AND YET...
...
ONCE I GET THE BOY SAFELY OUT OF LONDON...
...MAKE THE ANNOUNCEMENT THAT THE PRINCE HAS DIED.
SUCH MISFORTUNE.
I WANT TO...
...HAVE THE "FUNERAL" BEFORE THE BATTLE.
AND PERHAPS...
...A FUNERAL FOR ANNE AS WELL.

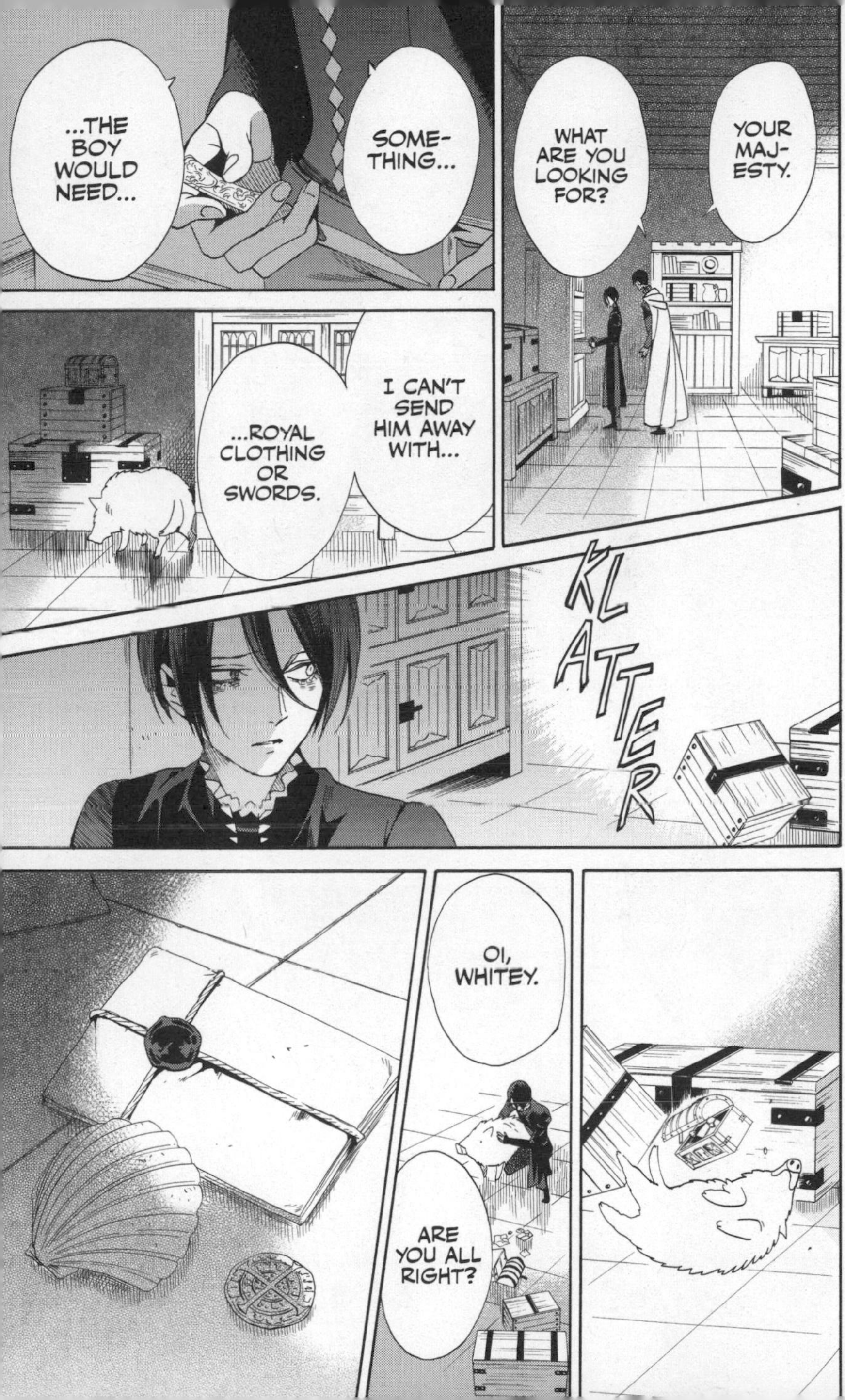
YOUR MAJESTY.
WHAT ARE YOU LOOKING FOR?
SOMETHING...
...THE BOY WOULD NEED...
I CAN'T SEND HIM AWAY WITH...
...ROYAL CLOTHING OR SWORDS.
KLATTER
OI, WHITEY.
ARE YOU ALL RIGHT?

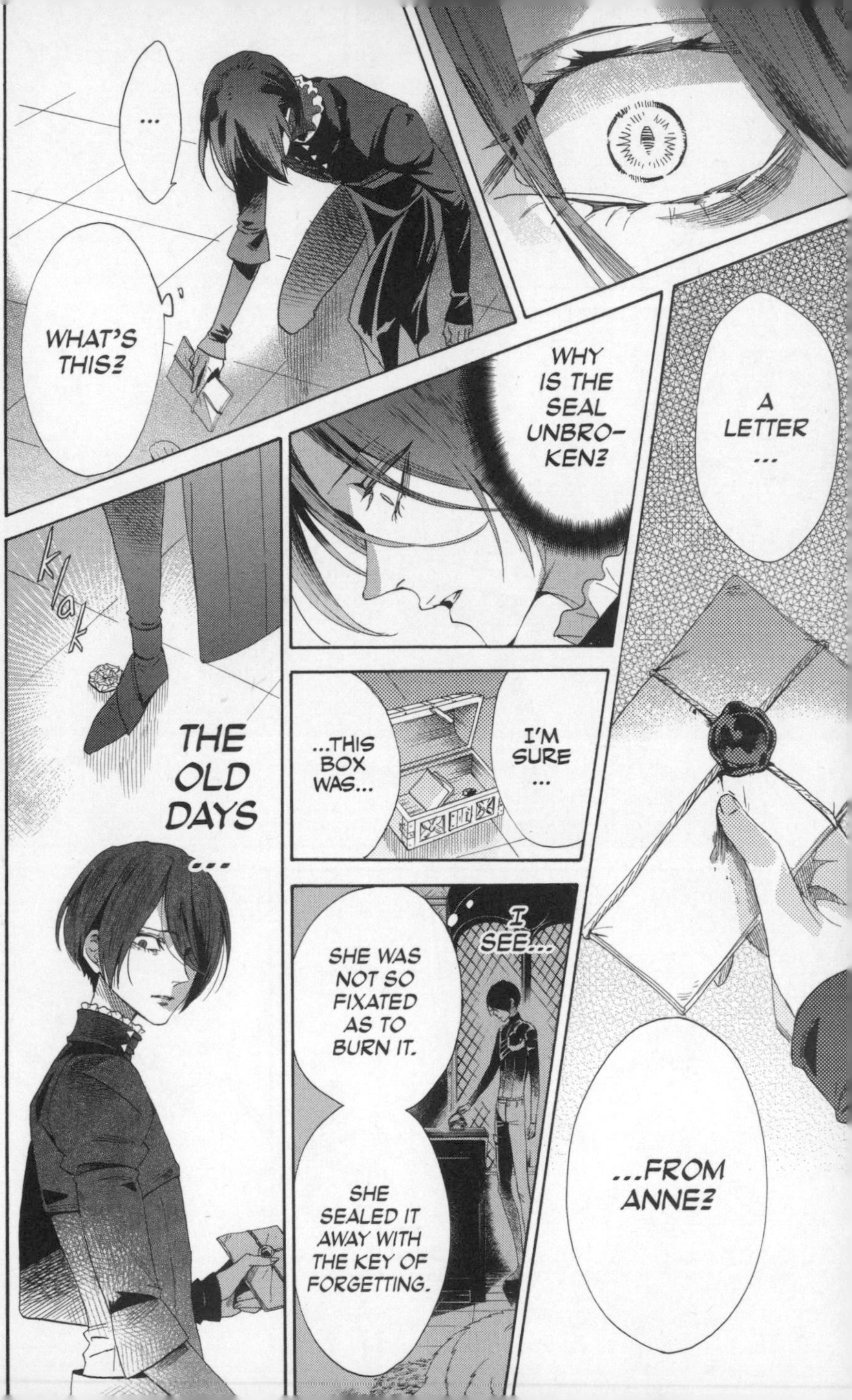
...
WHAT'S THIS?
A LETTER ...
...FROM ANNE?
WHY IS THE SEAL UNBRO-KEN?
I'M SURE ...
...THIS BOX WAS...
I SEE...
SHE WAS NOT SO FIXATED AS TO BURN IT.
SHE SEALED IT AWAY WITH THE KEY OF FORGETTING.
klak
THE OLD DAYS ...

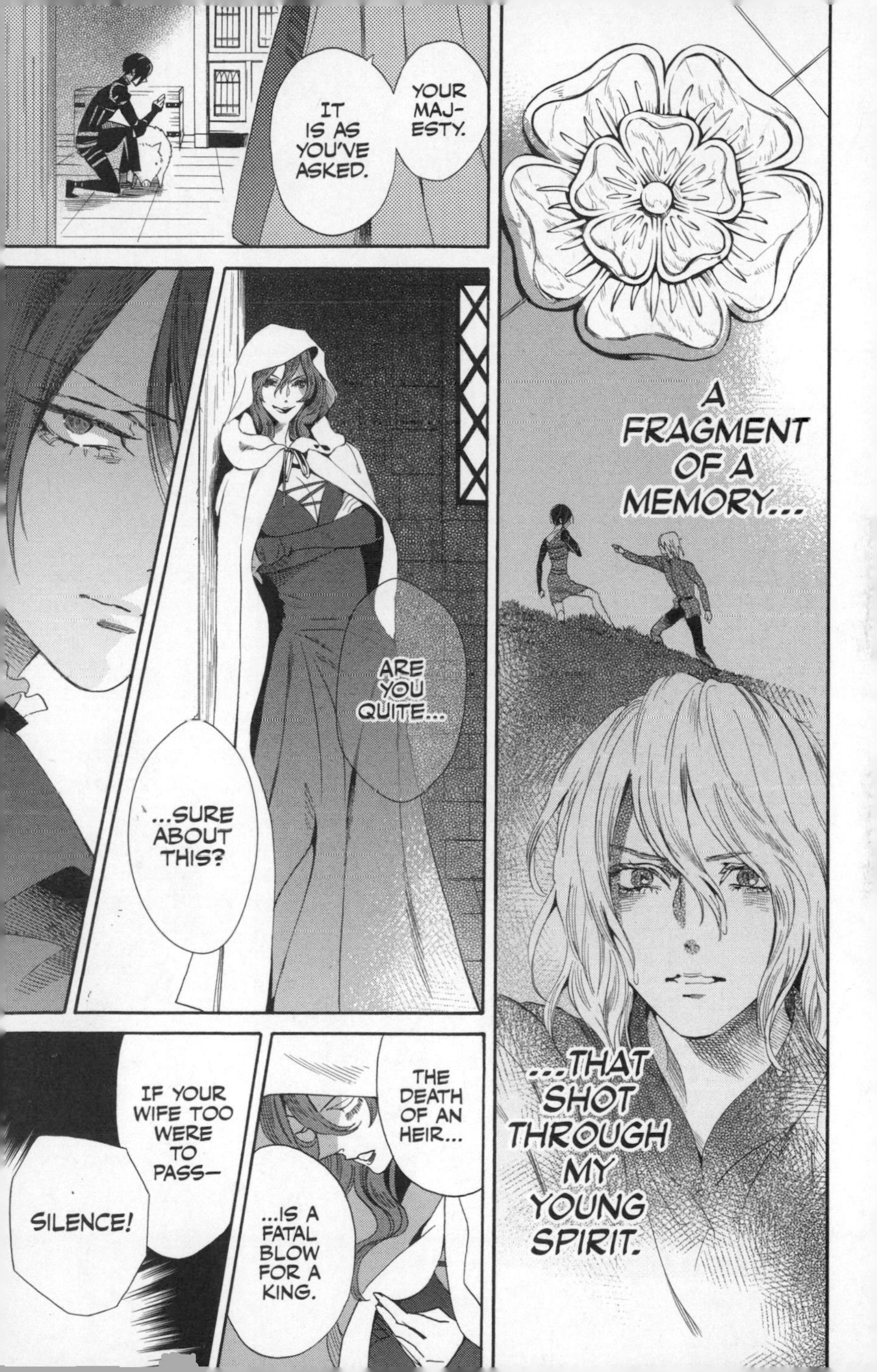
A FRAGMENT OF A MEMORY...
...THAT SHOT THROUGH MY YOUNG SPIRIT.
YOUR MAJ-ESTY.
IT IS AS YOU'VE ASKED.
ARE YOU QUITE...
...SURE ABOUT THIS?
THE DEATH OF AN HEIR...
...IS A FATAL BLOW FOR A KING.
IF YOUR WIFE TOO WERE TO PASS—
SILENCE!

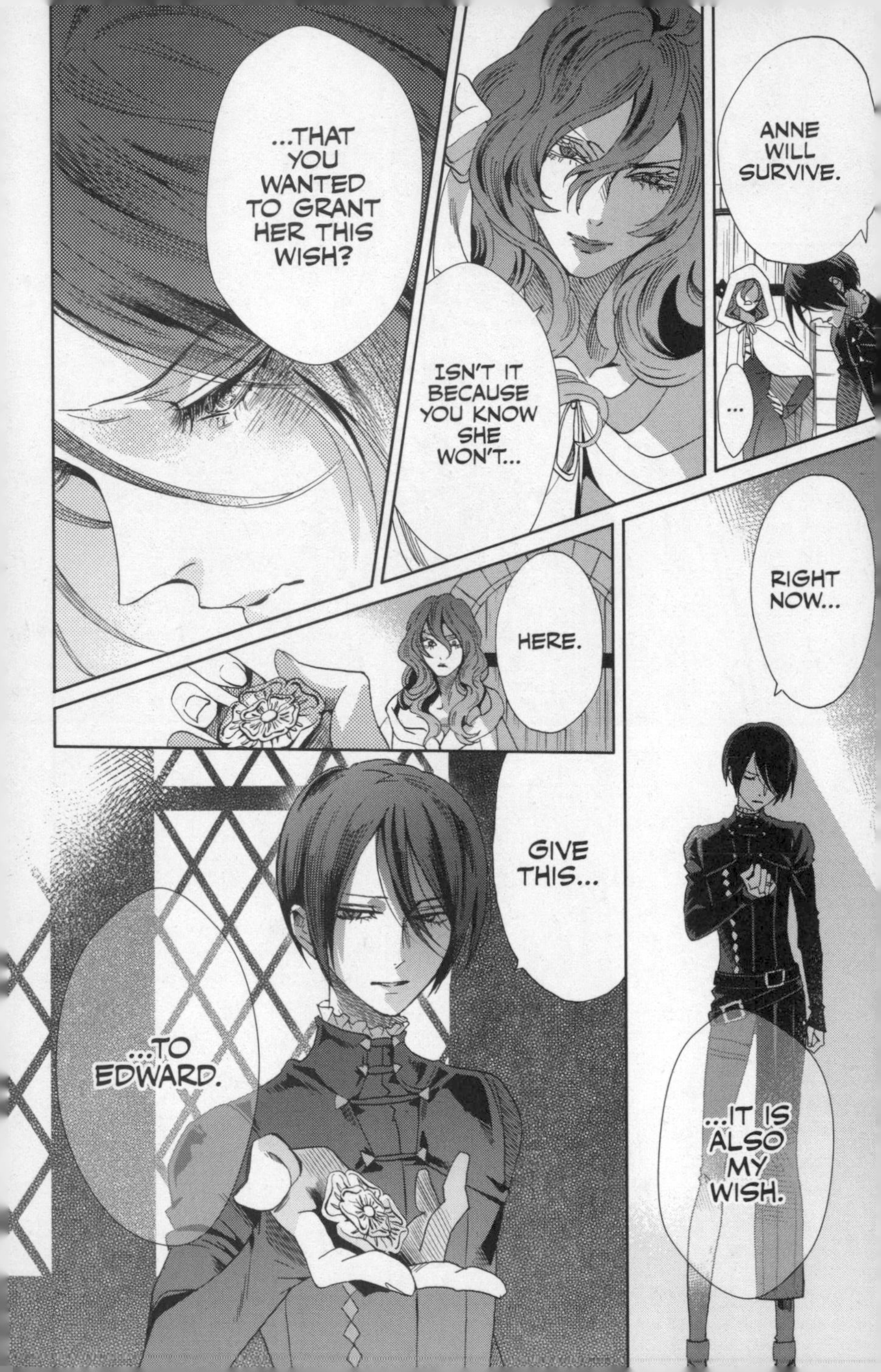
ANNE WILL SURVIVE.
...
ISN'T IT BECAUSE YOU KNOW SHE WON'T...
...THAT YOU WANTED TO GRANT HER THIS WISH?
RIGHT NOW...
...IT IS ALSO MY WISH.
HERE.
GIVE THIS...
...TO EDWARD.

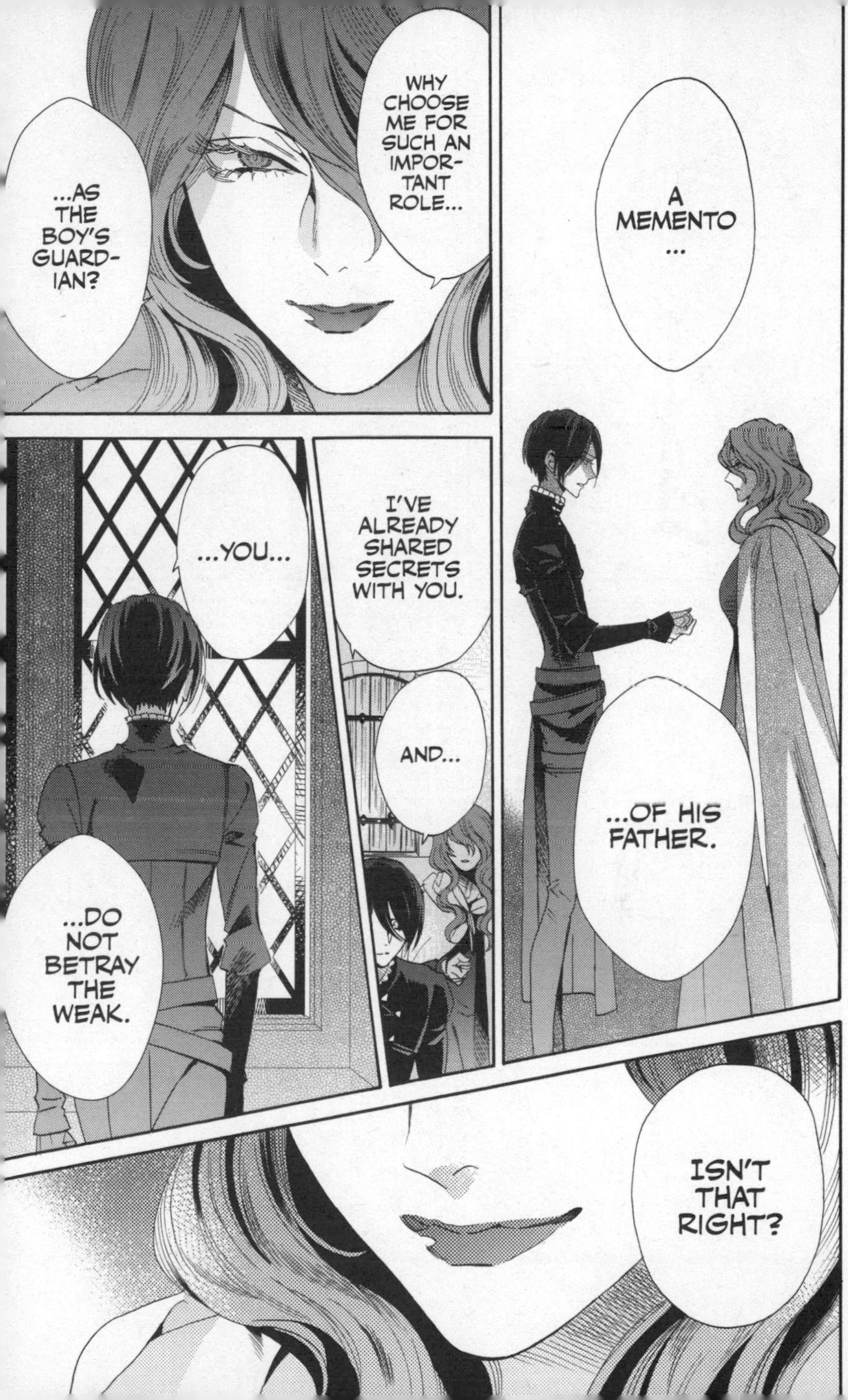
A MEMENTO ...
...OF HIS FATHER.
WHY CHOOSE ME FOR SUCH AN IMPORTANT ROLE...
...AS THE BOY'S GUARDIAN?
I'VE ALREADY SHARED SECRETS WITH YOU.
AND...
...YOU...
...DO NOT BETRAY THE WEAK.
ISN'T THAT RIGHT?

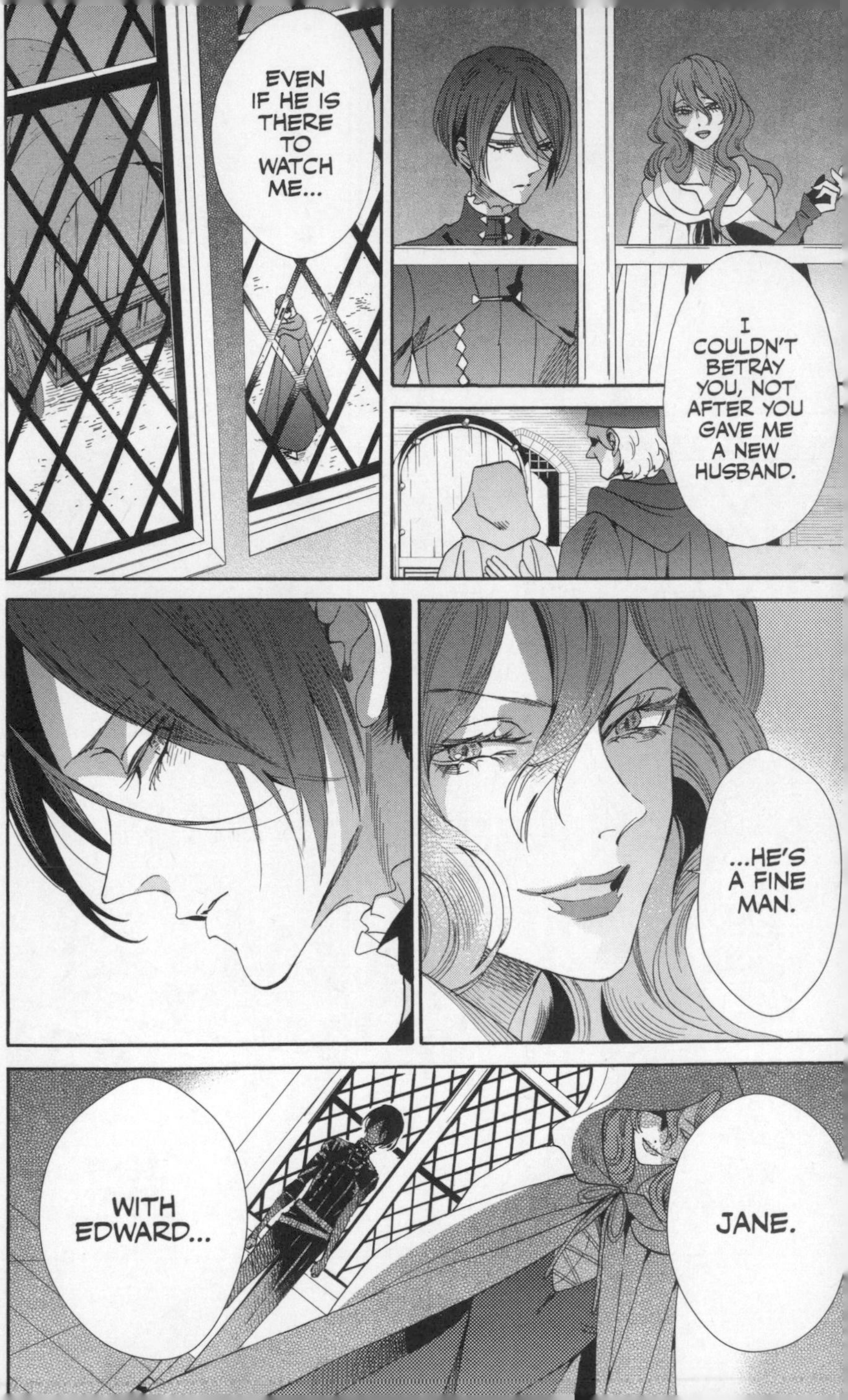
I COULDN'T BETRAY YOU, NOT AFTER YOU GAVE ME A NEW HUSBAND.
EVEN IF HE IS THERE TO WATCH ME...
...HE'S A FINE MAN.
JANE.
WITH EDWARD...

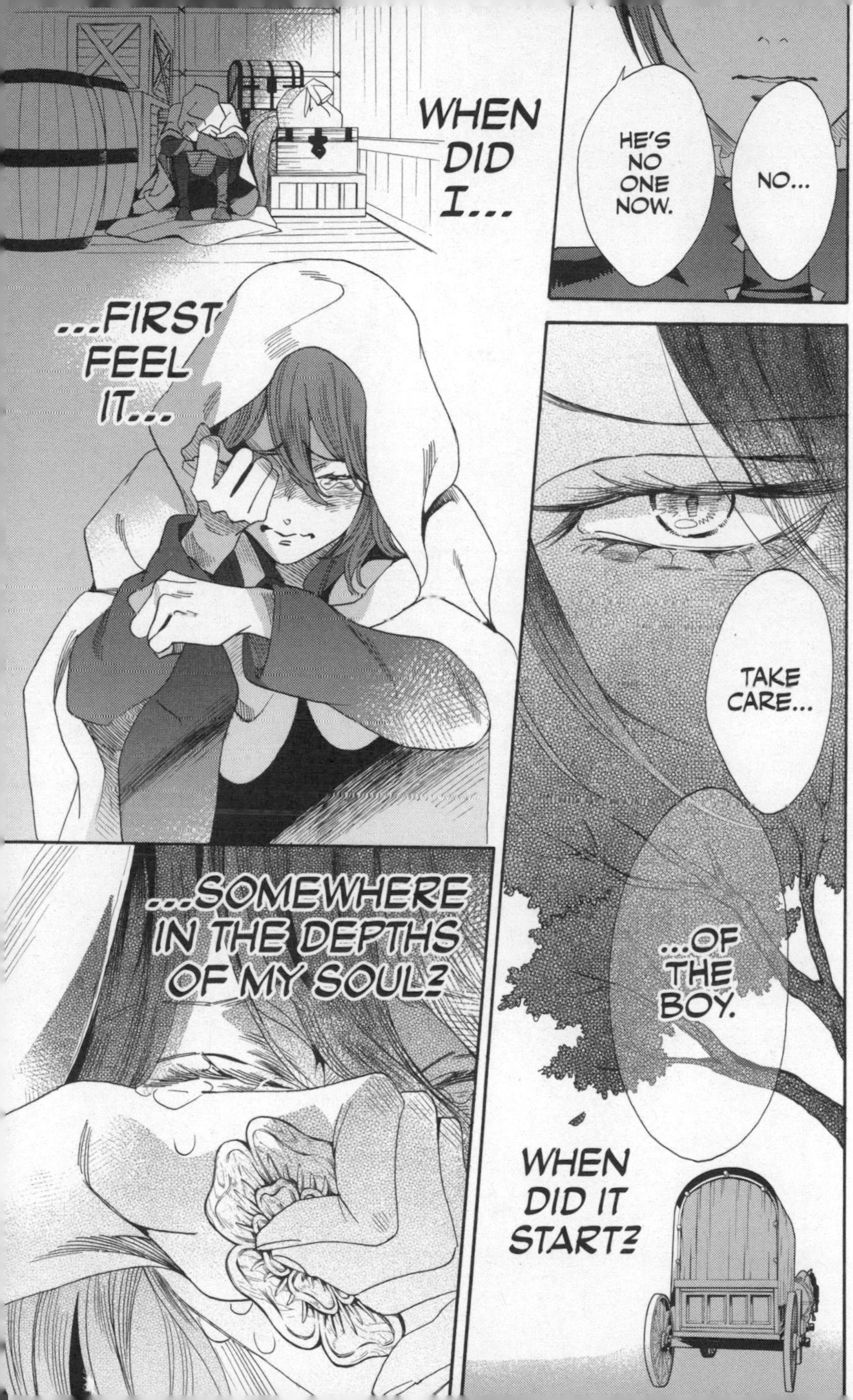
NO...
HE'S NO ONE NOW.
WHEN DID I...
TAKE CARE...
...OF THE BOY.
WHEN DID IT START?
...FIRST FEEL IT...
...SOMEWHERE IN THE DEPTHS OF MY SOUL?

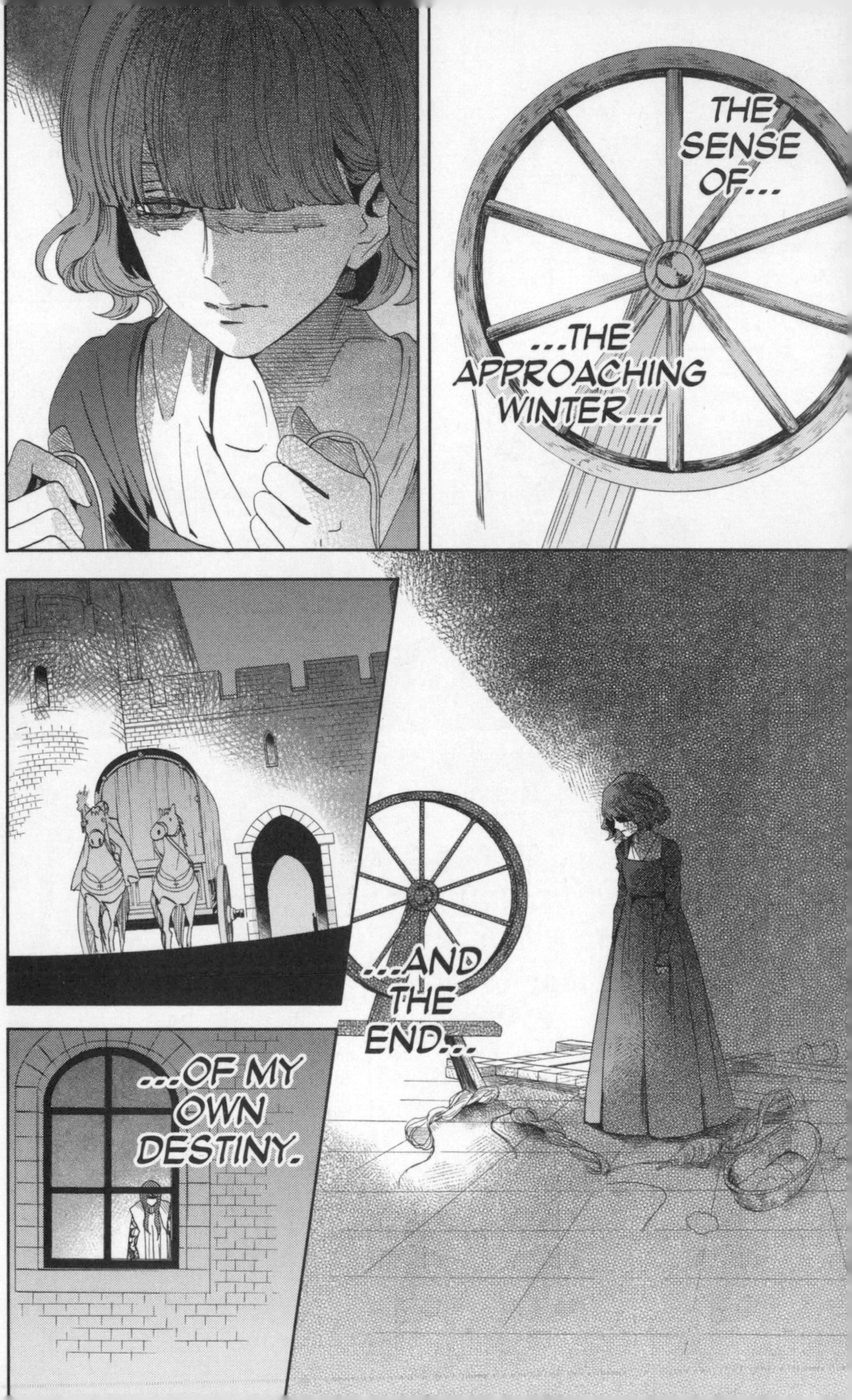
THE SENSE OF...
...THE APPROACHING WINTER...
...AND THE END...
...OF MY OWN DESTINY.

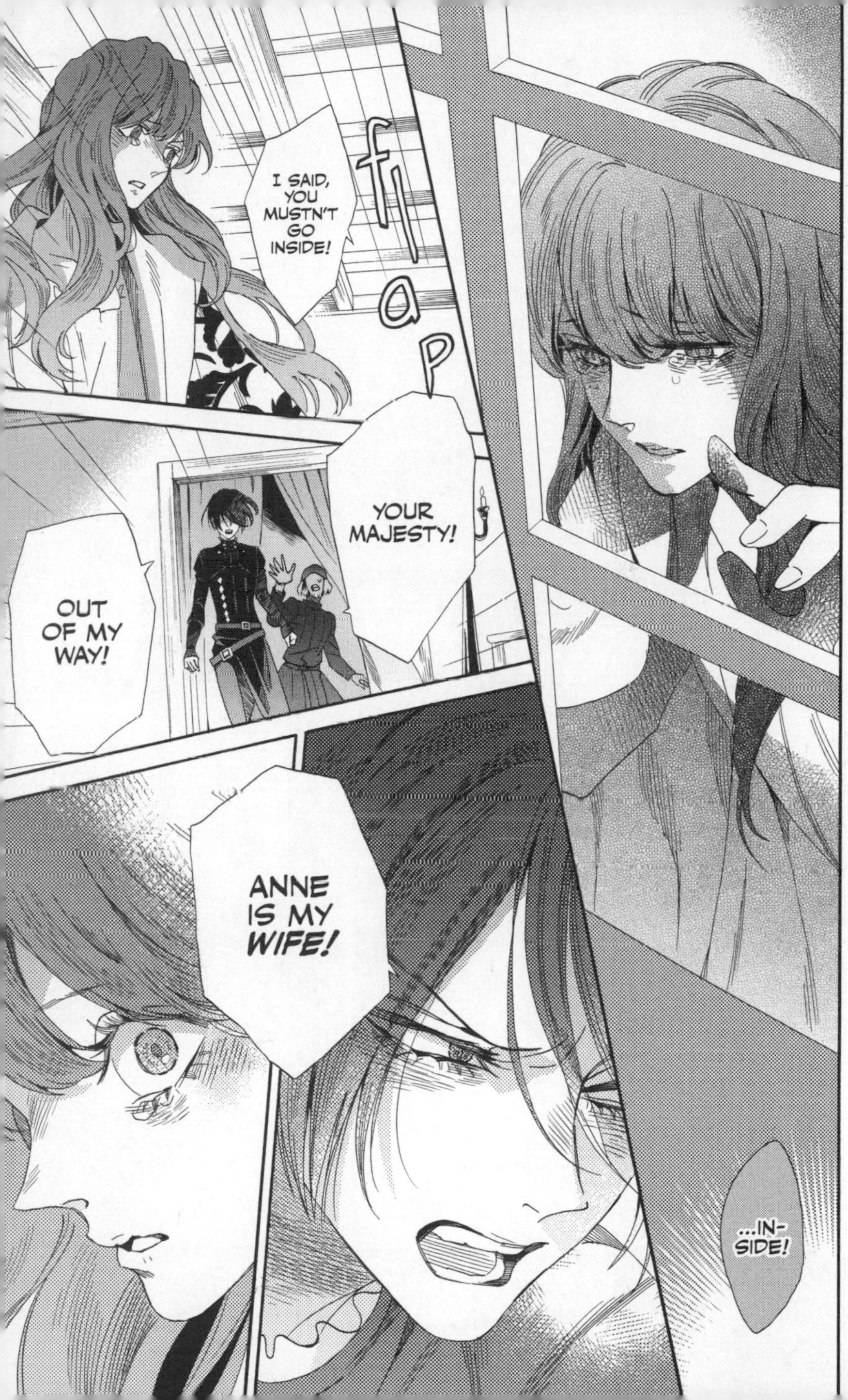
...IN-SIDE!
I SAID, YOU MUSTN'T GO INSIDE!
flap
YOUR MAJESTY!
OUT OF MY WAY!
ANNE IS MY WIFE!

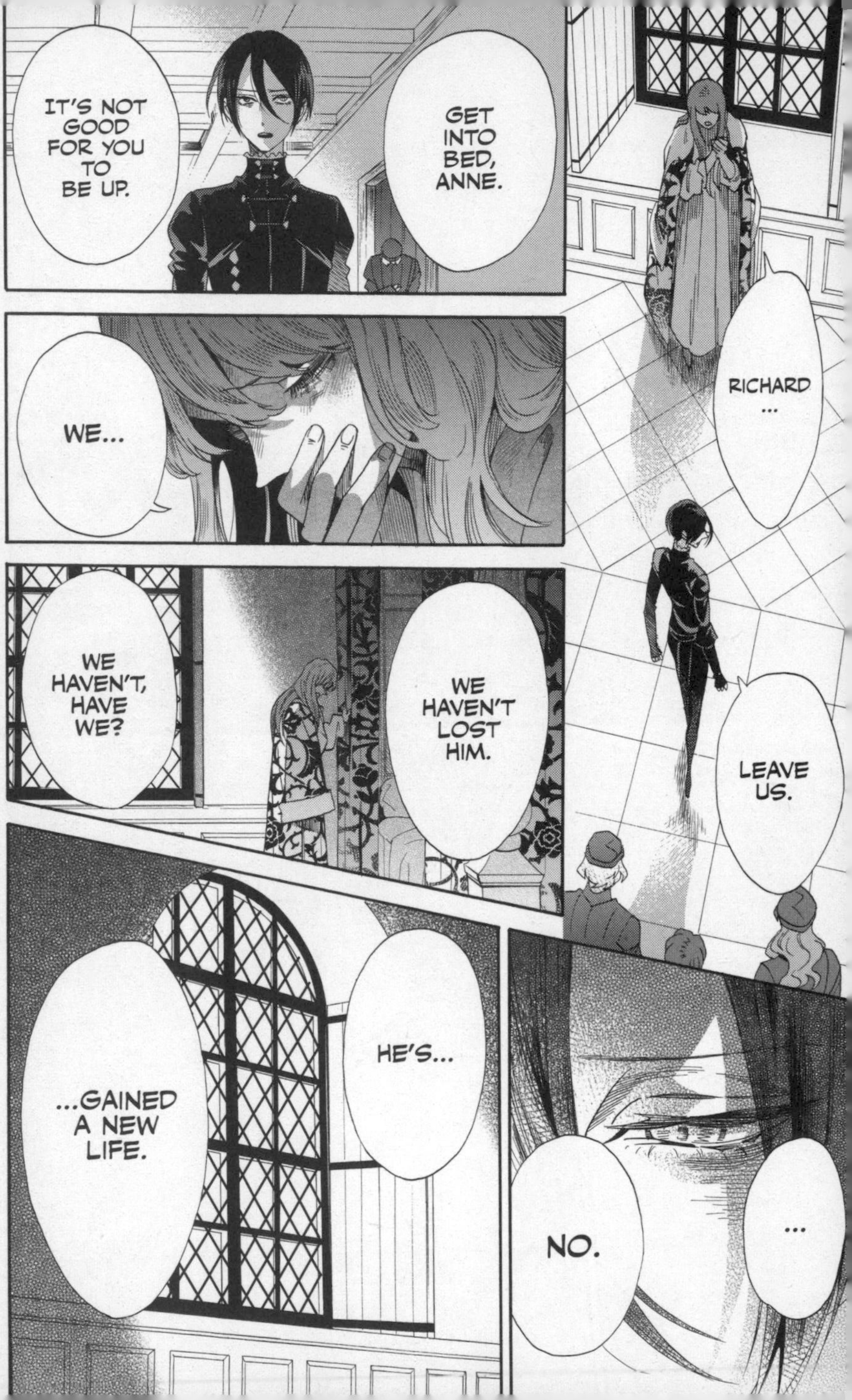
RICHARD...
LEAVE US.
GET INTO BED, ANNE.
IT'S NOT GOOD FOR YOU TO BE UP.
WE...
WE HAVEN'T LOST HIM.
WE HAVEN'T, HAVE WE?
...
NO.
HE'S...
...GAINED A NEW LIFE.

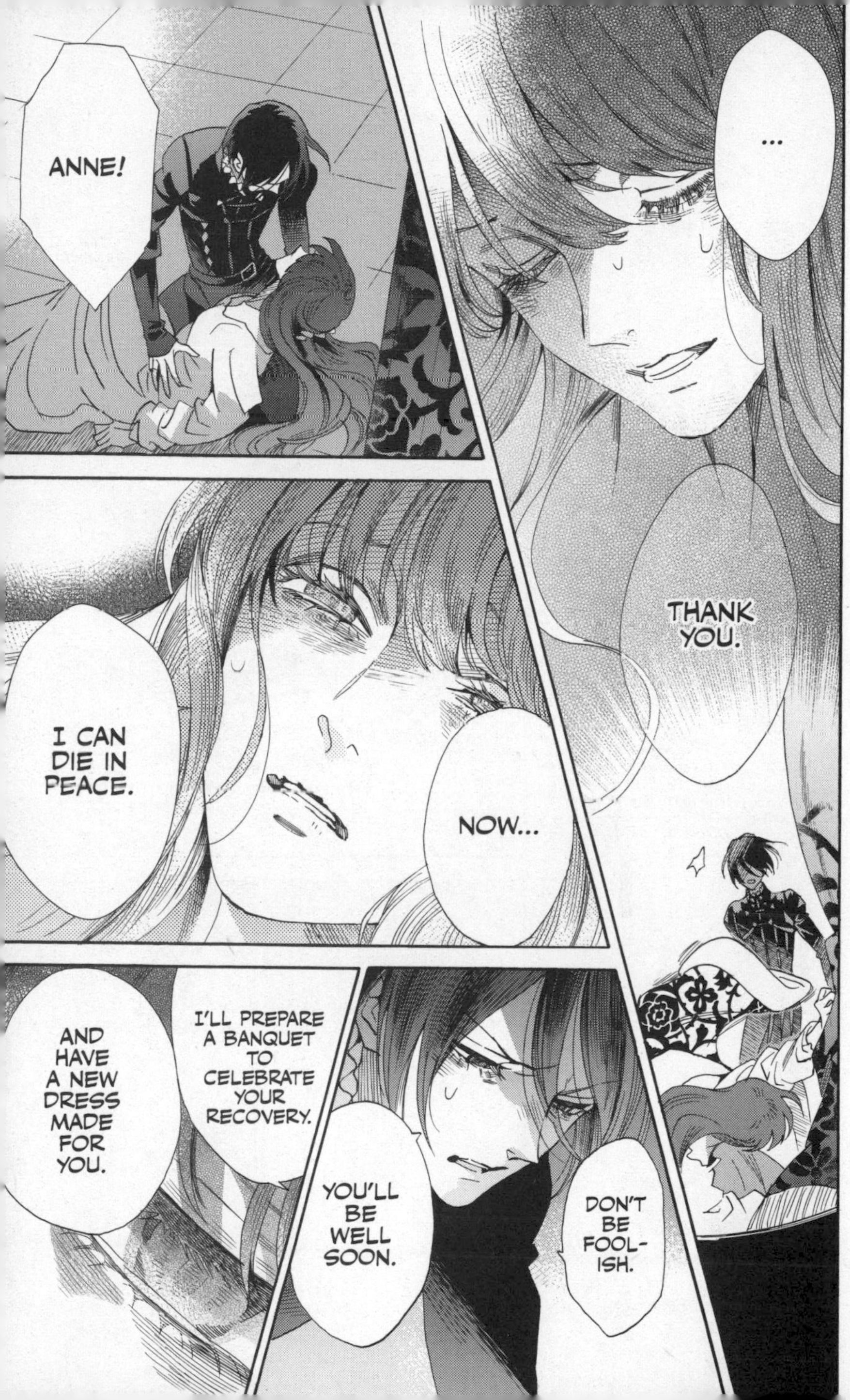
...
THANK YOU.
ANNE!
NOW...
I CAN DIE IN PEACE.
DON'T BE FOOL-ISH.
YOU'LL BE WELL SOON.
I'LL PREPARE A BANQUET TO CELEBRATE YOUR RECOVERY.
AND HAVE A NEW DRESS MADE FOR YOU.

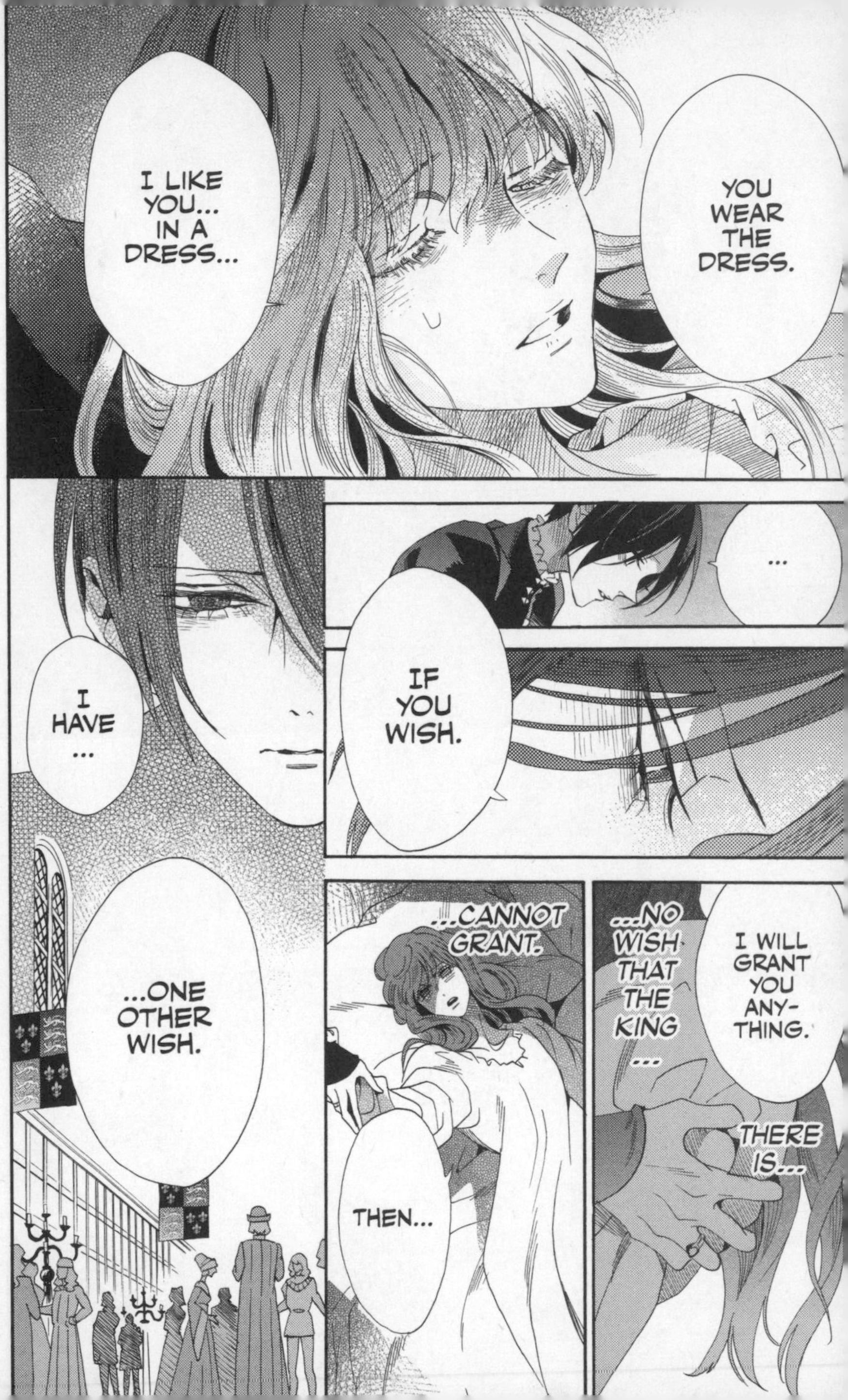
YOU WEAR THE DRESS.
I LIKE YOU... IN A DRESS...
...
IF YOU WISH.
I HAVE ...
I WILL GRANT YOU ANY-THING.
THERE IS...
...NO WISH THAT THE KING ...
...CANNOT GRANT.
THEN...
...ONE OTHER WISH.

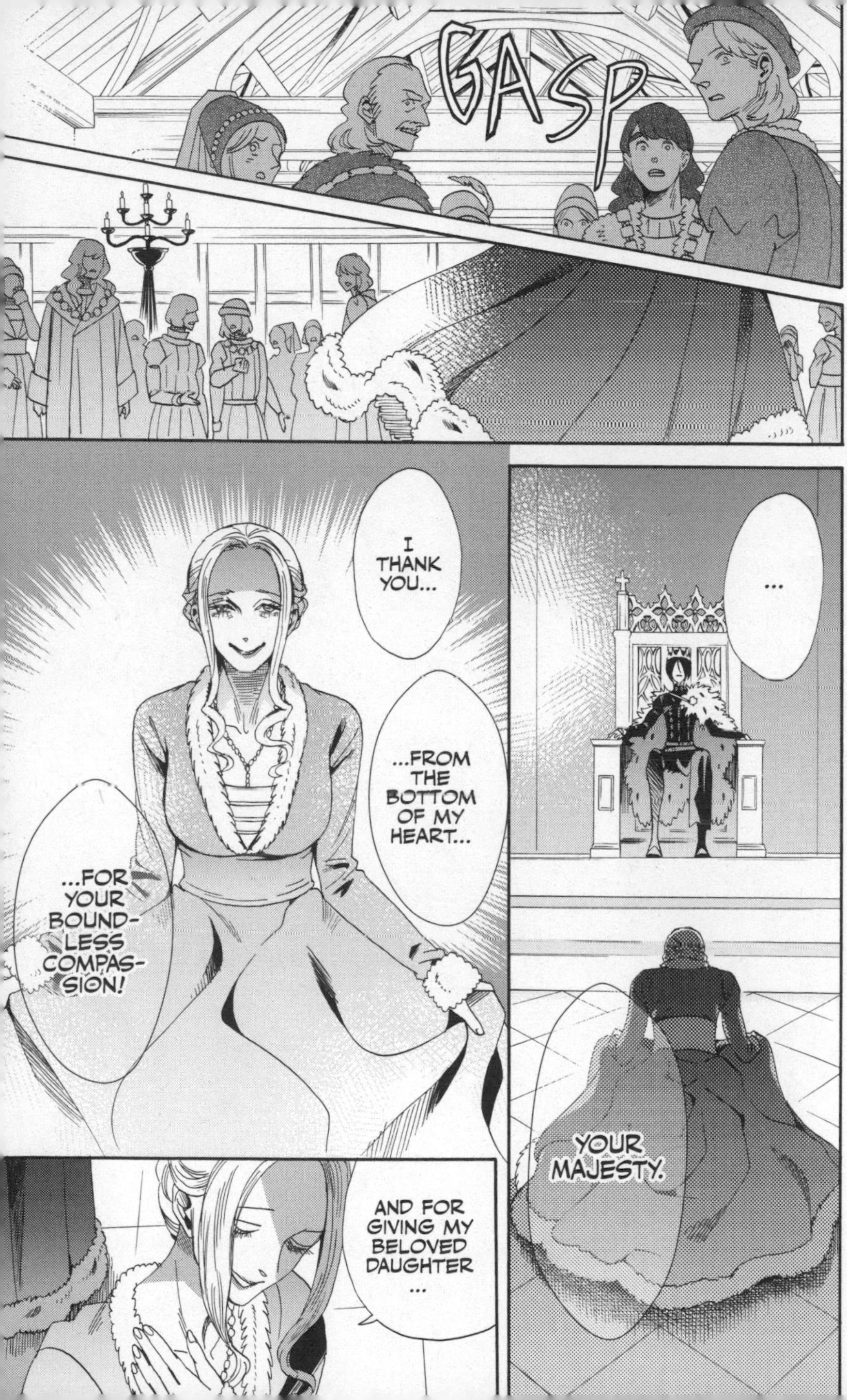
GASP
...
YOUR MAJESTY.
I THANK YOU...
...FROM THE BOTTOM OF MY HEART...
...FOR YOUR BOUNDLESS-LESS COMPASSION!
AND FOR GIVING MY BELOVED DAUGHTER ...

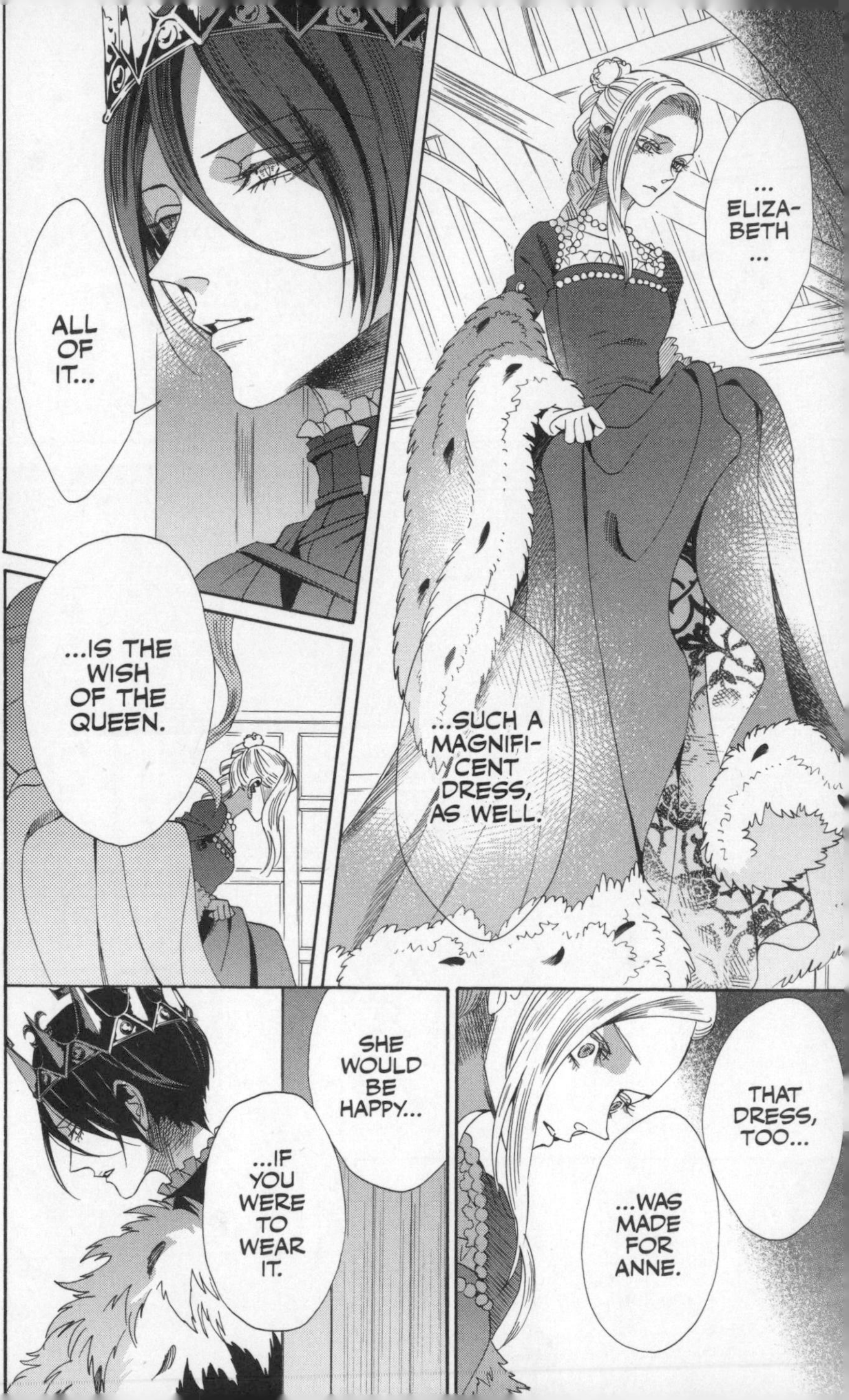
...ELIZA-BETH...
...SUCH A MAGNIFI-CENT DRESS, AS WELL.
ALL OF IT...
...IS THE WISH OF THE QUEEN.
THAT DRESS, TOO...
...WAS MADE FOR ANNE.
SHE WOULD BE HAPPY...
...IF YOU WERE TO WEAR IT.

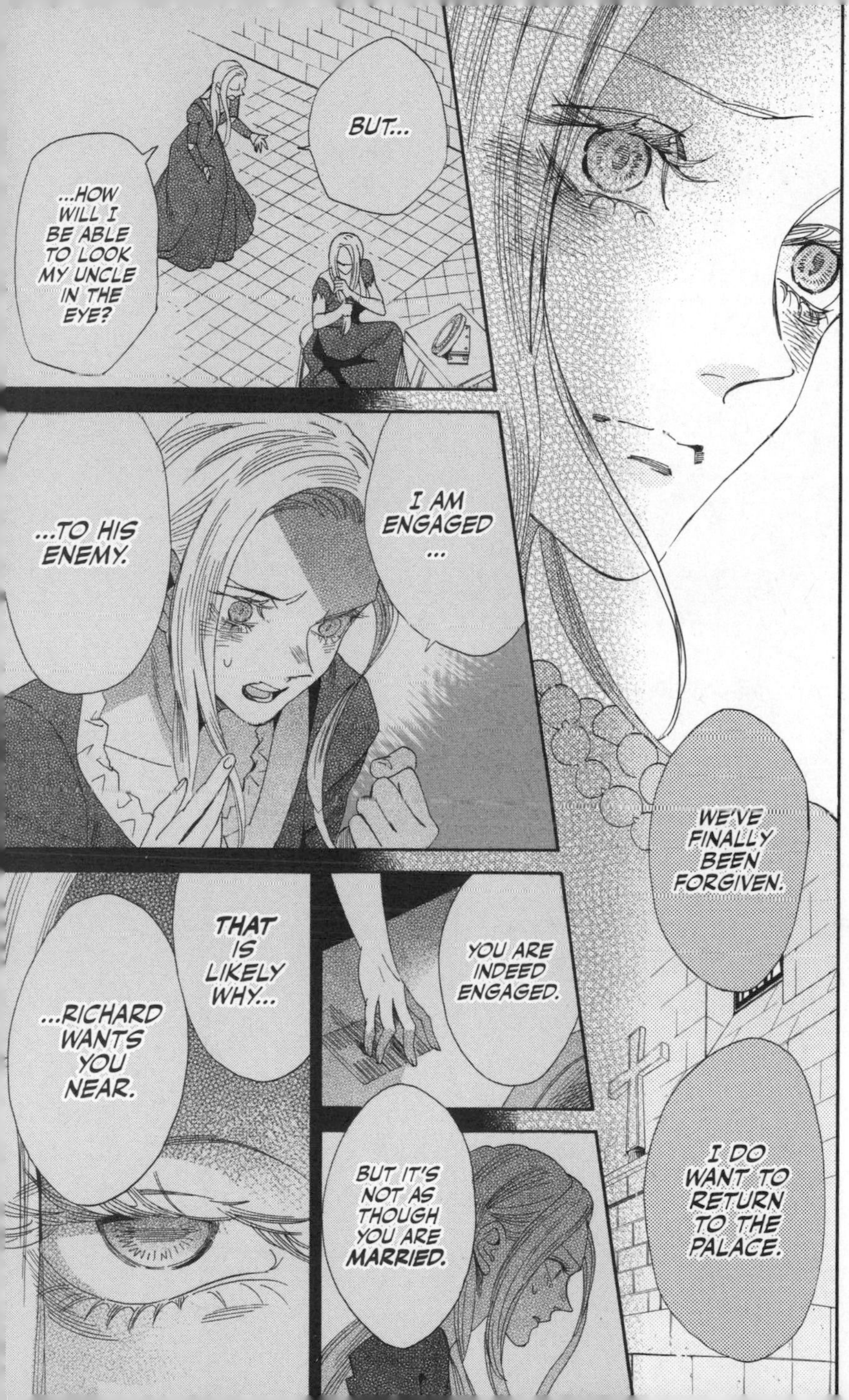
WE'VE FINALLY BEEN FORGIVEN.
I DO WANT TO RETURN TO THE PALACE.
BUT...
...HOW WILL I BE ABLE TO LOOK MY UNCLE IN THE EYE?
I AM ENGAGED ...
...TO HIS ENEMY.
YOU ARE INDEED ENGAGED.
BUT IT'S NOT AS THOUGH YOU ARE MARRIED.
THAT IS LIKELY WHY...
...RICHARD WANTS YOU NEAR.

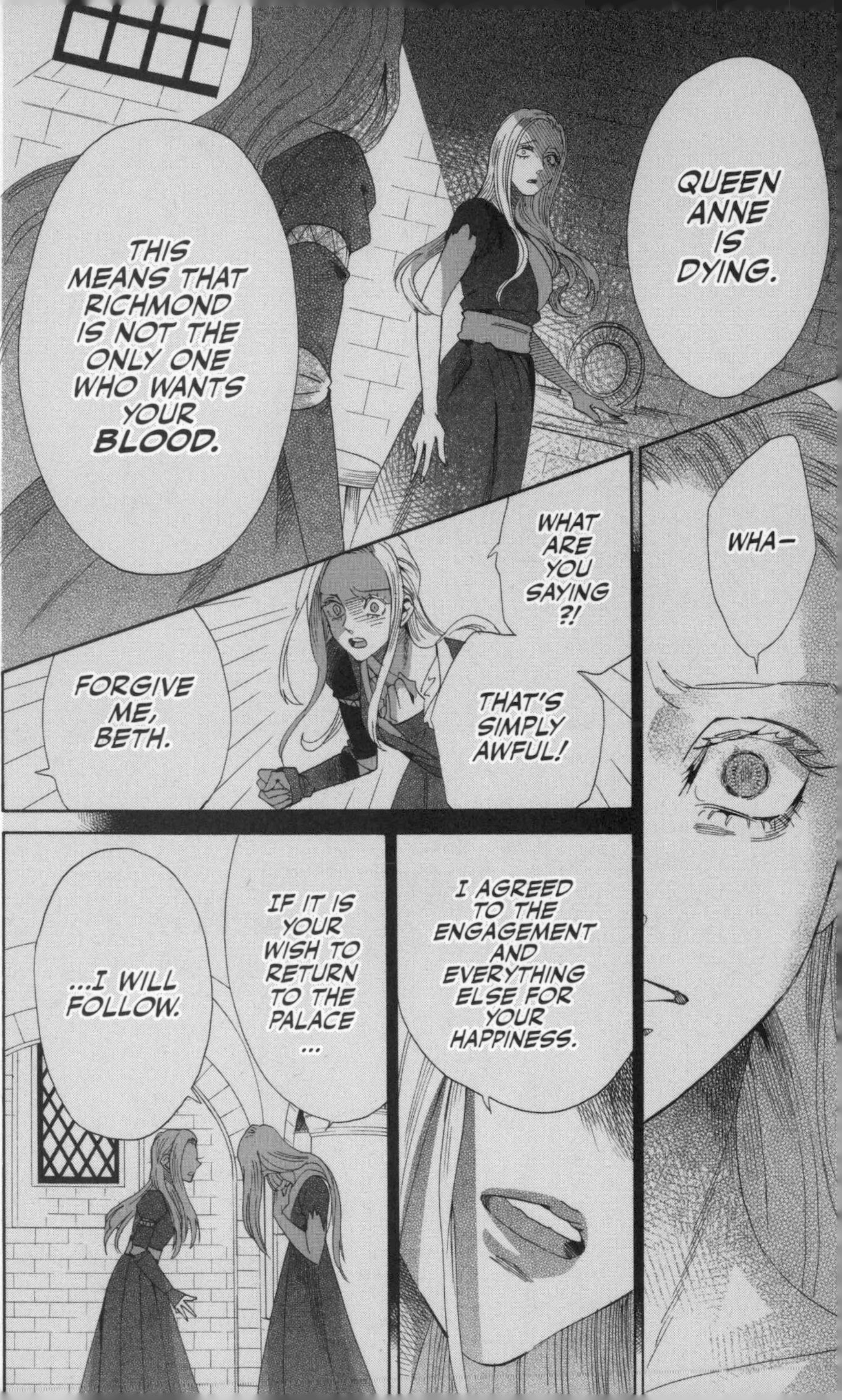
QUEEN ANNE IS DYING.
THIS MEANS THAT RICHMOND IS NOT THE ONLY ONE WHO WANTS YOUR BLOOD.
WHA–
WHAT ARE YOU SAYING?!
THAT'S SIMPLY AWFUL!
FORGIVE ME, BETH.
I AGREED TO THE ENGAGEMENT AND EVERYTHING ELSE FOR YOUR HAPPINESS.
IF IT IS YOUR WISH TO RETURN TO THE PALACE ...
...I WILL FOLLOW.

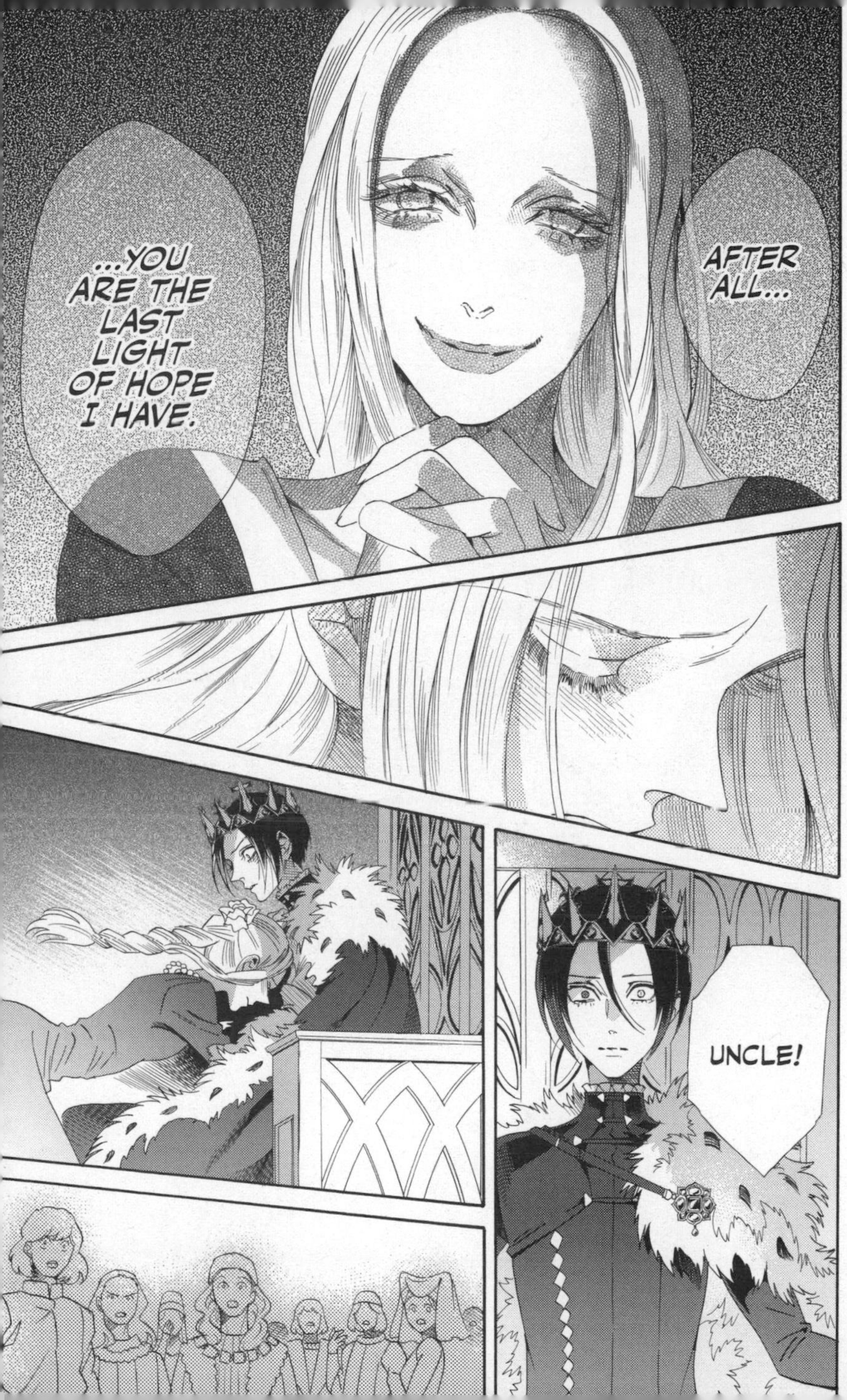
AFTER ALL...
...YOU ARE THE LAST LIGHT OF HOPE I HAVE.
UNCLE!

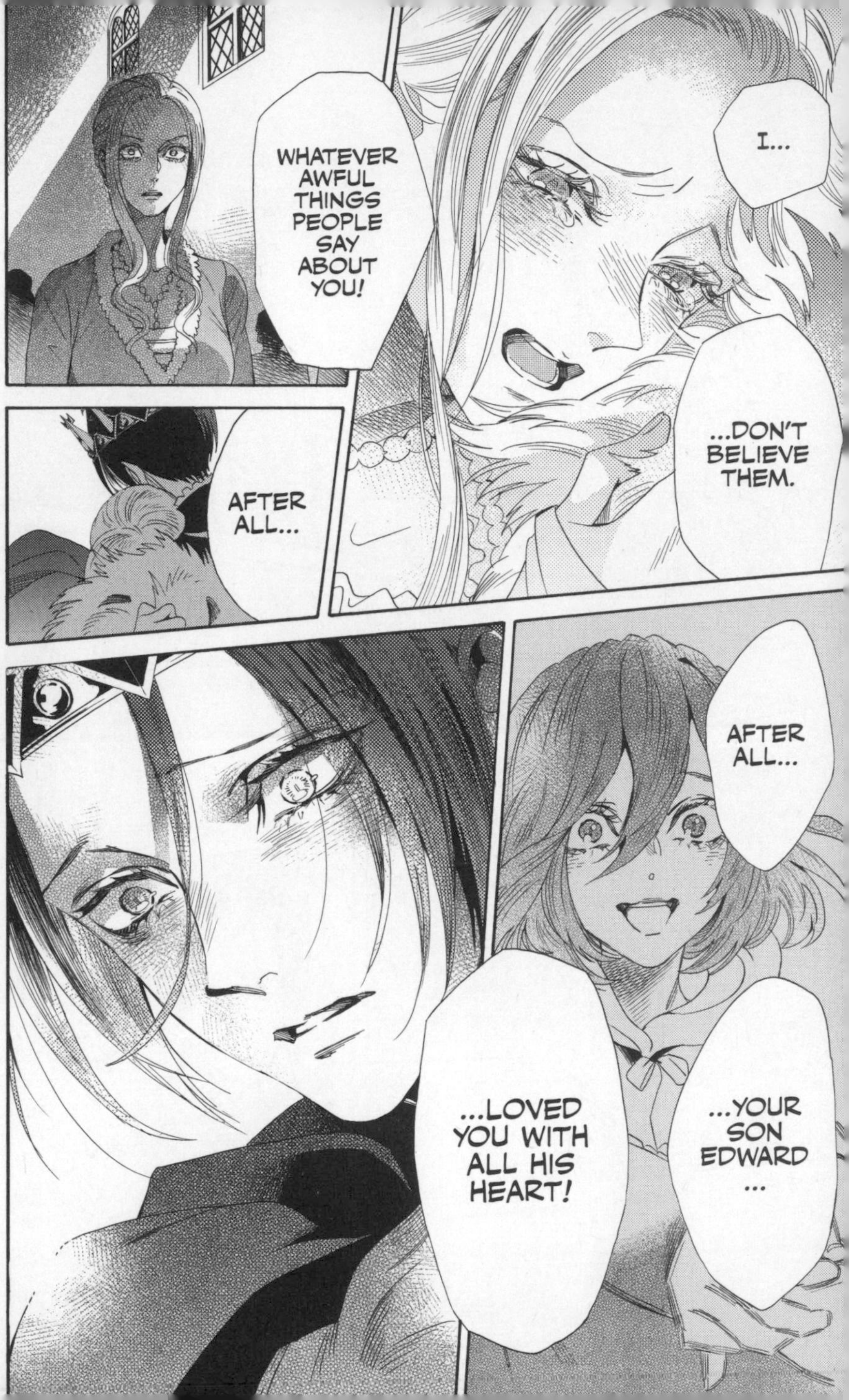
I...
...DON'T BELIEVE THEM.
WHATEVER AWFUL THINGS PEOPLE SAY ABOUT YOU!
AFTER ALL...
AFTER ALL...
...YOUR SON EDWARD ...
...LOVED YOU WITH ALL HIS HEART!

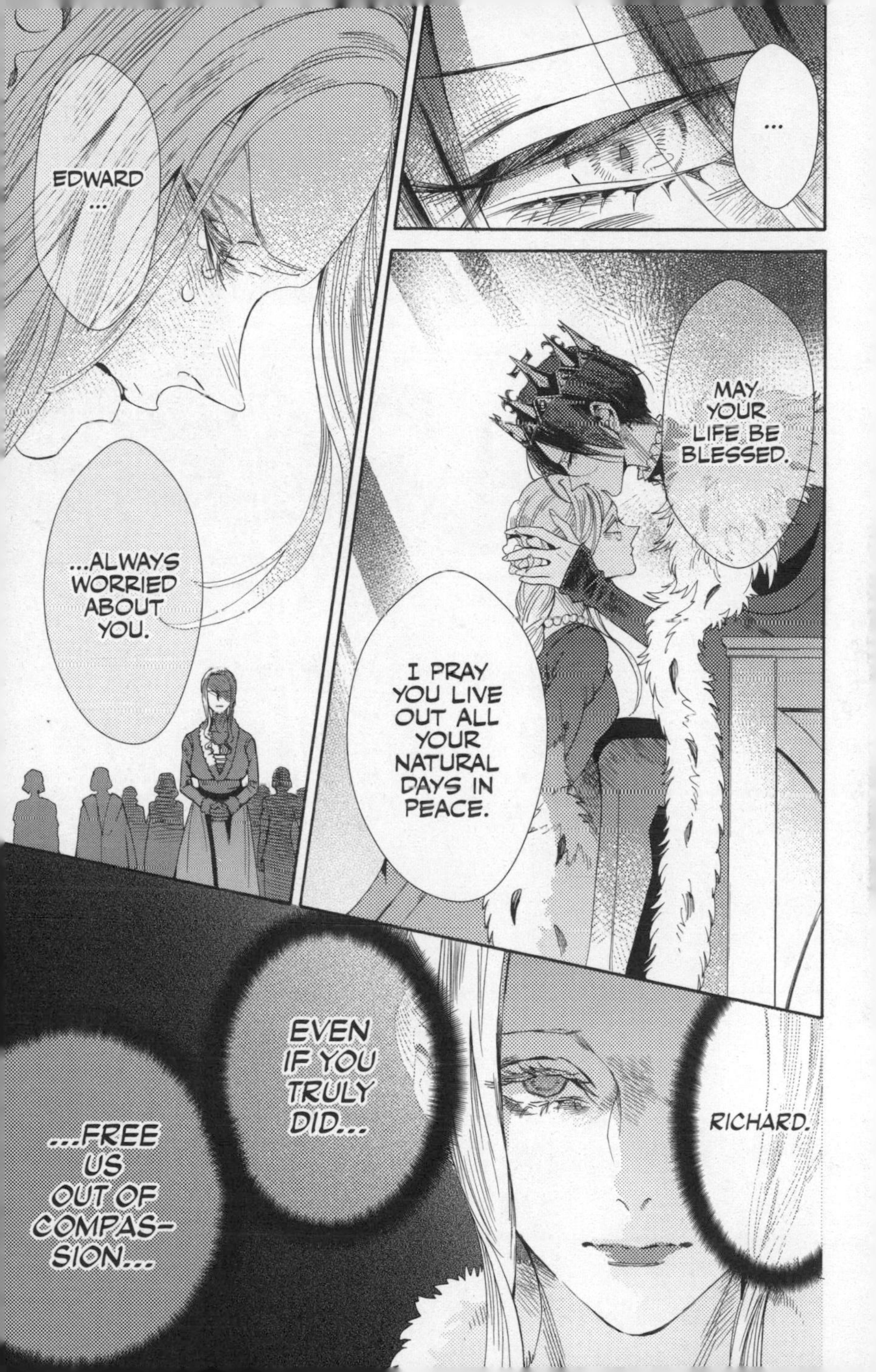
...
MAY YOUR LIFE BE BLESSED.
I PRAY YOU LIVE OUT ALL YOUR NATURAL DAYS IN PEACE.
EDWARD ...
...ALWAYS WORRIED ABOUT YOU.
RICHARD.
EVEN IF YOU TRULY DID...
...FREE US OUT OF COMPAS-SION...

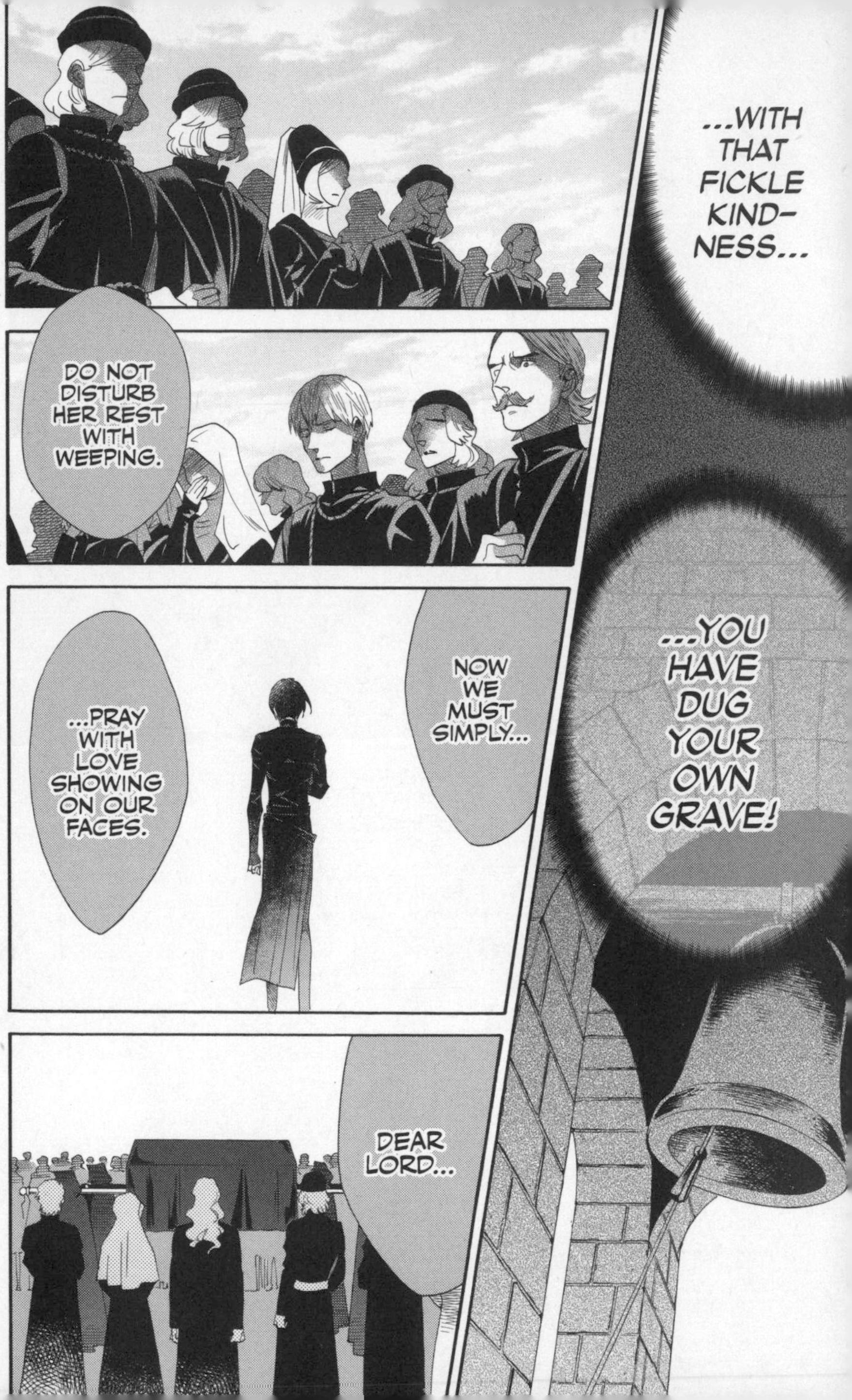
...WITH THAT FICKLE KIND-NESS...
...YOU HAVE DUG YOUR OWN GRAVE!
DO NOT DISTURB HER REST WITH WEEPING.
NOW WE MUST SIMPLY...
...PRAY WITH LOVE SHOWING ON OUR FACES.
DEAR LORD...

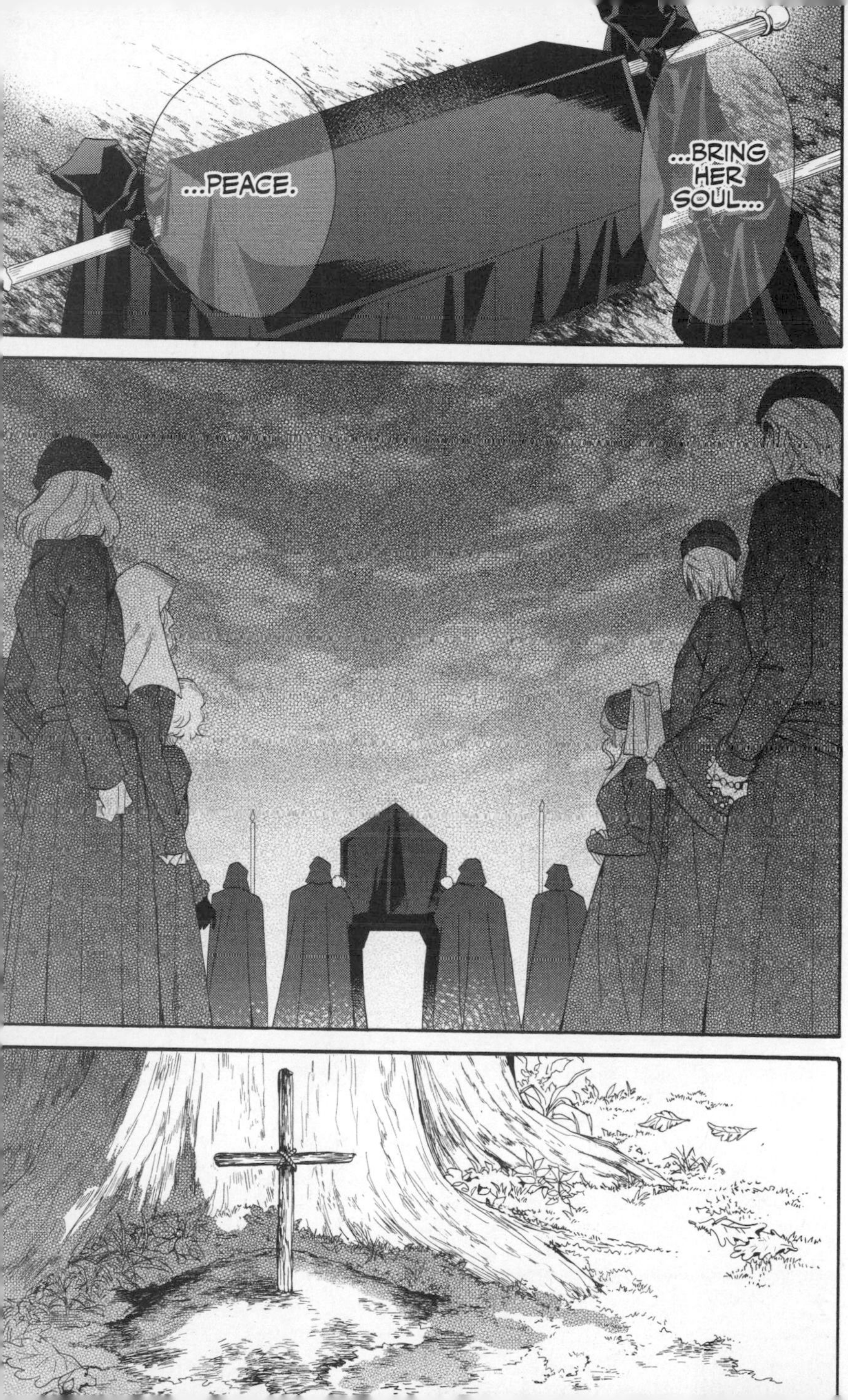
...BRING HER SOUL...
...PEACE.

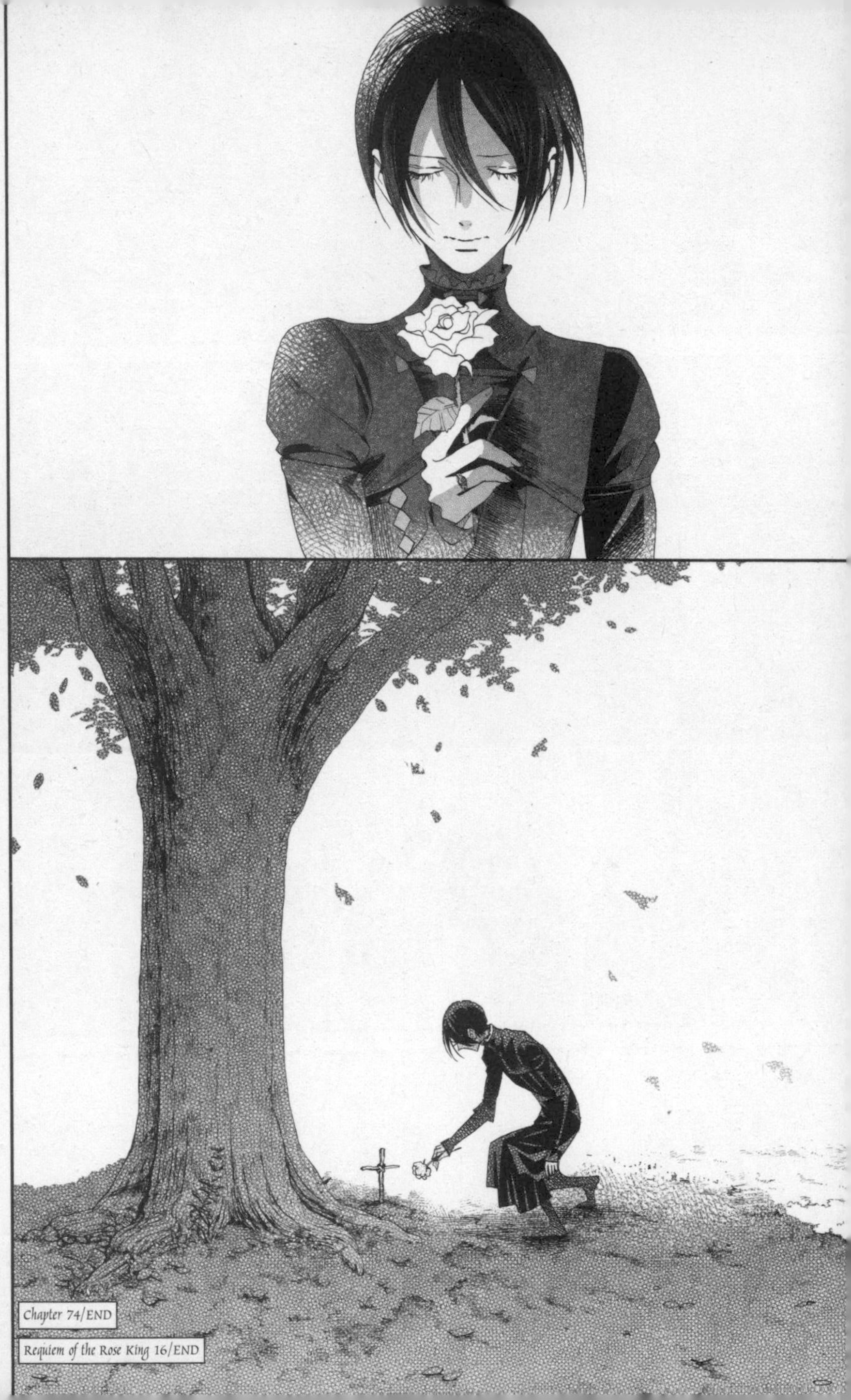
Chapter 74/END
Requiem of the Rose King 16/END